E 114-1-2 ✓ W9-CCW-628

LANGUAGE AND THINKING IN SCHOOL

Second Edition

97374

E. BROOKS SMITH
Wayne State University

KENNETH S. GOODMAN
University of Arizona

ROBERT MEREDITH
Wheelock College

HOLT, RINEHART AND WINSTON   New York   Chicago   San Francisco
Atlanta   Dallas   Montreal   Toronto
London   Sydney

Library of Congress Cataloging in Publication Data

Smith, E. Brooks, 1917–
    Language and thinking in school.

    First ed. published in 1970 under title: Language
and thinking in the elementary school.
    Includes bibliographical references and index.
    1. Language arts.   2. Children—Language.   I. Good-
man, Kenneth S., joint author.   II. Meredith, Robert,
1923–   joint author.   III. Title.
LB1575.8.S56   1976   372.6   75–11519
ISBN 0–03–089248–1

PREFACE

This book was both originally designed and now recast to synthesize some modern views of language and linguistics, of literature and symbolism, and of thinking and knowing that are pertinent to the educative process. Because language, in a broad sense, is the main medium of instruction and pupil learning, the authors feel that a *language–thought-centered view* of teaching and learning has become indispensable to planning curricular strategies and instructional tactics for all subject areas. When focused on education, studies in the nature of language and processes of thinking bring new significance and vitality to some of the older ideas of the child-centered era. Such studies lend support to many modern approaches in the new curricula, including "open" inquiry education, and suggest wholly new possibilities, especially in the teaching of reading and language arts.

The book is divided into seven major parts, each dealing with an aspect of language and thinking studies. The first chapter of each part presents scholarly concepts, positions, and views drawn from pertinent disciplines. It is followed by chapters that discuss educational implications of the ideas with specific examples of recommended classroom activities. Earlier practices are reviewed in the light of a language focus and are given new dimensions, while recent innovations that hold promise are cited as examples and are explored for their potential in promoting *language–thought-centered teaching*. But the basic thesis presented here is the authors'. This is a thematic book exploring many possible relationships among language, thought processes, and education. It is not an eclectic summary. Rather it develops theoretical positions and proposes practical applications for the consideration of both beginning and experienced teachers who have seen the power of language and thinking in their classrooms and who would like to investigate these phenomena further in relation to their work. Key recommendations to teachers are italicized. School administrators of curriculum and college teachers of education may find that a language–thought-centered view of curriculum and teaching can illuminate a rationale by which they can assess the soundness of present programs and the potential of new proposals. Practical means for building and assessing curriculum and instruction based on such an approach are presented.

The second edition of this book, though firmly rooted in the basic ideas and approaches of the original, has been expanded and altered to respond to new school needs and teacher questions. The authors are indebted to the many readers and reviewers who commented approvingly on the book's literary style and format in contrast to conventional methods-book text; we are grateful for their suggestions for improving and updating content in light of new *accountability* demands being made upon professional personnel for raising quality levels of *language and thinking competency* in schools.

The change in title to "in School" reflects the book's focus on the use and development of language and thought in school life, in school environment, and in school teaching–learning situations that range from nursery through primary, elementary, middle, and secondary education. Yet there is substance enough in the elementary school references for the book also to serve as a text in reading and language arts courses. The changed emphasis on school life has brought new material into the book on *British primary school education*, on *American "open" education*, and on *teacher competency* in planning and evaluating programs with *"expressive" and "action" objectives* in mind consistent with a language–thought-centered view of instruction. Practical suggestions for trying out new ideas and assessing their impact are included. The reading sections have been updated and expanded to present the latest findings from psycholinguistic research and their aplications to practical reading activities, including *language experience* approaches and *individualized reading* methods. The *literacy skills and mechanics* section has been augmented as has been those sections dealing with *multimedia symbolic systems* now including discussions of *mathematics education*. Substantial expansion and reorganization have been accomplished in the sections dealing with *modern curriculum planning* and *instructional analysis* and assessment to the point where the book can now serve as a guide for teachers in curriculum development and instructional improvement in all fields where language and thinking are the educational focus.

The next decade or two is the time for a scholarly consolidation of educational ideas and methods around themes like "language and thinking" rather than continuing the chase of chimeras labeled "the latest thing." This book is an effort to bring a fresh view to old educational problems and to open new pedagogical prospects by making "language and thinking" focal in discussions of curriculum and instruction. The authors' attempt to do this will be adequately rewarded if the book encourages greater educational use of the full resources of the versatile language that is ours and of the thinking potential of young people.

E.B.S.
K.S.G.
R.M.

August 1975

ACKNOWLEDGMENTS

The authors are indebted to the scholarship of the following persons who made contributions to the text or reviewed various sections for consistency and accuracy of argument. Special appreciation is given to the late Lawrence V. Frank for inspiring the authors with his able synthesis of a number of key modern ideas from psychology and philosophy and from cognition and language studies as related to education. Appreciation is also given to Edward Chittenden for review of the Piaget formulations and ideas about evaluating "open" education; to John Camp for contributions on mathematics literacy; to Thomas Davidson for contributions on the analysis and evaluation of communication in the teaching act; to Lawrence Gagnon for assistance in writing the section on "questioning"; to Joseph Grannis for ideas about curriculum design; to Dwayne Huebner for ideas about the arts of teaching; to Carolyn Burke, Dorothy Menosky, Yetta Goodman, P. David Allen, Barbara Greene, William Page, Rudine Sims, Dorothy Watson, Mervin Thornton, Patricia Rigg, Hughes Moir, and Peter Rousch for sharing their research studies in applied linguistics; to William Curtis, Ruth Moline, and Yetta Goodman for special contributions to the children's literature section; to Robert Williams, Gene Yax, and Richard Snell for classroom activity suggestions in the language arts and social studies; to Peter Dow and Ruth MacDonald for social studies curriculum ideas generated in discussions with them; to Costa Leodas and Lansing Wagner for ideas in the science education references; to Gary Kilarr for assistance in the section on competency-based curriculum designing, instruction, and assessment; to Greg Davenport for help on classroom interaction observation instruments and pupil attitude inventories; to Paul Jacobs for a contribution on cognitive styles; to Bill Greenwood and A. J. Light for basic ideas and a review of the sections on British "open" education, national curriculum planning, and teachers' center developments; to Joseph Sales, David Wallace, and Patrick Johnson for ideas on cooperative teacher education; to Pierce McLeod for ideas on inservice education; and to several teachers for contributing examples of their planning or practices: Harry Woods, Haig Derderian, Ann Crile, Norine Donaldson, Marion Risborough, and Jean Fuqua. Special appreciation is given to Jonathan Smith for permission to use his stories, to Elizabeth K. Smith for devoted editorial assistance, and to Yetta Goodman for her helpful suggestions.

CONTENTS

LANGUAGE
AND THE
PERSON

1

Speech is a human activity that varies without
assignable limit as we pass from social group to social
group, because it is a purely historical heritage of
the group, the product of long continued social usage.
It varies as all creative effort varies—not as
consciously, perhaps, but none the less as truly as
do the religions, the beliefs, the customs, and the
arts of different peoples.

EDWARD SAPIR, Language
(New York: Harcourt, 1949), p. 4.

TEACHING FOCUS

What kinds of language experiences do young people need, both in and out of school, for expanding their life-space while making sense of it?

Why do youngsters learn language, and how do they acquire its subtleties before schooling and refine them during the school years when taught with a "language-expansion" view in mind?

What impact do the sociocultural, historical, and geographical aspects of the development of the English language have on the learning of young people, and how do they participate in that development?

How can teachers deal with dialect differences and language prejudices in middle-class and ghetto neighborhoods?

What are the key elements in a "language-expansion" school program?

1

Creating One's World through Language

THE ANIMALS

They do not live in the world,
Are not in time and space.
From birth to death hurled
No word do they have, not one
To plant a foot upon,
Were never in any place.

For with names the world was called
Out of the empty air,
With names was built and walled,
Line and circle and square,
Dust and emerald;
Snatched from deceiving death
By the articulate breath.

But these have never trod
Twice the familiar track,
Never never turned back
Into the memoried day.
All is new and near
In the unchanging Here
Of the fifth great day of God,
That shall remain the same,
Never shall pass away.

On the sixth day we came.[1]

[1] From *Collected Poems 1921–1958* by Edwin Muir. Copyright © 1960 by Willa Muir. Reprinted by permission of Oxford University Press, Inc., and Faber and Faber Ltd.

Coming into a World with Language

Until the child assumes language he cannot separate himself from the all-consuming moment. Like the other animals, he is in the world without knowing he is in the world. Language makes it possible for him to objectify and conceptualize his world and himself and to share the responsibility for his destiny.

The child comes into the world with the physical and mental potential for language and finds a ready-made symbolic structure, the end product of thousands of years of development awaiting his assumption of it. In assuming language he races along, retracing swiftly the trails built so tediously over the centuries. He cannot simply start where the previous generation left off; the whole development must be re-created in him. It is this legacy of language and man's capacity as heir that set him apart from all the other animals.

The basic and primary role of language is to embody reality, to be the carrier of the world image. A child sees a tree, hears it called a tree, chants "tree, tree, tree," and goes around forever after with a tree in his head, which he can conjure up in the dark, in the middle of the desert, or multiply into a forest at will. This first freshness of symbolic embodiment is reinforced by the reception it gets from other speakers of the language and by endless experiences with other trees. The landscape of word symbols that looms in the child's mind forms the scene in which his every act is laid. What he does with his world, how he makes relationships within it, and the impact of his sensuous awareness of it go far beyond that. However, this aspect of language—personal recognition—should never be forgotten, for it remains central to language at all levels.

Finding Reality through Language

A reality coterminal with the limits of language may not be reality in some absolute sense, but it is as much of reality as the individual and the language community will ever know. Eskimos reflect their own environment and their interest by their many classifications of snow unknown to inhabitants of the Temperate Zone. Arabs may distinguish endlessly among camels, and Brazilian Indians have hundreds of words for different birds without a generic term for *bird*. Slum children have many colorful words for policemen. The fact that people from other language communities can learn Eskimo or Brazilian distinctions does not destroy the validity of these as examples of language–culture delimitation. It is possible to learn other languages, including nuances and refinements, but one still only knows *about* them. The psychological depth and sensuous involvement that grow out of extended interaction of the individual and his environment through the medium of language will always be lacking to some degree when he learns another language. The particular grasp of reality is determined by the structure of the language as well as by its lexical reference.

Everyone and every language community starts with the same physical world (at least, we postulate a common world), but each sees it from a slightly shifted perspective. Our common humanity predetermines what we shall find in reality, but our common humanity also allows room for community and individual differences. Although we have begun to find ways of radically shifting our perspectives to those of other persons or cultures, ultimately all will be qualified by the final individual perspective. All world views, no matter how wide the horizons, turn on the axial "*I.*"

Using Language in the Particular and in the Universal

Language scholars speak of individual language (idiolect) at one end of a scale and the speech of a community (dialect) at the other, and there are many gradations between. Within a broad dialect, there are many sub-dialects that may be refined to the particular words and expressions peculiar to a family that causes the family's total language to differ somewhat from that of the community. The language of a region such as the southern United States—or even a city block—will have its differences. The language area might be extended to larger areas such as major languages, families of language, and the final category, human language. In going from the smallest unit to the next largest, something is lost and something is gained. The broader groupings file off the rough edges; the smaller areas exclude more and more of mankind for the sake of sensuously richer, psychologically deeper particularity. *Literary* language tries to preserve a dynamic tension between the richly particular language of a person and the broadly representational language of a culture. The ultimate in literature is achieved when the universal is realized through the smallest particular, as in Blake's

> To see a World in a Grain of Sand,
> And a Heaven in a Wild Flower . . .

Language cannot exist in a vacuum. It depends on the sensuous particular as a firm foundation for the ladder of abstraction. The physical grasp of the senses is extended into the world by means of the symbolic process of language, much of which, in its roots, leads back to the parts of the body, figuratively extended into the world, from the face of the cliff to the foot of the hills, from the mouth of the river to an arm of the sea.

Language gains life and strength through the psychological and aesthetic grasp of reality centered in the individual. Though it is the codification of centuries of human experience, transformed by man's creative intelligence and preserved from generation to generation by the means it itself supplies, language still must be re-created in the individual. It binds man to the earth as well as separates him from it. As an ideational means, language separates him from total immersion in the particulars of life by making objectification possible, while at the same time it permits him to grasp immediacy and makes possible his relation to the things of the earth preventing his alienation from nature.

Projecting Language into the World

Man speaks and a resonant world responds. He projects his voice, and the echo gives him the contour of what is out there. A danger for modern man has been the prevalent conception that nature is unresponsive, made up of dead matter, that even the other man is an object spoken at. When a man who projects such a concept ahead of his voice speaks, his voice trails off into the crevices and craters of the blighted landscape of a dead planet, killed by his own hand. Language is projected into the world, and if we listen carefully we know what world this is and who we are in relationship to in it. The preservation of this constant and ever comforting relatedness prevents man's alienation from his environs.

The process of resonance can be observed most readily in children. The following poem projects the idea of resonance and the correlation of a child's self to her world.

DEFINITION: FOR JANE

I am, I shout.
Hop-hoppers in the grass
hop round me as I pass
through the sunlit scene,
pulsing yellow on green,
flower opening all day long
to a whirring song,
I, mid arcing petals,
bright enameled metals
of summer. Fields lie still
before, behind. At will,
like poets ringed in rhyme
that beats and meets in time,
I move my circle round
me anywhere. No sound
can be beyond my ear,
a silent world until I hear,
no sight beyond my seeing,
O worlds await my being.
Through the fields of choice,
called to life by my voice,
I sing from morning to night,
then darkness dims my sight.

A light goes on ahead
to light my way to bed
and after, out.[2]

Shaping Reactions to the World in Words

Part of a new experience is naming, describing, and classifying it. Fear of the unknown collapses in the presence of experience organized into concepts and expressed in language. All fear may not be destroyed, but fear of the unknown is. Roman troops panicked when first faced with war elephants. In the next encounter, the troops perhaps said something like, "Well, here come those war elephants again," opened their ranks to let them pass through and then closed their ranks again. When Sputnik I first went into orbit, we witnessed a widespread attempt to make the awesome feat tolerable by saying just what it was and how it worked. We could not let it fly around up there undescribed. Fear and curiosity required that it be put safely within the controlling lines of language.

Man speaks to himself as well as to the world. He carries on a dialogue with himself, rehearsing his being constantly. Adults often misread the changing pattern of child language. They see the discontinuance of monologue and the gradual diminution of egocentric language as putting away childish things and developing a more mature and social language use. Desirable as the development of social use of language is, it should not supersede the ego-centered grasp of reality that takes place in language, which should be continued and extended rather than supplanted. It should not kill the animistic grasp of nature but should put it in perspective.

Language, from beginning to end, is shot through with sensuous elements that are basic and necessary to scientific and rational language. A prosaic approach to language tends to kill its psychologically and aesthetically satisfying aspects and in the end even defeats the purpose of prose. A narrow "correct" language dries up the wellspring of language.

The growing child learns to submerge his dialogue with himself, his dramatization of his role in the world; but substantially the same process goes on beneath the surface. In the mature man the quality of thought and decision making depends on inner representation of opposing sides, and in the judicial hearing of causes and actions. Even "unrehearsed" actions are based on precedents established in past rehearsals.

Assuming Language

The assumption of language is not a passive process. A dynamic interaction takes place between the individual and the pre-existing language pattern. The child racing along the well-worn path of language is not just

[2] Robert Meredith, "Definition: for Jane." From *Quicksilver*, 1959, by permission of the author.

being initiated into the dialect of the tribe or the neighborhood; he acquires an idiolect, a personal language that interacts in an intricate way with the dialect.

The individual has the potential for extremely rapid and widespread language extension, but this is not to say the growth cannot be blocked, slowed, inhibited, or distorted. Whether the individual has a rich, sensuously rewarding world with wide horizons and dynamic and stimulating inter-relationships within it, or a colorless, dwarfed world depends to a large degree on whether language growth is confirmed, enriched, encouraged, and whether the individual is able to reach out and extend himself into the world through language. Independence depends on whether a person uses his language as the instrument of his own will in creating a personally authenticated world or whether he uses others' language for working their will upon him and forcing their fixed and "safe" world upon him. Language must, in any case, be personal, but whether it is richly personal or atrophied and weak depends on the formative language experience.

If the expanding of his world through language is discouraged in the classroom and in the home, the child will take it to the playground and the street—although he may run the risk of cutting himself off from the most highly civilized aspects of his culture for the sake of vitality. To inhibit the child in his assumption of language and the world is to limit his life-space and to take some of the life out of what remains. Teaching the true structure and nature of language and supporting its assumption by the individual can enrich and extend his world. Language is the carrier of experience insofar as we are aware of experience, and any effort by society, parents, or teachers to restrict it or deny it to the child can only make him a lesser person and can lead to the very chaos the teacher claims to fear. *A child's language development can be stunted whether he lives in a restricted ghetto, in a protected suburb, or in an isolated farm community. The child should no more be excluded from the rich range of personal language than he should have all evil and threatening representations removed from his literature. The child must be given his world—all of it.*

2

The Child
Learning Language

Every language is a vast pattern system, different from others, in which are culturally ordained the forms and categories by which the personality not only communicates, but also analyzes nature, notices or neglects types of relationship and phenomena, channels his reasoning, and builds the house of his consciousness.[1]

Language is the most useful and marvelous invention yet achieved by man, and it is amazing that virtually every child achieves near mastery of at least one language by the time he is five or six. Over the last decade and a half, studies have confirmed that by school age most children's speech is a close approximation of adult speech in their communities.[2] Adults tend to overlook the immensity of this achievement. Because virtually every child learns to talk, adults presume it is a part of the natural growth of the child. They also tend to pay more attention to the relatively few signs of immaturity in the speech of children than to the high level of mastery they display. They remark the one or two sounds a five-year-old cannot yet produce but not the fact that he has mastered all the other phonemes of the language. They notice the occasional misuse of a word by a child but not

[1] Benjamin Lee Whorf, *Language, Thought, and Reality* (New York: Wiley, 1956), p. 252.

[2] Courtney B. Cazden, *Child Language and Education* (New York: Holt, Rinehart and Winston, 1972).

the extensive vocabulary that he uses accurately. Many adults find it hard
to accept repeated studies of the vocabulary of school beginners that have
indicated that the average child knows at least 8000 words and may know
over 20,000. They are aware of the sentences that children produce that
are not grammatical by adult standards, but they often do not realize that
the bulk of children's speech is entirely grammatical. The child can produce
sentences that he has never heard but that are nevertheless grammatical.
Even his errors tend to be overgeneralizations of common language patterns. For example, he may say "he bringed it" rather than "he brought it."
He could not make this error unless he had a well-established notion of how
past-tense verb forms are usually produced. Studies by Strickland[3] and
Loban[4] have established that kindergarten and first-grade children use all
the basic sentence patterns of English in their speech. However, some of the
more complex forms are established and refined during middle childhood,
as the youngster learns to embellish on the basics.[5]

Adults who are closely associated with infants and small children during
the period when they are mastering language are vaguely aware that there
is a learning process involved. They know that the child moves from
babbling, through first words, through a phase of immature speech commonly labeled baby talk, to speech that falls within the language norms of
the community. But even parents focus more on the cute, the quaint, the
charming, than on the process. In fact, parents tend to be unaware of the
vital role they play as language models and suppliers of linguistic raw
materials. Sometimes a parent is startled to hear his own remark, complete with intonational detail, coming back at him from the mouth of his
child. Sometimes the replication is all too accurate and timely, as when the
four-year-old says to his maternal grandmother, "Daddy said, 'I hope the old
battle-ax doesn't stay too long,' " and then turning to Daddy, "What's a
battle-ax, Daddy?"

Each child invents a system for expressing his needs, wishes, desires,
and thoughts to persons around him. This personal communication system
eventually coincides with the language of his family and subculture. He
acquires the sounds and units of this language, and the structure of the
language embeds itself in his mind and personality. This internalization of
the structure of language not only influences the way a child expresses his
reactions to the world around him but may help structure his perceptions
as his world and language expand.

[3] Ruth Strickland, "The Language of Elementary School Children," *Bulletin of
School of Education* (Indiana University), *38*, No. 4.

[4] Walter Loban, *The Language of Elementary School Children* (Urbana, Ill.:
National Council of Teachers of English, 1963).

[5] Carol Chomsky, "Language Development after Six," *HGSEA Bulletin, XIV,*
No. 3 (Spring, 1970), 14–16.

Why Children Learn Language

Linguists, psychologists, and students of child development have begun to examine closely the process of language development in children to discover how this mastery comes about. Before one can consider *how* children learn language one must consider an even more basic question: *Why* do children learn language?

Language learning is not a natural organic part of growing up. Children who grow up isolated from human society do not develop language. Human beings have the capacity to produce a great variety of sounds. The use of phonemes, significant variations in sounds, as the unitary symbols of the language is a social invention of man. Choice of which features of sound variation will be significant in particular languages is entirely arbitrary. Some languages utilize clicks, which are almost totally ignored in English. Some languages (Chinese, for example) make much more significant use of pitch variation than does English.

Complex languages can be built that do not use sounds at all but that utilize systems of visual symbols—signs made with fingers or other body parts, puffs of smoke, pictures, or abstract graphic designs such as letters.

Language systems utilizing symbols based on other sensory stimuli could also be constructed. Some tactile stimuli, for example, have the symbolic quality of a rudimentary language; a squeezed hand, a pat on the head, a slap on the shoulder, or a kick in the shins under the table are all symbols that convey simple messages. Braille, of course, utilizes tactile symbols. However, human beings can produce and discern an almost unlimited variety of sounds, whereas our control over production and discrimination of other sensory stimuli is more limited.

All human societies known developed languages that utilized sounds as symbols. Other animals (parrots, for example) have a similar ability to produce a range of sounds but have not developed a spoken language, although a few apes have been taught to use sign language. Two human qualities explain the development of language. The first quality is the capacity of man's mind to imagine and use symbols; the second quality is man's faculty for complex and varied communication. So universal is his need for communication that man invented language not once but perhaps many times, wherever, in fact, man congregated.

The ability of children to think symbolically and to produce sound symbols makes it *possible* for children to learn language. The need to communicate makes it *necessary* for children to learn language. The child learns a particular language not just because it is the only one available but because it is the one that makes communication possible with the people around him. In fact, if he needs to learn two languages to communicate effectively, he will learn both, as has been amply demonstrated by children who grow up in bilingual homes. Bellugi has studied language learning in deaf children of deaf parents. She finds that such children learn sign as a first language as easily, as early, and as well as hearing children acquire speech.[6]

Studies in language development have given disproportionate attention to physical development in children. Physical development, control, and coordination are necessary prerequisites to the physical acts involved in producing sounds, and the child who cannot produce sounds cannot talk. All children who are physically and mentally normal do develop control over the speech apparatus. But the ability of the child eventually to produce exactly the sounds that are the symbols of the language of his society is determined by his need for effective communication. Because almost all children are born into societies that have oral language, it is the oral language that is learned first and that becomes primary to all hearing children. The need to communicate is ever present; the choice of language is social. *As language develops, it becomes a tool of the child's striving to derive meaning from his world. In turn, language is expanded by this striving.* There must be purpose in learning, and communication is the immediate reason for language learning.

From this axiom of communicative need in language learning several corollaries follow:

The closer the language of the child comes to the language norms of the adult community, the more effective becomes his communication.

There is a continuous tendency, therefore, for the child's language to move toward adult norms.

The more opportunity the child has to communicate, the more skill he will develop in use of language and the more acceptable will be his language by adult standards. He needs to be spoken to, listened to, responded to.

Anticipation of his needs by a parent or teacher before he communicates them will tend to retard a child's language development.

In literate societies, communicative need will play the same prime motivational role in the child's learning to read and write as it does in his learning to speak and listen with understanding.

Before change can be achieved in an individual's idiolect, the individual must strongly feel that the change will help him to communicate more effectively.

Language, Experience, and Situation

Philosophers for centuries concerned themselves with the relationship of *the word* and *the thing*, and most people tend to think of language as a series of words that stand in close relationship to objects they name. But language does not confine itself to naming the things in the world. Language must be capable of conveying the most abstract feelings and relationships

---

[6] Ursula Bellugi, "The Language of Signs and the Signs of Language," paper presented at the Michigan Conference on Applied Linguistics, January 1971.

as well as of conveying concise, concrete descriptions. Actually, language development in children moves from vague associations between utterances and their referents to precise ones, from general meanings to particular, from large language units to small.

Consider the encounters the human infant has with language, for instance this episode:

> The child, a four-month-old boy, is lying in his crib. An adult appears. The child feels discomfort and begins to express it through body movements. He starts to cry. The adult changes the baby's diaper, lifts him, holds him, pats his back and bottom, all the time talking: "Oh your diaper's wet. Well, Mommy will fix that." Other persons are present. "Karen, hand me the powder. Here, Daddy, hold the baby while I get his food ready." The child is carried into another room. The talking continues amid other sounds. Other voices are heard: the high pitched voice of a five-year-old sister, the deep voice of the father, the dimly heard voices of a television program in an adjacent room.
>
> The child feels himself placed in a reclining seat. The feeling is a familiar one. He has experienced it many times before. His mother begins to feed him. The taste is new and unexpected but pleasant, a new strained fruit; but the spoon and the process are familiar. And all the time, the language continues. Some is directed to the baby, "I have something new for you, Tommy. Open your mouth. That's a good boy. Aren't the peaches good? Yes, Tommy likes peaches."

This episode is not a particularly complex or unusual one. The child experiences repeated variations of it. The episode is really a *situation*. Everything that happens to the child is experienced in the context of the total situation. He can focus his attention on some aspect of the situation, but the particular aspect cannot be isolated from the context of the situation. Some aspects of the situation are closely related—the dish and spoon, for example. Some aspects of the situation are experienced simultaneously, such as the feel of spoon and the food. Others occur sequentially; the sight of the spoon and the dish usually precedes the taste of the food.

Language is always experienced by the child in the context of the situation. The child starts by associating the whole language utterance with the whole situation, or at least with the aspects of the situation that he experiences at the same time he hears the language. To acquire effective control of language he must sort out of the situations recurrent associations between language and particular aspects. He must be aware, for instance, that when the language includes the recurrent element *Mommy*, the situation almost always includes the presence of a particular person.

Sometimes adults simplify the situation, the language, and the focusing problem of the infant. The mother will point to the father while repeatedly uttering, "Daddy, Daddy, Daddy." Still, the child must sort out of the situation that it is the person pointed to rather than the speaker to which the term refers. He must also delimit the term; he may, for instance, apply it to all adults or all male adults. Nor has it really become language for him until he can use it to communicate. He must become aware that by producing a recognizable approximation of *Daddy* he can summon adult aid or produce a desirable reaction in an adult present, such as a hug or a pleasant stream of language.

The child's reaction to the situation is also a part of the language-learning process. His emotions and his developing ability to think, to process his perceptions, and to begin forming concepts actually become part of the situation as the child experiences it.

The sounds that compose the speech the child hears have many variable dimensions. He must learn which of these variables are the significant ones. He must learn that recognizing the difference in voices is useful only because it tells him which person is speaking. In some Chinese-language communities he would need to learn to attend to many different pitch levels, because the same sounds said at different pitch levels are different phonemes.

Essentially, the early language of an infant is made up of whole language utterances that he associates with generalized experiences. When language becomes purposeful, the purpose is a generalized one also. He says "Daddy," but he is conveying a message that is a general "I need help!"

Adults tend to think that children learn words as individual units, which are then joined in longer and longer sentences. This misconception, is partly due to the limited ability of young children to repeat utterances in speech, even though they may have the whole idea in mind. The child is limited to uttering short sound sequences by his lack of physical coordination and by other factors. When he imitates adult speech he fixes on the most prominent characteristics, because he cannot repeat it all. Brown and Bellugi report that children they studied tended to repeat the most heavily stressed words in an utterance.[7]

The child does not begin to speak in words, then, but in abbreviated utterances—a kind of telegraphic language. He expands these utterances until they eventually are complete in virtually every detail. They sound like carbon copies of the adult utterances.

There seems to be a play aspect to the language development of children. Babbling, experimenting with sounds, getting control of the apparatus for producing sound variations, imitating sounds and adult speech are all part of this play. These phases of language development are noncommunicative and nonrational. But the close relationship between language and experience in the context of recurrent situations brings about an important interplay between the language and thought of the child. Bits of language become closely associated in the child's mind with bits of experience. Recurrence of an experience brings to the child's mind the language that he has come to associate with it. Hearing familiar language, even his own speech, recalls

---

[7] Roger Brown and Ursula Bellugi, "Three Processes in the Child's Acquisition of Syntax," in J. Emig, J. Fleming, and H. Popp, *Language and Learning* (New York: Harcourt, 1966), pp. 3–12.

the experience. The child's early utterances are often quite appropriate to the situation, because the experiences suggest them to him. The language is his reaction to the situation, but it is not yet purposeful, nor does it yet represent a developing concept in the mind of the child. But as adults and other children respond to his early speech, the child begins to use it consciously and communicatively.

As language becomes a means of expression, it becomes rational. Vygotsky believed that speech and thought have separate roots. "Up to a certain point in time, the two follow different lines independently of each other. At a certain point these lines meet, whereupon thought becomes verbal and speech rational."[8] When speech becomes rational, not only does the child begin to use it to express his needs but also he begins to manipulate his perceptions of the world by mentally manipulating language. Thus, thought becomes verbal. It is not that he cannot think without language but that language becomes a convenient symbolic medium for thought. In the process, the perceptions themselves are sorted into categories that are available in the language. Thus, the language to some extent structures the child's developing life-view. The categories of the language, of course, are those of the culture into which the child has been born. He begins to see things the way others in his society see them. His ability to communicate with others is thereby increased; he not only speaks the same language but also sees things their way too.

The language errors and misconceptions of the child have the same genesis as his correct language and his accurate concepts. These errors are very important in the development of thought and language in the child. They represent essential stages in development. The child must be able to compare situations in which language is effective or ineffective, in which concepts work or do not work. Suppose, for example, the child wants to be picked up and he says to his mother, "Up, up." When she picks him up, his communication has been effective. But suppose she is holding him and he wants to be put down, but he says "Up, up." The mother may do nothing; the language then will be ineffective. Or she may guess from his body movements that he wants to be put down. As she does put him down, she will very likely use appropriate language: "Oh, you want to go *down*." The child learns language in a number of situations and uses subsequent situations to verify his language and to refine and limit it.

Or consider how the concept of *brother* might be developed by the child. It may be associated with situations in which children are present, then siblings are present, and, finally, male siblings are present. His understanding begins to acquire the status of a concept when the child generalizes that other children also have brothers—that, in fact, *brother* is a category of

[8] L. S. Vygotsky, *Thought and Language* (Cambridge, Mass.: M.I.T. Press, 1962), p. 44.

relationship between people. Through many experiences in many situations the concept develops, takes on subtlety, acquires emotional overlays. As the child grows older, the concept becomes more abstract, and he is able to describe a brotherlike relationship. Eventually, he may grasp the significance of brotherhood. Then only can he deal rationally with the question, "Am I my brother's keeper?" The misconceptions and early concepts that he abandons along the way are as much a part of the process of conceptualization as the final concept.

How Do Children Learn Language?

Studies of the child's language development have provided much new information about how children learn language. Still, there is no general agreement on the total process and sequence involved.

One simple but important explanation of the development of language in children that has recently gained considerable acceptance among linguists and language psychologists (psycholinguists) is that the human brain is uniquely equipped for the development of language. In this view, a kind of universal grammar is supplied to all human brains just as the procedure for pecking is preprogrammed in the brain of a newborn chick. Language is therefore, in this view, an *innate* human attribute, not an acquired one. It is instinctive. All that is required for its development is exposure to a natural language. Under such exposure, the human infant adapts his universal grammatical system to the particular *surface structure* of the language he hears. In this view, learning to walk and learning to talk are much alike; both are inevitable when given the characteristics of the human organism, unless physical or mental impairment intervenes.

Perhaps the strongest argument in favor of this view is the research evidence that a child's language development far outstrips his other intellectual achievements, notably his concept development. Language in all its complexity is learned with such ease and at so early an age that it does seem possible that instinct (albeit a complex one) may be at play. However, the "innate" theory leaves much still to be explained. The reader is urged to read McNeil's cogent and well-documented statement of the theory in *The Genesis of Language*.[9] Some issues raised by this view follow, and then an alternate position is stated.

The innate theory does not sufficiently explain the errors that both learners and adults make in language (here an error is something that is outside the system of the language).

The theory does not account for or concern itself sufficiently with language

[9] David McNeil, "Developmental Psycholinguistics," in Frank Smith and George A. Miller (eds.), *The Genesis of Language* (Cambridge, Mass.: M.I.T. Press, 1966), pp. 15–85.

change, a universal characteristic of language. The result is that significant differences between dialects are treated as unimportant.

The theory so minimizes the development of language as a learning process that it is counterproductive. If all children learn to talk, why be concerned about the process?

For educators, this lack of interest is unfortunate. Understanding the processes of language acquisition promises too much for understanding the acquisition of literacy, reading, and writing, which are also language processes. There is also too much still to be learned about the differences in effectiveness among adult users of language and among children whom we seek to help become more effective language users. One thing on which we can agree is that language is uniquely human. How much it is social invention and how much it is instinct remain to be seen.

An Alternate Theoretical Model

The following is a theoretical model of the process of language learning that is consistent with recent research and that does not depend on the assumption that language, particularly its grammar, is an innate human attribute. Throughout the process of language acquisition there are four continuing cycles: *increasing experience, increasing conceptualization, increasing communicative need,* and *increasing effectiveness in communication.* The last can be considered synonymous with increased control over language.

Child language development can be viewed as a series of stages through which the child passes. These stages overlap; the child enters into higher stages well before he has completed earlier stages.

THE RANDOM STAGE In the random stage the child is in a prelinguistic phase. His babbling and experimenting with sounds that he can produce are not language. He does, however, produce sound as part of his reaction to discomfort. He cries when he is hungry, dirty, wet, in pain, too hot, too cold, or frightened. Because adults around the child respond to the noise he makes, he does, during the random stage, acquire a generalized ability to use sound purposefully as an attention-getting signal. He learns that sound can provoke responses from people at a distance who cannot respond to his body movements and other visual signals.

Studies of Russian, German, and American babies all confirm that during this phase, physically normal children produce all the sounds that are significant in the language of their societies, as well as sounds that have significance in other languages.[10] There is no selection process at this stage. The child varies the way that he uses his tongue, mouth, lips, and so on,

---

[10] Hans Tischler, "Schreien, Lallen und Erstes Sprechen in der Entwicklung des Saüglings," *Zeitschrift für Psychologie, 160,* 1957, 210–263.

much as he kicks his arms and legs and flexes his fingers and toes. He produces a random assortment of sounds, although adults hear these sounds as phonemes of adult language and repeat them, presenting the child with what to the adult are corrected models.

The random sounds the baby produces are usually pleasant to him, although he may occasionally startle himself. He plays for long periods at noise making. Often his babbling is composed of consonant-vowel links such as "ma-ma-ma-ma, goo-goo-goo, da-da-da." The peak of babbling is between eight and ten months of age.[11]

It is likely that toward the end of this stage the child is engaging in some intentionally selective behavior, which begins the process of his control over the sounds he makes and which leads to his ability to produce particular sounds at will. He may experiment with varying the intensity or pitch of the sounds he produces. He may mimic lip movements he sees. Thus his development of the physical coordination necessary for speech begins before speech, but language development does not wait for physical maturation and coordination. The two processes, language development and physical maturation, go on simultaneously. At times, in ensuing stages, speech is limited by the level of physical development, but at other times language seems to leap ahead, at least in its receptive phases, and to stimulate the physical development and control necessary for the expressive phases.

THE UNITARY STAGE   At seven to eight months of age, infants show no preference for vocal sounds over other sounds. But three months later they can learn to respond to verbal signals much more quickly than to other sounds.[12] In the unitary stage the child begins to produce sounds purposely to express a need or desire. Sometimes babbling stops just before this stage begins, but it often continues.

In some cases early intentional sounds may not have a communicative function but may be produced on cue. A parent may repeatedly urge a child to say "bye-bye" until he does; the child parrots the adult. The response of the adults around the child when he succeeds in such a task are highly gratifying to him, and the desire for such responses may become the communicative function of the utterance for him. Eventually, the situation itself becomes the cue. Every time the child sees someone with a coat, he says "bye-bye."

This stage is called the unitary stage because the child develops units of language. We must not be misled by the general shortness of each utterance, often limited to a single syllable. The length of each utterance is a function of his level of physical development and control over the

[11] Tischler.

[12] Susan M. Ervin and Wick R. Miller, "Language Development," *Child Psychology*, NSSE Yearbook 62, Part 1 (1963), p. 135.

sound-producing apparatus. But the child has generalized needs and feelings to express; his language has its referents in the total situation in which it is uttered. And the particular syllable used will be the child's approximation of a feature of language that he associates with a situation such as feeding time.

Brown and Bellugi report that in their study of a boy and a girl learning to talk, the children, who were named Adam and Eve, repeated statements of their mothers in a kind of telegraphic language composed of utterances two to four morphemes long. These morphemes were the most heavily stressed words or parts of words in the utterances the child was repeating. Adam, for example, said *"He go out"* when he heard his mother say *"He's going out."*[13] In English the words that get the greatest stress are the ones that carry the most meaning, so that the child's abbreviation carries enough meaning for an adult to reconstruct a total utterance and respond to it. Studies by Menyuk and Bernholz have shown that even the one-word utterance of an 18-month-old child may have several meanings, depending on the intonation. Door, for example, may mean "That's a door," "Is that a door?" "Shut the door!"[14]

The telegraphic abbreviations of Adam and Eve almost always preserved the word order. This would seem to be evidence that the early sentences of children are not lists of words put together but are utterances learned as wholes by the child, independent units of language. Because word order is an important signal of contextual meaning, the child's retention of word order incidentally makes his communication more effective. His speech gives adults a feeling of grammatical consistency, although it is devoid, for the most part, of inflectional markers and function words.

In this stage of the child's language the phonemes (the significant sound units) of his language do not coincide with the phonemes of adult speech. He has fewer phonemes, each of which may function in place of several adult phonemes. This is partly because of his limited control over the organs used in speech and partly because of his limited ability to discriminate fine differences in sounds. Roman Jakobson has suggested that there is a certain economy in developing a stock of phonemes. The child may possess four consonant phonemes. When he has divided one of these phonemes into two, a voiced and an unvoiced form, for example, he may suddenly have eight consonant phonemes, because the physical process that he now controls can be used in the case of his other three original consonants to make each a pair: voiced and unvoiced.[15] In this process, as in all language processes,

[13] Brown and Bellugi, p. 136.

[14] Paula Menyuk and N. Bernholz, "Prosodic Features and Children's Language Production," Quarterly Progress Report, No. 93, M.I.T. Research Laboratory of Electronics, April 1969, pp. 216, 219.

[15] Roman Jakobson and Morris Halle, *Fundamentals of Language* (The Hague: Mouton, 1956). Also see Jakobson, *Child Language, Aphasia, and Phonological Universals* (The Hague: Mouton, 1968).

the child hears differences some time before he can produce them. In fact, even babies as young as one to four months old can distinguish adult phonemes.[16]

In the unitary stage, then, child language is a collection of utterances, each an independent unit. The utterances are abbreviated. They are limited in length to a few highly stressed *morphemes* (idea units) and are composed of a more limited number of phonemes than adult speech. There are notable giant steps toward sounding more like adult speech as the child gains control over his speech apparatus. The word order of adult speech is maintained in the child's abbreviation.

THE STAGE OF EXPANSION AND DELIMITING In the stage of expansion and delimiting, language is still a collection of utterances, but the utterances move in two directions at the same time. They are expanded and delimited. The expansion is from the one- or two-syllable utterances to fuller and fuller approximations of adult speech. This is not a process of combining words to make sentences. It is an expansion of the nucleus so that minor features are included. *Eat* may become *wanna eat* and then become *I want to eat*. It is important to understand that the child's more complete utterances are not built up; they are filled out. They come to correspond closely to adult utterances, but they are still independent wholes.

At the same time that the child is filling out and expanding his utterances, he is delimiting their use. The utterances come to be more and more precise in expressing more and more particular needs or wishes or feelings. The situations in which each utterance is used become increasingly narrow. In the process of striving for more effective communication, the child learns the precise limits within which adults will accept each utterance as appropriate. If he says something in a situation that is meaningless for the utterance, the result is either unsatisfactory or unexpected. The child will tend not to repeat the utterance in similar situations. When he uses an utterance in an appropriate situation, the response is the desired one, and he will tend to use the utterance again in similar circumstances.

Brown and Bellugi report that in their study the mothers of Adam and Eve tended to repeat and expand the utterances of the children to complete simple utterances appropriate to the situations. When the child said, "Baby high chair," the mother said, "Baby is in the high chair."[17] The mother, when she does this, indicates to the child that his utterances are appropriate, and then she adds more language elements to make the baby's speech a complete whole that is not only grammatical but that expresses what to the

[16] P. Eimas, E. Siqueland, P. Jusczak, J. Vigorito, "Speech Perception in Infants," *Science,* 1971, 303–306.
[17] Brown and Bellugi, p. 141.

mother is significant in the situation. Not only is the child being aided in learning language but he is also being guided toward the expression of a view that is meaningful to the adult. This view is likely to be one shared by the culture in which the family lives. Thus, as the adult responds to the child and assists him to move toward the norms of adult speech, the child's perceptions of the world are also shaped to the cultural norms.

Because children's utterances are abbreviations for more complete utterances, it sometimes appears to adults that their language explodes overnight. Velten reports that his daughter developed prepositions, demonstratives, auxiliaries, articles, conjunctions, possessives, and personal pronouns, and suffixes for past tense, plurals, and possessives all in the brief period between 27 months and 30 months of age.[18] All these were implicit in the utterances that the child had used in abbreviated forms, but as the child's speech expanded toward complete utterances they began for the first time to appear in her speech.

By 36 months of age some children are using all varieties of complete simple English sentences. These may be up to 10 or 11 words long. By the fourth year the child's phonological system, with one or two minor exceptions, is within the norms of adult speech. His speech is composed of complete utterances that preserve the word order and inflectional suffixes of adult speech.[19]

Through the processes of expanding expression and delimiting use, the child has come to speak a language remarkably like adult speech. His language is still largely composed of discrete wholes, but, because they have all the features of adult speech and sound like adult speech and because the utterances are usually used in acceptable situations, the child language is very effective.

THE STAGE OF STRUCTURAL AWARENESS Prior to this stage of structural awareness, the child has acquired a large vocabulary of language utterances and has become highly sophisticated about the parameters of their use. This collection of appropriate utterances is quite satisfactory as long as the child's communicative needs are relatively uncomplicated and his experiences are repetitious. But this process of learning language in wholes, one by one, is a slow one. It would eventually be impractical to learn all possible English utterances as units, and the child would be limited in his ability to deal linguistically with new situations and to express his increasingly abstract ideas and feelings.

Fortunately, he is also developing the *ability* to *generalize,* to find pattern and order in the situations he experiences. In his language de-

---

[18] H. V. Velten, "The Growth of Phonemic and Lexical Patterns in Infant Language," *Language, 19* (1943), 281–292.

[19] Ervin and Miller, pp. 116, 125.

velopment he begins to notice the common elements in similar utterances. He may notice that *no* or *not* occurs in many utterances that have a common negative attribute. He may thus experiment with creating his own negatives. Because these are not the wholes he has used before, his early attempts will not be quite like anything he has ever heard. He might say, "*No, I want to eat*," grafting his negative to a positive utterance but not sure of the means. Eventually he induces a rule for negation which then makes it possible to generate new negative statements. McNeil cites an example of a child who developed a double negative rule, "Nobody don't like me." This rule was so strong that the child kept saying, "Nobody don't like me," when he was asked to repeat, "Nobody likes me."[20]

Children will also begin to notice parallel elements in utterances that are otherwise the same. They generalize a pattern in which certain elements can be interchanged. An example of such a pattern that could appear quite early is one in which a series of things or people are inserted in the object slot, such as: *I want milk, I want apple, I want cereal, I want Mommy, I want chair*, and so on.

Ruth Weir reports that her two-and-a-half-year-old son actually engaged in linguistic play that revealed his pulling out of his experience utterances with similar patterns that he then experimented with. He would, for instance, while falling asleep at night, repeat groups of related utterances, such as: what color, what color blanket, what color mop, what color glass.[21]

This process of generalization about patterns and rules[22] for their formation and for the interchangeability of elements is much more abstract and complex than the process of expansion in the previous stage. In expansion the child merely becomes more complete and precise. In generalization he must reflect on the utterances he uses, generalize a pattern, induce a rule, generate an utterance consistent with the rule, and then, on the basis of the effectiveness of the utterance he generates, evaluate the rule and modify it. Just as he had to learn the limits of each utterance he must now also learn the limits of each rule.

As he learns the limit of generalizations he has made about the similarities and differences between utterances, the child slowly becomes aware not only of words and phrases but also of the complex interrelationships of these words and phrases. He becomes aware of very common patterns in the structure of utterances such as the subject-verb-object, *I see you*, pattern. He also becomes aware of less common patterns. He discovers that some patterns are one-of-a-kind idioms with no parallels.

---

[20] McNeil, p. 61.

[21] Ruth Weir, *Language in the Crib* (The Hague: Mouton & Co., 1962).

[22] A *rule*, as used here, is not externally imposed by a grammarian but is in fact a law by which language behavior is governed. To generate new sentences a learner must acquire control of the rules of language.

Prior to this stage the child's speech is remarkably grammatical, because it retains the exact surface structure of adult speech models. But as the child becomes aware of the *deep structure* (underlying forms) of language and begins to construct his own utterances according to his half-defined rules, his language goes through a stage of being ungrammatical by adult norms. His early attempts may be clumsy graftings of the type cited before. Later he overgeneralizes, regularizing irregular forms or structures. By analogy he creates forms that conform to common rules. He may say, "*I taked it*" (or even, "*I takted it*") because he is aware of the most general rule for indicating past tense.

Adults are sometimes disturbed about the errors in children's speech in this stage. They regard it as sloppy and often react in annoyed or sarcastic ways. Actually, the child could not acquire control over the rules, patterns, inflectional endings, function words, and intonation systems of language without testing his generalizations as they were formed. *Children who are prevented or discouraged from making errors in this stage may be reluctant to try out generalizations and remain in the less effective stage of learned wholes.*

It is in this stage of structural awareness that words or phrases begin to take on meaning. Previously, only the whole utterance had any meaning. Now the child begins to be aware of the element of meaning that is contributed by each word or phrase to complete the meaning of the sentence. This is a complex process, indeed, because every word in an utterance has not only a lexical, dictionary meaning but also a contextual meaning. The child must encounter a word or phrase in many utterances before he begins to know the limits of the lexical meaning of the word. An indication that children become concerned with the meaning of words and phrases during this stage is that they frequently ask adults, "What does _____ mean?" Sometimes they ask right after they hear the expression, but they are just as likely to ask hours or even days later as they mull over an expression that was not completely understood. Luria reports that Russian children at about four-and-one-half years begin to respond to the semantic qualities of words. Prior to four-and-one-half years they respond impulsively to whole utterances.[23]

The child's large vocabulary of learned whole utterances serves as a check on his generalizations about language structure and word or phrase meaning. He develops a feeling for the language, a kind of intuition that is formed of many not wholly analyzed and understood language experiences.

During this discussion frequent mention has been made of *words and phrases* rather than just *words*. This phraseology is preferred because children do not break language into words as literate adults might. They become aware, during this stage, of *particles* of language that are smaller

---

[23] Ervin and Miller, p. 137.

than whole utterances, but these *particles* are not exactly the same as words. Groups of two or three words, like *all-gone, out-of-doors, pick up*, and *fire engine*, are heard so frequently together and are so closely bound that the child considers them and treats them like single elements. He may even say, *"I pickuped my toys."*

The process of induction by which each child discovers the fine points of structure of language is long and slow. Berko reports that American children from four to seven years of age tend to avoid derivational suffixes like *worker*, preferring compounds like *working man* or syntactic constructions like *the man that works*.[24] On the other hand, pre-schoolers can identify nonsense words such as *was* sibbing, *the* sib, or *some* sib as verb, count noun, or mass noun, respectively, by the markers. Ervin and Miller conclude that by age four most children have learned fundamental structural features of their language.[25]

The process of acquiring less important structural generalizations and of learning unusual exceptions continues well past the point where the basic structure has become automatic. An example is an expression such as *he gots it. Got* is in the process of replacing *has* in some uses. Americans are likely to say *I've got it* or *I got it* rather than *I have it.* Similarly, Americans say *he's got it* or *he got it* but seldom *he has it* and hardly ever *he has got it.* Because the child does not hear *he has got it,* he does not know that the *'s* in *he's got it* is equal to *has*, so he regularizes *got* as a third person singular verb, making it *gots* and hence *he gots it.*

In the stage of structural awareness, then, the child becomes aware of the constituents of the whole utterances he has learned. He forms generalizations about the structure of the utterances, induces rules for generating them, acquires precise meanings of words and phrases. He begins generating original utterances, which he tests in situations that seem appropriate to him.

THE AUTOMATIC STAGE When the child reaches the automatic stage of language development, he has internalized the grammar of his language. But he doesn't just rely on a large vocabulary of whole utterances that he can use appropriately; he can generate utterances that he has never heard but that are fully grammatical. He can move words and phrases from one structure to another and know with considerable confidence whether they are acceptable in these settings. He does all this with little conscious reasoning. He can tell whether something is wrong or right but cannot begin to explain why. He just knows.

[24] Jean Berko, "The Child's Learning of English Morphology," *Word, 14* (1958), 159–177.

[25] Ervin and Miller, p. 125.

The average child has reached the automatic stage of language by the time he begins kindergarten. The basic grammar of *his* language, which is of course that of his home and community, is deeply embedded in him. It is continuously reinforced by the language he hears and uses at home and play.

At the time he reaches this stage, the child is greatly increasing his conceptualization and greatly increasing the quantity and effectiveness of his language. His language has moved rapidly from highly individual attempts at communication to an idiolect that falls well within the norms of his community's dialect. Whatever this dialect is, when he has reached the point of automatic control over it, it is adequate to meet the communicative needs common to persons of his age in his immediate society.

THE CREATIVE STAGE As he begins to develop language the child literally invents his own. But the need for effectiveness in communication is so strong that he is constantly pushed and shoved in the direction of the language of his community. Like a plastic mass, his language develops within the language mold of his community, eventually taking on the same structure and dimensions. All this is in the direction of conformity. Language becomes for the most part, and for most users, a vast collection of clichés. Most of everyday communication is carried on with trite expressions linked in trite ways. To a great extent, this conformity reflects the manner in which language has been learned. It also reflects the degree to which language has become the automatic reaction to repetitious situations.

But it must not be forgotten that language is man-made. However trite and systematic it becomes, it never becomes completely static and unchanging, because man, individually and socially, never loses his ability to create language. Children pass into a stage of creative manipulation of language. Perhaps this is due to their increasing ability to conceptualize and think in metaphors and abstractions. They push language beyond its conventional limits. This may be related to the need children have for testing all adult limits.

Children, of course, have needs and interests in common that they do not share with adults. In a sense, a child subdialect develops. This is passed on from each wave of children to the next. But there are always some new needs and new ways to meet old needs, and new language is created to express them. Teen-agers, particularly, tend to create language. To some extent this may be because language is so closely related to perception and life-view. To use the language of adults would imply acceptance of adult categories, values, and attitudes. The teen-ager must have a language that is uniquely his and uniquely able to express life as he sees it. The limits of some terms are even inverted so that generally negative adult terms such as "crazy," "mad," "tough," "bad," and "wicked" become positive terms in the teen vernacular. Positive terms like "nice," "sensible," "square,"[26] "bold," and "good" become negative. Other groups in society share with the adolescent the need for a special language to express a nonconformist view. A recent example is the language of the hippies.

Regardless of the forces that bring new language into being, some of it will find its way deep into the common language of society. New language tends to be colorful and a welcome relief from the clichés that are repeated endlessly. Then again, the perceptions of life and the world that are common to the society are also in evolution. It may be the young who first sense this and supply the language to express it.

All people create language to some small degree, but only the great language artists rival the young in creative use of language. The literary giants and storytellers of all time have had in common the ability to use language in artistic and novel ways, to find unique ways to communicate fine images and emotions with great effectiveness and understanding. They become masters at stretching and varying language to avoid repetition. In their hands, language does not so limit the human capacity for self-expression; it becomes the supple tool of thought and communication. So much a master of language is the great writer that he transcends all language conventions; he makes rules work for him.

Creative thoughts require creative language to express them. Emphasis on conformity in language in school or at home stifles not only expression but also thought. Fortunately, the tendency of children to be creative with language is almost universal. Parents and teachers can encourage this tendency. If they do, perhaps there will eventually be more adults with the courage to use language creatively.

Language in School

A longitudinal study of the language development of elementary school children over time was made by Walter Loban. He followed the language development of eleven kindergarten classes (which were selected as representative of all ethnic and socioeconomic groups in Oakland, California) until the children had completed the twelfth grade. This important study has shed much light on the directions and variations in growth of children's language and the correlation of language development with other abilities and achievement of children.[27]

Except for children whose native language was not a dialect of English, all the children in this study used all basic patterns of English sentence structure, even in kindergarten. There were, of course, considerable differ-

---

[26] Compare George M. Cohan's "There is something there, that seems so square" with the meaning of "square" to modern teens.

[27] Loban, pp. 81–89.

ences in size of vocabulary of children in the study and differences in the fluidity and completeness of their utterances.

Loban found that the difference between groups of children who were rated high or low in language ability was not in the patterns they used. He found that children who were rated "poor" tended to use more partial utterances. Those who were considered better users of language used more complete utterances and more complex fillers of the slots in the utterances. More subordinate clauses were used by the "high" group.

Loban found these general directions of growth as children became older and more effective in use of language:

> They tend to use more language, and more communication units when they speak (the communication unit corresponds roughly, but not exactly, to a traditional sentence).
> The communication units tend to get longer (include more words), and to get more complex grammatically.
> The language tends to express more tentativeness, supposition, hypothesis, and conditionality as it becomes more articulate; it is less disjointed.

Loban found that children had a tendency to grope for words, sometimes in the middle of an utterance. He labeled this phenomenon in the speech he studied "a maze." Here is an example he cites of a maze: "I saw a hunter program last Sunday, an he an snow time he had to have lot uh, wah-h when he, uh, not too many dogs, he . . . . and that's all I think of that picture."[28] The child appears to be literally wandering in a linguistic maze trying to find a way to express his thoughts.

The frequency and length of mazes in children's language is an indication of their ease of expression. Loban found that children whose language was rated high in kindergarten tended to use mazes less until the third grade, at which point they leveled off. Children rated low in kindergarten used mazes less when they were in grades four, five, and six but still used mazes much more than the "high" group. Throughout elementary school they continued to find it relatively difficult to find the language for easy expression.

Boys, in the Loban study, were found at the extremes. As the researcher puts it: "Whatever the causes, genetic or cultural, boys in this study do very poorly in language when they are low in language ability and excel when they are high in language ability."[29]

In this study a number of interesting correlations were found:

> Reading, writing, listening, and speaking were all positively related. Children who were low in general oral language ability tended to be low in reading and writing achievement. Children high in language ability tended to do well in gaining literacy skills.

[28] Loban, p. 9.
[29] Loban, p. 89.

A positive correlation was found between health and language proficiency. Reading and writing were related to socioeconomic position.

Oral language ability and vocabulary correlated highly with success on group IQ tests.

Chronological age, effective use of language, and socioeconomic status correlated positively with complexity of grammatical structure in the speech of the children.

From the Loban study and older, less comprehensive studies, it is possible to pinpoint the major categories of language difficulties that elementary school children are likely to have: (1) language that is limited and inflexible and that does not serve the expanding needs of the child, particularly in school tasks; and (2) language that is considered nonstandard or socially unacceptable for educated members of the society to use.[30]

Failure to keep these two problems distinct may have caused many school programs to be self-defeating. If teachers and school programs confuse language that is inadequate with langauge that is different, they may, in well-meaning ways, so inhibit learners that they become totally inarticulate.

Kellogg Hunt has demonstrated through the use of *transformational grammar*[31] in analysis of the written language of children at various points during their school years that a key feature in their language development is increased use of language structures that are both compact and complex. He developed the concept of the T-unit, the shortest language sequence that can be terminated without leaving any fragments, as a unit of anlysis. He found that successively older subjects had longer T-units, longer clauses, and more clauses per T-unit.[32]

To illustrate this phenomenon here are sequences that express essentially the same ideas:

I have a friend. His name is Jimmy. Yesterday he got a new bike. It's red. Somebody stole it already.

Somebody already stole the new red bike my friend Jimmy just got yesterday. The new red bike my friend Jimmy got yesterday has already been stolen.

The ability to *generate* these more complex and compact language units not only may reflect the increased control of the youngsters over the transformational rules involved but also may be an indication of the ability of children to relate the complex ideas involved rather than to handle them one at a time. *In any case this well-defined progression of transformations suggests an area in which schools can contribute to development and generation of effective language.*

---

[30] Loban, p. 89.

[31] See Chapter 8, Section 3.

[32] Kellogg W. Hunt, *Grammatical Structures Written at Three Grade Levels* (Champaign, Ill.: NCTE, 1965), p. 63.

3

Language Development in Social and Historical Context

Those who have been persuaded to think well of my design, will require that it should fix our language, and put a stop to those alterations which time and chance have hitherto been suffered to make in it without opposition. With this consequence I will confess that I flattered myself for a while; but now begin to fear that I have indulged expectation which neither reason nor experience can justify. When we see men grow old and die at a certain time one after another, from century to century, we laugh at the elixir that promises to prolong life to a thousand years; and with equal justice may the lexicographer be derided, who being able to produce no example of a nation that has preserved their words and phrases from mutability, shall imagine that his dictionary can embalm his language, and secure it from corruption and decay, that it is in his power to change sublunary nature, and clear the world at once from folly, vanity, and affectation.[1]

section 1

The English Language in Time, Place, and Culture

The story of the English language is one of differentiation through constant change from its Germanic cousins; it is a story of a peasant language disdained by the nobility as unworthy of noble discourse and

[1] Samuel Johnson, *A Dictionary of the English Language*, 1755.

official business; it is the story of a language that in many variants has come to pre-eminence among the world's languages.

High-status dialects of English have displaced the classic Latin and the noble French as the language of the elite. But the process of change continues, always responsive to the shifts in the needs and culture of the language's users.

Yet, each modern dialect of English echoes its antecedents. The language and its background form a commonly received frame of reference. No language exists only at the surface, and only surface ends can be achieved by treating it as if it did.

Origins of English

Most of the European languages, as well as Persian and several of the languages of India derived from Sanskrit, have been traced back to a hypothetical parent language called Indo-European. The comparative studies of languages that led to the establishment of these relationships were a great triumph of nineteenth-century scholarship.

English is a Germanic language, belonging to the same general family as Dutch, Flemish, modern German, and Scandinavian tongues. This family is derived from a Germanic tongue that was related to Greek, Latin, and the early Slavic language. All of these were more distantly related to Persian and Sanskrit. It has not been possible so far to establish relationships with such non-Indo-European languages as Chinese, Malay, or Arabic.

In addition to these common origins, English has been built up from cross-fertilizations and borrowings; isolation and differentiation also complicate the picture of language development. When the Angles, Saxons, and Jutes left the continent of Europe for what was to become England (Angle-land), they separated themselves from the other Germanic tribes that remained behind and began to change their language to adapt to a new environment. Also, the natural changes in language varied among those who had emigrated and those who remained behind. Later, with Viking invasions, the North Germanic language of the Scandinavian peoples came to England, although the languages were still alike enough for the two peoples to communicate. Some of the Scandinavian invaders settled and blended in with the English, leaving recognizable traces of their language differences in the *sk* words, *sky, skirt, skin,* and *skull.* The Celtic people of Britain had been eliminated, enslaved (in small numbers), or driven into remote corners of Britain—to Wales, Cornwall, the Scottish Highlands, or across the sea to Ireland. Very little Celtic influence was left on English other than in place names, many of which are Celtic or Latinized Celtic origin. Had the Celts become a subject people in large numbers, they might have influenced English, but the few who remained were in no position to maintain a social group to sustain their language.

Influence of the Norman Conquest

William and his Norman-French followers carried a French-speaking ruling class to England in 1066. Unlike the earlier conquests of Celts by the Germanic tribes, William's conquest of a stable society maintained that society relatively intact. Although the ruling class spoke French and the populace had, of necessity, to learn a certain amount of French, the language of the majority of the people prevailed. By the thirteenth century the ruling class was speaking English more and more, although English itself had changed radically.

The presence of French-speaking rulers led to a vibrant vocabulary, which has typified English ever since. The point could be made that words having to do with the enjoyment of the fruits of labor were French, while those having to do with producing them were English. *Pork* is of French origin, while *swine* is of English; *beef* of French and *cow* or *ox* of English. Words having to do with government come largely from French—*govern, reign, realm, sovereign, country*—but the claim of legitimate continuance of the English system is shown in certain key English words, such as *king, queen,* and *earl.* Words having to do with luxurious living are of French origin, and as education and the church were taken over by the Normans, religious, spiritual, and cultural terms are of French origin. The Norman Conquest, with all its social and cultural side effects, left a permanent mark on the English language. In many cases French and English words existed side by side and both survived. Usually, however, these are not duplicates; they are used to express different shades of meaning.

More important than what French did to English was what English did to itself during the period of French-speaking leadership. Many changes in Old English (Anglo-Saxon) were accelerated. Without educated leadership, which normally acts as a conservative force, speakers of Anglo-Saxon (and the few who wrote) moved swiftly toward a reduction of inflected forms and a reliance on positional features bringing a greater simplicity of language. The basic grammatical form became a much more streamlined Germanic language with a strong admixture of Norman-French vocabulary.

Middle English and Early Modern English

By the end of this period the language was so changed as to require a new designation, Middle English. The Middle-English period may be dated roughly from 1100 to 1500. The language of the sixteenth century is Early Modern English, the language of Shakespeare and the other great Elizabethan writers. Their language presents no major difficulties for the educated reader[2] of today, although it may do so by the end of the twentieth

---

[2] Shakespeare's continuing popularity in the theater has helped to keep Elizabethan language alive as has continued reading of the King James version of the Bible.

century. It should be pointed out that these writers wrote without the benefit of schooling in correctness of usage or grammar. They used the language freely and un–self-consciously, and that was their strength. It is quite possible that academic inhibitions would have cramped their style, particularly if the inappropriate Latin grammar had been applied to it. This is the form of English that the early settlers brought to North America and that constitutes the early colonial literature, the William Bradford and John Smith histories.

Borrowings from Other Languages

Some attention should be paid to a long history of borrowing from languages other than French and to its impact on English. Cultures have always shown a tendency to borrow from perceived higher cultures when they come in contact with them. Sometimes this is done in a slavish way, sometimes in a very selective way, when only those things needed are chosen and adapted to the language. The Romans borrowed heavily from Greek culture, recognizing its superiority in many areas; they borrowed and adapted words to express concepts and ideas for which they had no words in Latin. The Germanic-speaking people on the Continent, some of whom were later to emigrate to England and become the English, came in contact with Roman civilization, mainly through traders.

As the Germanic peoples were not literate at the time, Latin words were borrowed orally, and when they came to be written later, it was not easy to recognize their Latin origin. From this period came such words as *wine* (from Latin *vinum*) and *wall* (from Latin *vallum*), *mint* (from Latin *moneta*), *pound* (from Latin *ponde*), *inch* (from Latin *uncia*), *mile* (from Latin *mille*), *chest* (from Latin *cista*), and *kettle* (from Latin *catillus*). Objects of trade not known to the purchasers would be likely subjects for word borrowing, although not necessarily. In this case, as in all others to follow, it was always possible to use native language elements to give a sensorially, psychologically, and semantically sound translation. A desire to associate an item with the language and people it came from might lead to the adoption of a foreign word. At later stages, second-language snobbery might lead to its use. At a still later stage, when the new fused culture becomes strong and begins to look with pride on its roots, the borrowed word may be dropped and an older term revived.

After the Germanic-speaking peoples migrated to England and eliminated the Britons—the Celtic and Latin-speaking inhabitants—they were Christianized over a period of years by St. Augustine in the south and by the Irish Christians in the north. Christianity brought Latin terms into use again, and with them came the Latin cultural elements of philosophy and literature that Christianity continued to foster after the fall of Roman political power. Words having to do with Christianity, such as *pope, arch-*

bishop, priest, Mass, monk, nun, and *shrine,* were borrowed from Latin; but many terms were translated, such as *gospel* (Anglo-Saxon *god-spell,* meaning literally "good teaching") instead of Latin *evangelium* (borrowed from the Greek). Throughout the Anglo-Saxon period, the tendency was to use native elements of the language rather than to borrow words. Any language is adequate to the culture it embodies and is capable of expanding to meet whatever cultural developments become necessary, within the terms of its own form and vocabulary. There are other successful ways of extending the cultural limits (as English has shown), but it can probably be done more efficiently with native resources. Modern German is the product of an attempt to use native elements (although somewhat self-consciously as an instrument of nationalism in the nineteenth and twentieth centuries) in the manner of the Anglo-Saxon.

It seems quite likely that the undermining of Anglo-Saxon national spirit in the Norman period changed the attitude of speakers of English toward borrowing, and this attitude has never been the same since. Even so, a parallel native term has often been available, providing great range and nuance to the language for those who care to avail themselves of the possibilities. Thus, for aesthetic or psychological reasons or for semantic exactness, an English-speaking person can use native elements going back to the roots of the language, or he can use borrowings that create quite a different effect. This is not to say that borrowings have no psychological depth or aesthetic texture. After four or five hundred years, they are honestly English. *Cry, poor, change, war,* and *peace* are such words. But apart from such short and familiar words, the shadings of difference are always there. In literature, they loom large; in science also, but for other reasons. A doctor, in discussing internal organs with a patient, might not want to emphasize the psychological and sensory impact of *guts.* On the other hand, such a euphemism as *intestines* might strangle a poem.

Influence of the Renaissance and Scientific Age

The Renaissance (mainly sixteenth century in England) brought an influx of Latin terms to accompany the revival of Classical civilization. A climate of thought was created that seemed to call for the wholesale borrowing of Latin words, even where French borrowing going back to the same Latin roots was present, as in *adventure* and *debt.* At the same time, there was effort to create a vernacular literature of a quality comparable to that of the Classical age. Many writers took pride in native vocabulary, scorning the use of "inkhorn" terms, which they regarded as undigested and unnecessary Latin borrowing.

Eventually, usage sifted out many unnecessary Latin borrowings. This was a period of intellectual ferment, and the process was fed from many sources. The result was the heady wine of Elizabethan literature. English developed the range of vocabulary that made refined gradation of feeling and thought possible, while retaining a central native tradition that made for psychological depth and artistic simplicity. The language developed an extensive system of qualifying terms with an underlying grammatical structure that made the language highly analytical at a time when scientific thought could make use of it.

The development of commerce and communication led to a new eclecticism in word borrowing and quickened the process. Speakers of English have borrowed from all lands and languages in the modern period, reflecting mercantile, military, and colonial interests in various areas at different times. Modern science has led to the use of neo-Latin and neo-Greek words for scientific classification and for describing newly discovered processes.

Each speaker of the English language calls it to life, as he has been doing for over a thousand years. *The language has changed and will go on changing, but there is a continuity that ties the present-day speaker with the past and the future. He finds his way through riches on every hand, some familiar, well-worn, and of proven worth, some waiting to be discovered, mined, and minted. The teacher may lead him to these riches if he knows of them.*

The Geographical Context

The land was ours before we were the land's.
Robert Frost[3]

The finding of common forms in the various Indo-European languages led to identification of the family and to the establishment of a hypothetical parent language. Those words appearing in a number of the languages were assumed to represent something of the common culture and its original geographic setting. From the beginning it was assumed that the parent language flourished in a limited geographic area before it spread across Europe and Asia. Words appearing only in isolated languages of the group were assumed to reflect a geographic setting of that language, after its speakers wandered away from the homeland. The presence of common words for snow, beech, pine, bear, wolf, ox, sheep, and bee, taken together, suggest a temperate setting; the absence of common words for elephant, lion, tiger, rhinoceros, monkey, rice, bamboo, and palm adds negative evidence.

In the late eighteenth century, after the identification of the Indo-European family through the discovery of similarities between European languages and the Sanskrit-derived languages of India and assisted by the

[3] From "The Gift Outright" from *The Poetry of Robert Frost,* edited by Edward Connery Lathem. Copyright 1942 by Robert Frost. Copyright © 1969 by Holt, Rinehart and Winston, Inc. Copyright © 1970 by Leslie Frost Ballantine. Reprinted by permission of Holt, Rinehart and Winston, Publishers, and Jonathan Cape Limited.

commonly held idea that Mesopotamia was the site of the Garden of Eden, it was held that the Indo-European homeland was in Asia, despite the fact that most of the members of the family were in Europe.

More recently, scholars have postulated the location of the homeland as Europe, somewhere east of the Germanic-speaking area, extending from Lithuania into southeastern Europe and possibly including Anatolia. These interpretations grow out of language detective work, based on trying to match language (or hypothetical language) and geographic context. However, extreme care must be employed in making judgments about a long-dead, unwritten, prehistoric language in an uncertain geographic setting. Tracing associations of language and geography in recorded history or modern times is much easier.

Influence of a New Land
on Emerging English

When Anglo-Saxon people went to England they began to differentiate their Germanic language from that on the continent to reflect their new environment. Their interaction with a new part of the earth, together with their isolation from the old, helped to make English a distinct language. There were dialect differences among Angles, Saxons, and Jutes on the continent, and when they settled in different parts of England, these differences were continued. Although the common experience of migration and of association in driving out the Celtic Britons might have served to reduce differences, this was a relatively brief experience as language experience goes. When political unity of England did come, the lack of communication typical of all Europe after the fall of the Roman Empire left the dialects so isolated that they continued to develop along their own lines. The general language was realized by each particular human organism and in each particular geographic context.

Cleaving to the mother tongue was understandable in the early days of North American settlement. The American wilderness may have seemed like chaos to the first settlers, and one way of avoiding slipping into it was to stick to the safely ordered language of society that maintained in England. But the new environment called for new language to express its concepts. The American Revolution was in part the result of the realization that the British Parliament and British civilization had little relevance to the American situation; to continue to vest power in a body without the possibility of cognitive and perceptual understanding would indeed be tyranny.

The Adjustment of English
to the American Scene

Psychologically and aesthetically, the need to adjust English to the American geographical and cultural context was extremely important. The immediacy of perceptual grasp and its feedback from the conceptual were slowed by the requirement that every experience be referred to England. The organic and symbolic importance of the colonial pine-tree shilling had its counterpart in language. The need for a thoroughly acclimated and domesticated language was even more important in literature, and a very great advance in American letters took place when writers such as Mark Twain and Walt Whitman finally made the break complete, cutting England out of the circuit. They evaluated the American experience in its own terms. Once, this kind of turning away from source would have meant a new language, considering the size of North America. But changes in communication now seem likely to maintain a widespread language community.

Meeting the American
Experience with Language

From the beginning, English-speaking settlers used Indian place names, recognizing that there is often some special connection between the place and the conventional name it bears. Just so, the Anglo-Saxons, while obliterating the previous inhabitants of England, did not tamper with some Celtic and Roman place names. The feeling for the country in its national manifestation, as against cultural features, has come to be expressed in Indian names—Oklahoma, the Penobscot, Massachusetts, the Chickahominy, Alabama, and so on. Words for new flora and fauna and experiences were also borrowed from the Indians: moose and caribou, pow-wow and pecan, opossum and pone, squash and succotash, wigwam and wickiup, sachem and wampum, skunk and quahog, tomahawk and toboggan, canoe and tobacco (these two from the West Indies), chili and chocolate, tomato and tamale (these four from Mexico). Terms were translated from Indian languages: warpath, paleface, big chief, pipe of peace, bury the hatchet, war whoop, and war paint. Words were contributed by non–English-speaking settlers: from the New Amsterdam Dutch, cruller and coleslaw, sleigh and span (of horses), dope and spook and Yankee (derived from *Jan-Ki,* diminutive for John); from the Spanish settlers (mostly after the westward movement), corral and ranch, lasso, bronco and pinto, arroyo and canyon; from the French, bayou and levee, cafe and portmanteau, portage and prairie. Perhaps most important of all in conjuring up the quality of American experience were the new combinations of old words: gartersnake and grizzly bear, slippery elm and snap bean, sourwood and sugar maple, corn patch and corn crib, bullfrog and backwoods (the latter an interesting contrast to the Australian *outback*), sweet potato and bluegrass, butternut and catbird, lightning bug and pond lily, statehouse and selectman, hoe cake and husking bee, quilting bee and spinning bee (and a whole hive of other social activities followed by "bee"; contrast the later rash of "ins"— love-in, sit-in, teach-in, and so on); land office and bottom land, backlog and drygoods, eye gouging and rough-and-tumble. The first English settlers to come to America had grown up in the age of Elizabeth and were Elizabethans in their language. But the life of the frontier did not lend itself to the restraints in language that overtook the stay-at-home Englishmen in the eighteenth century, so that Elizabethan ebullience and inventions continued to characterize the language of the New World.

The English Language in America

Like Dutch settlers in South Africa who gave themselves to their environment and, with the added element of isolation, evolved a new language, Afrikaans, the new settlers arriving in America from England brought the language of the homeland, but immediately began to find new words or to use old words in new ways. Continuing political relationship and new immigration served for a time to keep the differences between British and American English to a minimum. Because the migration was mostly one way, the attitude of those in England was that the language was degenerating in the New World.

When Americans began to accept their language as the valid means of defining the unique American experience, they could at last give themselves to the land they had held aloof from by pretending they were still Europeans, dwelling in a wilderness and in exile from their native heath.

Early English travelers, within a few years of the first settlements, commented on the changes wrought in the language by the New World. Although dialect differences came to America and, in some instances, were isolated in pockets, as in some southern Appalachian areas, the fact that the settlers were funneled in through the East Coast served to provide a common language denominator. Also, continuing and relatively rapid mobility of people across the continent and new forms of communication made the old isolation less possible. West African pidgin with its English word-phrases set in African language structures came to America with the slaves, sometimes via the Caribbean islands. It has enriched the American language as it combined with southern black dialects, together strongly influencing popular language and finding their way into American literature. For all these reasons only a few major dialects with the degree of difference comparable to that of the 30-odd dialects of England have persisted in the United States.

American Dialects Today

Does a peach have a pit, seed, stone, or bone in it? Is the same thing found in a cherry or is that known by another name? Your answer will be different depending on where you live and where you grew up. Do you carry the groceries home in a bag, a sack, a poke, or a tote? One or more sounds natural to you and the others are either strange-sounding or you may argue that they have quite another meaning. A speaker from southern Illinois amuses his Chicago listeners when he says he will "warsh" his clothes and then "arn" them. A listener in Milwaukee notes inwardly the lack of culture of an educated Kentuckian when he hears him say *dived* instead of *dove*.

All these are aspects of the differences between the well-established regional dialects of the United States. Such differences have been studied and documented by linguistic atlas field workers who have been engaged for decades in the task of interviewing speakers in all parts of the country to determine the boundaries and overlaps of dialect regions. The task is not yet completed because of the limited number of trained field workers and the lack of the substantial financial support that would be required to complete it.

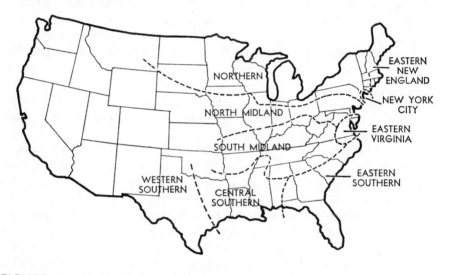

FIGURE 1.   Major Dialect Areas of the United States. Adapted by Roger W. Shuy in DISCOVERING AMERICAN DIALECTS (Champaign, Ill.: NCTE, 1967); from E. Bagby Atwood, THE REGIONAL VOCABULARY OF TEXAS (Austin: University of Texas Press, 1962), p. 80. Used by permission of University of Texas Press.

The map in Figure 1 is a relatively up-to-date one showing the boundaries between America's regional dialects as far as they have been drawn. The influence of the generally westward population movement across the northern, middle, and southern states since colonial days explains the division of the country into the basic dialect groups. A certain degree of insularity explains the more contained dialects of New England, New York City, and eastern Virginia. The areas of earliest settlement on the East Coast developed the smallest and most easily defined dialect areas.

When the map is finished it will partly represent an extension of the existing lines westward and partly reflect major changes in the speed and methods of transportation in recent decades. The population movement into California, for example, represents leapfrogging from distant parts of the country. Similarly, southern Florida has had strong northern dialect influences.

CLASS DIALECTS The dialect patterns of the major northern cities are influenced by a decided South-to-North movement established as industrialization became a magnet to those leaving more rural areas. This has led to complex socioeconomic dialect patterns within the major cities. The different social classes have been recruited from different parts of the country. Particularly after the immigration of Europeans in large numbers ended in the 1920s, industrial workers were recruited from the black and white poor in the South and Midlands. World War II accelerated this migration.

Studies of socioeconomic dialect patterns within urban complexes of the United States have only recently begun. In the geographic atlas work there was a strong tendency to concentrate only on the most stable and well-established language in an area. Studies of urban dialect patterns require a look at the speech of all groups in the area across ethnic, racial, and class lines. The patterns of dialect distribution within a metropolitan complex relate to the population shifts in that complex. Immigrants have tended to arrive in the central portions of the complex, to spend a generation there, and then to shift outward toward the outer part of the city and the suburbs. In American cities the pattern has been for successive waves of European immigrants to replace each other, followed by black and white immigrants from the South. Transplanted regional dialects are superimposed on pre-existing ones in the cities; and all are in continuous evolution, as is language everywhere. The net result is a picture of great variation with social-status factors becoming intermixed with linguistic ones in the attitudes of urban people toward the language of their neighbors, their friends, and themselves. Some language forms, phonological, grammatical, and semantic, become prestigious, while others are accorded the low status of their users. All dialects influence each other to some degree, but upwardly mobile individuals will tend to shift toward prestige forms to gain greater acceptance from high-status groups in the community and to conceal their more humble beginnings.[4] *Each dialect, however, is a bona fide language system. Teachers need to be well aware of this fact in daily instruction.*

[4] Roger Shuy, *Discovering American Dialects* (Champaign, Ill.: NCTE, 1967).

section 2

Children's Role in the History of Language

Children have played key roles in the history of American English and will continue to make their influence felt as the language is molded today for the future. They are protectors of the language that was, conveyors of the language that is, and innovators of the language that will be.

Child-Folk or Play Language

A remarkable and fascinating book, *The Lore and Language of Schoolchildren*, by Iona and Peter Opie, reveals English-speaking children at work in their language. The Opies have differentiated the juvenile tongue from the mother tongue of the adult world by making a distinction between the nursery rhyme and what they call the "school rhyme," which is language of the playground, whether it is used in a street, in a barnyard, or upstairs in the attic.

> While a nursery rhyme passes from a mother or other adult to the small child on her knee, the school rhyme circulates simply from child to child, usually outside the home, and beyond the influence of the family circle. . . . It [the nursery rhyme] is a rhyme which is adult approved. The schoolchild's verses are not intended for adult ears. In fact part of their fun is the thought, usually correct, that adults know nothing about them.[5]

This child language of rhymes, jokes, parodies, tricks, testing codes, nicknames, and epithets is the symbolic content of a universal subculture of childhood society. It is a subculture in which the child learns the language and all its possibilities at the same time that he is learning adult culture and its language. The new language of each generation emerges from an interplay between the child tongue and the mother tongue.

Conservation of the Language by Children

Children protect or conserve the language that was and thereby assist in the stabilization of the language. Oral transmission is a stabilizer of the language. Transmission of folk tales, folk songs, and rhymes is a good example of how the old language persists for centuries. Children learn some of these rhymes and tales by heart in their early years, but more important than the fact of exact or near memorization of words is the children learning the old syntax, the old flow of line, the old rhymes, and assonance that delight. Some words persist for generations because of this oral tradition

[5] Iona Opie and Peter Opie, *The Lore and Language of Schoolchildren* (London: Oxford University Press, 1959), p. 1, by permission of the Clarendon Press, Oxford.

even though there is no need for the words any longer. *Porridge* is such a word. It is firmly seated in "Pease porridge hot, pease porridge cold," even though porridge has been replaced by cornflakes for most children in the United States.[6] Overly modernized versions of such tales, songs, and rhymes may help the child grasp the ideas they express, but could also begin to shake the language loose from its roots.

Children also tend to conserve the old language in their own tongue. Contrary to what many had believed, the Opies found that children's language in play has changed surprisingly little over the centuries. Although much of the slang of children is inventive and gains prominence for the moment, dialect lore passed down in regions and neighborhoods from one generation of children to the next persists over many generations. Names and places change, but the old jokes and themes of play language are the same. The Opies quote an old ballad of 1725 from which a common playground song obviously developed.

> Now he acts the Grenadier,
> Calling for a Pot of Beer:
> Where's his Money? He's forgot:
> Get him gone, a Drunken Sot.   (1725)

They then quote the British Museum's record from an eight-year-old child who noted his own version of the ballad almost fifty years later:

> Whoes there
> A Granidier
> What dye want
> A Pint of Beer   (1774)

From that date until now it has been children's coinage and theirs alone.

Rat a tat tat, who is that?
Only grandma's pussycat.
What do you want?
A pint of milk.
Where's your money?
In my pocket.
Where is your pocket?
I forgot it.
O, you silly pussycat.   (1916)

Mickey Mouse
In a public house
Drinking pints of beer.
Where's your money?
In my pocket.
Where's your pocket?
I forgot it.
Please walk out.[7]   (1950)

The catch is altered in each generation, but not substantially. Perhaps play language remains much the same because it is passed on so quickly. A generation for children's language is only six years to eight years.

---

[6] To Canadians, however, *porridge* has come to mean specifically "oatmeal."

[7] Above verses from Opie and Opie, pp. 10–11.

Many items of the British collection by the Opies sound very close to American play language. Oceans of distance have not held back the carrier-children. One of the "tricks inflicting pain" is as common in America as in England.

> Adam and Eve and Pinch-me
> Went down to the river to bathe.
> Adam and Eve were drowned,
> Who do you think was saved?[8]

From most categories of child language collected in Britain, there are echoes and even repeats in the American child culture. Crybabies on both sides of the Atlantic are rebuked with some version of

> Cry baby, cry,
> Put your finger in your eye,
> And tell your mother
> It wasn't I.[9]

Children's play talk pervades the child culture and stabilizes the movement of language at an impressionable period in the child's language development. Both schoolyard language passed from child to child and the nursery rhymes, tales, and old songs transmitted by adults preserve the oral traditions. Children carry the language they learn in this way into the next generation, when, as adults, they pass some of it along to their children. They put away child language as they put away childish things, but the sense of rhythms and sound-play remains.

Children Expanding the Language of Their Generation

Children are more than just the conveyors of the language between generations. They actually remold or remake it as they play with it. Even though they tend to be conservative in their imitation of adult language, they also break away from accepted patterns as they innovate and use shortcuts.

Here are a group of circle games collected from some inner-city black children. These are called circle games because the players stand in a circle. Usually sung, some have motions or movements that go along with the words. The rhythms, like the sounds and grammar, change to suit the singers.

[8] Opie and Opie, p. 59.
[9] Opie and Opie, p. 188.

LITTLE SALLY WALKER

(Someone is Sally and sits in the middle.
A boy would be Tony Walker.)
Little Sally Walker, sitting in a saucer,
Crying and weeping for someone to come.
Rise, Sally, rise, Sally.
Wipe your weeping eyes, Sally. *(Swivel hips during next line.)*
Put your hands on your hips and let your backbone slip.
Oh, shake it to the East, Sally. *(Shake hip to left.)*
Oh, shake it to the West, Sally. *(Shake hip to right.)*
Oh, shake it to the very one that you love best, Sally.
  (On the last line cover eyes with one hand and
  swing around while pointing with the other. The
  one pointed to at the end is the next Sally or Tony.)

LONDON BRIDGE, MY BABY

(The Tune is a variation of London Bridge.)
London Bridge is oo-atcha-koo, my baby, oo-atcha-koo, my baby,
  oo-atcha-koo, my baby,
London Bridge is oo-atcha-koo my baby,
All right, Karen. *(Child chosen "rocks and rolls.")*
She got to hip and ho[10] and rock and roll. *(Three times.)*
All right, Karen. *(Now repeat and Karen calls another name.)*

Of course there are lots of folk songs that children sing. Here is a version of one that boys sing showing their response to changing cultural events.

MOCKINGBIRD (THE BOYS' WAY)

Hambone, hambone, have you heard?
Papa's gonna buy me a mockingbird
If that mockingbird won't sing,
Papa's gonna buy me a diamond ring.
If that diamond ring don't shine,
Papa's gonna buy me a bottle of wine.
If that bottle of wine gets broke,
Papa's gonna buy me a billy goat.
If that billy goat runs away,
Papa's gonna buy me a Chevrolet.
If that Chevrolet won't run,
Papa's gonna buy me a BB gun.
If that BB gun won't shoot,
Papa's gonna buy me a baseball suit.
If that baseball suit won't fit,
Papa's gonna say, "Aw shoot, I quit!"[11]

[10] Note rhyme of *ho* and *roll.*
[11] Circle games and song collected by Yetta, Debra, Karen, and Wendy Goodman.

Purists who try to keep the language from "degenerating" object to the noun–verb transformation more than any other, yet it was a powerful device in the hands of Shakespeare, and it accounts for some of the livelier changes in English. In *Richard II* the Bishop of Carlisle warns against furthering the civil strife initiated by Bolingbroke: "The blood of English shall *manure* the ground" (IV, i, 137). It may be that, as the language passes through the minds of children, some of these changes become a part of the language because children's transformations are so colorful. One six-year-old certainly discovered a striking noun–verb transformation to describe a man with a new crewcut: "He was porcupined."

The language might be radically changed by each generation of children were it not for their strong need to communicate with adults. When adults are not present, as in the instances of isolated children (so-called feral children and real victims of extreme adult cruelty), only grunts and groans emerge from the complex speech-sounding apparatus all human beings possess. In a society of only peer relationships—no child–adult confrontations—there could be only minimal language development.

However, as the language is passed on from generation to generation, children, like poets, seem to brighten it and stretch it when they discover new things already commonplace to adults. Even though it would be impossible to find out whether some startling pieces of a child's language ever got into the mainstream of the national language, the freshness and rightness of some of their phrasing suggest that it must have influence. This freshness can be a mighty resource for imaginative adult speaking and writing if it is not submerged by the formalities of socially acceptable, conforming language taught in school and required for advancing oneself.

The following rope-skipping chants collected from very different parts of the world not only reflect the psychic world of child–familial relationships but also add spice to the oral folk literature of the world.

For example, children in large families are often forced to tend younger brothers and sisters, and their frustration may come out in rope-skipping rhymes. In Belfast one child commented that her mother didn't like her to skip too much, since it wore out her shoes. Then she began:

> My wee brother is no good.
> Chop him up for firewood.
> When he's dead
> Cut off his head,
> Make it into gingerbread.

Another skipper in Belfast added this one:

> Eni eni mino mo
> Set the baby on the po [pot]
> When it's done

Clean its bum
And give it a lump
Of sugar plum.

And in the United States, baby care is a problem, too.

I had a little brother,
His name was Tiny Tim.
I put him in the wash tub
To teach him how to swim.
He drank up all the water,
He ate up all the soap.
He died last night
With a bubble in his throat.[12]

The slang of the street and the schoolyard has substantial effect on the history of the language because a certain amount of slang from one generation lodges in the matrix of the language and becomes an acceptable word or phrase for a cycle of years. Children, particularly the older ones, take hold of current slang, using it, stretching it, and adding to it. They do this with all the zest of defiance against parents and their standards. To use slang frowned on by parents is one safe way to revolt. Following the launching of Sputnik and the emergence of the drug culture, a spate of slang emerged, which the young quickly exploited. Being "in orbit" came to apply to more than just satellites.

The intense popularity of a certain slang theme seems to last no longer than one child generation. However, some slang words and phrases hold and are carried into adult life. "O.K." was one of these. A variant, "oaky-doaky," was dropped, but "O.K." has swept across the seas and it now appears in many languages. "Cool" in its slang meaning may or may not persist, but there is hardly a youth in the "cool" generation who did not use it to describe the car he would like his father to buy or the posture he would like to present to the world. Heaven forbid that he should blow his "cool."

Fostering Children's Language Play

Children play an important role in the development of language, and that role should be respected by teachers. Traditional language is a valuable inheritance, but fresh and new language should be encouraged. It is improper for adults to intrude upon play language, for once they do, it is thwarted and is no longer an important aspect of the child's language. Teachers need to be aware of its existence because it gives them clues to what sorts of language interest children. The rhyme, the chant, the joke,

[12] Francelia Butler, "The Poetry of Rope-skipping," *N.Y. Times Magazine*, Dec. 16, 1973, p. 92.

the parody, the shaggy-dog tale, the scary story, the word trick, the pun, the riddle, and the taunt and tomfoolery that protect a child from other children and allow him to get back at the adult world are all literary forms children enjoy reading and writing. Children delight in the teasing puzzle of an unfinished story or in a story that starts off sensibly and then takes a foolish turn. These forms can be crudely or artfully executed. Children seem to prefer the artful ones with strong rhythms, delightful shapes, good rhymes, or interesting assonance. Yet many trite, ineffective verses labeled "poetry for children" get into children's readers or into teachers' plan books:

> I know a little zig-zag girl,
> Who flutters here and there;
> She never knows just where to find
> Her brush to fix her hair.

Sometimes what teachers think is "silly" talk or writing is sincere language play. At other times, children will direct silliness at the teacher which has no validity. The better acquainted the teacher becomes, through his own listening to the play talk of children, the better he will know when he is being hoodwinked into accepting language that is not valid. Ignoring the possibilities of child language or fighting against them may well be a disservice to more than a child or a class, for the re-emergence of the language in each generation is the burden of the children.

With the world's people having to learn to live together using different speech—and there seems no likelihood of a truly universal language being developed—children need to grow up with a healthy respect for their own dialects, for other languages, and for the history of language. They may not be aware that they share in this history when they go to school, but by the time they leave they should feel their part in the process of language growth.

section 3

Dialect Differences and School Programs

When a child enters school he brings to it five to six years of language and experience. Because his world, prior to entering school, has been largely confined to his family, his home, and his immediate neighborhood, both his language and experience are heavily rooted in his subculture. The language he speaks is his mother's tongue. No matter what other language learning he achieves in his lifetime, this first one is most deeply rooted.

His language has been so well learned that no conscious effort is involved in its use. It is deeply internalized. The child's language is as much a part of him as his own skin. Rejection of his language may more deeply upset him than rejection of the color of his skin. The latter is only an insult, the former strikes at his ability to communicate and express his needs, feelings —his self.

When he hears language the child can judge whether it sounds right or wrong on the basis of the language norms of his dialect. He can detect very fine differences in sounds when these differences are significant in his dialect. He has learned to ignore differences in speech sounds that are not important to his dialect. He has learned to use his dialect's patterns of rhythm and pitch with great subtlety. He enjoys, at an early age, puns on the language that depend for their humor on slight differences in stress, pitch, or phrasing. The puns may be funny only within his dialect of English. Many a teacher has unwittingly created a pun in the dialect of his pupils that is not a pun in the teacher's dialect (sometimes with embarrassing results).

The child, at the age of school, has virtually mastered the grammar of his dialect to the point where he can create sentences that he has never heard but that are grammatical *within his dialect*. His vocabulary falls largely within the vocabulary of his speech community. He has begun to develop concepts based on experiences common to his culture and has learned to express these concepts in his mother tongue. He becomes ever more effective in communicating with *his* language.

In all respects, the process of language learning and development is the same whether the child is learning a socially prestigious dialect or learning one considered substandard. When he enters school his language is well learned and is just as systematic and just as important to him, regardless of the social value attached to his dialect in the general culture. It is his means of communication with humanity and with those who are closest to him.

The Child with Divergent Speech

Perhaps the greatest handicap to more effective language programs in the schools has been the mistaken assumption that language that deviates from the standard (however defined) is bad, sloppy, or ineffective. In a national conference on social dialects and language learning, linguists expressed surprise that anyone would believe that any dialect of any language could exist without a system of its own.[13] Linguists have learned through studies of countless dialects of countless languages that each dialect is basically systematic and that speakers of each dialect use its system with great consistency. Gleason says, "All languages are approximately equally adequate for the needs of the culture of which they are a part."[14] So long as the schools treat learners as poor users of standard American English rather

[13] Reported by Albert Marckwardt, National Council of Teachers of English, Cleveland, November 1964.
[14] H. A. Gleason, *An Introduction to Descriptive Linguistics* (New York: Holt, Rinehart and Winston, 1961), p. 9.

than as speakers of other systematic dialects, schools will be unable to deal adequately with the language learning of all children.

Children who do not speak high-status American English have language that has been adequate to their needs up to the time of school beginning. That same language continues to be an effective means of communication in the child's daily life, outside of school. This effectiveness is increased and the dialect is reinforced through contact with adults and peers in the subcultural group. The teacher may say that "I done it" is wrong, but the subculture says over and over again to the child that "I done it" is right.

It is only when the child comes into increasing contact with other sub-cultures and the general culture that his language may become inadequate for his changing needs. Normally, new communicative need will stimulate the expansion of the child's language. But the teacher may frustrate the child's language development rather than facilitate it if he continually attacks that speech as incorrect or substandard. The child may be driven to defend himself, his family, his friends, and his culture by resisting all attempts to change his language. He may be forced to regard rejection of his language as rejection of himself. Growing movements stressing ethnic pride, however, have made speakers of low-status dialects aware that there is power and beauty in their language.

Social and Regional Divergencies

For the purposes of this chapter, standard English is used to mean the dialect form which carries the most social prestige in the larger community. The child who speaks a dialect different from standard English will be referred to as a *divergent speaker*. This term is preferred because it is not value laden. It does not label the child's language as worse or less correct, in some qualitative way, than standard English. We use the term *divergent* also because of the variety of idiolects and dialects found among American children, particularly in urban areas. Whereas one might find relatively pure forms of geographic dialects in communities with relatively immobile populations, the big cities have populations who have moved more or less recently from other parts of the country. They bring varied social and regional dialects with them. Their children grow up with many language influences—the speech of their parents, the other transplanted dialects of their friends and neighbors, the regional dialect of the city in which they live, and the standardized speech of radio and television.

The language each child brings to school may vary in important ways from all other children's language. A group of children may have speech rooted in the same dialect, but their personal languages—their idiolects—will vary widely, depending on how much they have absorbed other language influences. The idiolects of urban children vary from distinctly divergent dialects toward the standard speech of the community, depending on such variables as origin of the family, the degree of isolation from the general culture of the community, and the recency of movement to the new community. Attitudes are also important; parental aspiration, personal motivation, and self-esteem will undoubtedly influence the degree to which the individual seeks, accepts, or rejects language influences.

Divergence beyond the Pale: Bilingualism

For the child whose divergence goes as far as speaking an entirely different language, the problems accompanying divergent dialects may assume even larger proportions. However, it is easier in many ways for the teacher and the educational system to give recognition to the language of the child in a way that will reassure him and give him pride in his native tongue, just because the gap is so wide and obvious. In the case where some children speak a language or languages other than English, the bilingual situation opens an avenue for the children to achieve greater understanding of language in general, to enhance their awareness of the way their dominant language works as a result of seeing it from the perspective of another language, and to receive cultural enrichment that comes from knowledge of a second language-culture. Bilingualism can be developed in varying degrees, from elementary awareness of alternate ways of saying things and naming objects to full fluency in a second language; at any level it is beneficial and broadening. It is important that the bilingual program not be conceived by its initiators as induction of speakers of a foreign language into the dominant language. Patronizing and self-congratulatory approaches amount to rejection of the child along with his language and culture.

Questions of divergent dialects arise even with children who speak languages other than English. Too often children in Texas speaking the dialects of northern Mexico are told they do not speak real Spanish, children in New England speaking Canadian French are told they do not speak real French, and children speaking dialects of southern Italy are informed that the Tuscan dialect is the only true Italian. The polarity of the pure language of the capital and the vulgar dialects of the provinces is no longer accepted by language scholars.

There has recently been a trend toward treating some dialects of American English as sufficiently divergent to be taught as foreign languages. This approach may highlight significant differences, but is self-defeating educationally because it fails to make use of a fully developed base of English, in addition to the negative social assumptions usually involved in such an approach. American English dialect differences are relatively minor compared to those of England or those of the German language.

Divergent versus Immature Speech

Many teachers fail to distinguish between speech behavior that is dialect based and speech behavior that is immature. Some fine points of grammar, inflection, and vocabulary may still not fall within adult language norms when the child starts school. He may even retain a slight problem with the sounds of the language, not being able to differentiate the initial consonants of *free* and *three*, or *red* and *wed*, for example. Also, school-age children are still experimenting with the limits of generalizations about language they have acquired. Regularizing of irregularities in language (for example, *bringed* for *brought*) is not uncommon among young school-age children. Such immaturities exist in all children regardless of the dialect they speak. The important difference between immature speech and divergent speech lies is the direction of language growth of the child. Immaturities stem from stages in language growth that are part of the process of development and will give way to more effective forms that fall within adult language norms. But divergent speech already lies within the norms of the dialect; it is reinforced by the systematic nature of the dialect—that is, it obeys the dialect's rules. One way for a teacher to differentiate divergent and immature speech is to consider how the child's parents would say the same thing. Only by comparison with the speech of the mature members of *his* language community can the child's language be judged immature. Even then there will be some contrast since changes within dialects are constant and tend to be more easily noticed in young speakers.

The Myth of Nonlanguage

Lately, a myth has grown up among the general public, and among many teachers and educators as well, that may be called the myth of nonlanguage. Somehow, the belief has developed that children, labeled variously as culturally deprived, culturally disadvantaged, low income, language-deprived, or just slum kids, are virtually without language. This belief is reinforced for many teachers by their observation of youngsters who are inarticulate and unresponsive in the classroom, who appear not to understand what to the teacher is simple, clear language. But the overwhelming evidence of linguistic research should begin to clear up this myth. All groups of people ever studied have language. All normal children learn the language of their subcultures, and they use it on the playground, in the backyard, the empty lot, and the street. The observed lack of language of some children in the classroom, then, is not a real lack of language but is a lack of "appropriate" acceptable language and a lack of "appropriate" acceptable experience to express.

Perhaps two examples will illustrate this point:

1. A teacher noticed that one of her first-graders was unable to participate in the general discussion after the class returned from the trip to the zoo. She was, in fact, unable to answer the simplest question about the animals. She did not even seem to know the names of such common animals as lions, tigers, elephants, and bears.

A few days later, the teacher tactfully raised the question with the child's mother during a parent–teacher conference. "You know," she said, "it would be very good for Mary if you and her father took her on trips to places like the zoo. She needs experiences like that."

The mother was puzzled. "As a family we go on many trips," she said. "We get to the zoo several times a year, as a matter of fact. It's one of the children's favorite trips."

Now it was the teacher's turn to be puzzled. "But Mary doesn't even seem to know the names of the animals or anything about them," the teacher said.

"Oh, she does know about animals," the mother explained, "but, you see, my husband is Old World Chinese. He is very anxious that our children learn to speak Chinese and appreciate their cultural heritage. So when we go on trips he insists that we speak only Chinese. Mary knows the Chinese names of many of the animals in the zoo. I'm sure she could tell you a lot about them in Chinese."

2. A second-grade teacher had prepared to introduce a story to her reading group. The children all lived in a housing project near the heart of Detroit. The story was about a squirrel. Assuming a lack of experience with squirrels, which she associated with suburban residential districts, the teacher had prepared a large cutout of a squirrel to show the children. "I'm thinking," she said, "of a small animal that likes to climb trees and has a bushy tail." Hands shot up and several children, bursting to answer, almost shouted, "I know, I know!" Triumphantly the chosen child said, "Squirrels! We got lots of squirrels where we live." "Really?" said the teacher in polite disbelief. "Who can tell me about squirrels?" She called on a black child, literally falling off the front edge of his seat in his eagerness to tell about his experiences with squirrels. "My daddy, he go huntin' for squirrel," he said. "Sometime he take me 'long." "Hunting?" the teacher said in a dull tone. "What do you do with the squirrels?" "First we skin 'em. Then we cook 'em," he said. "They goo-ood!" he added, drawing out the last word for emphasis. The teacher responded with a silent look of revulsion. An Appalachian youngster then said, "I know how to skin squirrels!"

Another boy spoke out without the teacher's permission. "My brother, he ten. He catch squirrel and tie tin can to they tail. Man, they sure fun to watch." "That's enough, Thomas," the teacher said coldly. "Class, open your books to page 37 and begin reading."

The first story involves a bilingual child, rich in experience but unable to express it in language acceptable to the school. The second story illustrates the more complex problem of the child who finds neither his experience nor his language acceptable in the school. Unable to understand the subtle limits and unstated standards for acceptable language and experience in the classroom, hurt and rejected in his initial attempts at using his language to discuss his world in the classroom, the divergent speaker retreats to the safety of silence. Those who doubt this phenomenon have only to listen to the rapid, flowing speech of young divergent speakers as they speak among themselves on the playgrounds and in the halls as they approach the classroom. The speech is rich in idiom, and its effectiveness in communication is obvious from the response and repartee that ensues. Suddenly the speech ceases at the classroom door at the first sight of the teacher. Only then is the child who is a divergent speaker transformed into an inarticulate, tongue-tied nonuser of language.

Children have concepts that they can express in their own language, but they find that this is not the language of the classroom or of the basal reader. In fact, they find that commonplace expressions at home may not be understood by the teacher. Worse, yet, the teacher may be shocked by the expressions, because they have an entirely different significance and connotation to the teacher. Occasionally the opposite may occur. The teacher may find that the language in the book sets the class to embarrassed snickering or to outright laughter. Such was the fate of the music teacher who attempted to introduce to one first-grade group the time-honored children's song "Pussy Willow." Another teacher, in preparing her second-grade class for a visit to the fire station asked how many had seen a house on fire. To her utter amazement she discovered that these slum children had not only seen such fires but a majority had had fires in their own dwellings. It seemed astonishing to her that fire hazard was a fact of life for slum children.

Labov reports that inner-city black youngsters observed to be nonverbal in schools and in interview situations became extremely fluent when the situation was made less school-like and peers were present for interaction.[15]

Teachers tend to prejudge what kids are saying on the basis of their dialects. They reject the low-status speaker's ideas because they reject his language.[16]

Divergent urban speakers are linguistically handicapped in school only by the rejection of their dialects. In fact they have linguistic advantages over speakers of high-status dialects. In general, people learn language in order to communicate with those they interact with. Inner-city kids learn to understand dialects used by others in their communities such as storekeepers, policemen, and teachers. This receptive language control is well developed by the end of the sixth grade though the speaker may never move to productive control, that is, speaking in the higher status dialect. Ironically teachers tend to expect their pupils to understand them without always seeing the need to reciprocate by learning to "dig" the dialect of the learners.

[15] William Labov, "The Logic of Non-Standard English," in DeStefano, *Language, Society and Education* (Worthington, Ohio: Jones, 1973).

[16] Frederick Williams and Jack L. Whitehead, "Language in the Classroom," *English Record, 21*, No. 4 (April 1971).

The Myth of Cognitive Deficit

A related, and even more poorly based myth, is that the language of some children is not suitable for use in learning. In its extreme form this theory relates to a general view that some ethnic or racial groups are genetically different than others in the extent and way in which they can learn. The language difference is seen as an indication of their general cognitive abilities; limited language comes from limited intelligence.

Arthur Jensen has become a spokesman for this position.[17] In his view, black Americans perform more poorly on intelligence tests because of genetic differences. They can learn, he asserts, but not as much and not as easily.

Englemann, in the teacher's manual to Distar, uses the following illustration to support the view of a language-based and genetically rooted cognitive deficit.[18] Three children are in a classroom. One is a speaker of black dialect, the other a Mexican-American, the third a recent immigrant from Holland. Who, asks Englemann, will learn standard English first? The Dutch immigrant, he replies, because he already speaks a language adequate for learning, while the others lack such a language. Chauvinism is hidden under a blanket of empathy for the poor unfortunate black or Chicano.

The argument for this conclusion is summarized by Labov in six steps.[19]

1. The lower-class child's verbal response to a formal and threatening situation is used to demonstrate his verbal deficit.
2. This verbal deficit is declared to be a major cause of the lower-class child's poor performance in school.
3. Since middle-class children do better in school, middle-class speech habits are seen to be necessary for learning.
4. Class and ethnic differences in grammatical form are equated with differences in the capacity for logical analysis.
5. Teaching the child to mimic certain formal speech patterns used by middle-class teachers is seen as teaching him to think logically.
6. Children who learn these formal speech patterns are then said to be thinking logically, and it is predicted that they will do much better in reading and arithmetic in the years to follow.

In programs based on this set of premises students are drilled in patterns until they respond quickly and uniformly. The teacher holds up a pencil. "Is this a cup?" she asks. In unison her class responds, "No, this is not a cup. This is a pencil." No other response is acceptable. If a black youngster replies "That ain't no cup," his response is rejected. Because he uses a double negative his response is assumed to be illogical and his control over the concept of negation is questioned. Yet clearly he has understood and clearly

---

[17] Arthur Jensen, "How Much Can We Boost IQ and Scholastic Achievement?" *Harvard Educational Review, 39,* No. 1 (1969).

[18] Siegfried Englemann, *Distar Reading I, Teacher's Guide* (Chicago: Science Research Associates, 1969), p. viii.

[19] Labov, pp. 34–35.

his double negative is not illogical but a matter of dialect preference. In many languages double negatives are required. N'est-ce pas? Are French and Russian illogical languages? No, they are only different.

The danger in these programs is that they turn linguistic strength into weakness and justify elitist views that treat the language of low-status learners as unworthy.

Labov summarizes his case in this manner:

> There is no reason to believe that any nonstandard vernacular is in itself an obstacle to learning. The chief problem is ignorance of language on the part of all concerned. Our job as linguists is to remedy this ignorance. Bereiter and Englemann want to reinforce it and justify it. Teachers are now being told to ignore the language of Black children as unworthy of attention and useless for learning. They are being taught to hear every natural utterance of the child as evidence of his mental inferiority. As linguists we are unanimous in condemning this view as bad observation, bad theory and bad practice.[20]

Influence of Prestigious Forms

Although no one dialect of American English has established itself as *the* prestige dialect to be imitated by all others (as, for example, Florentine Italian is *the* preferred Italian dialect),[21] there is a common assumption that a standard American English exists. But there are really a number of regional standards, each approximating the speech of high-status speakers of the region. Perhaps it can be more accurately stated that there are a number of aspects of language that are commonly regarded as nonstandard. These mark the speaker, in the view of the general society, as uncultured, crude, and ignorant. Labov's study of dialect in New York City indicates that there is considerable agreement among people of all social classes, who differ considerably in their actual speech, on what are preferred and rejected forms. In fact, many people think, or say they think, that they use prestige forms when they actually do not.

The Child's Language and Social Attitudes toward It

To some extent, this common agreement on prestige forms may be due to the prescriptive efforts of schoolteachers, but this can only explain part of the phenomenon. Labov suggests, in fact, that language differences can be divided into three categories: (1) *differentiating factors with no social-discrimination components* (the differences, in a sense, are socially neutral), (2) *social markers* (these differences are widely considered to indicate non-

---

[20] Labov, p. 18.

[21] Raven McDavid, "Dialectology and the Teaching of Reading," *The Reading Teacher, 18,* No. 3 (December 1964), 208.

standard speech; examples are *nuttin', we was,* and *didn't have no*), and (3) *stereotypes* (these items, such as the use of *ain't,* are so widely regarded as "bad" that they disappear from the speech of almost all Labov's New York subjects in even the least formal contexts). It is in this last category that the effect of prescriptive teaching may be felt, but the second category of the socially important markers is the key one.

Labov has found in his studies that there is a pattern of change among all social classes toward prestige forms, but significantly he has found that this pattern does not begin to form to any significant degree until after the age when most children have learned their literacy skills. He suggests six stages a person goes through in the movement toward socially prestigious language norms.

1. Mastering the basic communicative apparatus of language. The child learns this at home from his family. What he learns is the relaxed, informal, unguarded speech.
2. Mastering the street vernacular.
3. Social perceiving. At about puberty the child begins to be aware of which aspects of language and kinds of language behavior are more prestigeful. Adolescents, of course, may well deliberately reject the prestigeful forms they have identified in favor of what they regard as distinctively adolescent speech.
4. Learning stylistic variations, that is, not just to hear differences but to produce the preferred form. This, of course, is not an easy task, because the preferred form may involve phonemes, inflections, and syntax outside the deeply learned patterns of the native dialect. An example of such a difficult acquisition for many New Yorkers is the final *r* in such words as *fear, car,* and *fire.*
5. Maintaining prestige forms.
6. Being completely mobile in language. Few divergent speakers are likely to reach this last stage.[22]

Anxieties Caused by Language Differences

Studies of social attitudes toward language indicate a great deal of language anxiety on the part of many Americans, particularly those in the lower middle classes. Anxiety may lead to supercorrectness. This might take the form of overpronunciation, particularly of final sounds in words, or use of such forms as "she gave it to he and I," or "aren't I."

Increasing language anxiety may produce more careful speech, but at the cost of its expressive ability. The speaker devotes so much attention to his language that he is unable to give adequate attention to his thoughts.

There are, of course, economic reasons for teachers, parents, and minority group leaders wanting young divergent speakers to achieve socially prestigious speech. They feel that a person who does not speak "properly" will be

[22] William Labov, address to National Council of Teachers of English, Cleveland, November 1964.

denied many jobs and promotional opportunities as an adult. There is some truth to this fear. But educators are well aware that children aged six or seven are not easily motivated to learn on the basis of what someone says their future needs as adults will be. For most young children the need is for language here and now: at home, at play, and at school. Further, although young children can perceive differences in dialects (they may well be able to say, for example, "I say it this way, but you would say it *this* way"), they are quite likely to be unaware of the social approval or disapproval that applies to one or another way of saying something.

Adolescents are likely to have learned the social lesson too well. "Ya, man, alls I got to do is learn me some pretty ways to talk and they goin' to make me President of the United States" is the way one teen-ager summed up his awareness that the solution to all his problems does not lie in learning to "walk right and talk right."

Efforts to sell either children or adolescents on the need to change their language because of their future need for socially approved language are likely to be largely unsuccessful. The youngster who feels a pressing drive to move out of this subculture will be motivated to change his language as he will be to change his dress and habits. But, as Lloyd has said, "Change of speech will follow, not precede, his decision to make his way out of the world he was born to."[23] The decision to move out of his subculture literally forces the child to disown his own heritage, to reject the folkways and values of his culture. It involves an intense effort, and the possibility of failure is all the more frightening, because if he does fail, he will be left in limbo: no longer what he was nor yet what he aspires to be.

The only approach that may help any large number of divergent children is expansion: not the rejection of their mother tongue but expansion outward from the idiolect and subcultural dialect to the expanded language of the general culture, giving up only what is no longer needed and adding to meet new needs. Teachers can be of enormous help in this process.

Transplanted Regional Speech

Earlier, reference was made to the problem of transplanted regional speech. It is obvious that a teacher in Atlanta ought not to strive to impose the dialect of upper-class Boston or middle-class Chicago on children whose speech falls within the norms of high-status speech in Atlanta. But our country is one of great geographic mobility. What to do with the transplanted Atlantan when he arrives in the Boston or Chicago classroom is not so obvious. What complicates the problem is the ethnocentrism that most people feel for their language. If language is different, it must be bad. Too often, children are shunted into "speech-correction" classes because they have

[23] Donald J. Lloyd, "Sub-Cultural Patterns Which Affect Language and Reading Development," copyright by the author, 1962.

phonemes that differ from those of their new speech communities. Sometimes they are ignored or admonished when they have said a word or gleaned the meaning of a phrase but in their own dialect. Too often, differences in vocabulary, usage, and choice of words are lumped with all other language labeled "incorrect."

Ignorance, as the proverb says, is no excuse. The teacher cannot plead ignorance in the case of language phenomena. Educators must know what regional speech is, what immature speech is, what a lisp is, what an idiosyncrasy of one child's idiolect is. *Surely, schools must not attempt to stamp out individuality in speech.*

The following humorous editorial, from the Pine Bluff, Arkansas, *Commercial*, expresses some of the problems, the futility, and the unfairness involved in any attempt to obliterate regional speech:

CHUNKIN' IN ON FIXIN' TO
Another Detroit educator, _____, reported that tape recorders have been used successfully in that city to change the dialects of children whose parents bring them to Detroit from other parts of the country, particularly the South.

Samples of these dialects, she said, include the use of such coined words as "onliest," "unlessen," "carry" for "take," "chunk" for "throw," and the frequent use of "fixing-to."

First off, _____ is a punk speller to be trying to teach English to other folk. It's "onlyest," not "onliest"; "onlessen," not "unlessen"; and, by all the verities, "fixin' to," not "fixing-to."

Secondly, those people in Detroit have more vanity and less sense than even we were prepared to believe if they imagine that the abandonment of the verb "chunk" is an improvement in anybody's vocabulary.

We'll take our Southern chunkers against _____'s sanitized throwers in any competition, from beanbag catch to rock fight, and will pound 'em into the ground.

Then there's "fixin' to," which _____ wisely refrained from suggesting a synonym for. She alleges that the word is used frequently but this is, we are sure, a canard based on inadequate listening. Nobody down here, and nobody from down here who has gone up there, is fixin' to do anything very frequently—but when fixin' to time has come, events of great moment will not be far behind.[24]

Dialect and Learning in Teaching and Learning

The significance of dialect differences in language arts instruction in schools has been largely overlooked. The reasons for this oversight have been touched on earlier: the mistaken assumption that there is one correct standard English, the lumping together of all deviations from the mythical standard as incorrect, the language ethnocentrism of most people, the social and cultural positions of teachers and writers of texts, the myth of nonlanguage, and the cognitive deficit libel.

[24] Reprinted with permission of the editors.

Dialect-influenced aspects of language learning are not confined to the groups we have called divergent. Because every child speaks a dialect, each one's further development in language will be rooted in his dialect. Consider, for example, the following list of words: *frog, log, dog, fog, cog, smog, bog, hog.* Some of those who read this list will pronounce these all as rhymes; the vowel in all the words will be /a/[25] as in *dot; dog* and *dot* will be the same except for the final consonants. For others, the words will all rhyme but the vowel will be /ɔ/ as in *law.* But for many people the words will divide into two groups: *frog, log, dog, fog, hog,* and *cog, smog, bog;* or perhaps the two groups will be *frog, log, dog,* and *hog, fog, cog, smog, bog.* Perhaps *dog* is the only word in your idiolect that does not rhyme with the others. There is no one correct way to say any of these words.

If these dialect differences are ignored, unconscious errors are made by teachers and texts. In readiness lessons children may be asked to identify words that rhyme for the teacher but not for the learner. The generalization in a spelling lesson may not be a generalization at all for some learners. Because the lessons make an inaccurate assumption about the prior language experience of the learner, both the teacher and the learner are puzzled by why learning does not occur.

As we have said, a major block to language development and school success is the rejection of the child's language. But dialect differences also enter in many specific ways into the process of acquiring literacy skills. Several aspects of language differences will be explored here.

Divergent Dialects but Only One Spelling

An important point to remember is that, although there is great diversity in oral language, there is only one accepted spelling for all American English (different in minor respects from Canadian and British spellings, for example, labor/labour, civilize/civilise). There is a well-known story about a little boy who asks his teacher (as she hears it), "How do you spell *rat?*" "R-a-t" she responds. "No, Ma'am," says the boy, "I don't mean *rat*-mouse, I mean *right* now."

Most dialects of American and British English have the same inventory of vowel and consonant phonemes. But few words have the same phonemes, particularly vowels, in all dialects. Moreover, each phoneme, since it is not a single sound but a range of sounds, varies its limits from dialect to dialect; some sounds at the extremes will be identified as one phoneme by speakers of one dialect but as another phoneme by those who speak a different dialect.

---

[25] An attempt has been made in this book to avoid being overly technical. But when it comes to comparing the ways words are said in different dialects, no adequate way exists except to use the phonemic symbols devised by linguists to precisely describe the sounds of English.

Dialect in Phonics Programs

All phonics programs attempt to get the learner to associate sounds and letters. Such programs in reading and spelling instruction either must be adjusted to the phonology of the dialect of the learner, or the learner must first be taught a new dialect if these phonics programs are to be usable for all learners. Teachers sometimes appear to be unaware of contradictions between their own speech patterns and the phonics program: "I can't *git* those kids to hear the short *e*," one teacher complained. A study by Rystrom showed that when rural black Georgian first graders were taught the sounds of "standard white speech" before reading instruction they actually did somewhat more poorly than a control group of similar learners with no dialect training. The instruction appeared to interfere with learning.[26]

If a child says *duh* /də/ instead of *the* /ðə/ and *nuffin* /nəfɨn/ instead of *nothing* /nəθɨŋ/, it may confuse him more than it helps if he learns that the digraph *th* represents the initial consonant in *the* and the medial consonant in *nothing*. The generalization is not appropriate to his speech.

Even if he should learn to say /nəθɨŋ/ when he sees the printed word *nothing*, it is possible that he does not realize that this is his word /nəfɨn/ and that it represents the same concept. Does the child know that *four* /for/, which is the name of the *4* he must say in school, is the same as /foh/, which he knows to be the number of wheels on a car? Even adults often have the experience of meeting what at first seems to be a new word or phrase in speech or print and of not recognizing until later that it is one that they know, but know in another form. Dickens *victuals* are the same as Appalachian "vittles" /vitəlz/.

Dialect and Spelling Programs

Misspelling may vary considerably from dialect to dialect; again, little attention has been given to this factor in learning, so the extent and nature of differences is not known. Logically, for example, dialects that soften or only slightly pronounce some final consonants will not relate in the same way to standard spellings as dialects with more distinct terminal consonants.

Homophones, words which sound alike, will vary from dialect to dialect. The geographical linguists' favorites (*merry, Mary, marry*) are good examples. Whether two or all sound alike to you or all are different depends on your dialect. *Been* may be a homophone for *bin* or *bean* or *Ben* in your dialect. Most spelling programs ignore these differences. Teachers need to be tuned in to children's dialect. A teacher who asked her children to use the word *so* in a sentence was surprised with the response she got. "I got

---

[26] Richard Rystrom, "Dialect Training and Reading: A Further Look," *Reading Research Quarterly, 4*, No. 4 (Summer 1970), 581–599.

a *sore* (/sow/) on my leg," said one young pupil. Another teacher, a native Californian, was surprised by her Boston pupils' use of *pack*. "My father found a place to *park* the car."

Still another teacher (a New Yorker by origin) was startled by the definitions her Midwestern pupils gave of *borough* (a new word in their fifth-grade social studies text). "I think it's a hole in the ground rabbits dig," said one. "No, it's some kind of donkey," said another.

Phonics programs, if they are effective, may only heighten the spelling problems of some divergent speakers and of speakers of some regional dialects. Some will not only say /aydiər/ but also spell it *idear*. Others will say /pənkin/ and spell it *punkin*. Every dialect contains many words that are spelled in unpredictable ways. Strong phonics programs produce phonic misspellings.

A major problem with ITA (Initial Teaching Alphabet) and other approaches to achieving one-to-one correspondence between letters and phonemes in teaching reading is that they must either be based on one dialect or they must abandon the principle that there is only one spelling, no matter how diversely a word may be pronounced in different dialects. The word *levers* is spelled, using ITA orthography: lïv3rz.[27] If *lever* rhymes with *beaver* in a child's speech, this spelling is fine. But if he says *lever* to rhyme with *never*, he will have a mismatch.

The peculiar belief persists among the public and among many teachers that how a word is spelled determines how it should be pronounced. If this were true it would mean there were no dialect differences in English. It would also mean that written language was invented before oral language, an obvious fallacy.

Inflectional Change

Inflectional changes in words involve the use of suffixes or internal variations in words to achieve changes in case or tense. Although inflectional differences among American English dialects are minor compared with phonemic differences, they are still important. When some children say *he see me* instead of *he sees me*, it is not because they have dropped the word ending; it is because in their dialect there is no *s* form of present-tense verbs after third-person singular subjects.

In terms of spelling, the *s* in this use becomes silent. Telling a child that it does not sound right to leave off the *s* or that he is wrong if he does not say /siyz/ because the written word has an *s* on the end contradicts his past experience with language. Some children may learn to give the response that school demands, but in so doing the children develop a gulf between their oral language and school language tasks. In any event, problems in

---

[27] *The Story of ITA* (New York: ITA Publications, 1963), p. 11.

reading, spelling composition, and grammar will result; a continuous effort will be required of the divergent speaker to do what to him is unnatural. The problem is not a reading error but is a consistent language divergence. *Any change sought by the teacher must be treated not as a shift from wrong to right in reading but a shift to a socially preferred dialect.*

Morphemic Differences

Gleason cites an example that illustrates a morphemic difference between dialects. Most Americans add /ɨz/ for the plurals of words ending in /s/ (*buses*), in /z/ (*mazes*), and in /š/ (*washes*); but after /sp/, /st/, and /sk/ they add /s/ (*wasps, posts,* and *tasks*). But in the Blue Ridge Mountains, speakers use /ɨz/ after these consonant blends also. In their dialect the plurals are: /waspɨz/, /pohstɨz/, and tæskɨz/.[28]

The difference Gleason describes is systematic, that is, it applies to all words that fall into the categories. Children who speak this dialect will carry this difference over into their schoolroom language, and it may be reflected in spelling and reading.

Syntactical Differences

Similarly in dialects where final consonant clusters are reduced, the form of the plural *s* morpheme will change. When *test* or *desk* become /tes/ or /des/ then the plurals become /tesɨz/ and /desɨz/ rather than /tests/ and /desks/.

When a child who is a divergent speaker responds during roll call with, "I here, teacher," he is not being "careless" in his speech any more than he is a few minutes later when he volunteers the information that James is absent because "He sick." In his dialect the present tense of the verb *to be* (or the copula, as some linguists prefer) is omitted. There is a *syntactical* difference in his dialect. Use of verb forms and verb markers is one well-known area of dialect divergence. *We was going; they done it; we come* (rather than *came* or *had come*); and *he clumb* are examples. Hawaiian Pidgin uses only verb markers with no inflections: *I go; I stay go; I wen' go; I been go; I goin' go.*

Fortunately, such syntactic differences among American English dialects are relatively minor. The basic structure of the language, the sentence patterns, and the use of function words as structural signals are fairly uniform to all dialects.

Children will tend to carry these aspects over to their reading and writing. *As the child reads orally, he will tend to read his own dialect from the printed page.* He may "correct" the grammar of what he reads to make it fit the norms of the grammar of his own dialect. Such "corrections" are good

[28] Gleason, p. 62.

indications that the child is using his past knowledge of language to obtain meaning from the printed page. Here is an example of this phenomenon.

> A group of second-graders were reading in round-robin fashion. It was Jim's turn. "There was a lot of goats," he read. "There was black goats and white goats."
>
> His teacher smiled encouragingly. "Would you repeat that, please, Jim," she said.
>
> Somewhat puzzled, Jim reread: "There was a lot of goats. There was black goats and white goats."
>
> Still smiling, his teacher stepped to the board. In excellent manuscript she wrote two words. "Do you see a difference in these words?" she said.
>
> "Yes, they have different endings," said Jim.
>
> "Can you read these words?" the teacher asked.
>
> "Was, were," Jim read.
>
> "Good," said his teacher.
>
> "This is *was*, and this is *were*. Now read again what you just read from the book."
>
> "There was a lot of . . ." Jim began.
>
> "No, no!" his teacher said with some annoyance. "It's *were*. 'There *were* a lot of goats.' Now, please reread."
>
> "There were a lot of goats. There was black goats and . . ."[29]

The teacher, in this example, has assumed that the child is confusing *was* and *were* on a perceptual level. But in reality what he is doing is translating; he is reading his dialect from the printed page. He is using his language system.

Divergent speakers may master some specific tasks in English lessons on correct forms, but they are unlikely to carry the lessons over into their written and oral expression. They may be able to underline the correct choice: He *did* (done) it. But they will still say and write *he done it*, or, having become uncertain, they may avoid the expression altogether.

Intonational Difference

Dialects differ also in their *intonation*, the rhythm of stress, pitch, and pause or juncture, which characterizes the flow of language. Perhaps the greatest barrier to communication between speakers of different dialects is this difference in intonation. Teachers frequently complain, when they first begin to work with children who speak a different dialect, that they cannot understand the children at all. This is not just a result of the variation in the phonemes of the speakers' language but is also because of the teachers' being out of tune with the intonational pattern of the divergent dialect. After a week or two the children appear to be speaking more clearly. In reality, the teachers have become accustomed to their intonational patterns. Paradoxically, people

[29] Kenneth S. Goodman, "The Linguistics of Reading," *Elementary School Journal,* *64* (April 1964), 7.

are often struck with what to them is a poetic quality in dialects they have not heard before. This sense of a poetic quality stems from the listener's attention to the intonation of the strange dialect; he has lost his awareness, on the conscious level, of the rhythmic qualities of his own and other very familiar dialects.

Children for whom English is a second language tend to use the intonational patterns of their first language in speaking English. They are thus impeded in effective communication with people unfamiliar with their speech. They may also find it difficult to appreciate the subtleties of meaning that depend on slight but significant differences in intonation. For teachers, it is important to remember that no feature of language has any intrinsic meaning; any device in language, intonational or otherwise, has only the significance assigned to it by the users of a particular language or language dialect. Just as identical-sounding words may mean very different, unrelated things in different languages, so also may change in pitch or variations in relative stress. In comprehending oral language the listener gets cues to the pattern from the speaker's stress, pitch, and pause patterns. In oral reading, intonation follows from the decisions the reader makes about the syntactic patterns he ·is dealing with. If a pupil reads without acceptable intonation it may mean that he is not getting the syntax or meaning of what he is reading. A nonnative speaker will frequently read each word as if it were a word on a list. That's a more likely sign of poor comprehension than shifts toward the intonation of his native language. It indicates he is naming words rather than processing language.

Problems of Vocabulary Divergence

Divergent speakers may experience two types of *vocabulary divergence*. First is the type that stems from difference in word preference and word meanings. Examples of this were mentioned in the editorial cited earlier. Speakers may prefer to use *chunk* instead of *throw* to convey similar meanings. In some dialects, if you *carry* something, you physically transport it on your self, but, in other dialects, you can *carry* a friend to work with you in your car but you *tote* your books. In some uses, both dialects would agree. Some uses are acceptable in one dialect but not in another. The second type of divergence stems from the relatively limited vocabulary all speakers bring to unfamiliar topics or situations. Basically, this means that the divergent speaker will have a more limited vocabulary stock from which to draw in the situations that schools stress that are foreign to him. He will tend to use his basic stock more widely in his expression, using a single word or phrase in place of several, with subtle differences in connotation. He will use metaphors and similies as well: "the piece that looks like a lady's shoe" rather than "the triangular piece."

It would be well to remember that it is harder for a child to learn to spell, read, or write an unfamiliar word than one already part of his vocabulary. An unfamiliar use of a familiar word or phrase may cause a learner problems because in his dialect that usage may be incorrect. Mere manipulation of lists of words is not a solution to these vocabulary problems. Relevance becomes a key word here. Relevant instruction and relevant materials capitalize on the language and experience of each learner. Vocabulary differences between cultural groups reflect differences in cultural experiences. One is not a deficient example of the other.

Language and Culture-Bound Tests

Young divergent speakers are at a distinct disadvantage when they are judged on the basis of readiness tests, intelligence tests, and aptitude tests that are based on the assumption that all children have common experience and language. Even so-called nonverbal tests involve pictures of things outside the common experience of many children. The child who has seen and experienced but has not learned is not at all the same as the child who has not seen or experienced. But the tests show them both the same.

The logic of relationships and analogies built into many test items may not hold in the context of the divergent subculture. Do churches have steeples? The store-front churches that some urban children attend do not.

Even if an attempt is made to keep the test itself culture-free, the instructions are usually provided in a dialect other than the learner's, and the results are evaluated on the norms of the dominant culture. Perhaps for some time to come, all that teachers can do about the disadvantage of divergent speakers on standardized tests is to remember that these tests are inappropriate and to temper the use of the results of the tests in predicting and evaluating learning.

The significance of dialect differences in general has been neglected in teaching language and literacy skills. Children who are divergent speakers are often doubly handicapped. Not only is their language rejected and their form of expression misunderstood and thwarted, but also they tend to be children who are not highly motivated to meet school demands and achieve. They will give up easily and reject education if the school rejects their language.

If teachers and schools are to achieve success with divergent speakers, they must first accept and understand the mother tongue of the learners. Teachers must be very careful to separate immature speech from dialect-based speech. They must avoid complicating the difficulty that divergent speakers have in acquiring literacy by making unrealistic and inappropriate language demands.[30]

---

[30] Kenneth S. Goodman, "Dialect Barriers to Reading Comprehension Revisited," *The Reading Teacher* (October 1973).

Divergent speakers can build on the base of their own language. They can be encouraged to experiment with language and to meet the increasing need for societal communication by expanding their language. The goal is to move outward from the mother tongue, not to replace it or stamp it out. Dialect differences are inherent in language, and teachers must come to accept difference and to work with it. Divergence of dialect or a different home language can be a source of personal and linguistic enrichment.

4

A School Program Based on Expanding Language

Expansion is the key word in the language program: expansion of communicative need, expansion of experience, expansion of confidence in the use of language, expansion of conceptual ability, expansion of control over the structure of language, expansion of vocabulary, expansion of the range of language that is understood, expansion of the range of language used in expression and the ability to communicate with many different people. A time-honored adage of education is that it must always start where the child is. For the school language program this means:

That the school language program must be flexible to allow for the range of language abilities children have when they come to school.

That the school and the teacher must be concerned with understanding the language of the community or communities the children come from. The teacher must know the language of each child and must build upon it.

That the teacher must value and appreciate the language of each and every child. The child must not feel that his language is considered bad. The teacher must not just tolerate it, the teacher must cherish it, making the child feel pride and confidence in his language and his ability to express himself in language.

That the teacher concentrate on developing ideation in widening experiences with children, thereby stimulating an expanison of language.

To start where the child is in language, the teacher must listen to the language of the child carefully and without prejudgment. If the teacher disdains "the terrible English" of the learners, a barrier is created that not only undermines the confidence of the child in his ability to use and learn language but also makes it impossible for the child to communicate to the teacher. The teacher, perhaps without realizing, may refuse to listen or understand. In some cases, the negativism can be so strong that the child is literally forced to defend himself. If the teacher will not listen to him, then he will not listen to the teacher. For the child to build on his present language ability, his confidence in himself must be unshaken; otherwise, there will be a separation between his speech and language activities of the school and the larger society that may never be bridged.

Language Opportunities in the School

In order to expand language there must be no artificial exercises in recitation or copying someone else's language from the board but actual opportunities for children to use their own language to communicate. Children need the opportunity to stretch their language to the limits, to express their reactions to experiences, and to interact with each other. In this process they will strengthen and refine the generalizations they have internalized about language, while at the same time they will feel the need for growth in language. Children can discover limitations on their language ability only if they have many opportunities to use it. As communicative needs occur that they cannot meet, they will reach for more language; they will be self-motivated to expand their language.

Every available opportunity for children to use their language in school should be exploited. Whenever there is a time for natural conversation, it should be utilized. When children arrive in the morning, they have things to tell each other and their teacher. It is natural for friends and acquaintances to want to talk over what has happened since they saw each other last. This informal, spontaneous conversation is more valuable than any kind of before-school board-assignments could be. This is a particularly good time for the teacher to become aware of any interesting events or experiences children have had that they would like to share with the whole class in a more formal sharing time. Recess and lunch periods are also natural occasions for informal language. How unnatural it is to see hundreds of children sitting and eating their lunches in silence, furtively trying to communicate with each other without getting caught by a teacher or a monitor! Noise may indeed be a problem in many school situations, but if the importance of language opportunities is recognized, solutions other than bans on speech will be found.

When a child has something to say, it is at that point that he is most motivated to use language. It is important that children learn to listen as well as to speak, but in too many classrooms the times when speech is "appropriate" are to few. A sharing period may stimulate children to express their experiences and ideas to others, but language must not be confined to a formal half-hour period a day.

Children also need opportunities to talk about the new concepts and ideas they encounter during the schoolwork. Class discussions meet this need to some extent, but there are also times when it is beneficial for two or three pupils to discuss the mathematics that they are doing, to compare notes on African cultures they are researching, or to share their reactions to a science demonstration. In such situations children have the opportunity to seek effective language to express new concepts in a less threatening situation than they have when they must address a whole class. It is not enough that children have heard the teacher use language to describe a new concept or that they have read about it in a book. They must ultimately be able to communicate it to others and to get the immediate feedback from others that indicates whether they have been successful.

Some children seldom are listened to seriously at home. School must be a place where they know that people will listen. Communicative need stimulates expression, but if no one wants to listen, then there is no point in talking. Eventually, children who are not listened to stop trying to communicate. The curriculum, the weekly lesson plan, the daily sequence of lessons should be constructed to make it possible for children to use language in many ways.

Throughout these language opportunities, children must be encouraged to find pleasure in their own language. They should be helped to feel pride in a choice idiom, perhaps based in a regional dialect, that expresses an idea or emotion that cannot be expressed in any other way. They should be assisted in exploring the ways that language can be manipulated to produce variety of form and subtle differences in connotation. They should be guided to discover more effective ways of making themselves and their ideas maximally understood. They should be encouraged to be creative, not only in the uses they make of language but also in the language itself. Language must be constantly created and re-created to meet the changing needs of its users.

Some innovations in school organization and curriculum facilitate language use while others do not. The open-school movement is, by intention, an opening of space, of structure, of limits. If it is well executed it can be an excellent vehicle for stimulating varied, easy use of language in highly informal settings. It can also provide for one-to-one interactions as well as small- and large-group activities in which language will be used. But the structure itself will not bring about these beneficial effects. They must come from the planning and commitment of the professional staff. Their minds and the concepts they hold of language, curriculum, teaching, and learning must be open for the classroom to become a truly open learning environment.

Under the heading of individualized instruction many schools have all but eliminated any kind of linguistic interaction between learners. This is particularly true in those highly structured programs where, in fact, only the pace at which pupils may proceed through a rigid program is individualized. *Instruction can be personalized*, made relevant to the particular needs and interests of learners, while still making possible thought and language interactions which are essential to human learning.

Expanding Interests, Experiences, and Concepts

School-age children are by nature expanding their horizons, widening their interests. There is much in their world that is new and wonderful to them that they must express. They must know what things are; they must know where they come from; they must know how things work. They must have language to ask, to name, to share, to explain, to manipulate mentally. Eventually, children must be able to use language to expand concepts and solve problems, but the foundations for this ability must be built in situations where language accompanies experience. Before children can arrive at new mathematical concepts through the use of mathematical symbols such as 2, x, y, $=$, $+$, %, and ¢, they must first acquire the concepts they represent through the manipulation of representative objects and by hearing language in real situations involving real lengths, quantities, sizes, and intervals. The danger of creating a gap between language and experience is ever present because teachers as adults are accustomed to speaking in abstractions from their backlog of experience.

When language is learned in relation to many real situations, it acquires definition and limits in relation to the varied experiences that the child has had with it. A dictionary can confirm a definition the child has arrived at, or it can clarify which of several possible connotations is appropriate. Thus the dictionary is an aid in language acquisition. But a dictionary definition is of no use to a child if he has not encountered the words in situational contexts. There is always the possibility of one word being defined in the dictionary by another word, which, in turn, is defined by a third word, until the unfortunate student is led back to the original word—a chain of words all related to each other but none related to anything in the experience of the dictionary user that could give substance to the words.

Perhaps a cardinal precept of a school language program must be: *No language without experience and no experience without language.*

Using Language More Effectively

The first concern in expanding language is aiding children to have more to say and more language to say it with. Of equal concern must be increasing the effectiveness of communication.

During their school years, the language of children becomes fully grammatical within the norms of their own dialect. Not only do they gain control over the structure of the language, but in a sense, the latent structure of language gains control over the language of the child. As the child fully internalizes the structure of the language, it comes to determine the precise patterns and choice of words of his speech, thus increasing his effectiveness in communication. But a wide range of language is acceptable by adult standards. Some language is more effective, interesting, precise, or euphonious than other language that is equally correct. In short, beyond the point where language becomes fully acceptable grammatically, increasing the effectiveness of communication becomes something of an art.

The school can assist children in this art of effective communication. It can:

Encourage creativity in language as is done in the arts.

Encourage children to experiment with varying the fillers in the structural patterns they use. (Remember Loban's conclusion that more effective users of language use the same structural patterns in language but use more varied and complex fillers.)

Encourage children to listen to their own speech and read their own writing while considering: Have I said what I wanted to say as well as I could?

Avoid demanding absolute conformity. If there are many school situations where an answer or idea must be expressed in only one way, and that way is someone else's way, children are not likely to become more effective in communication. If the teacher says, "Put it in your own words," but then rejects those words and demands the words of the text or teacher, children will give back not what they are asked for, but what they know is wanted.

Expose children to a wide variety of language. They should hear and read "good" language ("good" here defined as highly effective), but it is a mistake to limit their experience to "good" language. How can a child tell what language is effective unless he encounters language that varies in effectiveness? How can he appreciate the language artistry of the great writer unless he can compare it with the triteness of the hack?

Increase vocabulary. There is, of course, a reciprocal relationship between the child's striving for greater language effectiveness and his expansion of the fund of language available to him. He is more effective if he has more language available. But it is not profitable to short-circuit this cycle by teaching language in isolation.

Vocabulary grows as the learner requires it to deal with new experiences and new concepts. The road to greater vocabulary, then, is through a rich, exciting, expanding curriculum. Directing children to work with word lists and dictionaries can have only a superficial effect on any learner's vocabulary.

Encourage bold experimentation with language. Children tend to be somewhat hesitant in trying new things. They will tend to do things in safe, tried ways rather than in new ways that may not succeed, particularly if they feel they will be judged by the results. They also tend to use safe, sure language rather than new terms, phrases, or constructions. To overcome this tendency, they must be given the feeling that school is a place for experimentation with language. Their experimental efforts should be praised, not laughed at, ridiculed, or red-penciled. Intrinsic, positive responses for using effective language must be provided. Praise always helps, but the success of communicating one's own ideas lucidly and powerfully to someone else is sweeter.

The pleasure that the teacher takes in language use in its full variety can be as encouraging to linguistic ease and experimentation among students as the narrow, up-tight view many teachers take is discouraging to such linguistic risk-taking.

Trying something new always involves risks. Traditionally pupils have been least willing to face risks involving expanding language in school, more so in fact than in any other place. Only teachers can turn that situation around, not just by what they say but how they act in response to the language of their pupils and how they use language themselves.

Increased effectiveness in language must not be confused with increased formality or floweriness in language. The goal is natural, effective language use. Within this goal, there is a place for the incomplete sentence, the contraction, the newly coined slang phrase, the new use of old words. When a child is asked, "How many kittens are there in this story?" "Three," is an effective answer. If one insists that the child must respond in a complete sentence, by saying "There are three kittens in this story," it does nothing to improve the effectiveness of the response. Great writers of dialogue would never use such a response. It is not even grammatical, for the rules of discourse elements in questions are never repeated in the answers except for special emphasis. Furthermore, it is unnatural. Language can be rich, varied, even elegant, without becoming unnatural. Language lives. It grows, changes, and adapts to the changing needs of its users. It is better to help children understand language change and be part of it than to insist on a static view of language. Such insistence can't prevent language changes but it can interfere with the language effectiveness of learners.

Teaching Strategy for a Program of Expanding Language

The process of language expansion and increased effectiveness is essentially a continuation of the induction the child has been using in all his language learning since birth in which communicative need has been the prime motivating force. The school is relying on the process of uncontrolled induction when it encourages the process of language growth by providing stimulating interests, by providing opportunities for experiences, by encouraging concept development, and by providing many situations where language is needed and used. When the school attempts to influence the pace and direction of language growth, it becomes more directive. Even if language instruction is based directly on the language of the learners, the examples are selected to lead the learner to generalizations that are predetermined by the curriculum or the teacher. Such instruction, then, must involve controlled induction. The teaching strategy for a school program designed to expand language and improve its effectiveness is a mixed strategy of uncontrolled and controlled induction.

The teacher and school select aspects of language development that would not develop as fully or rapidly without assistance. They develop a curriculum, a series of controlled learning activities, designed to achieve this language development. The sequence of learning activities directly concerned with language learning is important, but it must not be considered the entire school program for language development. Equal attention must be given to the ways that the school facilitates the child's own induction of language as he responds to his environment.

Helping Children To Achieve
Variety in Language

Children frequently fall into comfortable language ruts, as indeed their elders do. The school can help children to avoid this pitfall by asking children to play with language structures to see how the fillers of the slots in these structures can be varied.

For example, in a simple subject-verb-object pattern such as *Bobby has a puppy,* children can be helped to explore possible fillers of the slots held by *Bobby, has,* and *puppy.* They could begin with substitutions that do not alter the basic meaning.

He has a puppy.	Bobby has it.
The boy has a puppy.	Bobby has him.
Robert has a puppy.	Bobby has one.
That guy has a puppy.	Bobby owns a puppy.
Bobby has a pup.	Bobby's got a puppy.
Bobby has a dog.	Bobby owns Blackie.

Next, modifiers can be added that make the meaning more precise or complete.

My best friend, Bobby Miller, got a little, fuzzy, black, cocker-spaniel puppy yesterday.

Complex constructions can be used to fill the slots of the original elements and the modifiers.

The boy who lives across the street has a puppy.
Bobby really wants to have a puppy.
Bobby has a cocker spaniel named Blackie that looks like the puppy we saw yesterday.

This sort of experimentation in language variation is not entirely new in language instruction. The important difference here is that at the same time that pupils are encouraged to use varied language, they are being helped in a planned way to extend their feeling for how language patterns work. They are being guided to become more fully aware of what is possible and not possible within the limits of English language structure. Children should not be asked to experiment with embedded structures and modifiers merely for the sake of teaching the parts of speech. The goal is to help them realize the kinds of words, phrases, and clauses that can be modifiers and the grammatical devices available for their use so that their language will become more pliable in serving their communicative needs. It may be that as the children become aware of the function of noun modification we may wish to put a name on this function for the sake of ease in discussion, labeling it *adjective*. But knowing what an adjective is is much less important than knowing its function and then achieving flexibility in its use.

Children can also be helped to achieve variety in language through experimentation in transforming sentence patterns. Chomsky has suggested a view of language as composed of deep structures that can be transformed through a series of controlled operations into a number of derived patterns.[1]

John owns a bicycle becomes a question by adding a question mark: *Does John own a bicycle?* Add *not* and it becomes negative. *John does not (doesn't) own a bicycle.* Through a series of operations the same statement is transformed into a passive: *A bicycle is owned by John.* If *will* is added, the statement is projected into the future (*John will own a bicycle*) or into another question (*Will John own a bicycle?*).

The purpose of this sort of experimentation is not to teach language structure; as we have indicated, even young children use all basic language structures. Our purpose is to make children more confident in their use of structure to achieve variety.

In a series of studies, Kellogg Hunt has demonstrated that one of the primary ways in which language becomes more mature as children get older (comparing different children in fourth, eighth, and twelfth grades) is in the increased use of complex structures that embed several clauses or base structures in single statements.[2] The result is more powerful and economic use of language. Younger children might say, "Jim lives next door to me. He is a big bully. Yesterday I saw him beat up Tom. Tom is a little kid. Jim wanted to use Tom's bike. Tom didn't want him to." An older child might say, "Yesterday I saw Tom, that big bully who lives next door, beat Tom up because he wanted to use Tom's bike and Tom wouldn't let him."

Some of this shift toward complex, economical language must result from the learner's wide contact with varied language in his own reading and listening experiences. Some also must result from his own continued

---

[1] Noam Chomsky, *Syntactic Structures* (The Hague: Mouton, 1956).

[2] See, for example, Kellogg W. Hunt, *Grammatical Structures Written at Three Grade Levels* (Champaign, Ill.: NCTE, 1965).

attempts at using language in varied situations in both written and oral language. In fact, research has tended to show that the most effective way to improve the effectiveness of writing and speaking is to stimulate the learners to do a great deal of writing and speaking. Some direct instruction in syntactic and rhetorical devices may help, but only when children see the instruction in relationship to the desire they have already developed to be more effective in their use of language.

Sinclair-de-Zwart, a psycholinguist working with Piaget, has demonstrated that language follows rather than precedes conceptual development.[3] In studying children who did and did not have the concept of conservation (volume's constancy despite shape) she found that those who did conserve used more relational terms (e.g., more than) and more varied terms rather than polar opposites like big and small. They also used more coordinated terms to describe (He has more marbles but they are smaller.). Her research suggests that there is little merit in trying to get children to use more complex and advanced language before they have developed the cognitive structures and patterns of thinking, which require such language.

The child learns language because he needs to describe his universe and communicate with those around him. He learns language by wholes and eventually induces from these learned wholes the underlying structures of the language. If the school works with the child toward greater efficiency and effectiveness in his use of language, eventually, as his language becomes more effective, it will also come within the more general language norms of the society. Language and its structure are interwoven with cultural values and cultural perceptions. Expansion in language must closely parallel the learner's expanding views and perceptions of the world around him.

In developing language effectiveness in a pragmatic way, communication of meaning should be the guide to decisions about usage. Is meaning enhanced or diminished by a certain expression? A phrase may have low status in certain social settings, but it still may be the most effective way to state the idea. *Ain't* sometimes falls into this category when the polite form is too roundabout. On the other hand, a more widely used expression may carry a meaning that a localism, expressing the same idea, may diminish or make meaningless to an outsider. In-group language, although understood among small, intimate groups, in wider communication is no substitute for polished and aesthetically pleasing rhetoric.

Language is changing constantly, but social acceptance of change lags far behind. At appropriate ages, children need to learn about this social dimension of language; then they will understand why certain expressions are useful at one time but not at another time. *If the teacher concentrates on expanding their language, children with varying dialect backgrounds can*

---

[3] H. Sinclair-de-Zwart, "Developmental Psycholinguistics," in Elkind and Flavell, *Studies in Cognitive Development* (New York: Oxford University Press, 1969), pp. 315–336.

eventually achieve a flexibility that meets the demands of society for an appropriate English.

Priorities and Objectives for an Elementary Language Development Curriculum Based on Expanding Effective Use of Language

A key decision in planning any language arts program is what it will include. Some programs are narrow, confining themselves to presenting a system of grammatical descriptions and selected aspects of language etiquette labeled usage. But an effective language arts program in elementary education must be broad. The time and energy devoted to any single aspect must be keyed to a hierarchy of purposes based on a point of view of the role of the school in language development.

A modern point of view is based on two key premises: (1) All children have achieved a high degree of language competence in at least one dialect of one language by the time they come to school; and (2) this language is at the same time their means of expression and communication, their medium of thought, and the central tool in all their learning.

The vital role of the school in language development is built on the existing competence. In exercising this role, teachers and curriculum planners must keep in mind that all aspects of language, oral and written, are developmental. Growth in effectiveness, not perfection, must be stressed.

In the hierarchy of purposes, a minor role must be assigned to the presentation of knowledge about language. Knowing about language and how it works is important, but only as it contributes to using language effectively.

No language curriculum could or should isolate reading and literature from the rest of the language program. Language activities can draw heavily on literature and lead outward to literature from many oral and written language activities. The reading program, integrated with the total language curriculum can help to develop taste, interest, and critical insight into literature. Spelling and handwriting are directly related to effective written language. An effective curriculum should treat both as means toward this end rather than as ends in themselves.

The common division of English curricula in college and the secondary school into language, composition, and literature is not a useful framework. A more appropriate division is into language processes: reading, writing, speaking, and listening. These, however, create a dichotomy between oral and written language that is unnecessary. Many lessons and activities can deal with related aspects of both.

A SUGGESTED LANGUAGE CURRICULUM The following suggested language development curriculum has eight basic strands and one optional strand that get varied emphases as children progress through school. These strands fit under three general headings: those designed to increase language effectiveness, those that provide insight into language and how it works, and those designed to change language.

INCREASING LANGUAGE EFFECTIVENESS
Listening: This deserves far fuller and more sophisticated treatment than it now gets in most programs.

Informal Language: Language in its most basic and fundamental uses: conversation, discussion, argument, persuasion, questioning, answering.

Creative Composition: Imaginative use of language to achieve aesthetic as well as communicative effects.

Expository Composition: Reporting (describing and communicating complex ideas, instructions, and directions in effective ways); research technique; library skills.

Reading: Since reading, like writing, extends language competence into a new medium, it may be considered as part of the general objective of increasing language effectiveness in all areas of the curriculum.

Literature: The literature strand is also primarily an extension of the learner's language effectiveness because through the study of literature he expands his effectiveness in dealing with the aesthetic uses of language. To some extent, the structure of literature may be studied and would involve learning about language (in this case, literary language). But such study has only minor importance in the elementary curriculum compared with the more basic attempt to build comprehension, interest, taste, and a feeling for literary language. Without these basic goals, study of the form of literary language is barren and futile, and may in fact build a strong, early distaste for literature.

LEARNING ABOUT LANGUAGE
Grammar: The structure of language, how it works, linguistic terminology to express these concepts: surface and deep structures, transformations, and morphemics.

Other Language Aspects: History of language, semantics, comparative linguistics (the study of relationships between languages), dialectology and linguistic geography, etymology, language and logic, language games.

CHANGING LANGUAGE
Social Preferability: This should be considered an optional strand or, rather, several alternate options that must be keyed to the school populations: rural or urban, transplanted regional groups, speakers of low-status, indigenous dialects. Perhaps the most complex programs will be needed in the urban ghettos where a wide range of dialects exist side by side. However, the development of positive attitudes toward language or dialect differences should *not* be optional.

Figure 1 illustrates the changing importance of these strands as children progress in school and in development.

This curricular model is built from the bottom up on the base of the existing language competence of the learners. There is an unfortunate tendency to build curriculum from the top down, starting with college entrance requirements and orienting the secondary school curriculum to these, then gearing the elementary curriculum to the demands of the

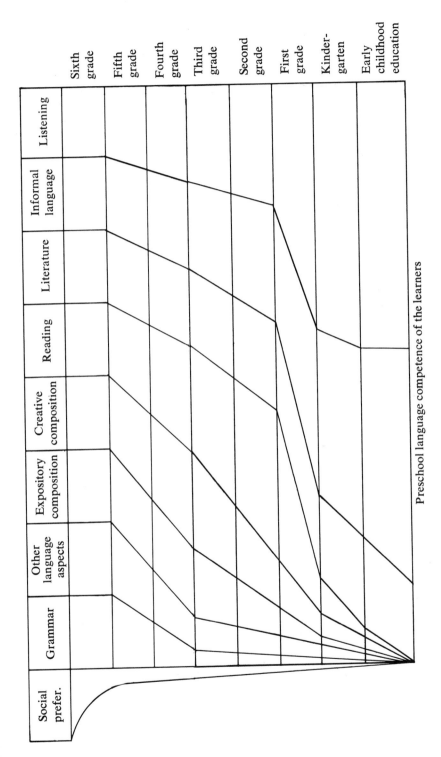

FIGURE 1   Strands in an elementary language arts program.

secondary school. Such an approach ignores the opportunities to expand on the pre-existing competence of the learners at each stage.

The preferred opposite model assumes that in early childhood education, the focus is on informal language and listening with some introduction of literature in the form of stories told and read by the teachers, rhymes, songs, and plays. Such literature may be in books but it may also be in films, records, television, and other media.

Kindergarten continues the heavy stress on listening as informal language expands on the introduction of children's literature and begins activities that will lead to reading instruction later. Small beginnings are made on the other strands, particularly composition through oral language activities and dictated stories.

In the primary grades (1–3), listening and informal language continue to be of considerable although diminishing importance. Reading assumes a major role in the curriculum, particularly at the beginning of the primary years, and diminishes somewhat through the years. Composition, both expository and creative, assumes increasing importance as the learners progress. Grammar and other language aspects get quite minor attention throughout the primary years.

In the upper elementary grades there is a gradual shift in stress so that it is approximately equal in the sixth grade on each of these strands. This curriculum model assumes gradual transitions with no abrupt shifts in focus and no sudden terminations. Although we have indicated grade levels, a nongraded school would facilitate both the gradual shifts in focus and a desirable adaptation of the basic plan to the needs and abilities of specific groups of learners. The social preferability strand, which must be keyed to the learners, does not really begin to get much direct attention until the end of the sixth grade, when the children are beginning to gain insight into social values and to become concerned about social acceptability. In the secondary school this becomes a major focus along with expanding involvement with literature of all kinds.

Testing Ideas against Reality

Teachers may wish to find out how their language development and that of their students relate to the developmental, sociological, and historical ideas presented thus far. The following validation activities are suggested as examples:

Tape-record an informal conversation between yourself and a colleague from another speech community background. Listen to it together, and then each mark down the speech divergencies of the other person: the vowel sounds, idiomatic structures, unusual vocabulary or special meanings for words, accent, and rhythmic flow. Speculate on what responses are dialect, idiolect, or "inconsistencies" ("mistakes") in the language patterns, special gestures, and intonations.

Tape-record youngsters from different speech communities reading a slightly above-level passage orally. Listen with the youngsters to the replay while following the actual text. Note the divergencies in sounding of words, in the flow of phrases, in the efforts to relate the printed words to language patterns and language knowledge of the reader. Speculate on what responses are due to dialect, idiolect, or confusions within the basic language pattern being used by each reader as it confronts a "standardized" or prestigious pattern on the page.

Tape-record several youngsters with divergent speech patterns as they tell about an event they have all recently witnessed. Note divergencies and ask the raconteurs, after hearing the tape, whether everything said sounds "correct" and if not, why.

Jot down or tape-record if possible the game rhymes, slang, and jokes or "funnies" used or shared at recess or on the playground after school. Ask youngsters where they learned them. Think about your findings in terms of child folk heritage and of child or teenage refreshment of the language.

Turning Ideas into Practice

Many of the ideas about language development in cultures and in persons can be applied to teaching–learning situations. Some suggestions follow:

Locate passages of similar content, such as "about spring," from writings in Chaucerian, Shakespearean, eighteenth-century, and modern English. Compare and contrast spelling, vocabulary, idioms, phrasing, and punctuation. Make attempts to "translate" the passages into present-day English not as an admirable activity, but as an investigation into the changes of a language through time. Ask pupils to read a passage from the originals of such early Colonial documents as the Massachusetts Bay Colony Laws establishing public schools or Bradford's HISTORY OF PLIMOTH PLANTATION.

Select dialect passages from literature such as Jim's famous near-monologues in HUCK FINN or dialogues from present-day black, Italian-American, or Irish literature. Ask students to practice reading them for presenting the dialect flow. Analyze them for consistency. Relate them to tape recordings that students and/or the teacher might make of the informal language of dialect speakers in the community or those heard during vacations in other parts of the country.

Listen to folk song recordings in the Library of Congress Collection from different speech community areas. Describe the differences in vowel sounds, intonation, and phrasing from the speech of those in the local school community.

Suggest Language Encounters for youngsters to write and/or draw descriptions of themselves, family, and friends. For older youngsters, suggest they keep diaries that describe their responses to the activities and confrontations of each day. Focus on parts of the body such as their feet or hands and write or talk about what those extensions of the body's cognitive–affective systems would like to do such as walk on soft grass or moss or let sand fall through the fingers.

LANGUAGE
AND
KNOWING

In Greek philosophy the very term LOGOS always suggested and supported the idea of a fundamental identity between the act of speech and the act of thought.

ERNST CASSIRER, Essay on Man
(New York: Doubleday Anchor, 1956), p. 163.

Even if the thing is not there to represent the meaning, the word may be produced so as to evoke the meaning. Since intellectual life depends on possession of a store of meanings, the importance of language as a tool of preserving meanings cannot be overstated. . . . Without words as vehicles . . . no cumulative growth of intelligence would occur. Experience might form habits of physical adaptation but it would not teach anything; for we should not be able to use an old experience consciously to anticipate and regulate a new experience. . . .

JOHN DEWEY, How We Think
(New York: D. C. Heath, 1933), p. 234.

TEACHING FOCUS

What are some of the reasons why young people develop misconceptions of scientific, sociocultural, and psychological phenomena?

How can teachers constructively influence the development of the thought-language-symbol process while utilizing instruction that considers the stages and continuities of language–thought growth?

What instructional methods and organizational procedures can teachers use that will produce independent and open inquiry in their classrooms as modeled on some British primary and American "open-education" schools?

How can the teacher make use of the organized disciplines of study in giving authenticity, recency, and authority to his planning of substantive school studies that will be relevant to the experiences of young people?

5

Coming To Know

And this our life, exempt from public haunt,
Finds tongues in trees, books in the running brooks,
Sermons in stones, and good in everything.[1]

Children could not achieve by themselves the state of knowing that
Shakespeare describes, nor could they reach it with their fellow children only.
They would see the trees, the brooks, and the stones, but not being able to
engage in discourse about them, they would not come to "know" them in
relation to each other and to other events in the "Forest of Order." Trees
can speak only when the human being observing the trees has the power of
language at his command to make trees a part of his cognitive map of the
world—a map that places environmental happenings in meaningful relationship with each other.

Knowing is more than thinking, although thinking is one of the processes
by which people come to know. Knowing is a very personal process, involving imagination above all else. Some of man's thinking procedures can be
isolated and scientifically explained, but perhaps only the poet has the kind of
vision that can capture a full concept of knowing.

There was a child went forth every day
And the first object he look'd upon
That object he became,

[1] Shakespeare, *As You Like It*, II, i, 15–17.

And that object became part of him for the
day or a certain part of the day,
Or for many years or stretching cycles of years.[2]

Knowing is becoming. As events in the world become part of a child's world and as he gains his own view of people and things about him, he begins to become a person.

Once Paumanok,
When the lilac-scent was in the air and fifth-month grass was growing,
Up this seashore in some briers,
Two feather'd guests from Alabama, two together,
And their nest, and four light-green eggs spotted with brown,
And every day the he-bird to and fro near at hand,
And every day the she-bird crouch'd on her nest, silent, with bright eyes,
And every day I, a curious boy, never too close, never disturbing them,
Cautiously peering, absorbing, translating.[3]

Whitman was not the only poet to discover and extol the freshness and intimacy of childhood learning, but certainly he showed a profound sensitivity to it in the line "Cautiously peering, absorbing, *translating*." Because poets never seem to outgrow this precious quality of childlike experiencing, they reiterate the childhood situation of meeting the world head on and coming to terms with it through the wonder of translation. Somewhere along the educational road to adulthood the wondrous quality of experiencing and knowing in language can be lost, and personality can stagnate. Perhaps the prime role of teachers should be to prevent intellectual stagnation from happening.

A Language-Centered Meaning for Intellectual Education

The educational problem lies with the place of language in a definition of intellectual learning. Language may be viewed as either an external verbalization about things or as an integral part of the personal process of experiencing and knowing. In the latter view, the thing is not known until it is named, and its interrelation with other things is not understood until language embodies the idea. If this function of language is accepted, intellectual education is neither the memorization of words and facts, nor the possession of significant experiences, but is the constant interplay of interrelated experiences and language toward knowing. Language is pivotal in a person's knowing through experience. Therefore, language is the very core of the teaching–learning process rather than a necessary evil that teachers

---

[2] Walt Whitman, from "A Child Went Forth."
[3] Walt Whitman, from "Out of the Cradle Endlessly Rocking."

and pupils are forced to use. Dewey and Bentley describe knowing as a transactional process between the individual and the environment, with language at the center of the process: "Transaction is the procedure which observes men talking and writing, with their word-behavior and other representation activities connected with their thing perceivings and manipulations."

In a final section in the book there is "A Trial Group of Names," and "language" is among the definitions: "Language: to be taken as behavior of men. . . . Not to be viewed as composed of word-bodies apart from word-meanings, nor as word-meanings apart from word enbodiment. As behavior, it is a region of knowing."[4] Coming to know—experience interpreted and intellectualized in language—would then be viewed as the goal of education.

Dewey's concept of interpreted experience has been misunderstood by some as being nonintellectual. He meant, however, that experience could not stand alone as learning but that it must be interpreted through a process of reflective thinking to be made consequential. *Knowing* is a transaction between the individual and the environment in which both are, in a sense, transformed. There is no such thing as absolute knowledge, only a process of knowing involving actions and word-meanings together. The young child's search for answers to his questions about every new item he sees and handles is a natural example of the transaction between the individual and his environment that Dewey describes. This process is always happening, and it never becomes final or fixed. The teacher's role is to keep the way open and the means available for the richest and fullest possible transactions.

One of the most powerful statements of the difference between knowledge and knowing is the one-act play "The Lesson" by Ionesco.[5] Herr Professor, his student, and his maid are the characters. The play opens innocently enough with the arrival of a new, young lady student, but soon the maid interjects a note of foreboding by admonishing the professor not to let "it" happen again. However, the teacher, by impressing his knowledge (verbiage) upon the pupil through the means of monotonous recitation, finally overwhelms the pupil and symbolically (although on stage literally) kills her. The Herr Professor could have achieved the same end had he used the more subtle modern methods of tightly programmed materials or carefully conditioned group processes. The aim would still have been the subjection of the pupil to the disembodied verbalization of the culture. The only possible rejoinder to "The Lesson" is to view language as the matrix in personal knowing. Then the process of education becomes a process of personal discovery under the guidance of a teacher who is aware of the validity of this process in his own learning.

---

[4] John Dewey and Arthur Bentley, *Knowing and the Known* (Boston: Beacon, 1949), pp. 123, 297.

[5] Eugene Ionesco, "The Lesson," *Four Plays* (New York: Grove, 1958), pp. 43–78.

section 1

Personality Development and Knowing

An individual's cognitive posture in the world—his idiosyncratic view of his environment—is a manifestation of his personality which guides his actions. Psychologists of personality speak of an individual's conceptual schemes or patterns, which are basic to the development of personality. Thus,

> The stored organized effects of past experience . . . we have labeled concepts.
> . . . Concepts in their matrix of inter-relatedness serve the critical cognitive function of providing a system of ordering by means of which the environment is broken down and organized, is differentiated and integrated into its many psychologically relevant facets. In this capacity, they provide the medium through which the individual establishes and maintains ties with the world. . . . It is on this basis, hence, that one's self identity and existence are articulated and maintained. Threat to such ties or severance of them leads to a psychological mobilization at maintaining or restoring them, efforts, which if unsuccessful may result in a major re-orientation and organization of ties to the world, or more drastically, even to breakdown or destruction of the self.[6]

Conceptual systems, using language in great part for constructing their webs, become the basis for self-identity and focus in a world otherwise confused by myriads of disconnected impressions. If the system is thrown out of kilter by too many misconceptions, then the personality can become distorted as self-identity weakens through a state of confusion.

The fact that language is the medium of the psychoanalyst's interview or therapy sessions suggests that language is the main conveyor of these conceptual systems. It is only by language that the human being can have them at all. Even the ephemeral emotions are expressed mainly through various language means: gesturing, crying, laughing, and speaking all at the same time. Conceptual systems can be heard at work when we listen to our internal arguing with ourselves before we make an active choice or when we "Monday morning quarterback." We reiterate our ideas in the pleasure of being right or defend what we did even when we suspect we were wrong, or we try to figure out how we might better approach a similar situation another time. Notice that the words for all these kinds of activities are words describing language activities: "arguing," "second guessing," and "figuring out."

People are constantly coming to terms with the world by forming their conceptions of it. They are making cognitive adjustments to the world—in a real sense, cognitive conquests of the world. From sensory deprivation experiments it is clear that when a man is deprived of the stimulation of

---

[6] O. J. Harvey, David Hunt, and Harold Schroder, *Conceptual Systems and Personality Organization* (New York: Wiley, 1961), p. 10.

novelty or even the passing parade, he stops transforming experience into symbol, stops knowing, stops playing with his world, and goes mad. Evidently, the process of ideation cannot sustain itself for long without the stimulation that comes from playful curiosity about things in the environment. Man strives to know more, but when deprived of the stimuli, he panics and requests relief from monotony.

Motivation for Coming To Know

Everyday life does not necessarily generate situations that challenge the person to know because of drives to be satisfied or instincts to be gratified. Much learning can be explained by drive psychology only in the most roundabout way. To explain a child's desire to know about pets by saying that he needs the security of a friend that cannot talk back to him is a roundabout explanation of motivation to learn. Robert White's ideas of "competence" and "effectance" seem more appropriate as explanations of motivation for knowing. The individual is motivated by a generalized need to explore his environment, to come to terms with it by gaining *competence* to cope with it, and by finding a "feeling of efficiency (*effectance*) in it.[7]

This need to explore is evident even in the behavior of the chimpanzee when it continues to search for playful activity even though all its drives are satisfied. It is this need to explore that keeps the crawling baby active in the discovery of his world and continues to sustain the wandering ornithologist in the discovery of *his* world. The scientist and the baby are gaining competence in coping with their environments as they discover meanings in them. Parents or educators can thwart this natural curiosity by stultifying it or putting it to sleep through denial of the opportunity to explore.

Positive cognitive activity is as essential to well-being as are physical activity and the exercise of the emotions. If children do not accomplish cognitive adjustment to the world, they may maintain into maturity misconceptions that can adversely affect their emotional adjustment. A child growing up with a marked misconception of a racial or religious group can become emotionally upset in his relationships with these groups in later life. A child who develops the misguided concept that material gain is *the* measure of an individual's success may find in maturity that his view of life is so lopsided that he is lost when material gains do not truly satisfy him. Had he not been so convinced, he might not have been so unhappy.

Education from the earliest time, guided by parent and teacher, is the only means for assuring that a child's cognitive map (consisting of patterns

---

[7] Robert White, "Motivation Reconsidered: The Concept of Competence," *Psychological Review*, 1959, pp. 297–333.

of knowing) is as representative of reality as is possible. If it is, there will be no need for later "cognitive therapy."[8] The healthful extending of cognitive development is as important as healthful emotional and social development. *The use of language with the child in the interpretation of experience all through the preschool and school years is critical for sound personality development as well as for improved intellectual education.*

Each individual's conceptual system develops uniquely, depending on his basic capabilities of imagination, thinking power, and language skill for processing data from his environment. If any one of these factors is limited, the child's intellectual development is stunted. On the other hand, when his environment is rich in experiential possibilities, when his language culture is nourishing, and when his intellectual powers are utilized, his conceptual system can eventually incorporate the logic of the stellar system or the philosophy of an ethical system. *Educational potential can be made higher for many children when maximums are sought by teachers in the factors over which they have some control: environmental enrichment and language-culture expansion.*

Language in Personal Knowing

Two twentieth-century philosophers, Ernst Cassirer and Susanne Langer, have been particularly interested in the place of language in personal knowing. Their formulations about language and other presentational forms in the symbolic transformation of experience are useful for illuminating the educational situation. Their views embrace the whole of knowing through the arts, as well as the sciences, and show concern for values both aesthetic and moral. Language in all its forms becomes a focal concern to them. Langer built upon Cassirer's ideas and extended them. The following statement summarizes their argument:

> The transformation of experience into concepts, not the elaborator of signals and symptoms, is the motive of language.
>
> For language is much more than a set of symbols. . . . Its forms do not stand alone, like so many monoliths each marking its one isolated grave; but instead, they tend to integrate, to make complex patterns, and thus to point out equally complex *relationships* in the world, the realm of their meanings. . . .[9]

The transformation of experience into a symbol is a personal, humanizing process of education. In our daily living we respond to most happenings

---

[8] Lawrence K. Frank, *The School as Agent for Cultural Renewal* (Cambridge, Mass.: Harvard University Press, 1960). This is a most provocative essay on the ways of knowing.

[9] Susanne K. Langer, *Philosophy in a New Key* (New York: Mentor Books, 1956), pp. 105, 109.

in a habitual way because we came to know them early in life and have developed routine reactions to them. Being served eggs for breakfast requires no cognitive or affective reorientation. However, every so often in the daily round a slightly novel experience comes our way. We must come to terms with it by comparing and contrasting it with the familiar and, finally, by formulating it into a revised and extended version of what we already knew. We may inquire of others, even do some reading, but all the time we are transforming the experience into our own symbols. The process may be slight and only momentary when, for example, we are served an omelet for the first time instead of scrambled eggs. But were we to travel to Japan and experience the traditional tea ceremony, a great deal of symbolic processing of fact and feeling would occur before we fully understood and appreciated this experience and could make it ours.

Teachers have a responsibility for fostering personal knowing in their students by developing strategies for evoking personal response to experiences and making symbolic representations of them.

section 2

Open-Inquiry Education: A General Means For Fostering Personal Knowing in School and Humanizing the Program

The general concept of open-inquiry education[10] incorporates such ideas as child-centered learning, individualized and self-directed instruction, team or paired learning activity, and discovery learning that fosters the student's inevitable and constant search for meaning in his environment through the manipulation of materials and confrontation with real experience. Although the movement for open-inquiry education has roots in the "life-experiencing activity" programs of the progressive period it was given new impetus by educational application of the findings of Jean Piaget and his colleagues in their vast studies of children's thinking and valuing. Indirect approaches to teaching and learning have been explored extensively by teachers who have been developing the instructional techniques for advancing open-inquiry education. Materials and resources have to be prepared and organized for independent study by youngsters with the guidance of teachers. Convenient resource and study areas are designated for use by individuals and teams of learners to support the open-inquiry approach.

[10] Charles Silberman (ed.), *The Open Classroom Reader* (New York: Vintage Books, 1973).

The British Experience in
Child-Centered Education

Since models for open-inquiry education are well advanced in Britain and adaptations of them have been made possible in other cultural settings, a discussion of them is presented in terms of a response by one of the authors to an extended participatory visitation program in a number of typical British primary schools. Although the open-inquiry approach is most evident in the infant and primary school (nursery school through sixth grade) there are programs underway in many junior and secondary schools that continue the approach through adaptations to the higher levels of education. Even the older buildings have been found adaptable to a more open organization and to team work since they all have an assembly area with classrooms opening on to it that can be used for a common resource and study center. British youngsters do exhibit some different cultural traits from those of American children, but the similiarities between the English-speaking children of England and North America are very evident. However there is a work expectancy and a respect for intellectual pursuits in school that could find more advocates on this side of the Atlantic; the open-inquiry approach may be the means for doing so.

Earmarks of the Open-Inquiry Approach
As Observed in British Primary Schools

The following earmarks are presented to suggest adaptations that teachers can make in their school settings that will foster open-inquiry by attempting to meet the youngster's personal thinking and language systems head-on and by developing instructional means for extending and enriching his thought and language in school.

A mixture of informal and formal teaching is an outgrowth of the British pragmatic sense of a need for mixing ideologies in real life.

The *formal part* may be scheduled by the teacher or scheduled in time blocks by the head teachers. These periods are mainly set aside for practice in language and math skills. The time allotted to these formal periods is never more than one third of the total day. *Individualized* and small-group work prevails even in these formal periods. Tasks are set either by task cards or exercise books, but even so most of these materials have a modern look to them. Another formal characteristic is the unwritten assumption that *every child, every day will do some reading, some writing (composition), and some mathematics practice (computation), and this work will be corrected and evaluated by the teacher.* The daily writing and usually the math practice were done in an "exercise book," a special notebook that children have used in England for many years. The content of the writing in the new programs is likely to be creative or applied to some project in which the child is involved, but some writing is done and corrected every day. Here is a practice to be strongly recommended to every United States elementary school staff. This understood requirement may be one reason why English children are generally more advanced in language learning than American children are.

The informal part of the day's schedule and of the teaching and learning activities occupies about two thirds of the work time. These activities may occur in a room with a teacher or in the school or section of a school involving a team of two to four teachers, sometimes with a helper. If the program is room-organized there will be several *learning centers* with teacher-made and commercial materials. If it is a school organization these learning centers will be in different rooms with one of the generalist teachers of the formal periods serving as a specialist teacher in the informal part of the program. Resources and materials around certain content areas are available in these rooms and in the general assembly area outside the rooms. Some schools combine these organizational patterns in their own ways depending on the talents and "likes" of its staff. In all cases the staff, with the head, behave as a team and share responsibilities for maintaining materials and resources in the various content areas as well as for serving as resource consultants to the other teachers. Sometimes whole staff or several members are using Schools Council or other nationally developed programs. All rooms are full of books, other printed matter, and manipulative materials. They are stored and catalogued for the convenience of the child workers. Teachers use everything for storing from cartons, to cheap see-through plastic boxes now available for such purposes.

The chief curriculum posture taken by the staff, remembering that the school head and staff are quite autonomous, is that studies for children must be *relevant* and *interdisciplinary*. "Relevance" is a word used in England only when reference is made at the same time to the fact that English educators would like to be free from American terminology. They use their own terms for educational ideas that are developed in their educational culture. By "relevant," as used here, is meant child-focused study that deals with scientific and social-cultural phenomena that children have experienced or to which they can relate. "Interdisciplinary" has the same meaning in both educational cultures and refers to employing all the disciplines of study that are appropriate to the child's question, problem, or concern being studied. This point of view toward curriculum may have given rise to the term "integrated day" or "integrated program" that has been used to describe the new English primary-school program by some authors.

The main teaching–learning methods in the informal part of the program revolve around the concept of *self-selection of work* through child interest and concern. The teacher serves as a guide and resource. The teacher behaves as if he were a tutor, mainly. He asks leading questions to get at the interest or concern, leads the child toward formulating questions or problems, and suggests resources. An *inquiry* attitude is sought in every "teacher–pupil encounter." Skill in this teaching behavior varies a good deal but one of the thrusts of the instructional improvement programs has been to help teachers find their own ways for developing inquiry teaching skills. Some teachers manifest this approach as they study along with the children. Frequently teachers talked about how much they were learning about science, for example, as they developed new clusters of materials and resources around science themes. Another key method used is the *individualizing of instruction* through materials by which pupils can keep track of their own progress. Their problems, questions, and successes are recorded as they sense when they are able to move on to the next level of work. Most of the reading instruction is done this way. The "Lady Bird" series of individualized reading books has been a boon to the use of this method. Although teachers have some reservations about the contents, the books themselves make small readable and interesting individual readers cheaply available to children at all levels. They become the basis for classroom libraries to which many trade books are added from purchases and local library collections.

Closely allied to this method is wide use of *team learning*. Children do a great deal of their work in pairs or triads, rarely more than four in a work group. Children pair off with different children for different tasks usually with the guidance of the teacher. The "family grouping" structure in each room helps in this situation when it is used. Sometimes older children help younger ones, or more advanced children in a content area help less advanced children or even slow-learners. *Team learning* is used from the earliest age levels to the top of the school, often in the same way as the rural schoolteacher used this method, but with many more materials available for this purpose. Sometimes pairs or triads of children work together over long periods on a subject or some project with the teacher keeping an eye constantly on the productivity. When attentiveness and productivity begin to decline, new materials are presented, new questions are raised, or the work group is redeployed after some summarizing of what has been done so far. Individual records of progress, problems, and suggestions are kept on *each* child even though he is working in these small groups. All children keep individual folders of their work as well as their "exercise books." Their teacher writes comments on everything.

Even though children may work in pairs or triads *each child prepares his own report of the work done* and the teacher examines it and makes recommendations for improvement or accepts it as the accomplished task. The pupils can work independently because they are very accustomed to reading and writing every day. In writing they are usually allowed to prepare a first draft as best they can. Then they bring it to the teacher and usually through an inquiry-type process the corrections are made and a final copy is presented. In reading the children tend to work independently, keeping their own word lists and asking their team mate or teacher for help when they need it. Reading and writing activities are very frequently interrelated. Young children learn to write as soon as they learn to read and very often this occurs at five years plus. It might even be said that a sequence of reading, writing, and then reading again is one of the main methods for teaching reading. In the United States this method would be called a language-experience and individualized reading approach. Drill books in phonics were not much in evidence although teachers used "sounding out" as a means for helping students gain independence in word attack. With this rich language-learning background independent work becomes quite possible at quite an early age.

The most practical method for permitting the teachers to organize individualized, pair-, and small-group study based on child interests and concerns is the *work card*. Every so often in the history of education a practical device is invented that perfectly suits a new approach and advances the practice because it is a device the teacher finds easy to use. The "work sheet" has been such a device in the past, but the "work card" when properly prepared, using an inquiry approach, not only assists the teacher in tailoring work for individuals or small groups but it actually puts an inquiry burden and responsibility on the student. Each card is tied to available materials or ones that can be constructed easily. This method encourages the development of child-made materials that can then be used by the next group of students. The making of work cards brings focus to the teacher's own curriculum development. The informal part of the British schooling could not function without this device. Teachers prepare *interdisciplinary* resource study units of all kinds often based upon the new national curricular programs, and then they develop their own work cards to meet the aims of these units with their groups of youngsters. The result of the application of these methods, in the new organizational patterns, is a busy school with children working all over the school on all sorts of learning tasks and educational questions. An interdisciplinary approach is used and the language tools of reading and writing as well as the creative arts are employed. We see by the tokens of the children's work the system is working. Contrary to some reports, very little work that was nonsensical or immature for the ability level was observed. These young people *produce*.

The Open "Classroom Meeting" Technique:
An Instructional Model for
Encouraging Personal Knowing in School
and Humanizing Classroom Life

A major technique for personalizing inquiry, outlined in William Glasser's *"Schools without Failure,"*[11] is the *classroom meeting*—a class discussion with the teacher and students seated in a circle. What distinguishes

---

[11] William Glasser, *Schools without Failure* (New York: Harper & Row, 1961), Chaps. 10–12.

Glasser's class meeting from the typical class discussion is not only that children are seated in a circle—how much better it is to respond to someone when you can see his face—but also that a change occurs in the roles of the teacher and student. In the circle, conversation should primarily be between student and student. The teacher is there to stimulate thinking and student talk but neither to correct responses, offer opinions unless asked, nor dominate the discussion. The teacher should be listening. Children should be learning to converse with each other, to argue or disagree with peer opinions, and to listen before responding or asking for clarification. Traditionally teachers have viewed discussions as another way to deliver some information, to lead students to asking the "right questions" in the pursuit of more knowledge. Glasser stresses that teacher talk should be minimal; student talk is maximized as students "try out" their ideas with their peers. For young children, opportunities for decentering their points of view are increased as they listen to others respond to their ideas and experiences. The role of the teacher is most important in getting meetings started and sustaining them by stimulating children's thinking with open-ended, divergent questioning strategies. Once children run with the topic, the teacher's role is to ensure equal participation and a reasonable focus for discussion.

An additional difference between traditional discussions and "class meetings" is that class meetings usually focus on one topic. The teacher may find it necessary to intervene to help students refocus if they stray from the topic too far. At times this may be desirable if the new topic engenders more interest, although too many topics under discussion will limit opportunities for in-depth discussion and resolution of thinking. Class meetings are not free-wheeling, off-the-cuff discussions about anything and everything. They demand careful teacher planning. The questions to be used must be carefully thought out in advance. The success and length of any meeting is dependent upon student age, student and teacher experience with class meetings, and the amount of interest the topic may have for the children.

In the end, Glasser feels class meetings help youngsters develop a sense of success and worthwhileness. It is most reasonable here, however, to examine how class meetings might enhance the ability of children to present their ideas, concepts, and experiences to their teachers and classmates within an organized structure for discussion.

Glasser outlines three types of class meetings. One is the social problem-solving meeting in which individual and social-educational problems are discussed. The second type is the open-ended meeting within which learners' out-of-school experiences and interests are discussed. The third type, the educational-diagnostic meeting, provides teachers with the opportunity to evaluate student success in the attainment of concepts taught in classroom learning activities. *Discussion is always focused on how the learnings relate to student interests, experiences, and concerns.* The teacher remains nonjudgmental of student responses, and does not evaluate children in the traditional sense. Students must feel free to participate and express themselves without fear of being corrected.

Glasser illustrates the diagnostic meeting by describing an experience he conducted with an eighth-grade class that had just completed study of a unit of the American Constitution.[12] He surmised that the students had learned about the Constitution but, individually, had not internalized its meaning. His first question led the students to an examination of the Bill of Rights. He asked, "Do these rights pertain to you?" There was heated discussion which illustrated a real lack of confrontation with this question in their regular study. Glasser felt his next question was the key to testing the students' understanding: "What happens if you do something on your own property that is against the law? For example, may you drive a car on your own property even though you don't have a driver's license and are too young to drive?" This question did generate a lively discussion, one which led to issues related to the Constitution and allowed the teacher, who was present, to judge the effectiveness of her unit of study. Based on the student responses in this meeting, Glasser concluded that during their study the students would have profited from a more relevant look at the Constitution and its meaning to their life situations. In effect, the meeting had enabled the teacher to evaluate his learning activities. Student responses in the meeting should suggest to the teacher the need for new learning activities that will assist his students in arriving at a more complete understanding of the concepts related to the Constitution.

Glasser's class meetings provide the opportunity for students to learn the social and intellectual skills of discussing within a structure of minimum teacher talk or interference. Teachers need to be listeners, for much can be learned by listening to children—how they think, what they think, and what is meaningful to them. The suspension of teacher judgment, as suggested by Glasser, supplies the added benefit of encouraging all students to gain confidence in their ability to verbalize: to present their ideas and concerns freely. For many students oral presentation may be the primary means of success for presentation of their knowing.

[12] Glasser, pp. 139–141.

6

Educational Phases
in Coming To Know[1]

Education, conceived as coming to know through the symbolic transformation and representation of experience, involves three phases of mental activity: (1) *perceiving* new data in the environment; (2) *ideating* upon the perceptions (ideation includes conceptualizing and generalizing); and (3) presenting ideations to oneself and others. Each individual *perceives* new objects, events, or ideas in his own way. He tries to incorporate what he perceives into his conceptual schemes through the process of *ideation*. Then he *presents* them on his own terms to himself and others by symbolic representation in media appropriate to his life-style and to the types of ideas. The media of symbolic representation are language, art, music, dance, film, dramatics, or any combination of them. The cycle begins again as his presentations meet new events and ideas that have to be newly perceived and conceptualized.

These symbolizing processes of perceiving, ideating, and presenting one's conceptions go on continually in the waking hours of adults and children. Even during sleep, dream sequences often show that the individual works over the experiences of the previous day. A two-year-old's persistent questions reveal the spontaneous activity of the transformation process, as do the probings of college students. The teacher either tunes into an in-

[1] Constructed on a free elaboration of Langer's formulations for the purpose of bringing a focus on "knowing" into educational planning.

dividual's symbolizing process or he is tuned out of it by the pupil, who proceeds on his own without the teacher's guidance.

The following sections deal with various phases of the symbolic transformation of experience as they can relate to classroom activity. These theoretical formulations can give new focus and significance to some conventional language-centered classroom activities and can suggest new instructional strategies that the teacher can explore. Like all formulations of this kind, they do not account for the full range of cognitive-affective learning. The categories are not perfectly distinct, nor do the process phases that they represent always happen in sequence. Perceiving, ideating, and presenting overlap and interplay almost simultaneously as an individual attempts to come to terms with a new object or event brought into his life-space. Even so, a delineation of the symbolic transformation of experience into phases can be useful to teachers in helping them to see what is happening in situations with potential for symbolic learning and to construct appropriate teaching strategies for fostering such learning.

section 1

Perceiving Phase

Meeting a New Object, Happening, or Idea

The perceiving phase can be easily observed when children are meeting new objects and situations. A three-year-old accompanies his mother to the store. She is probably thinking of her shopping list; he constantly interrupts with comments about what he sees along the way. This mother, unaware, is witness to perception as the first step in building concepts of the world. The mother's thoughts may be far away and so far above the vision level of her investigating child that she does not literally see or perceive what he is perceiving: a smooth pebble looks like one of mommy's beads, or a puddle reflects like a mirror. Perceiving is that first contact through the eyes, ears, nose, or skin with an object or event that a person is drawn to or selects from the vast complex that surrounds him any time, any place. These individual contacts are sometimes referred to as environmental stimuli. In a sense the individual stimulates the piece of the environment that attracts him at a certain moment; it comes into focus for him while someone standing by may not even see it. Something from his past experience reaches out and pulls in the object or event for closer view and consideration. Students looking out a school window at rain coming down may perceive many different happenings, depending on their previous experience with storms, their attitudes toward thunder, or what they were planning to do in the recess about to begin. Others in the class may not have noticed the rain at all because they were absorbed in some activity. At times something in the environment attracts attention because of its bright color, its unusual sound, or its strange feel, and it is perceived in terms of past encounters with similar events. Some persons perceived the first orbital flight of an astronaut as an awesome accomplishment; others, as a foolish exploit; and others, as a blasphemous intrusion into God's heaven.

Misperceiving

It is not unusual for individuals to misperceive. They see only what they expect to see because of their previous experiences. People living in Western urban societies expect that a room they enter will be four-square or oblong, with parallel walls. Experimenters have demonstrated that persons with such a concept cannot know rooms without parallel enclosures. For example, they are unable to locate a corner of a model of a room prepared with walls of trapezoidal shape. They cannot act sensibly and effectively in a distorted space because they perceive it to be conventional, even after they are shown the distortions. Only with repeated successful experience of touching corners with a pointer do they overcome frustration and perceive correctly the distorted room and others like it.[2]

The child shows he has misperceived when he perceives every family and household as like his. This kind of misperceiving was evident when young children described the family of a president in terms of their own family life by insisting that the first lady washed the dishes, cleaned the house, and put her hair up in curlers. Older children perceived the President as a "father-boss" of all the people. One of the famous Ames experiments in perception makes use of a slanted window frame shape rotating on a pivot. Because observers expect the distorted frame to behave like a regular window shape, they see magic when objects placed on the pivoting frame seem to float in the air.[3] Such misconception is common in childhood learning. A four-year-old secure in his perception of a regular window asked his parents when the people on the television screen were going to climb out of the window and come to talk to him. Without historical illustrations a ten-year-old is likely to perceive Roman baths as modern public swimming pools.

Misperceiving may also arise because of differences in cultural setting. Slum children may perceive "stores" as "store-fronts," where suburban children will perceive them as "supermarkets" and rural children may still see them as "country stores."

---

[2] The initial experimentation and subsequent investigations by Ames and others, with implications for perceiving and learning, are discussed thoroughly in the following references: Hadley Cantril, *The "Why" of Man's Experience* (New York: Macmillan, 1950), pp. 72, 73. Earl Kelley, *Education for What Is Real* (New York: Harper & Row, 1947), Chaps. 3, 4. Franklin Kilpatrick, *Explorations in Transactional Psychology* (New York: New York University Press, 1961), Chaps. 8, 13, 14.

[3] See descriptions of Ames's experiments in Cantril, Kelley, or Kilpatrick, cited in previous footnote.

Language-Teaching Strategies
during the Perceiving Phase

In a classroom situation the perceiving *moment* is a strategic time for the teacher to help the child extend his perceptions and to assist him in validating or corroborating his perceptions with those of others, including his teacher. Although the perceiving act probably happens in nonlingual images—visual, auditory, or sensory structures—language cues can help limit the situation to be pereceived or can interrupt the perceiving process and cause another "look." After setting the environment to be perceived by the children through a field trip, a demonstration, prepared materials, or a film, the teacher limits the focus by bringing one aspect of the environment to their attention or by asking questions that will cause them to look at a particular aspect. On the other hand, the teacher may want to glean all the different perceptions that his class has about an object or happening; then he will use an open-ended question, for example: "What do you see there?" or "How do you feel about this situation?" The teacher's tactic of the day depends on whether his purposes require a widening or a narrowing of perceptions. For developing poetic expression a diversity of perceptions in the classroom is admirable; for observing the interaction of two chemicals, a teacher will narrow the perceptual field until all the students' perceptions are calibrated or matched somewhat with his own.

Sometimes children do not perceive what the teacher expects them to perceive. Their perception may be faulty, or they may simply overlook the factor the teacher is trying to bring out. Unless the teacher permits free talk at this moment he may not find this out until hours or days later when an idea he had been developing is stillborn. A globe in a kindergarten room is not perceived for what it is, but probably as a spinning ball. This may be the first phase of a growing concept that will eventually permit the child to perceive the globe as a map of the earth's surface, but in the early stage the perception desired by the teacher is not made. Pictures of the moon taken by spacecraft cameras look like aerial views of volcanoes, but to perceive the craters as a lot of volcanoes may be a jump in the wrong direction. Sometimes feelings may dominate or distort perceptions. A child who has a horror of snakes may be incapable of perceiving all (if any) of the interesting features of the harmless garter snake the teacher is holding.

Confrontation of children with significant objects and happenings to be perceived is the first teaching strategy on the way to the child's knowing his world. If teachers are aware of the fact that perceiving may be ruled by past experience, by a cultural set or a conforming view, by emotional disposition toward or against an object, or by the physical placement of what is being seen, they can plan confrontation and language strategies for both heightening and focusing perception. They can use classroom tactics that will cut down time wasted in hit-or-miss scanning and will help eliminate confusions in the first step to knowing.

As students encounter the world, they can be helped through conversation and discussion to perceive it richly and accurately.

The importance of *setting up a stimulus-provoking environment* of objects and materials cannot be overstressed.[4] Progressive educators weaned on Dewey's emphasis on experience will recognize this need for establishing concrete life-situations in the classroom and creating a felt need, but they may not see so clearly the need for structuring these situations in such a way that they will present a "cognitive dissonance"[5] that the child must resolve. The slightly novel situation is introduced purposefully to create challenge and curiosity. In the everyday world the child is naturally confronted with novelty to explore, but in the more formal classroom, teachers have to bring in life. An interesting, novelty-producing tactic reported by a seventh-grade teacher provoked a half-hour of constructive discussion. In the context of studying France the teacher showed without comment a picture of a cow in the kitchen of a peasant farmhouse. The children, surprised by the seeming incongruity of this situation, started immediately to try to explain it. When skill exercises dominate the school day the child's education is seriously retarded in a very real sense. He would fare far better in his intellectual and language growth were he left to wander, provided there were adults and other children about to interact and think with him regarding his experiential adventure.

section 2

Ideating Phase, Including Conceptualizing and Generalizing

Coming to Terms with an Object, Happening, or Idea

The moment the individual begins to talk and think about what he has perceived, the phase of *ideating* has begun. The organism must come to terms with what has been perceived. Language, affect (feelings), and cognitive energy come into play as the new "percept" is brought into relation with previous ideational and affectual constructions devised from similar past experience. Intellect and affect are stimulated by the novelty, usually for no other reason than ordinary curiosity, and the need to know just for the sake of knowing.

[4] Hilda Taba, in a speech delivered at the Merrill Palmer Institute, Detroit, March 11, 1963, stressed the need for children to make transactions with environmental stimulations Not all the environment is stimulating—only that which the child perceives and by which he is stimulated.

[5] L. Festinger, *A Theory of Cognitive Dissonance* (New York: Harper & Rowe, 1957).

As Langer suggests, this human need to transfer perceptions of experience into one's own symbols, is a "primary activity of man, like eating, looking or moving about. . . . It is the fundamental process of his mind and goes on all the time. Sometimes we are aware of it, sometimes we merely find its results, and realize that certain experiences have passed through our brains and have been digested there."[6]

Since ideation is an internal activity, it has been difficult for scientists to find out what actually happens. Only recently have neurologists and biologists found means for beginning to explore the chemical and electrical activity of the brain in response to the perceiving signals sent to it from the senses. In the absence of such data, investigators and, in turn, educators can consider only the expressions and actions of individuals, especially their language expression when they are ideating. As people are asked questions that call upon their ideas following an experience or are asked to tell what they know about a certain subject, their verbal formulations and gestures probably reveal in part the mental process. There are many ways to picture this activity. The *tabula rasa* concept, in which one impression is thought to be implanted on another, is one way to view ideation. Perhaps a more fruitful way for educational purposes is to look at how people, including scholars, formulate their ideas in language and assume that some internal process allows the brain to make connections, store the mentally digested matter, and release it at appropriate times through the complex human neurological system.

Forming Personal Conceptions

The major aspect of transforming experience into symbol can best be called *conceptualizing*, for more than immediate impressions are involved as ideation begins. Concepts must form before generalizing can emerge. "But just as quickly as the concept is symbolized to us, our imagination dresses it up in a private, personal *conception* that we can distinguish from the communicable *public concept* only by a process of abstraction."[7] Personal conceptions are thematic clusters of related facts, impressions, images, ideas, feelings, and value judgments around an order of phenomena. They are not simply intellectualized and verbalized restatements of public or scientific concepts. If other children or adults are present or an appropriate book is at hand, the individual's conception can be influenced by what others say or write about that event or a similar one, but he does the interpreting. A young child's *conception* of the moon may be more like an active space station than the barren landscape it is, because of his imaginings from television serials.

---

[6] Susanne K. Langer, *Philosophy in a New Key* (New York: Mentor Books, 1956), p. 32.

[7] Langer, p. 58.

Prior to the lunar landings a six-year-old child told his father when they were observing a brilliant full moon together: "I can see the volcanoes where the spaceships land. Maybe I'll go there someday."

A *public concept* is what is left of a general nature when all specific and personal aspects are taken away. "House" described as a building in which people live is a public designation for all the individual conceptions that may include a little bungalow, a mansion, or a grass-roofed hut. Sometimes a public concept is not scientifically accurate but expresses conventional wisdom or even mythology. "Water divining" and "UFOs" (unidentified flying objects) are as much examples of public concepts as are "rainfall" and "jet flight."

A *scientific concept* is the aggregate of personal studied conceptions of scientists and scholars, objectified by processes of verification and abstraction, resulting in agreements among the scholars. Examples in the physical sciences would be "atom" and "gravity"; in the biological sciences, "genes" and "homeostasis"; in the social sciences, "caste" and "enculturation"; and in the humanities, "style" and "justice." Concepts are nominative, the names of things or classes of things or the names of processes or actions.

Attribute-Classifying in the Conceptualizing Process

A personal concept can be further defined as the cluster of ideas of a thing or phenomenon that will always include key *attributes* that distinguish it from another concept. These attributes will be a mixture of affectual, judgmental, and factual matter. This cluster of meaningful and significantly related attributes can be labeled by a word-holder or at most a phrase[8] such as "farm" or "factory" or "polluted water." Concepts are never completed by any individual but are ever expanding and being altered. As new significant experience is incorporated into a person's symbolic structures attributes are added and old ones are rearranged, some becoming prominent as others recede. Language, as the describer of attributes, is one of the chief elements in the conceptual structure; it is also the mechanism that holds the other attributes together.

There are both inductive and deductive paths to the attribute collecting that makes for personal conceptions. The inductive method is seen easily in the young child's assigning attributes to an emerging conception of "mother." The baby starts with a vague conception of a live, warm object that feeds and cares for him. Eventually, he assigns special attributes to this person and distinguishes "mother" from all the other people who do things for him. He hears the word *mother* used by the adults around him in specific

---

[8] Joseph Grannis, unpublished papers, Harvard Graduate School of Education. We have elaborated upon some notions developed in discussion with Grannis.

contexts, and when he begins to speak, the word represents his conception of "mother." This inductive procedure is one way in which a person conceptualizes throughout life.

Because we live in a social framework, we also assign attributes in building conceptions by reacting in a deductive manner to public and scientific concepts already derived by others in the society. This procedure can be seen when parents see an object or happening that they think their young child should know about. On a visit to a farm, they might say to the child, "There is a cow and it gives us milk." The child then has to come to terms with this public concept and to try to relate it in a deductive manner to his previous experiences and to the attributes he had connected to "milk" and "animals." He may not gain a conception of "food processing" for a long time, but the public concept of "cow" has started the conceptualizing process on its way.

Actually, very young children often use a *transductive* process that is a loose, casual form of induction. The child strings together particulars that happen to be immediately available. All horned animals might be labeled "cow," whether bull, goat, or unicorn.

Much development of conceptions obviously entails an interplay of inductive, deductive processes as a child interacts with his environment and speaks with the adults around him. He is busy collecting and assigning attributes to things and events. *When the teacher asks children to talk about an object or picture brought to class, he is stimulating the process of selecting and rejecting attributes. If the teacher is aware of this process, he can lift the quality of ideating and can enhance the substance of such discussions by, for example, injecting negative attributes from other concept clusters into the talk in order to help children confirm their conceptions.* This technique can also start them on the forming of subconcepts such as "dog" to "hound" or of related concepts such as "cat" to "tiger." These categorizing exercises can have a game quality about them that stems from the basic fun of trying to put the world together, like the completing of a puzzle.

The Generalizing Process in Ideating

One's view of conceptualizing can be extended and refined by making distinctions between, on the one hand, concepts and generalizations and, on the other hand, conceptual themes that are developed over long periods of time.

A *generalization* is a statement of a propositional relationship between concepts. It is a tentative "law" or model of the world, which has been tested or could be tested but which is still open to question.[9] Putting concepts of "light" and "plant" into relationship under laboratory conditions suggests

[9] Grannis.

a general proposition that light significantly influences the growth of plants. A generalization usually has exceptions because man has yet to encompass the world with his thought. Also, the world, especially the social world, is irregular and not completely amenable to generalization. Generalizations are always under the surveillance of doubt, and therefore they are subject to reformulation as new evidence is discovered. They last only as long as they are useful as frames of reference or guides in investigating the riddle of the universe. The proposition of gravity continues to be a useful generalization about a relationship between objects and force. The proposition behind blood-letting in medicine is no longer a useful generalization from which to study bodily functions.

Sometimes a generalization about some phenomenon seems so assured after repeated testings that scholars call it law. The generalization that genetic material in the nucleus of the cell regulates the growth and development of that cell and determines its characteristics has been so tested. On the contrary, Freud's imaginative proposition of "ego strength" has not been found to exist as yet. Even so, it is a most convenient generalization for framing a study of the personality. Generalizations can be either working hypotheses or proven hypotheses or any set of positions between those two.

The scientific generalization "An object immersed in a fluid loses as much in weight as the weight of an equal volume of the fluid" contains several scientific concepts: "fluid," "weight," and "volume," as well as "force" and "buoyancy." A young child may develop early, vague conceptions that eventually become—after years of experiencing, conceptualizing, and general-izing—his version of this scientific generalization. A three-year-old was ob-served on a beach, filling a hole in the sand with water that he was fetching in a pail from the pond. He had been lifting the pail out of the water and carrying it to the hole. Then, as if by chance, he dragged the pail one time *through* the water until he got to the beach's edge instead of lifting it out immediately. His body posture showed relief from the weight of the water. His face showed delight in his discovery as he repeated the labor-saving action several times. A glimmering of a conception about water displacement came through in this sensorimotor experience. One could speculate how subsequent similar experiences of the child, such as bailing water from a rowboat or lifting heavy stones under water, might cause extension and refinement of the kernel of such an idea. Perhaps later in kindergarten, water play would include objects that float and sink. An aluminum foil toy boat might be constructed to float and might then be flattened out and sunk. Even later, in general science, a teacher might set up a discovery situation that would involve the weighing of the water that a floating hull displaced from a brimful tank. Quite possibly a boy's generalization that approximates the scientific one might be made at that juncture, but all the earlier ideation would have contributed to the derivation of the generalization finally drawn.

In the process of instruction teachers need to be wary of forcing the act of generalizing before conceptions are made clear through attribute classification and description. On the other hand, teachers need constantly to encourage the emergence of generalization by induction at the appropriate time and at the level appropriate to the children's ability to comprehend.

Many attributes of "sun" have to be clear and fully understood, as do certain critical qualities of "plant," before a relation between the two can be developed into generalization. A generalization on a simple descriptive level might be that green plants in sunshine grow faster than those not in sunshine, other factors being equal. This simple concept can then be extended into the sophisticated and logically abstract generalization of photosynthesis when the child is older.

The Growth of Conceptual Schemes

As individual generalizations emerge, when conceptions of a like kind become related, the ideational process continues ad infinitum. However, just as the individual tends to cluster small items around concepts, so does he seem to have the tendency to cluster his conceptions and generalizations around individual schemes. Viewing the world a certain way keeps "making sense" for a person. This kind of ideation may be evident in a man's choice of work or hobby. As he puts pieces of the puzzle together, he can begin to gain competence in at least one aspect of life. It can be said of him that he knows a lot about such and such. When one becomes an expert in a field, he tends to interpret the world through the conceptual schemes of that field. For example, economists tend to claim that the history of man at war and peace can be explained in large part by economic theory.

The child-sized glimmer of a concept eventually grows into the man-sized, full-blown conception that aids the adult in coping with the world about him. A few children become discoverers of unique conceptual views, and they are the scientists, artists, and scholars who construct new concepts that become the public knowledge of the times.

When two boys were observed at three-year intervals playing with the same miniature farm equipment in the same sand pit, a substantial advancement in the sophistication and extension of their concepts of farming into conceptual schemes was evident.[10] When the boys were six years of age they used the equipment generally for making a road and for cutting a hay field. At nine years, the two boys played through the whole cycle of plowing, planting, cultivating, and harvesting. The language, as well as the activity, was more sophisticated. The sociodrama at the earlier age was in short repetitive realistic episodes, and they used appropriately direct, explanatory language. The drama of the later age was highly developed into

[10] E. Brooks Smith, an unpublished investigation.

specific characterized roles using richer descriptive language in "Yankee" dialect, which explained reasons for some of their activities.

The development of personal conceptual schemes can be recognized over quite long periods of time when patterns of a child's interests and hobbies are observed. A twelve-year-old boy, when asked why he had made an ecological study of forest Indians for a science fair, replied that life in the forest had been his chief interest ever since he could remember. He told about spending many summers in the New Hampshire woods. He recalled knowing an Iroquois Indian who had been a family friend when he was younger. He said that he did not read much but that when he did, he always chose books about the forest and about Indians. When asked what he would like to do when he was grown up, he replied that he would like to be a forest ranger. Particular experiences and personal conceptualizing were developing in this boy a life-view around man's adaptations and relationships to the forest. Children from urban or rural slums may develop distorted life-themes because of the absence or inadequacy of models for them to admire and because of the lack of positive environmental stimuli. *Teachers must not only be ready to seize upon clues given them by children, but they may also need to inject appropriate models and experiences into the school environment to foster life-themes.*

Instructional Assistance to the Development of Conceptual Schemes

Advances over time in ideation and language are to be expected, but the dynamics of concept clustering into schemes may be overlooked because the gains are probably minute from day to day and are difficult for a teacher to see. They are there all the same, and the time for growing is when new aspects of a phenomenon are confronted.

Teachers should preplan their programs so that new complexities of a conceptual scheme are introduced in an orderly manner. They will also want to return regularly to concepts and generalizations developed earlier. This cyclical planning around conceptual schemes should, of course, be flexible. The sensitive teacher will seize an opportune moment for extending a concept, even though it arises from an unplanned situation. The abiding conceptual schemes of a student are often revealed when a child shows excitement about an idea in class discussion or freely chooses to write, talk, or draw about a subject. A nonreading fourth grader of the author's acquaintance did not start reading until the teacher discovered one of his conceptual themes—trains. The local suburban and national train schedules became his primer. Interest inventories and reading and television selection questionnaires can assist in revealing conceptual schemes. *Being aware of his students' schemes means that a teacher can relate new material to them for concept building and enrichment. In this way his expanding world can continue to make sense to the child.*

Faulty Ideating: Misconceiving and Overgeneralizing

As reality-oriented conceptions develop over the years, they pass through phases of misconception. A conception may be only partially conceived and meanings skewed for various reasons: misinformation, lack of experience, falsified perception, inadequate classifying of attributes, verbal confusion, distracting emotion, or overgeneralizing. "Boners" often reveal partial misconception within a framework of some sense. Because of the incongruity caused by the misconceived elements, they are funny. These examples are from a fifth grade.

Manhattan Island was bought for twenty-four dollars from the Indians. Now, I don't suppose you could buy it for five hundred dollars. (*Inadequate conception of the value of money.*)

We don't raise the silkworm in the United States because we get our silk from rayon. He is a larger animal and gives more silk. (*Misinformation and overgeneralizing.*)

Heat expands; in summer, days are long.
Cold contracts; in winter, days are short. (*Logic of the language is correct but generalizing has come before facts are in.*)

The dinosaurs became extinct because they were too big to get into the ark. (*Two opposing frames of reference are incorporated into one conception.*)

Overgeneralizing is mainly caused by hasty generalizing from too few instances of seemingly similar experiences or facts and by not bothering to alter the generalization when divergent instances appear. Many teenagers, for example, become enamored of quickly conceived and limited views of their parents' generation. Prejudiced and short-sighted thinking is the dire result of overgeneralizing.

Precedence: A Cause of Misconceiving

When examples of children's conceptualizing are gathered through individual or group interviews, they reveal in part how conceptions and misconceptions develop. In concept development there appears to be a phenomenon called *precedence*. Certain powerful developmental tendencies take precedence over a seemingly logical development of the concept. Several kinds of precedence can be identified.

MARKET-PLACE PRECEDENCE The reiteration of commonplace and stereotyped impressions picked up from overheard adult conversations, comments, and small talk may take precedence over the logical or sensible development of a view of world happenings. "You can't trust politicians anywhere."

AUTISTIC PRECEDENCE An overpersonal identification with events results in every conception's being the way "I" am or the way "I" do things. The individual is at the center of the concept, as in the following pre-*entente* view of Red China by a seven-year-old. "If I lived in China, I would kill myself, go crazy, or ask God to help me!"

OPERATIVE PRECEDENCE Children often tend to view objects in terms of operations, how something works or how it operates on the individual. "School is a teaching place."

AUTHORITY PRECEDENCE. At early school ages family-approved positions or teachers' pronouncements take precedence over ideas generated by peer discussion. "My mother says" or "my father says" is a common introduction for an idea presented in school. On the other hand, particularly at the time when the teacher becomes an object of secondary identification, the child disputes a family idea with a statement from his teacher. There is no argument; the teacher is right. Later, the peer culture becomes the authority. However, in political matters the child is likely to reflect the family position completely. "The President spends too much money. He shouldn't spend more than the government makes."

EMOTIONAL PRECEDENCE The emotional aspect of a happening can dominate the concept, sometimes distorting it. Khrushchev's shocking remark about "burying" us took hold in the memory of children of that time as it did with their parents, and dominated many statements about Russia by children. Another emotional word, *brainwash*, caught the children's fancy after the Korean War, even though they did not quite understand the word. "If Khrushchev were President, we wouldn't have school because he would brainwash us. We wouldn't have any brains, then, so we wouldn't have to go to school."

The emotional prejudices built up in wartime (hot or cold) seem to carry over in the child's minds many years beyond the period of conflict. Undoubtedly, television shows help these emotional epithets to persist in young people's culture.

LINGUISTIC PRECEDENCE A new adult word, not quite understood, may warp a concept. Eventually the word or phrase will, as it gains proper reference over time, enable the child to develop a sensible concept around it. A young child insisted that the Pilgrims "conquered" Massachusetts. Sometimes words are used from the common language of the street before they are understood except in a purely emotional reference. A child overheard chanting "the last one down the hill is a nigger" was asked what *nigger* meant. He did not know. If language molds the particular thinking or way of viewing the world in each cultural group having its own language, it would seem reasonable that the child's native dialect will sometimes have precedence over experience in guiding the concepts of the children of that culture.

PRECEDENCE OF IMMEDIACY What is most recently experienced dominates the path of a concept in development. Children's concepts of the role of the President are expressed in terms of the immediate public events involving the President. When children in the months following President Kennedy's election were asked what they knew about him, they stated separately that he went swimming, played with his children, lived on Cape Cod, and made speeches. When children were asked during the Cuban missile crisis what a President did, they inevitably said that he stopped wars, was boss of our ships, and told Russians off.

Implications of Precedence
for Teaching

If a teacher is aware of the various phenomena of precedence, he realizes that some precedences are too overwhelming to be changed. They simply have to be lived with as part of the processes of gaining independence from parents and from subcultural bounds. On the other hand, teachers may, with sensitivity to the growth pattern, strategically intercept a precedence tendency by injecting into classroom dialogue a countermeasure of logic or of opposing emotion at the time of the conceptualizing phase. The meaning of the word *conquer* could be clarified and amplified at the time when the child said the "Pilgrims conquered Massachusetts." In dialogue or discussion with the teacher and other pupils, meanings can, of course, be differentiated as the word is used in conventional contexts. Or meanings can be extended. There is a "conquest" element in the Pilgrim mission that is often brushed aside.

Teaching To Avoid
Unnecesssary Misconception

Misconceptions are often taught because parents or teachers are not aware of the most recent scientific concepts. Sometimes books or pictures used by a teacher convey the misconceptions of misinformed authors. Children's conception of the life of the Pilgrims has suffered more than most school subjects from this type of misconceiving-teaching. Most American children misconceive the Pilgrims as having been tall, idealistic men and women with stuffy moralistic characters, who lived in log cabins. The misconceiving can be ended when the teacher understands the generalization discovered by cultural anthropologists that socially consistent groups of people moving from one environmental setting into another tend to carry their culture with them into the new land. The Pilgrims, then, are rightly conceived as robust Elizabethans enjoying the earthly pleasures of beer-quaffing as well as visualizing themselves as new "Israelites." They would not build log cabins, but they would, naturally, construct models of English Tudor country cottages as best they could with the materials at hand.

Another usual cause of misconceiving stems from conceptualizing inadequacies in the adults who surround children. Unless the adult has kept an open mind and has avoided prejudice or has examined the folk wisdom of his culture, the child will pick up not only the adult's misconceptions but also his lazy process of narrow and sloppy thinking. "A penny saved is a penny earned" is not a sound economic concept. The "balanced budget" does not fit into modern economists' theme of productive financing. Uneducated adults surrounding children are likely to have common-sense concepts, which are passed on to the children in the manner of conventional wisdom.

A far more serious problem of misconceiving is apparent when adults of a cultural group and even the scholars among them fail to view a whole field of knowledge with objectivity because of their cultural blinders. The white community of the European-American world has failed until recently to recognize that it has written history only from its cultural viewpoint, disregarding the view of Asians or Afro-Americans, for example. New research needs to be done and new books written to consider the viewpoint of all peoples involved in history. Teachers can begin, however, to present the views of other cultures or at least to express the need for these views to be considered when new history is written or when past history is rewritten.

The child himself, because of the immaturity of his thinking processes, makes many misconceptions on his own. For example, in the early years he tends to overgeneralize. This is a phase in thinking when he has come upon the possibility of putting two likes together and saying, "These must be always the same." Two experiences with old ladies who are cross and constantly reprimand the child will develop the concept "fussy old ladies." He will perceive every old lady in this category until it is extended by sufficient experience with kindly, generous old ladies.

When the child is first making a relationship between phenomena (generalizing), he may fall into logical mistakes. Fifth-graders who had learned that hot air rises, misapplied this concept to account for the cooling process. When they were asked to talk about why some tin cans, filled with hot water and covered, would cool if left to stand, their reasoning became confused. One student suggested, and they all agreed, that if the teacher would make holes just in the top of the can, the water would cool much faster. The teacher asked them to suggest a simple experiment that might test their proposition.

Misconceiving seems to be part of the "growing up" of conceptions and generalizations at various stages of their development. Teachers made more aware of this possibility can judiciously allow some of the misconceiving to

*occur. At the same time, they can waylay some of the unnecessary miscon-
ceiving and inaccurate generalizing by constructive instructional tactics such
as challenges to experiment.*

Language in the Ideating Process

In the perceiving stage there are many cues from the environment that are nonverbal, although individuals do bring their own meaning to a word cue as they perceive it. However, language is crucial to the conceptualizing of both words and images perceived. "This phenomenon of holding on to the object by means of its symbol is so elementary that language has grown up on it. A word fixes something in experience and makes it the nucleus of memory, an available conception.[11] Language frames the thought and imbues it with communicable meaning so that it may be held in memory and used again in interplay with other thoughts. Frances Minor describes the lingual aspects of conceptualizing as an act of "owning" words in which the child takes possession of the word through a "multiplicity" of his own experiences; the language becomes his personal property. "Children shape the meaning of words from their experiences."[12]

Bruner has described thinking as a mediating process between stimulus input and an individual's response in which he is freed from the stimulus by varying his response after thinking the situation over or by keeping his response steady in a varying environment. Language is viewed by Bruner as the "instrument" of thought, not just as a medium of communication. The individual "instructs himself" in the art of "reformulating with language." An idea is shaped by talking it out, alone or with others. The young child's thinking, then, is shaped in large degree by the dialogue he carries on with adults, for it is the adult's grammar of thinking in language that interacts with the child's grammar of thinking. Bruner cites as an example the young child who might say, "Ma, coffee." The mother responds naturally with the full grammar, "Mother is drinking coffee now." The child may then reply, "Ma, coffee, now," showing that he is reformulating as he interacts with the adult language.[13]

In the conceptualizing phases of transforming experience to symbol, language molds thought as thought constructs the personal language of an individual's private conception of his world.

---

[11] Langer, p. 110.

[12] Frances Minor, "A Child Goes Forth: Ideas Invite Involvement," *Individualizing Instruction* (Washington, D.C.: Association for Supervision and Curriculum Development, 1964).

[13] Jerome Bruner, lecture at Teachers College, Columbia University, October 1963. Extended discussion of the instrumentality of language can be found in *Toward a Theory of Instruction* (Cambridge, Mass.: Harvard University Press, 1966).

Language Modes and
Style in Conceptualizing

The instrumentality of language in thinking can be seen in the language mode or style used in expressing different kinds of personal conceptions of public or scientific concepts. Youngsters pick up these modes and styles from the adults with whom they have dialogue whether that dialogue be with adult writers of books or directors of films or with teachers. The language mode is related to the content of the concept whether it be scientific and factual or value laden or, as most concepts are, a mixture of both. The mode of an adult's conception of "atomic power" will carry both factual and value content in a mode of "either–or" language. An example of such a combination follows:

> I shiver at the thought of the magnitude of force released by the atom. This is a terrible weapon and I fear it greatly, even though I fully realize that it can be applied to uses that will build up our civilization.

Adults are not very different from children in coming to terms with new awareness provoked by environmental stimulation, except that they have a backlog of experience and have advanced thinking capability. The concept of "sublimation" may be as unknown to an adult as Newton's concept of "falling objects" is to a four-year-old, yet they both live in a world with these phenomena occurring all about them. When the adult is in dialogue with the common scientific concept, the particular style of the language appropriate to that concept is acquired. In freely reacting to a word like *sublimation*, adults will use the mode of definition and example:

> Sublimation is a rational act that satisfies an undesirable and antisocial wish in a socially acceptable way. For example, some people have sadistic desires and they become surgeons.

An adult reacting to *hippy* will reveal not only prejudicial conceptualizing but also the style of imagery.

> I automatically picture beards, dark glasses and light jeans for the male hippies and dark, long hair, sallow complexion, heavy eye makeup, and black tights for the female.

A metaphorical mode is evident in this very young child's developing conception of sickness: "I am so sick to my stomach that I feel like I am killing myself." The mode of eliminating negative instances is evident in the statement a five-year-old made as he was watching an outboard motor boat speeding under the historical Concord Bridge: "That does not belong here; it is too modern for this place."

Teachers have always engaged their pupils in discussion, but when they keep in mind the instrumentality of language in the development of conceptualizing and generalizing, they can set the stage for exploring different stylistic types and can encourage the development of appropriate modes. A scientific conception might emerge from the child in imagistic and prejudicial language, but refinement toward a concept should be in the direction of the expository mode. A metaphorical mode may be more appropriate for conceiving certain aspects of the concepts "farmer" and "farming," such as "love of land" and "the rhythm of the seasons," than explanations in terms of the science and agronomy. Literary statements tend to be neglected in a technically oriented society unless educators make the effort to explore the literary modes of thinking with children.

Teaching for Ideation in Contexts

Children constantly traffic in both concepts and generalizations as they come to terms with new events in their environment and as they form conceptual schemes. For teaching purposes, environments can be conveniently conceptualized as various *contexts* in which conceptions and generalizations are likely to be developed. A context in this sense can be described as a chunk of events from the real world of the present or past that can be experienced directly or vicariously by children. It could be the geography of a place and the culture of a people living there. It could be the biography of an individual or the history of an institution or the activities of a community. It could also be the life of the ant. the evolution of a pond, or the phenomena of thunder and lightning.[14] Concepts and generalizations about environmental conditioning, for example, are most likely to develop in contexts of extreme environmental conditions such as "desert lands" or "life in Antarctica." The educating process is the interplay between concept and generalization in varying but somewhat similar contexts. The child, teacher, and scholar all strive for an approximation of reality.

The teacher, knowing the general background and characteristics of his pupils, selects contexts in which concepts and generalizations can best be nourished. For psychosocial reasons in relation to dependency, "pets" may be a good context in which to develop some concepts and generalizations regarding "domestication" at the early childhood level. On the other hand, in junior high school, contrasting contexts of a "hunting society" and an early "farming society" might be more appropriate for extending the same concept of domestication. Taba has found the use of opposing contexts of a primitive society and a modern urban society to be very useful in extending concepts and lifting thinking about "shelter," for example.[15]

The old-fashioned "object lesson," in which a teacher focused the lesson upon some natural object that was brought in, might be revived and re-

[14] Grannis, unpublished papers. See also Grannis, "Team Teaching and the Curriculum," in J. Shaplin and H. Olds (eds.), *Team Teaching* (New York: Harper & Row, 1964), Chap. 5.

[15] Hilda Taba, "Contra Costa County, Social Studies Curricula," Contra Costra County, California, 1964.

furbished as a teaching device for extending concepts and developing generalizations. The "object" to be studied can be a group of objects that imply relationships, such as a set of magnets, a compass, and some nails. Or the "object" could be in the social science domain, a film clip of an Eskimo seal-hunting expedition juxtaposed with a clip of Americans on holiday fishing for brook trout. The discussion of the "object" need not, as in past days, be based on a prepared schedule of questions. It could be a free-ranging colloquy in which the teacher, by astute questioning, can foster the clarifying of concepts and the deriving of generalizations.

The time-honored field trip can be revitalized for the development of ideation. Instead of just a visit to a farm for the experience of a trip to write or draw about upon return, a tactical plan can be made by the teacher ahead of time to insure that children see concept-provoking objects and happenings. The farmer can be asked to show how to milk a cow by hand and then to demonstrate how modern milking machines work. The intricacies of his office and bookkeeping paraphernalia can be shown along with his barns to highlight the business aspects of modern farming.

The world can be brought to the class or the class can be taken to the world in such a way as to promote or enrich symbolic transformation of experience into knowing. But to make the transformation from experience to knowing requires many teaching strategies as concepts are developed and interrelated into generalizations through the language interchange of guided discussions among students and with teachers.

Developing a Dialogue between Personal Concepts and Public or Scientific Concepts

Students can enhance and extend their worlds of knowing through a *mental dialogue* between *individual conceptions* of events and *public* and *scientific concepts* found in books, newspapers, magazines, lectures, films, and combinations of them. Scientific concepts are derived from summarizing activities of scientists in various fields of study as they digest the results of recent research and incorporate them into explanations that students and public can understand. Public concepts are those carried by public means of communication that vary from accurate accounts of events in newspapers to hearsay passed along in public places of work and commerce. They sometimes are merely bits of conventional wisdom that seem persuasive at the moment. Or they may be as profound as a public policy derived through a legislative process.

In school the teacher serves as both a resource person and a catalytic agent for getting a mental dialogue underway that causes an interrelating of students' personal concepts with those in the public and scientific domains. The strategies most available to teachers are the lecture-discussion, the project method developed around topics or issues, the debate, and the research study and report developed by an individual or small group of students. In open-inquiry education the small unit of work or learning activity is the means by which the teacher preplans the interaction of personal conceptualizing with public and scientific concepts.

One of the most useful teaching tactics yet devised for engaging a child in such a dialogue is the small-scale *study contract* between the teacher and a student or small group of students. Such contracts should be jointly developed and based upon the specific capabilities of the learner including experiential and conceptual background in the area of study and upon the specific resources and materials that the teacher can make available to the student or small team of students. A contract should specify the goals and scope of the study. These might be in the format of a series of mutually derived open-ended questions. The types of resources, their availability, and guides to their use should be designated. Alternative means for expressing the results of the study need to be suggested. A timetable for accomplishment of the tasks is advisable. Criteria for judging the level of conceptualization gained should be set down.

The *activity card* with a accompanying assemblage of packaged resources and materials is another useful means for encouraging the dialogue between personal and scientific concepts through independent work of individual students or students in pairs or triads. The attempt by any more than three students to engage in such intellectual activities is likely to be futile because too much time has to be spent on socialization factors that create interruptions or side-tracking in the ideating process. Activity cards need to be keyed to specific materials and to be small enough in scale to be accomplished within a reasonable time span for the particular age of the involved youngsters. The activity card must not ask more of the learner than he is generally able to comprehend at his age. Above all it must not be an assignment card of directions; instead, the questions should be stated in such an open-ended and appealing fashion as to induce self-directed concept learning.

section 3

Presenting Phase

Susanne Langer[16] has attempted to show that discursive, expository language is a very different way of presenting one's conceptions of the world from the direct, composite, simultaneous manner of the arts—sculpture, music, dance. Although this distinction between art forms and language serves

[16] Langer, Chap. 4.

well her discourse on the conveyance of meaning in the arts, she possibly underplays the potential of language by describing it as mainly discursive. The language of poetry has the same characteristics of compactness and directness that sculpture has. Only the most factual, descriptive language of science could be called purely discursive.

The important idea is that after an individual has conceptualized an event he has perceived, he then tries his conception out on the world. He gives it back to the world to be tested against the notions of others. He searches for an echo from reality much in the same way that the bat listens to his "radar." He announces to himself and the world that this is his idea of the situation. In a real sense, the presentational symbols that he constructs *are* his world. He can know no other, and the only way he can make sense of what he knows is to present his conceptions for reflection by himself or from others. This is as vital an aspect of knowing as is the need to transfer experience into symbols.

The presenting of symbols would seem to be for artists alone, but even though the ordinary person cannot give his presentational symbols the refined qualities of the artist's style, every person can present his conceptions in all the available modes. Indeed, modern social life would be more interesting if people were encouraged to practice the art and music modes of expression as folk cultures once did. Sometimes youth, on their own and usually outside of school, have used the musical mode to present their ideas. Young jazz musicians improvise in jam sessions. Puerto Rican children in Spanish Harlem create festive street music during summer evenings on motley collections of oil drums and tin cans. "Combos" of suburban youth make up their own music of social commentary with its grim absurdities. Children of the city have always been sidewalk artists while their country cousins have been whittlers and sampler makers. *The school curriculum should make good use of the many natural modes of presentation by children and youth.*

Differing Modes of Presenting

Just as there are different modes for perceiving, dependent upon the senses used, so there are different modes of presenting, dependent on the part or parts of the organism used to convey the meanings. The individual perceives through all the senses. Teachers unknowingly limit the possibilities for perceiving by allowing only two sense organs to be used. The eyes and ears are overworked as the other senses are neglected, especially in the school situation. Outside, in nature, the child is frequently seen fondling a new object, licking it, smelling it, and banging it against other objects. Langer points out this need for children to use all the senses by focusing on the kinds of sensations that children receive from objects: "Childhood is the great period of synaesthesia; sounds and colors and temperatures, forms and feelings may have certain characters in common. . . ."[17] Synaesthesia probably is not just a phenomenon of early childhood but probably continues to function all through life, opening channels for the play of preconscious intuition. Word–object relationships become vital ideas as they are infused with the effect that develops as the initial stimuli touch the senses. Sensations make ideas vibrant by stirring preconscious memories of feeling and form and by bringing them in relation to the newly developing conceptions.[18]

Similarly, conceptions being presented come alive as they are expressed through all the presentational modes—art, music, dance, mime—as well as through language. The organic means by which the various modes are conveyed are the vocal organs, the facial muscles, the movement of the body and the manipulations of the hands in writing, drawing, playing a musical instrument, or sculpting, or extensions of these through tools or instruments. The presentation, in turn, is prepared to stimulate the various senses.

Language in the Presenting Process

The language mode is used in four ways to present an individual's conceptions, his symbolic world, to himself and others: soliloquizing, conversing, discussing, and writing.

SOLILOQUIZING Like Hamlet, the individual presents his thoughts to himself for examination and consideration. He goes over these ideas in his mind as he "talks" to himself. Conceptions are refined in this way. Often the soliloquy is a precursor to writing or formal speaking. As in Shakespeare's play, it may be simply inner communication. When one stops to listen to himself objectively for a few moments, he may be surprised at his eloquence. It is not surprising, then, that in the hands of an artist, that inner thoughts can become great literature as demonstrated by the "stream of consciousness" writers of the early twentieth century. Time for reverie is essential to the fulfilment of the cognitive process, but rarely are such moments planned for in school programs. A child will find these moments himself, whether planned in school or not, but great opportunities are lost when he is so pushed from one activity to another from morning until bedtime that he is distracted from contemplation. *After the reading of a story, the presenting of a significant idea, or the viewing of an impressive sight, time should be given not only for discussion but also for reverie.*

CONVERSING In most instances conversing is soliloquizing to an audience. It is an egocentric activity in which the individual keeps presenting

[17] Langer, p. 100.
[18] Lawrence Kubie, *Neurotic Distortion of the Creative Process* (New York: Farrar, Straus, 1961). Preconscious processes are described and discussed in this book.

his conceptions. He does not hear much that his colleagues are saying, but he uses their remarks as cues for further extension of his own ideas. Conversation is parallel monologue in which each individual has the opportunity to talk out his ideas as he listens intently to them and looks at his listener to see how he is reacting. To hear how ideas sound helps the individual test them and refine them. Children, during play, talk past each other in their conversation, yet they seem to sense that playmates and guardians are sounding boards. This phenomenon continues in all conversation. Sometimes the speaker will say to his colleague, "You are not listening," and that is probably so, because the listener is too busy thinking about what he will present next. Conversation, as distinct from discussion, rarely accomplishes new extensions in the thinking of both parties. It does provide, however, for a presentation of concepts by an individual.

Conversation at relaxing moments in the day's classroom schedule should be encouraged. *A time set aside for conversation rather than for discussion might be useful after an important incident of confrontation.* Conversation may serve well as a "warming-up" activity for pointed discussion to follow immediately or the next time the topic is broached.

DISCUSSING True discussion requires acute listening as well as thoughtful speaking. It is a dialogue of ideas, one thought building on another, a concert of thinking as individuals present their conceptions in relation to those of others. During the act of discussing, conceptions are actually altered, even abandoned, as new ones take their place. The total process of perceiving, conceptualizing, and presenting occurs almost simultaneously in deliberative discourse.

Plato's record of the dialogues of Socrates are usually too one-sided to be considered literally as discussion. *The Symposium* does very much fill the requirements, however, as guests explore different positions with regard to all meanings of "love." Socrates, of course, has a firm hand on the outcome of these arguments. In a free dialogue, the several minds of the persons involved influence each other as they seek the truth.

Debate is a formal type of discussion, which in practice is valuable for learning to support a position consistently. It has limited value as an education device, however, because one's believed conceptions sometimes have to be altered to fit the tight pattern of pro or con. No compromised resolution is possible. However, in debate the structuring of the language for meaning is clearly evident. The formal grammar of debate is a reminder of the fact that even in informal discussion there is a special language structure that forces the co-respondents to come to terms with cause, proof, and the conditional. As children become involved in true discussion with adults, the grammatical forms of the dialogue enforce, in a sense, the development of children's thinking about relationships.

A discussion needs to be carefully planned by the teacher as to the kinds of questions to be raised and the "givens" upon which the discussion will be based. At the same time, spontaneity must not be thwarted by over-structuring. The genuine discussion happens in the classroom when even the teacher finds himself refining his preconceptions because of challenges raised by the students. *An effective strategy for stimulating discussion is to confront the children with an experimental situation in science or social studies, permitting them to describe what they see and then to speculate on why or how the particular phenomenon happened.*

DIALOGUE A fifth-grade class in science was studying the problem of body heat and insulation. The effects of fur was the topic of experimentation and discussion. The teacher posed the following question that prompted some interesting dialogue:

Teacher: If it is 120 degrees where the camel lives, what does his fur do for him?

The students immediately applied previous knowledge in saying that the fur kept out heat. Then a new thought occurred to them.

Child A: He must be hot. If I put a fur coat on at 120 degrees, I would be hot.
Child B: If fur keeps heat out, why don't we wear fur coats in the summer?
Child C: I think it is because nobody has tried it.
Child D: How about Arabs, did they go around in swim suits?

A number of the students were acquainted with the Arabs and stated that they do wear quite a large amount of clothing but that it is loosely worn. They pointed out that the cloth was very similar to wool.

Child E: If my mother had a fur coat, I'd wear it tomorrow and find out what happens.[19]

Discussion is the most common means for presenting one's conceptions to be tested against the ideas of others.

WRITING. Written composition is the form of presenting most abused in school. Children are often asked to use it when the written form is not the most appropriate means for expression but is merely the best way to keep them quiet and busy. On the other hand, writing in school is rewarding when it is used to hold conceptions for future reference, to pull loose thoughts together, to put thoughts into a form whereby they can be considered reflectively, or to form conceptions into memorable statement.

[19] Elementary Science Study, "First Trial with Animal Temperature at the Fifth Grade Level," mimeographed account of lessons (Watertown, Mass.: Educational Services, Inc., Summer 1962).

There are two kinds of writing to be considered, expository and literary. Expository writing deals with statements of fact and arguments based on them. A minimum of emotive language is present, because the writer is trying to be objective. Descriptions of scientific or social phenomena fall into this category. What was observed is presented. Literary writing is subjective and unabashedly emotional. It is no less meaningful, but metaphor and imagery convey the sense more than lucid simple statement. Poetry is the most literary form of writing, whereas a chemical formula is the most expository. In some writing the forms are ingeniously mixed. Children should have occasion to express their conceptions in the form that is appropriate. *Writing becomes a necessity when seen as presentation and not as an adjunct skill to the educative process.* The child's writing his impressions of the first snow is as important to his cognitive life as writing "Stopping by Woods on a Snowy Evening" was important to Robert Frost.

Nonlingual Presentations

The pictorial, musical, mimetic, and terpsichorean arts offer modes for presenting conceptions that cannot conveniently be expressed in words. Composers in these modes decry every attempt to translate their presentational symbols into words. The music, the sculpture, or the dance each speaks for itself. People when first introduced to modern dance or modern painting inevitably ask what a certain abstract painting or choreographic episode means, as if the meaning could be put into words. So-called primitive tribes have no difficulty creating or understanding dance, but so-called civilized man has been so conditioned to word literacy that the literacy of the arts often escapes him. Modern man obviously needs education in the modes of the arts as well as in that of letters.

Rather than pursuing the vague concept of *appreciation*, the arts in the curriculum should fill the need for *literacy* in these particular modes of presentation. *In a real sense, children need to learn how to present their ideas in art forms and how to "read" the symbolic presentations of others. Practice in the arts should be contiguous with practice in language presentation. The study of art, music, dance, and theater is not a frill but is an essential in the curriculum.* Dramatic art should hold a special place in the curriculum, because it combines the lingual and nonlingual forms of presentation.

The nonlingual modes of presentation can be used in exposition just as language can. In the pictorial mode, matters of fact can be presented in diagrams or pictograms. Indeed, many of the pictures that teachers ask children to draw after a field trip are not art products but are pictograms showing the facts they observed. Body movement can be used literally to give direction or to describe what someone did. Sculptured objects can literally depict atomic relationships or the anatomy of the body. Drama may be quite literal when role playing is used to describe factual happenings. The arts of all these modes, on the other hand, are similar to the literary kind of writing in which the emotive aspects of concepts are expressed directly. There are other sophisticated ways of presenting ideas, such as mathematical and chemical equations.

Presenting is both the culminating phase of knowing and the beginning of it, for every presentation offers something new to be perceived and considered.

Teaching Strategies for Presenting

If presenting is considered an essential phase of knowing, opportunities for its practice must find their way into the regular school program. Planned opportunities to soliloquize, converse, and discuss must follow confrontations of significance. When all ideas have been explored, a summarizing activity that will cause reflective and deliberative thinking must be arranged. The modes to be used should suit the subject. Writing is appropriate for either the literal matters (which can best be described by precise language) or the affective matters (which can best be presented in emotive and metaphorical language). The impact of a great winter storm or of a raging forest fire might best be conveyed by painting. Pictorial diagrams or charts are better suited than verbal exposition to the presentation of interrelated facts about such topics as rainfall and land productivity. The concept of Thanksgiving may best be expressed in song, and the toil of the fields may best be realized in dance. The teacher needs to introduce children to all the modes in their appropriateness. Children can experience presenting the same concept in several different modes to see which is most successful or to see how emphases are altered in the varied presentations. There are many new media, such as audio-tape, 8-millimeter motion pictures, Xeroxing, and portable television recording, that can be used by teachers to extend the modes of presenting.

Valid "Integrating" of the
Arts into School Programs

At one time in educational parlance the use of the various modes of presentation was called "integration of art and music with subject matter." A study of the mailman included the "making up" of a mailman dance, a mailman song, and the creation of a post-office mural just for the sake of integration. Some of these "integrations" were most incongruous because they were inappropriate. The pictogram mural might serve well to show in one long glance the various procedures in the handling of the mail, but a dance of a mailman walking down the street seems foolish.

Sometimes teachers mistakenly eliminate one of these modes because they feel that it does not suit the tenor of the age level. For example, not many teachers would dare to involve sixth-grade boys in modern dance, yet one brave sixth-grade teacher, with his boys, choreographed and dramatized Custer's last stand, using accounts of the battle as source material. The emotion of that dramatic incident lent itself especially well to the medium of dance. The boys were so impressed with what they could do in dance to present their idea about Indian preparation and white desperation that they forgot for the moment that dancing was "for girls only." The various modes are for all ages to explore, but within the child's levels of skill and comprehension. Dramatic presentation with music, dance, and scenery combines several of the modes and is therefore particularly useful in the school setting. Different children can work in different modes as they all center their attention on one comprehensive summary of their various conceptions. These are essentials in the curriculum, not just additions for special occasions.

Using the Presentations of Others for Extending Conceptions

The remarkable presentation of adult writers, painters, sculptors, film directors and actors, and composers and choreographers can be used in the educative process to enrich the content of children's conceptions. Fortunately, modern artists in all fields have applied their talents to presenting their ideas to children. Every year, book publishers offer many titles for children of all ages. Some of these books are good literature and are effectively illustrated and beautifully printed. Robert McCloskey's *Time of Wonder* with its colorful prose and dramatic illustration can add substantially to children's sense of awe about nature. Margaret Wise Brown's *The Dead Bird* with its poignant yet restrained language and its severe but touching illustrations gives children an opportunity to stop in the midst of their daily activities to contemplate the end and the beginning of things. The right book placed in the hands of a child at the right time can accomplish wonders that direct teaching could never do, because with a book the child is with himself. Then there are no thoughts unimaginable or unacceptable.

Modern informational books, like those of Herbert Zim and Enid Blough in science, structure the information with words and pictures in such a clever way that the child can build some science concepts vicariously. Modern encyclopedias and the better textbooks combine picture, diagram, and text in ingenious fashions to present facts and ideas. Films, filmstrips, and recordings bring into the classroom scientific phenomena that could not otherwise be presented in a structured manner. In carefully edited film, the science and the fury of a hurricane can be presented all at once by a sequence of pictorial images ranging from views of storm clouds and weather satellites to closeups of family tragedy.

In the social studies, presentations that create a sense of personal immediacy are important. In historical studies the firsthand account, a piece of literature from the time, or some music of the period, will heighten sensitivity and understanding. Smith and Meredith have prepared for children a presentation of eyewitness accounts of the founding of Plymouth, of Columbus's first voyage, and the early white explorations of the Mississippi in *Pilgrim Courage, The Quest of Columbus,* and *Exploring the Great River.* Authentic historical storybooks and biographies are other ways to capture the attitudes as well as the facts of a time. James Daugherty in a masterpiece of book writing and illustrating has caught the vigor and excitement of Daniel Boone's story that children will never forget. Esther Forbes's *Johnny Tremaine,* a work of fiction, accurately and vividly relates the beginnings of the American Revolution for children.

Studies in geography and the culture of peoples benefit immeasurably by presentations of life in children's books written by residents in the particular culture or by sensitive observers of it. Taro Yashima's *The Village Tree,* through language of simplicity and contemporary drawings of Japanese landscape, gives children a knowledge of life in Japan that an outsider could not produce. Ann Eaton's stories about the Indian cultures in America's Southwest and in South America bring children the feeling of living close to the land and places them in communication with the natural elements. Tom Feelings, author and illustrator, creates in *Black Pilgrimage* a fascinating story of his experiences as an artist in the ghetto and traveler through Africa. His stunning art work is accompanied by a sensitively written text. This book offers to children a personal sociocultural document in two media.

Using Folk and Regional Presentations for Enriching Conceptions

Literature, music, and plastic art by the folk or by artists from various regions of the world present the symbolism of those cultures. These presentations range from the music of a Watusi tribal dance to a Grant Wood painting of Midwestern farm life. Folk literature, music, painting, and dance are the symbolic presentations of a culture. They convey through myth, ritual, and language the essence of a people's beliefs and world-view. By experiencing folk creations, children can, in a sense, live in the culture they are studying and can learn to respect it. Through folk art from earlier times the child can participate in some of his own culture's rich symbolic background and the backgrounds of other modern children. "Greensleeves" and folk Christmas carols symbolize old England more adequately than hundreds of lines in a textbook. The designs on Grecian vases or the friezes on Egyptian tombs tell stories that no book could convey. The brief, epigrammatic American-Indian folk tales and the Japanese haiku tell volumes about those cultures. And no child can hear the bells of Bali or Jamaican drums without gleaning some knowledge of the differences and likenesses of those two island peoples on opposite sides of the globe.

Integration of literature, music, the plastic arts, and dance into the social studies should be for the express purpose of enriching the children's symbolic content about a topic. Integration should never be forced into the curriculum simply to enliven the activities in a social studies unit; the artless patter songs about little Dutch shoes and the like should be eliminated from both social studies and music curricula. The criteria for selecting supplementary integrating materials should be appropriateness of media to the subject and artistic quality of the presentational symbol. "America the Beautiful" conveys the exuberance and optimism of the American frontier spirit; whereas "God Bless America" is sentimental and superficial by comparison.

Using the Dramatic Modes

The dramatic mode most asscessible to schools is the cinematic form, and it is highly effective in the presentation of ideas to children. Unfortunately, many of the films for children are artless and, therefore, do not meet one of the criteria. However, a few great films are produced that are exactly right for children as well as for adults. Robert Flaherty's *Nanook of the North* is one of these timeless masterpieces. The one-to-one relationship of man to his environment has rarely been more effectively portrayed. A good teacher chooses this old film over the many other more recent selections about Eskimo life because this film catches so much more than the facts. Film loops from *Man, A Course of Study* have these same qualities.

Both radio and television production are forms of the dramatic mode with qualities all their own. Radio can weave a drama of sound that assaults the ears. There are many fine news "specials" and on-the-spot coverages of history-making events that can be taped and presented to children at the appropriate time. Not infrequently, these programs have been taken from phonograph recordings or have been turned into records that can be purchased. There are unusual presentations, for example, of the "Civil War Years" and "the F.D.R. Years."

Television has many of the same qualities as theater, cinema, and radio. At its best, it is a collage of sound, pictures, written words, dialogue, images, and designed patterns; and now color has been added. Television can bring important events such as the moon walks to people at once. It can take its audience back to the days of the Gold Rush or to ancient Rome. Because there is an intimacy about television in the home or the classroom, the personal and group involvement in watching it is new in the media world. Fortunately, the networks have taped some of the outstanding television "specials" of recent years, and they have been made available to teachers.

Television educational tapes are in abundance, but they are only effective as presentations when they use the full potential of the television medium. If the program is simply a recording of a lecture, it might as well have been audio-taped or printed in a book, but if the producer has used the camera to explore examples and to take students from a view of minute sea life to a view of the world from a space capsule, then television is an exciting means of presentation for instruction.

Importance of Using
All Modes of Presentation

Well-chosen examples of literature, music, art, and dance will not only enhance a study with children but may indeed present the essence of that study. Taba has suggested that a study for children might center about some significant children's books such as the African story *Brothers and Sisters*.[20] To this study might be added collections of art, song, and dance. These can become the focus of the study of places, as facts are collected to assist in the interpretation of the books, folkways, and artifacts.

The presenting phase of knowing is double edged. Children need to present conceptions and to experience the presenting of conceptions in all the modes. Some children will show unusual talent in one mode, and they should be given special training, because these students might become artists, poets, or musicians. But, for most children, literacy in the various modes is sufficient. *The experience of knowing, of coming to terms with the world, is not complete without opportunities to present one's conceptions, and teachers must see that times for presentation are available and fully used.*

General Teaching Strategies
in Coming To Know

In the *perceiving phase* of the symbolic transforming of experience, the teacher generally helps the student become aware of significances in his environment. He confronts the child with situations that spark curiosity, raise questions, and activate a discovering process.

During the *ideating phase* the teacher assists his pupils in finding problems to be solved and in organizing his thinking by raising the appropriate questions. He puts the pupil into dialogue with public and scientific knowings by presenting his own ideas and by offering the conceptualizations of others in books, films, and various instructional materials.

When the *presenting phase* arrives, teachers devise means for pupils to work through their ideas and present them in oral or written language or in

---

[20] Hilda Taba, lecture given at Merrill-Palmer Institute, Detroit, Mich., March 11, 1963. See I. Compton Burnett, *Brothers and Sisters* (New York: Zero Press, 1957).

other symbolic forms. They can set up problem-solving situations in differing contexts in which students can test and rehearse their conceptual learnings.

In a sense, each individual in each generation rediscovers, in part, the world's phenomena and their interrelationships. The aid and guidance of scholars past and present are available to each person in his schooling, reading, and listening if he wishes to call upon them. The excitement of discovery must be maintained as each child traverses the conceptual paths, but the student needs to use the guideposts of past and present scholarship to stimulate his thinking and to verify his conceptualization. Teachers act as guides and questioners, transforming the child's experiences into language and symbol.

After preparing the class environment with challenges, teachers engage children in a dialogue between their knowings and those established by the discipline. In the words of Whitman, the children "peer," "absorb," and then "translate."

7

Stages in the Development of Thought and Language

Thinking and reasoning are aspects of the search for meaning in the symbolic transformation of experience that has been systematically studied. Some of the findings have been selected for discussion here because they contribute to an understanding in the educational process.

The question of how much language there is in thinking is a useless one, because it is impossible to see or hear the inner thinking process. Investigators can only surmise from observing behaviors and hearing expressions that seem to be manifestations of thinking processes. Obviously, there are aspects of thinking that do not involve language, such as imitations in which a child copies adult behavior in one situation and then applies it reasonably to another. Manners and customs are of this variety of thinking. The little girl who always scrapes the imaginary toast in the sink when playing house because she observes her mother doing this one morning is thinking without words. Chimpanzees use wordless thought structures when they figure out how to get food placed out of their reach by using sticks as makeshift tools. Men, of course, use wordless thought structures of great complexity.

The ape, however, is able to communicate his thought structure only by doing what it represents or by giving simple signals and gestures; man can *tell* about his actions and give his reasons for them, even writing them down for someone's use a hundred years later. The human miracle, language, is crucial to the highly sophisticated thinking that distinguishes man from the apes. Thoughts above the habitual level—and human habit patterns can be quite complex—are so infused with language in longhand or shorthand and so dependent on its load of meaning in word and syntax that language surely is more than a mere carrier of thought. Obviously, in many instances language *is* thought. Wordless symbolic structures can be organized from observations, but to be recognized in terms of past experiences and the collective experience of man, these rarefied structures have to be infused with language.

Sign modes of communication other than language, such as music and the arts, behave in the same way as languages when they become infused with the artist's thoughts to the point where artists say, "I can see it on canvas" or "I can hear it in notes."

Language and thinking are so interrelated in most forms of sophisticated thinking that they must be dealt with together. Psychologists need to be interested in the question of where language and thought are *separated*, but educators need to be concerned with where they *fit together*, because language is the main vehicle for the teaching of thinking and reasoning. The verbal stages of thought are those that are most manifest and visible. Teachers, of course, must also be aware of the nonverbal aspects of thinking; some problems in geometry and in physics, especially those in which a pictured symbol conveys a thought, are of this variety. However, most of the thinking in classroom situations will involve language structures as well as personal sensorimotor and imagistic structures.

section 1

Kinds of Thinking

Several kinds of thinking must be considered. Robert Thomson begins his book *The Psychology of Thinking* by describing six possibilities.

1. *Autistic thinking:* daydreaming, fantasy-making, idle flitting from one half-formed notion to another, expressing underlying wishes and needs
2. *Remembering:* recalling happenings in the past and describing them, trying to think of how one did something
3. *Concentrating:* thinking about what one is doing, sticking with a problem
4. *Imagining:* thinking ahead to possible solutions and their feasibility, projecting present knowns into fanciful new combinations, playing around with ideas
5. *Believing:* valuing one thing or feeling over another, judging one action over another, expressing attitudes of taste or distaste, attacking or defending emotional stances
6. *Reasoning:* reflecting about a happening in the light of past experience, deliberating about an idea in view of knowns or givens, pondering over sev-

eral possible solutions, hypothesizing possibilities, checking out alternatives, raising questions.[1]

All these types of thinking may occur in the classroom and consequently may be nurtured there. Although "reasoning" is generally considered the highest form of thinking, the other forms are as important. Daydreaming may well be the means to intuitive flashes, particularly when it is combined with remembering. The affective or emotive ways of thinking are most responsible for artistic expression. Who is to say which demonstrates more knowing—a formula by Einstein or a fugue by Bach? The teacher must be sensitive to all the types; he must be able to recognize them and know how to nourish them. A program in the creative arts is not offered merely to provide activity or to permit a legitimate means for working off aggressions; the arts must be in the school program to generate and refine thinking and to teach children how to respond to these other-than-rational/literal kinds of thought.

Divergent and Convergent Thinking

In Getzel and Jackson's book *Creativity and Intelligence* the authors report investigations of Guilford's notion that there are two differing modes of thinking. Basically the two forms are:

> *Convergent thinking*, in which the individual converges on patterns in a logical manner, a narrowing of prospects in the field, a closing in of definition as already established. These are tested or seen in new situations.
> *Divergent thinking*, in which the individual moves out from a given situation and imagines many divergent possibilites, breaking away from formula and past or established interpretations, experimenting and exploring with novel combinations.[2]

Both modes are essential to the advancement of learning. However, experiments showed that in school, divergent thinking by children was generally ignored by teachers and that in many instances children were penalized for indulging in it. The divergent thinker is likely to be the child who is constantly interrupting an orderly discussion with a "far out" idea that sounds as if it were off the subject; actually, it may be very much to the point, even though it leaps out of conventional and conformist thought. Divergent thinking is the kind of thinking that moves the bounds of knowledge outward. This mode must be cultivated as carefully as the step-by-step processes

[1] Freely adapted from Robert Thomson, *The Psychology of Thinking* (Baltimore: Penguin, 1959), pp. 13–14.

[2] Jacob Getzel and Philip Jackson, *Creativity and Intelligence* (New York: Wiley, 1962). Freely adapted from pp. 14, 51, 76, 127.

of logical thought that are so highly rewarded in the school situations of exercises and tests. Language becomes flat and sterile when it is overrefined in the convergent mode; in the divergent mode it expands and extends as it does in the mind of the poet. Careful syllogism is the language of convergent thinking; expansive metaphor is the language of divergent thinking. Both of these modes of thinking and their language need to be cultivated in school.

In the following example, the sources of this six-year-old's syllogism are obvious and the combination is childish, but the form of thinking exemplifies a syntax of convergent thinking:

> This is Dick.
> Dick is eating snow.
> Snow is radioactive.
> Dick is eating too much snow.
> Dick is radioactive.

A teacher's questions and directions of the following types encourage convergent thinking: What is this most like? List all the ones that are the same. Knowing this, how would you account for that? A glance over the kinds of questions asked on standardized tests will reveal other examples of the language that encourages convergent thinking.

When a fifth-grader says that "a globe is a rolled-up map" instead of repeating the dictionary definition, the teacher must stop to listen and take the divergent route with the child. In such instances the child's thought may lead to a splendid discovery. When a child says, "God's eyes are the eyes of lobsters which can see all around," he is using the metaphorical language of divergent thinking.

Control of Language over Thinking

Language has a certain amount of control over thinking. The collective or public way of describing something or of analyzing the processes of some phenomenon persists if only through the confirmation of long-time repetition. Some linguists have conjectured that language patterns control thought patterns. This position may seem extreme to those who expect originality from the individual mind, but even they must admit that the power of language over thinking—especially in the young—is very strong. The sense of predication comes from the language and is evident in almost every sentence: It is the syntax that suggests causality—something acts upon something else, and the following is the result. Conditional ideas evoking proposals and possibilities are firmly rooted in the conditional sentence. As Thomson says, "Without the sentence, considered as a conditioning and generalizing device, elementary reasoning could not be carried out with efficiency and clarity" (p. 128).

Cognitive Styles with an Example[3]

Scholars have been studying the different ways youngsters approach a thinking task. There seem to be many variations, such as seeing wholes before parts and vice-versa, sizing up a situation before analyzing it, or plunging right in. Some youngsters tend to group categories on the basis of one thing being dependent on or related to another (dogs hate cats), while others prefer classifications (horses and cows are mammals).[4] Some people are visually oriented, whereas others receive messages more easily through auditory or kinesthetic means.

> An individual's cognitive style is determined by the way he takes note of his total surroundings—how he seeks meaning, how he becomes informed. Is he a listener or a reader . . .? Does he reason as a mathematician does, or in relationships as a social scientist does?[5]

Individuals differ in their approach to problem situations involving high response-uncertainty. Some individuals accept the first hypothesis generated, while others take their time and reflect over several alternatives before a final decision is made. This relationship between response time and choice of hypothesis in problem situations crosses over into a variety of cognitive events. Kagan[6] defines the *impulsive* individual as one who responds quickly to problems with high response-uncertainty at the expense of considering all alternatives. The individual who takes his time to consider all possible alternatives is defined as being *reflective*. Research has demonstrated that these characteristics are not linked to specific age groups or to sex, for the disposition to be one or the other can be seen in individuals of all ages; however, the pervasiveness of impulsiveness does decline with age in a developmental process.

When relating this dimension to school-aged children and achievement, definite differences are found between the two types of individuals. The reflective child is at an advantage in many school-related tasks. More fundamentally, the impulsive child has been shown to have greater difficulty demonstrating academic skills. When a child is unable to control his response rate and disregards accuracy, he immediately is at odds with the expectations of the school. Independent of intellectual ability, the impulsive child's output is inferior to grade-level peers.

[3] This section on cognitive styles was prepared with Paul Jacobs, Wayne State University, Detroit, Michigan.

[4] Irving Sigel and F. Hooper (eds.), *Logical Thinking in Children* (New York: Holt, Rinehart and Winston, 1968), p. 515.

[5] Joseph Hill, *The Educational Sciences* (Troy, Mich.: Oakland Community Colleges, 1970), p. 1.

[6] J. Kagan, "Impulsive and Reflective Children: Significance of Conceptual Tempo," in J. D. Krumboltz (ed.), *Learning and the Educational Process* (Chicago: Rand McNally, 1965).

Because of the significance of the reflection–impulsivity dimension and its relationship to achievement, attempts have been made to alter the behavior of impulsive children. At this time, the findings are rather inconclusive but a few are worth mentioning. Recent investigations have indicated that a wide range of response patterns can be transmitted to children by exposure to models. Based on the fact that the classroom teacher acts as a model for various types of behavior, Yondo and Kagan[7] attempted to look at the effects of teacher reflection–impulsivity on students. Their findings show that experienced, reflective teachers had a positive effect on changing impulsive children's behavior, while impulsive teachers had the opposite effect. Looking at control of motor behavior and its relationship to reflection–impusivity, Meichenbaum and Goodman[8] found that impulsive children exercise less verbal control of motor behavior and use language in a less self-directing manner than do reflective children. Based on these findings, a training procedure was devised to help impulsive children learn how to use language in a self-guiding fashion. This procedure combines exposure to a reflective model and training in verbal self-instruction. The results of this approach have been somewhat effective, but further study is necessary before this technique is put into widespread usage.

Through words and sentences the individual is able to "fixate, isolate, and relate aspects of his environment that otherwise would be a 'confused complex.' " Thus, man builds an "ordered world" and has a "map" for reference.[9] These relationships are stated in sentences or meaningful word groupings. They are available to other individuals and may be built upon. Cumulative abstractional thinking requires the use of linguistic structures. *Teachers continually need to build with children the language structures that carry the various kinds of thought.*

section 2

Two Views of Children's Thinking and Language: Piaget and Vygotsky

Language and thinking cannot be discussed without reference to the somewhat divergent positions of the two most esteemed investigators of children's thinking in this century, Lev Semenovich Vygotsky and Jean Piaget. Working separately, one at the University of Moscow and the other

---

[7] R. M. Yondo and J. Kagan, "The Effects of Teacher Tempo on the Child," *Child Development, 39*, 1968, 27–34.

[8] D. H. Meichenbaum and J. Goodman, "Training Impulsive Children To Talk to Themselves: A Means of Developing Self-Control, *Journal of Abnormal Psychology, 77*, 1971, 115–126.

[9] Thomson, p. 176.

at the University of Geneva, they developed similar concepts about the stages of cognitive development while basing their ideas on slightly different views of language. Twenty-five years after Vygotsky's death in 1934, Piaget responded to the Russian's thesis by pointing out their differences and agreements. A review of their positions regarding language and thinking is pertinent here, because it will summarize the significance of language in thinking and suggest implications for teaching children.

Piaget's Position

The following quotations present the crux of Piaget's argument that a purely sensorimotor type of *thought symbolizing* precedes and is separate from the *translation* of those *thought symbols* into the *signs* (words) of language.

> Words are probably not a short-cut to a better understanding. . . . The level of understanding seems to modify the language that is used, rather than vice versa. . . . Mainly, language serves to translate what is already understood; or else language may even present a danger if it is used to introduce an idea which is not yet accessible.[10]

Piaget views language as an outside agent in the child's developing thought that comes to serve him by translating his personal symbols or symbolic structure into collective or societal meanings. The child's use of speech and language does not substantially affect the development of personal symbolic structures. They are independently made. As he comes to understand language, he has to assimilate and then accommodate the lingual signs to his thought structures, but if he is to find his own meaning, the symbolic structuring must come first and not be confused by adult language structures. Following his own symbolizing, the child then translates his thoughts into language and comes to terms with adult signs. Of course, the symbolizing and then the verbalizing frequently occur almost simultaneously, but Piaget seems to view them as separate operations. Unless the teacher begins with the child's spontaneous structures, adult language as it influences the symbolic structuring is likely to confuse the child's thinking or allow him to settle for a verbalized statement of an idea without knowing what it means. Piaget seems to have been convinced of this position because of his vast experience in recording and analyzing children's symbolic play and their manipulation of objects. Children can show without words that they understand some ideas by the way they manipulate objects in play and in problematical situations.

Teachers of children need to take warning from Piaget's notion and to

---

[10] Jean Piaget, in Eleanor Duckworth, "Piaget Rediscovered," *ESS Newsletter*, June 1964, Elementary Science Study, Educational Services, Inc., Watertown, Mass., p. 4. These are quotations from discussions with Piaget on his American tour in 1964.

consider his advice. Teachers have, in the past, presented children with an idea to be learned in adult language (that is, in the watered-down adult language of textbooks or in "teacher talk"). Then teachers call for examples or set up experiments or demonstrations to show the concept. Any typical science or social studies text or teacher-made lesson plan reveals this process. The recent trend of educators to structure concepts from the organizational patterns of the disciplines for presentation to children can fall into the same trap. It can force adult language structures upon children's thinking as "subject-matter" teaching did. Piaget's advice is worth consideration: "The question comes up whether to teach the structure or to present the child with situations where he is active and creates the structures himself."[11] He points out that the goal of education is to "create the possibilities for a child to invent and discover" and then warns:

> When we teach too fast, we keep the child from inventing and discovering himself. . . . Teaching means creating situations where structures can be discovered; it does not mean transmitting structures which may be assimilated at nothing other than a verbal level.[12]

Piaget does, however, view language as a key element of social interaction. It is only through an exchange of ideas with adults and other youngsters that the developing child moves from a subjective point of view (egocentricity) to a objective and socialized outlook.

Vygotsky's Position

In contrast to Piaget's emphasis on the structuring of thought symbols by observation and manipulation of the environment prior to the injection of language, Vygotsky's emphasis is on the language of the children and the adult teacher in the creation of thought.

> The language of the environment, with its stable, permanent meanings, points the way that the child's generalizations will take. The adult cannot pass on to the child his mode of thinking. He merely supplies the ready-made meaning of a word, around which the child forms a complex [concept or idea cluster]. . . . The lines along which a complex develops are predetermined by the meaning a given word already has in the language of adults. . . . Verbal intercourse with adults thus becomes a powerful factor in the development of the child's concepts.[13]

From Piaget the impression is gained that the schemata or cognitive structures are pure thought connections involving language but not built of

---

[11] Piaget, in Duckworth, p. 3.

[12] Piaget, in Duckworth, p. 3.

[13] Reprinted from *Thought and Language* (trans. E. Hanfmann and G. Vakar) by L. S. Vygotsky by permission of The M.I.T. Press, Cambridge, Massachusetts. Copyright © 1934 by The M.I.T. Press. Pp. 67, 69.

language necessarily, whereas from Vygotsky a picture of conceptual structures made of shorthand language is conceived. The early interaction between the child's complexes (similar to Piaget's notion of structures or schemata) and the language of the environment is crucial. The child's egocentric speech becomes the inner speech that is the shorthand of thinking. This speech is not accompanying thought; it "serves mental orientation and conscious understanding." "Inner speech is not the interior aspect of external speech—it is a function in itself."[14]

It still remains speech—that is, thought connected with words. Vygotsky views pure thought as nonlingual, a "subtext" that is conceived all at once, not in a linear grammar like language; he places inner speech, however, just prior to the emergence of a pure meaning and sees it as the first step toward preparing a thought for communication. He closes his book with these words:

> Thought *and* language, which reflect reality in a way different from that of perception, are the key to the nature of human consciousness. Words play a central part not only in the development of thought but in the historical growth of consciousness as a whole. A word is a microcosm of human consciousness.[15]

From this position Vygotsky shows great concern for the *dialogue* between children and adult teachers, in contrast with Piaget's concern for self-discovery before adult language is introduced. The environmental language is as real in Vygotsky's view as the objects in the environment and is pivotal in the development of the child's thinking. There is a suggestion that words have vague meaning for children even before the children can speak, and therefore language helps share their first thinking. The development of thinking is enhanced by the presentation of scientific concepts (collective adult statements, knowledge) to children as the child's spontaneous concepts become organized in relation to the adult structure. Vygotsky says, "It is our contention that the rudiments of systematization first enter the child's mind by way of his contact with scientific concepts, changing their psychological structure from the top down."[16]

Experiments showed that children could deal more readily with "because" and "although" thinking in scientific concepts developed in school than in everyday concepts developed spontaneously.[17] However, this does not mean that concepts are only realized from the top down. Scientific concepts, on the other hand, cannot develop unless certain basic generalizations have developed in the spontaneity of living; for example, historical concepts can develop only when the child has a generalized sense of "in the past and now."

[14] Vygotsky, p. 133.
[15] Vygotsky, p. 153.
[16] Vygotsky, p. 93.
[17] Vygotsky, p. 107.

When making his investigations for writing *Language and Thought,* Vygotsky was primarily concerned with educational psychology. He was, therefore, more aware of the effect of environmental language and adult instruction on thinking than was Piaget in his purely developmental studies of the growth of children's intelligence. Vygotsky may, perhaps, have overstressed the influence of adult language on thinking. *Nevertheless, teachers need to be wary of the influence of their language and their structured concepts upon the learning of children.* What the teacher says when developing ideas in the classroom has a profound effect upon children's conceptual development. A faulty concept or misconception presented to children could seriously delay the child's development of a scientific concept.

A Compromise Position

A middle position between Piaget's and Vygotsky's could be taken, which would be more useful educationally than the extremes professed by some of the followers of the two men. This middle position embraces a concept of "dialogue" in which the language of children and the language of the adult teachers are brought into interplay at every stage of the development of language and thinking, including an initial "discovery" period. The collective language of the adults in a society is as potent a factor in the development of thinking as the child's own spontaneous formation of structures of relationships drawn from experience. Even though Piaget did not stress language in developing his notion of developmental stages in thinking, certain forms of adult dialogue with children are obviously most appropriate for supporting and encouraging the development of thinking at a particular stage, especially if the adult talk raises questions or alters the situation. This process causes a decentering of the older child's point of view, thus fostering objective thinking. The limitations and potential of the child's egocentric and developmentally emerging speech-thoughts need to be recognized. At each stage of the child's intellectual development, the adult's teaching language must be appropriately congruent with the child's learning-language.

section 3

Overall Processes in the Development of Thinking

Both Piaget and Vygotsky postulated and described several stages in the development of thinking. Although the descriptions were built from different data, they correspond roughly and can be combined to aid teachers in considering the thinking capabilities of their students.

Readers must not mistake either Vygotsky's *stages of concept development* or Piaget's *stages in the growth of thought* as distinct periods or ages in a child's life when a certain behavior is exhibited, as is done in the usual development psychology. Rather, these stages are descriptions of a style or mode of thinking, which the child uses in coming to terms with his environment. When the child has exploited and explored a way of thinking sufficiently to have developed the schemata (Piaget) or the complexes (Vygotsky) that will support the next way of thinking, he moves on. Thought structures are built that will support new relationships and connections. Children will move from one stage of complexity to the next, depending on richness of experiential background, quality of dialogue with adults and peers, and concomitant neurological development. Teachers need not only to keep these stages in mind as they plan experiences and "dialogue" activities for their children, but also recognize the limitations and exploit the possibilities of each stage. If children do not have sufficient practice (perhaps *play* is a better word) in each stage of thinking, they may remain in one phase longer than necessary. In extreme cases, they can become fixed in a stage, much as they may become trapped in immature psychological phases. However, these stages are not discarded once the child enters the next one, for the adult probably uses different types of thinking in all stages, depending on the situation and the level of his thinking about a certain matter.

Decentering the Child's View:
From Egocentricity to Objectivity

Language and cognitive development are just as important as emotional or social development. They are all closely related. Teachers may either underestimate the stage of development of pupils and never stretch their thinking or may overestimate their stage of development and never reach them. Baby talk and oversimplification of ideas and language can hold children's thinking back just as effectively as overly formalized language tactics can leave them behind. The value of dialogue between children and their peers and between younger and older children cannot be overstressed. Arrangment for such occasions which will assist in "decentering" points of view, can be a part of the teacher's strategy in exploiting a stage and leading toward the next. Teachers do not think and speak as children in these stages, but they question and present adult structures at strategic points in the classroom dialogue. They should listen to the children and watch their manipulations, reset situations, introduce new materials, add information, raise appropriate questions, and talk with the children about what they see and think.

Assimilation and Accommodation

Before a description of stages is made, some discussion of a general process of learning to think is needed in order to show what is happening in each stage and what brings a child to the climax of one stage and prepares him for the next. Piaget's formulation has been systematically devoloped and is congruent in part with Vygotsky's general view of process.[18] As the individual meets a new situation, new data is *assimilated* into old related material; at the same time, these older ideas are *accommodated* to the new. This is an adaptive process much like biological adaptation. These clusters of thought (connections of inner speech, meanings, images, and feelings) that form much as cells grow and multiply are called structures, schemata, or complexes of concepts. These are not viewed as linear additions of associations or of stimulus–response connections, but more as *gestalten* (configurational totalities whose properties exceed the mere sum of the parts). In concept they are more biological (like cellular growth) than psychological in the connectionist sense. Vygotsky gives the proper impression in a general description of the process.

> The development of the processes which eventually result in concept formation begins in earliest childhood, but the intellectual functions that in a specific combination form the psychological basis of the process of concept formation ripen, take shape and develop only at puberty. Before that age, we find certain intellectual formations that perform functions similar to those of the genuine concepts to come. With regard to their composition, structure, and operation, these functional equivalents of concepts stand in the relation to true concepts as the embryo to the fully formed organism.[19]

Formation of
Thought Schemata

Schemata become extended and enriched through both a *horizontal* process of *decalage* (coupling) happening within a stage, and a *vertical decalage* happening through maturity in the next stage. Horizontal decalage is a rehearsal of a cognitive structure gained in one situation by working it out in a slightly different situation. A child in the concrete operational stage has classified rowboat and sailboat as boats in a seashore situation. When he visits a lake and sees a canoe for the first time he assimilates it into his class "boats" and then accommodates to it with some differences noted, regarding shape and kind of locomotion. Several years later in the stage of formal logic, upon the child's seeing an ocean liner, a vertical decalage would occur. Rather than simply adding to his conglomerate classification by the criterion of one attribute, "goes in water," he would build generalized classes and subclasses based upon a concept of the difference between boats and ships, taking first the viewpoint of a sailor and then that of a vacationer. A new type of thought process, logical abstraction, has extended and made more complex the earlier and simpler schema.

---

[18] John Favell, *The Developmental Psychology of Jean Piaget* (Princeton, N.J.: Van Nostrand, 1963), pp. 16, 24. This book is a modern summary of all of Piaget's work to date, directly stated and clearly arranged.

[19] Vygotsky, p. 58.

The main difference between the early and later schemata is that the earlier "boat" is viewed from only one position (the egocentric) and is held together by one simple attribute, whereas the later schema has developed from taking the view of different people (objective and social) and is intricately bound by a principle. The older child can hold the concept of boats as objects that go in water while he considers them as carriers. He can then *conserve* those two ideas as he looks at "boats" according to naval tradition. This is the process of growth of schemata or concept clusters. The developmental goal is *decentering*, moving away from cognitive egocentricity toward objectivity. The result will be socialized, cooperative thinking in abstractions of principles and guiding themes that encourage hypothesizing and testing of new ideas.

Motivation for Thinking and Language Learning

Vygotsky and Piaget differ somewhat in their explanations of motivation for intellectiual development, but they agree that neither the systematized "drives" of the behaviorists nor the primary "instinct" of the Freudians will suit this situation. Instead, they suggest that there is a kind of self-activation to growing in the intellectual dimension, just as there is in the individual's physical growth. Vygotsky, from his Soviet Union orientation, suggests that the tasks with which society confronts the child prompt initiation of the cognitive processes; if this process does not occur naturally, he suggests that it is the role of the adult and teacher to so set the environment that these tasks will be more evident.[20]

Piaget, on the other hand, from his individualistic Swiss background, suggests that independent exploratory drive and the urge to mastery are responsible for motivating the thinking processes. The child is seen as striving to structure his world with meaning, the pupil as an active participator in the world who converts it into his own terms.[21] There need be no devised incentive; the life processes of knowing and adapting are sufficient to explain learning to think.

Both these views of learning are optimistic and positive. They challenge the teacher to enhance the process of thinking and not to impede its natural progress. In general, the stages of development of thinking as envisioned by Piaget and Vygotsky are supported by mounting evidence through experimentation in many cultures with many individuals. There will undoubtedly be alterations in this concept as experimentation continues, but for the present the following description can be useful as a way of looking at the development of thinking processes. *Teachers need to stretch children's thinking horizontally in the stage they are in as well as to lead them vertically*

[20] Vygotsky, p. 55.
[21] Duckworth, p. 3.

toward the stage that is coming. They should remember that because of individual differences a child may be at different stages in different areas of cognitive content and that children in the same age group may be generally at different stages.

section 4

Stages in the Development of Thinking and Their Implications for Education

Piaget and Vygotsky suggests five major stages or phrases of development in thinking.[22] Certain developmental language patterns pervade these phases, although the stated age levels may differ among cultures and subcultures as well as among individuals. For Vygotsky, the primitive phases appear at all ages prior to adolescence and the development of conceptual thinking, but some comparison with Piaget's stages can be made. Each stage of thinking has an obvious relation to its counterpart in the stages of language development described earlier.

Stage I (Birth to around Two Years):
Sensorimotor (Piaget)
and Primitive (Vygotsky)

In this period, in which is formed a foundation for all thinking, the child begins to explore his universe of objects. He handles them, manipulates them, and watches them. In time, he discovers that they have some permanency. A brightly colored toy boat is not designated as anything in particular. but it is grabbed, fondled, thrown, lost, and found again. The child becomes aware of the parts of his body. Eventually, he learns that certain tools are used for eating, even though he may use the toy boat for that purpose in his still unorganized, hit-or-miss scheme of things. Eventually, he "follows objects through sequences of placements and his behavior implies objective space, causality, and time."[23] His understanding of causality is only an observation: he sees that his kicking makes dolls hanging from his bassinet sway; but he has no notion of how this happens.

Toward the end of this period, imitation of adults and symbolic play develop. These are steps that begin to take children out of themselves and

---

[22] The stages as described by Vygotsky and Piaget are not identical, but they are close enough for consideration together in this context. Readers interested in further study are referred to the works of these scholars.

[23] J. McV. Hunt, *Intelligence and Experience* (New York: Ronald, 1961), p. 168. This book summarizes and interprets Piaget's theory and experimentation, relating it to other modern theories of the development of thinking.

show them holding schemata that they rehearse in play. The symbolic structures revealed in his early play are nonlingual thinking.

Vocalizations, crying, cooing, and the like appear to be unrelated to these cognitive activities, but as these sounds become more like the gross sounds of language, especially the vowels, snatches of words may appear in the play. Piaget noted at 15½ months that his daughter used "no no" in a playful episode of sucking her thumb as if she were starting to sleep. The fact that some of the symbolic play appears without language, being only imitative action, shows that language develops with symbolic representation but is not always necessary to thinking. Be it noted, however, that the child shows signs of hearing adult language and understanding it long before he begins to speak. Language may well influence his thought structure prior to his speaking his first words. Thought is undoubtedly a combination of purely symbolic or representational structures and language structures intertwined persistently through the stages of life, with language becoming more crucial as the child finds it a convenient means for holding ideas.

Although the parent does not formally teach the child at this stage, it is important for the parent–teacher to keep the child's environment alive with appropriate objects, to place the infant in the family circle of activity, and to go along with him as he reaches out to try new activities. Whether she knows it or not, a mother is orienting a baby to language when she chats with the baby while she feeds and changes him. Isolation and protection of the infant at this time will be as damaging to his cognitive development as to his psyche, for the child cannot develop the foundations for thinking *in vacuo*. As Harlow's famous experiments demonstrated, even apes remain stupid and ineffectual when they are deprived of nurture that allows for the developmnet of imitation and play. A stage is completed when the child can think adeptly in the modes of a level, when he can see reversibility; that is, the object can be found when hidden or can be hidden to be found.

Stage II (Two to around Four Years): Preconceptual or Preoperational (Piaget) and Syncretic "Heaps" or Conglomerations (Vygotsky)

During the second stage the child actively explores the world. He walks and travels about, investigating everything. He gets underneath things, on top of them, and inside them. He experiments with all objects in play, imitating the adults' use of them and trying out new combinations of his own.

As he explores this world, his thinking about it develops in several ways. By imitating the activities of adults and older children, he internalizes his observations, and they become the basis for imagery.[24] These new symbolic

24 Thomson, p. 94.

structures or images stand for more than they did previously, as related ones are imitated and incorporated with the old impressions. This is the time for the beginning of real language development, because words begin to stand for the images. Play becomes symbolic of these imitations as language begins to accompany the play. The child begins, in other words, to imitate the adult language in approximations. Semiwords become transitional between the pure symbolic structures and the true signs that are the words. "Ch-ch" applies to all moving vehicles. "Dada" designates any man. Then begin the naming and the constant "What is it?" question. Interestingly, the early nouns are not really names but are abbreviations for expression of the whole action,[25] a leftover development from the sensorimotor period. They designate the whole operation, not the thing. A "cup" is to drink from or to bang with for attention or to hold milk. "Book" means being read to.

Slowly the words are used not only to accompany action but also to represent something or to describe it. And finally, in this period the child begins to classify. "What is it?" is a request to know what it belongs with, where it fits into the scheme of things.[26] As Vygotsky notes, these primitive groupings are very random and are derived mainly by trial and error. They are egocentrically considered: How does it fit into my view? The bonds are subjective.[27] Teddy bear and bedtime go together. These are preconcepts. Some immediate association with an object will stay connected with it even though it does not make adult sense. Piaget notes that his daughter saw a red insect at about the same time that she saw a lizard. At the next sight of the "red animal" she asked, "Where is the lizard then?"[28]

This process of thinking is called *transductive reasoning*. The child proceeds from particular to particular rather than from particular to general, as he will do later in inductive reasoning, or from general to particular, which he will accomplish much later as he reasons deductively. Transductive reasoning is still prevalent in the third stage; therefore, teachers of preschoolers and kindergarten children need to keep this fact in mind as they listen to children and as they wonder why the children are not following the inductive process despite all maneuvers to help them. Many transductions need to be made as a foundation for inductive and deductive thinking. Slowly the transductions become true inductions. Piaget tells of his daughter's talking about a little neighbor who was a hunchback. After he was sick with influenza and was out of bed Jaqueline expected him to have lost his hump.[29] Such transductions, which confuse two different orders, sometimes lead to mistakes and sometimes make sense. Which way they fall

[25] Hunt, p. 186.
[26] Hunt, p. 187.
[27] Vygotsky, p. 63.
[28] Hunt, p. 189.
[29] Hunt, p. 191; Piaget example retold by Hunt.

depends mostly on chance until egocentricity is put aside and relationships are seen. Transductions are not made because objects appear one after the other in the child's immediate chain of events but are made because the objects have something in common.[30]

The adult teacher working with children of this age should keep the environment "busy" with objects and happenings. Opportunities to talk about relationships should be encouraged, even though the results come out as unreasonable transductions, because this kind of thinking is a precursor to the inductive mode.

Children can only develop their thinking potential at each stage through practice by discussion with adults and other children. They will check out their transductions with the adult. If they do not get some response, they will assume that their reasoning is correct. Teachers should not constantly correct children but should, in a natural way, state their own reasoning, just as Piaget would have responded to his daughter's question by saying that the hunchback still had the hump because it was not connected with influenza. Children sort out these matters when they occur in normal dialogue with adults and older children.

It is very important at this stage that the teacher encourage symbolic play by providing the setting and the materials for manipulative and visual exploration of objects and realia of all sorts. The toys do not have to be extravagant—sometimes a closet of pots and pans will do—but toys and objects there must be. The adult must be on hand a good deal of the time, not just to protect the exploring child, but to talk with him and answer some of his questions. The adult's full response, not too formal in grammar, is useful because it helps the child sort out the logical relationships the grammar of language encourages.

By the end of this second stage many youngsters can use language quite effectively. During these years an incredible amount of learning can be realized if children engage in dialogue about significant and real experiences with other children and with adults.

Stage III (Four to around Seven Years): Preoperational Intuitive Thought (Piaget) and Associative Collection and Chain Complexes (Vygotsky)

This stage is a precursor to concrete operational thinking when classes, relations, and numbers are systematically used. Although "operations" begin in the third stage, an intuitive, subjective, and egocentric mode still dominates. The child bases relationships in classifying on strictly perceived attributes. If the same number of beads has been poured from a round container into a square container, the child will think that the number of beads

---

[30] Hunt, p. 191.

has changed, even though he counts them out. The perceptible change in the shape of container dominates his thinking. He imagines the representation of beads inside because of the change in container shape rather than "conserve" in his memory the number of beads and reason from there. He would classify "rowboat" and "seaplane" together if he saw them both on a lake. Although he exhibits strong subjectivity in making bonds at this stage, the child will begin to relate things with practical ties, and he can change his criterion for choice; however, he can handle only one criterion at a time.

For the first time the child really begins to put things together in the third stage. He is still full of questions about what things are and where they belong in a scheme. The teacher needs to encourage this curiosity by setting up many situations in which objects can be described by their likenesses to some things and their differences from other things, remembering not to expect the child to consider more than one attribute at a time. Once things have been classified according to one attribute, they can be considered from the point of view of another attribute. This kind of thinking activity is exercise in thinking about things in the world around the children or things brought to the children: the world of plants, of animals, of people, of houses, of workers, and the like. Seeing, feeling, hearing, and manipulating real objects or multi-media representations of the real world while discussing responses are the main means for advancement through this stage.

The grammar of children's language in thinking is implied simile: Something is like something else in "this" way. The adult–child dialogue includes many statements of similarity and contrast. Concepts can be broadened and enriched in this way. A programmed series of pictures is useful in prompting discussion and dialogue among children and with a teacher; for example, first- or second-graders studying the farm can extend their concept of "farmer" by viewing, talking about, and categorizing pictures of farmers on tractors, at the market, in the office, milking cows, and riding the range; or pictures of a series of farmers with a hand hoe, with a horse plow, with bullock plow, and with a tractor plow.[31] When children are confronted with things that can be categorized, practice in thinking can take place. Describing a phenomenon and comparing it in one way to a similar phenomenon is a worthy exercise of the mind at this stage. Science and social studies can be the context for these thinking activities. Language development, including the skills of reading and writing, will be fostered admirably by this kind of activity as by the necessary practice of those skills. Language skills are best learned in contexts that have substance rather than

[31] Joseph Grannis, unpublished mimeographed reports of categorizing experiments using picture sets, Harvard Graduate School of Education, Cambridge, Mass., 1960–1963.

insularity from interesting ideation. School opportunities should be provided for young children to be with older ones, in family-type groupings, when ideas are discussed, thus allowing for a natural introduction of the advanced thinking stage with its language.

One kindergarten teacher invited students from the sixth grade to explain medieval castles to her children. They brought pictures, stories and a model they had built. The kindergarteners had heard about castles from folktales they had been told, but they seemed to be having difficulty in visualizing what castles were and how people lived in them. The sixth-graders talked with them and answered their questions to the delight and edification of the five-year-olds. Prince and princess, high walls and drawbridges became more meaningful each morning as the sixth grade contingent met with them for fifteen minutes every day for a week.[32]

In many ways teachers can recover the best of the one-room school where children of all ages were in dialogue with the teacher and with each other.

Stage IV (Seven to around Eleven Years):
Concrete Operations (Piaget), Pseudo-concepts
and Potential Concepts (Vygotsky)

In Stage IV, the child is not likely as yet to work in formal logic, although many school programs and teaching strategies are built on the assumption that the school-age child can think widely in abstractions. Other very important kinds of thinking must be practiced before the child can conceptualize in abstract principles and generalizations. The concrete operational stage leads children toward that capability, but unless they have sufficient experience with *concrete operational* thinking they will only be able to verbalize their generalized concepts and will not be able to glean their meaning or develop their own new abstractions for ordering their universe. The term "concrete operations" in this context refers to mental operations that are concrete rather than abstract. They involve a system of interrelating ideas that are realities in the experience of the child at a particular stage. For example, numbers are abstractions for very young children, but a real or "concrete" system for older youngsters. Simple plane geometry could be a concrete operation for children using manipulative representations or triangles that fit into squares or rectangles or parallelograms.

CONSERVATION The child develops the capacity to *conserve* one attribute or idea while he is considering another. He can accomplish groupings and seriations in space, in time, and in number. He can keep at least two

---

[32] Reported by Catherine Goodrich, a kindergarten teacher.

variables in mind as he considers categories or classes. These are great accomplishments. Children enjoy using these new powers if they are not pushed into formal logic before they are ready and if they are permitted, instead, to deal with concrete propositions.

Vygotsky points out in his discussion of pseudoconcepts why teachers are sometimes fooled into thinking that children are truly conceptualizing at the adult level.

> The child produces a pseudo-concept every time he surrounds a sample with objects that could just as well have been assembled on the basis of an abstract concept. . . .
> [In reality the experimentation shows that] the child is guided by the concrete, visible likenesses and has formed only an associative complex limited to a certain kind of perceptual bond. Although the results are identical, the process by which they are reached is not at all the same as in conceptual thinking.[33]

Vygotsky's notion of the pseudoconcept is very similar to the concrete operational idea of Piaget in that the associations are based on practical, action-bound thinking.

These observations by Piaget and Vygotsky give added support to the old "progressive" position that stressed the importance of an experience-oriented curriculum reaching beyond simple practice in life situations. The elementary school child must have the opportunity to think in "concrete" terms. Verbal abstraction is not for him yet, although he is coming to it very soon and will be reaching for it. He can think propositionally, form hypotheses, and look at a phenomenon from at least two points of view. He can hold an idea while he is considering another related one, but these processes all must be in terms of the concrete. He must have many such experiences as he prepares for the full realization of conceptual thinking and abstract logic. Depriving him of these opportunities in the school years may stunt his potential for mature thinking. Teachers are tempted to push students prematurely into the next phase of abstract thinking because it is the one they, the teachers, are in. They falsely assume that the child is there, too, because he can perform at a high level in concrete operations. Categorizing exercises with pictures could include negative or marginal instances that would lead the child to alter the category, thereby moving him toward abstract propositional thinking. This would be the time, for example, to introduce the concept of simple sets and subsets using realia in mathematics and in scientific classifications of things. The language of the dialogue at this stage should teem with "becauses," "althoughs," "ifs," "givens," and "supposes," provided the teacher keeps in mind what is "concrete" in the mental operations of his learners.

[33] Vygotsky, p. 66.

Stage V (Eleven Years–):
Propositional or Formal Logic (Piaget)
and Genuine Concepts (Vygotsky)

The main difference of this stage from the others is that the child can think beyond present tasks and form theories.[34] He can deal with propositions, probabilities, correlations, permutations, and aggregations. He can be truly experimental, setting up factors to be investigated, interrelating or separating them as need be. He can hold several factors in his mind while he considers others. According to Vygotsky, the child can now cope with a "scientific concept" from the collective knowledge and apply it or test it. The deductive process as well as the inductive is open to him. The language of experimentation, with its hypothetical statements, its searching question, its propostitions, and its analytical grammar, can now become the language of the classroom dialogue as studies in the sciences and social sciences are made along with the mathematics of proposition. Adolescent and adult students may need to use the operations of earlier stages of thinking in new fields of study to prepare a groundwork for their abstract thinking.

Matching Environmental Circumstances
with Developing Thought Schemata

Hunt suggests that the teacher can take advantage of this concept of stages of development of thinking by practicing what he calls "matching." He encourages the teacher to match environmental stimuli and classroom language with the stage in thinking of the children involved.[35]

Piaget's description of the successive stages of intellectual development removes the necessity for some of the trial and error in determining an appropriate match between environmental circumstances and the nature of the central processes already developed fo sustaining a positive interest in the environment and promoting accommodative growth by those central processes that underlie intelligence.[36]

Although there has not been sufficient experience with the effects of various attempts at matching the classroom "circumstance"[37] with the individual and collective schematic or mental structures of children at various levels, study of the developmental psychology of thinking suggests some general implications for teaching. *Teachers more than ever before need to listen to their children and observe their behavior from the point of view of thought and language development.* The place of a child or a group

[34] Thomson, p. 100.
[35] Hunt, pp. 270–288. This section includes a full discussion of "matching" on which these statements are based.
[36] Hunt, p. 287.
[37] Hunt, p. 273.

of children in the stages is revealed in large part by the syntax of the language used by the children and their accompanying behaviors as they encounter novel situations and struggle with the questions of "why" and "how." Teachers may be surprised to discover how much of the language and ideation of their children they had previously missed because they had not been listening for cognitive processes in development. For example, a young child was observed[38] making a mess on his desk during snack time by breaking up his crackers into tiny pieces. When asked by the observer what he was doing, he replied that he was making an "infinity" of crackers. When asked what that meant, the reply was that he was breaking them into pieces until he could not count any more. A teacher bent on socializing the child and keeping the classroom tidy would have completely missed this evidence of a child's thinking.

Before the presentation of a study in science, mathematics, or social studies, teachers can *pretest* for thinking level and concept attainment by holding a discussion of topics similar to the ones being planned for. Such discussion can be aroused by selected pictures, demonstration materials, or described episodes. The teacher would not enter the dialogue at this time but would listen and record the interplay of the children's talk, their proposed solutions, their propositions, and their questions.

Summary of Stages and Pedagogical Strategies

Critical periods for cognitive development become evident when all stages of schemata building are considered. Full development of schemata can only be assured toward the end of each stage if maximum opportunity for thinking with the dominant type of schemata of the stage has been offered.[39]

In the *sensorimotor phase*, variation in stimulation that will encourage the functioning of all the senses should be planned. Confronting similar things repeatedly brings pleasure, and the play of practice is fostered especially when, as the child becomes mobile, he can meet many new and old friends in and about his fast-expanding universe. The environment does need to be prepared, but it should not be restricted except for safety and for preventing undue annoyance to adults.

In the *preconceptual stage* the child is building symbolic structures through his imitative play. The more models he has to imitate and the more environmental range for play, the more he can be expected to advance. Hunt has made the interesting conjecture that television may have the desir-

---

[38] Reported in Kenneth Wann, Miriam Dorh, and Elizabeth Ann Liddle, *Fostering Intellectual Development in Young Children* (New York: Teachers College Press, Columbia University, 1962). Many other interesting examples of young children's statements are reported in relation to description and classification of young children's concepts.

[39] Thomson, pp. 272–275.

able effect of enlarging the source of models and situations for imitative play even though some of the models may be undesirable from other points of view.[40]

During the *intuitive stage*, "corrective" discussions with adults, teachers, and parents would seem to be crucial.[41] Without someone to answer the question "What is it?" and the question "Why?" the child becomes cognitively deprived in this phase. If there is a confusion from the presence of too many children, or if adults are too busy to talk with children, retardation in cognitive development is possible. This is obviously the crucial period for injecting objects, simulations, or pictures.

In the *concrete operational stage*, structuring ideas from what is real to the child is the key. The temptation to rush the abstract at this stage can be detrimental. The structuring of concrete situations and related questions to "perplex"[42] the child is a important as making the realia available. Suchman's[43] experimental teaching in science is one example of how children at this stage can be stimulated by reality structures. A scientific phenomenon is presented on film, and the children frame "yes-or-no" questions for the teacher as a means of testing individual hypotheses.

At the stage of *formal logical operations*, presentations of general principles or collective categories in which the specifics can be arranged seems to be critical. The child's need to deal constantly with the "concrete" does not seem to be as necessary as in the preceding stage. Combining material already known with new conjecture can be done by language alone, provided the referents remain clear. Propositions can be made and thought out abstractly before the most likely ones are tested.

Success in *matching* of environmental circumstances to thought schemata will depend on more information from experimentation in educational psychology and on the developing acumen of teachers. In the meantime there is much to be gleaned for teaching from the proposition that youngsters proceed through various stages of thinking and language development, and that students at all levels may need to go through prior stages when dealing with completely new situations. Scientists working with children in curriculum projects have been observed getting fresh ideas for their own experimentation from their dialogue with youngsters. For stretching thinking in a natural way, "family" or "cross-age" school grouping plans can be helpful as an alternative to conventional age-level grouping. As in extended families and closely knit village cultures, old and young mix in work and play, and a natural influencing of expanding idea patterns takes place.

---

[40]Hunt, p. 277.

[41] Hunt, p. 279.

[42] Hunt, p. 283.

[43] Richard Suchman, *The Elementary School Training Program in Scientific Inquiry* (Urbana, Ill.: College of Education, University of Illinois, 1962).

8

Structuring in Thought and Language

section 1

Categorical Thinking

Psychologists Gordon Allport and Jerome Bruner have found the formulation "structuring categories" helpful in describing and analyzing a major aspect of thinking and language. Such a process of categorizing characterizes the individual as classifying and categorizing events in various ways for the sake of mental economy. The human mind cannot hold, nor does it need to hold, all the specifics of the world. It needs only to collect and combine in categories of relationships those specifics which, when put together, help the individual make sense of the world and guide him in acting. To put a number of events together into one category is an easy way to remember them and provides a convenient means for deciding on reactions to similar events. Sloppy, overly simplified categorization brings stereotype and prejudice, whereas reflective and deliberative categorization can bring insight and effectiveness of action. Interrelated clusters of categories become structures of knowing for individuals; when formulated by communities of scholars categorical and propositional structures become accepted "knowledge."

150

Studies of Prejudicial Categorizing

The late Gordon Allport, in *The Nature of Prejudice*,[1] developed the concept of categorization in relation to the problem of racial and religious prejudices. Categories, in his view, are little generalizations drawn from instances in experience.[2]

In their simplest terms they are first-order generalizations tying one simple concept to another according to a theme. After seeing many instances of houses—our house, the house across the street, the house in the city, the hut of a Bantu, the log cabin of a pioneer, the tepee of an Indian—the child generalizes "house," and a category is formed. Then Aunt Sara's apartment, Dad's office, and the hospital are eliminated from the category "house" as they are perceived, although they may have been so included when four walls and a roof were the defining attributes that differentiated "house." A category may be extended and revised by finer distinctions; it may become clustered with related categories as the process of making sense out of the world proceeds. Each person's categories and the language that shapes and holds them are his own.

On the other hand, the individual may be overly economical—a polite word for lazy—and settle for a few strongly impressionable instances to make up his easy category. The young white children who wrote the following reactions to "Negro" have, insofar as these expressions reveal their categories, a very limited concept of "Negro."

The first one, by a six-year-old, has some positive value content. Even so, his category excludes the Negro from the category "Americans." Given a young boy's interest in sports, it is not hard to imagine how this category developed.

> They are good athletes. Most Negro men are good tackles, good in basketball and baseball. They are good jumpers and they are strong. Negroes are stronger than Americans.

Some negative instance, reinforced by parental agreement, left this impression with another six-year-old. Even if the following represents only one aspect of his category of Negro, it is already a prejudiced, *closed* category that may take years to open.

> Negroes have brown skin. They usually don't work. They are asleep on the job. Negroes don't understand our language and I don't think they can learn it.

Some children, even very young ones, are disposed to keep their categories open-ended and tentative. As one seven-year-old stated:

> I think they're kind of nice and it isn't right to separate them. People are people whatever color they are.

[1] Gordon Allport, *The Nature of Prejudice* (New York: Doubleday Anchor Books, 1958.

[2] Allport, p. 19.

Categories may be rational, irrational, flavored with emotionality of all sorts, or coldly calculating. Some are "autistic," very personally and even selfishly centered; others are freer in their associations and more objective in their outlook. They are built in language, and *words become their labels.* The speaker who uses racial, religious, or ethnic epithets probably holds a very different category from the one who speaks of Irish-Americans, Afro-Americans, or Italian-Americans. The importance of category labels is well illustrated by the recent drive among many "Negro" groups to refuse that label as one imposed by hostile whites and to accept for themselves the labels "Afro-American" or "Black."

Generally, categories tend to resist change, since they are built by incorporating each new but similar exemplar. However, the open-minded person keeps his categories tentative. The ability to *tolerate tentativeness* is in part a personality trait and is difficult to cultivate in someone who does not possess it. On the other hand, open-mindedness *can* be learned, especially when an individual realizes that he will find advantages and satisfaction in being able to *look at alternatives.* The mind and emotions can be disciplined when personal goals are developed that require self-discipline. In homes and classrooms where judgments are not hasty, children can learn by example to be more deliberative about making categories. The inquiry or discovery method of teaching can discourage the making of *closed categories* and encourage the habit of creating *open categories.*

Allport's view was not optimistic, because he felt that the individual modes of categorizing are learned so early in the social, emotional, and conceptual set of a family that little can be done through education. Change in categorizing would mean personality change, and that is a slow, complex process. His view that personality is behind categorization points up the close tie between the development of language and that of personality. Parental categorizations impress the child, especially when the categories carry high emotional content. *Because teachers are viewed by children as parent surrogates, they need to learn how to listen carefully to themselves for the prejudiced categories they may be passing on.* They are the models of secondary identification for children. *Teachers also need to listen more intelligently to the child's emerging category, for it may reveal the way the child is viewing life about him and show the shape of his attitudes.* "All categories," writes Allport, "engender meaning upon the world. Like paths in a forest they give order to our life-space."[3] Despite Allport's pessimism, he did, in his closing chapters, state that educators can lead pupils to open-mindedness and tolerance for ambiguity. *Categories can be altered, widened, and extended by strategies of teaching that assault the closed category with opposing proofs and highly emotional attributes of a positive nature.*

The study of *emotive language* in journalism, advertising, oratory, and schoolyard fights can be useful. Demonstrating its power and influence can

[3] Allport, p. 171.

be helpful in teaching children to objectify categorization. Children need to be shown that the emotive language that expresses categories is not good or bad in itself but that judgments based on value decisions and expressed in language are crucial. Children will understand, because they are accustomed to name-calling. Perhaps middle childhood is the strategic teaching period for opening up prejudiced categories. Gillham reports an experimental social studies program for extending children's "life-space" in a Western community bordering on an Indian reservation. It included class experiences with a third grade designed to attack the category "dirty Indians."[4] After a positive experience with Indian children who had made a visit to their school, constructive dialogues between teacher and children and then between children and parents succeeded, for a while at least, in altering the category to "our neighbor Indians." Leaving categorization to pure chance is abdication of education. In guiding children's judgmental thinking toward rational categories, teachers and parents can contribute to the sanity of society.

The Categorization Process

On the subject of categorizing, Allport was the activist, and Bruner was the investigator. Because Bruner is mainly concerned with the "how" of categorization, his experimentation deals mostly with nonlingual matters in order to give objectivity to the experiments. In searching out the strategies individuals use for concept attainment—the locating of "predictive *defining attributes* that distinguish *exemplars* from nonexemplars of a class"—the experimenters used abstract pictograms, each slightly different from the others.[5]

Even though language was not stressed in these studies, it is clear from other writing by Bruner that without the "instrumentality" of language, categorization could not take place in much of everyday life. Words permit the holding of categories in memory and create the possibility of altering them and using them in prediction.

The theory of categorizing is based on the apparent need of the human organism to "reduce the complexity of his environment" by "sorting out" and structuring aspects of it that for one significance or another are useful in understanding the environment and in being instrumental in it. Man can put happenings in place and can anticipate future events by this means.

[4] Helen Gillham, *Helping Children Understand Themselves* (New York: Teachers College Press, Columbia University, 1958).

[5] Jerome Bruner, Jacqueline Goodnow, and George Austin, *A Study of Thinking* (New York: Wiley, 1956). Italics are ours. For a thorough account of the study of categorizing, the reader is referred to Chaps. 1–7 in *A Study of Thinking*. Its relation to linguistic studies is amplified in the Appendix, Introduction, and Chap. 6 of Roger Brown, *Words and Things* (New York: Free Press, 1958). Further related studies of thinking not discussed here are reported in Jerome Bruner, Rose Oliver, and Patricia Greenfield, *Studies in Cognitive Growth* (New York: Wiley, 1966).

By "ordering and relating classes of events" and "establishing categories based on defining attributes" he can "reduce the necessity of constant learning."[6] A concrete example can serve to explain Bruner terminology (even though actually carrying one set of categories to this extreme would be unnatural).

> The child *identifies* food that he eats as something outside himself. Eventually some of that food is *identified* as vegetable, fruit, meat, etc. Food in this situation is an *identity category*. At the some time, the child might be making further identifications about the same object but in such a different situation that a separate category is set up for the time being. As he crawls through the grass in the backyard he *identifies* plants as he grasps at pretty blossoms in the flower bed or pulls a hanging leaf from a lettuce plant in the vegetable garden. As his language develops, words begin to stand for the category as further differentiations are made.
>   The eventual putting together of these several identities into a hypothesis of relationships is *concept formation*. Some plants are edible and called food, and/or some plants grow in moist places while some grow in drier places. Determining whether certain observed events—i.e., eating a plant, finding that it tastes good, and noting it as an exemplar of the category "edible"— is the process of *concept attainment*. A boy buys a plant at the dimestore which he does not know is a cactus. At home he waters it frequently as he does other plants, but it dies. His eventual decision, after relating the event to previous concepts of "desert" and "plant" to place it in the category of "desert plant" is part of the process of *attaining* a concept of environmental relationships.[7]

Bruner and his associates have observed other forms of categorizing based on different types of equivalences that people draw. They also investigated the ways that people develop categories and the ways they test their validity.

The exciting lingual–cognitive procedures of categorizing in identifying new instances or playing with the possibilities of new categorical themes are ways for a person to discover new relationships in the universe. In this manner, he constructs his own cognitive map of the world, a reference for his intelligent living. It is the teacher's duty and privilege to be his assisting cartographer.

Educational Implications
Regarding Categorical Thinking

Although more research is necessary, this view of a personal way of cognitively structuring one's world suggests possibilities for curriculum planning and instructional methodology. A number of categorical themes crucial to an understanding of the environment could be set down, and samples of subcategories that support the themes might be delineated. Categories involved in man's relation to water might be one such theme. Teachers could

---

[6] Bruner, Goodnow, and Austin, pp. 12–15.

[7] Adapted from the text of Bruner's discussion of categorization in *A Study of Thinking*. Examples are the authors.

build strategies of categorization that would eventually reveal the themes (important generalizations). However, the teacher's main strategy, after thinking about some of the subcategories, would be to set the stage—the classroom environment—in such a way that the children would develop their own categories and relationships between categories. The *empty category*,[8] Bruner's term for an open-ended category, should be encouraged; in this category the student goes beyond the conventional groupings and imagines his own. The teacher encourages the use of cues already identified to anticipate what might follow and what might be possible. With careful questioning, attributes can be eliminated or incorporated.

CATEGORIZING GAMES Students can take a theme and categorize objects or situations in one way; then they can change the theme and point of view and categorize the same instances in another way, eliminating and adding as required by the testing. Different strategies for attaining concepts can be explored while the efficient ones are encouraged. Present categories can be used for predicting future possibilities to encourage children to do some original thinking. The theme "man's work" in a career-education curriculum suggests many opportunities for categorizing occupations and their relation to various social and economic factors. The open questioning strategy for group categorizing games is as follows: (1) Make a list on chart paper of everything we can think of about "work and jobs." (2) Now designate with an appropriate symbol all those that seem to fit together. (3) Choose a label for those with the same symbol. (4) If some fit under two or more labels, think of new labels for them. (5) Which label would you like to be the focus for your study? Teachers must, however, be aware of "teaching at the child's level" by accepting all responses and letting the learners decide which items are valid under which category.

The injection of a "noisy" attribute into discussion can disrupt the process. Very often the affective or emotional equivalence will dominate the categorizing of children and obstruct more important equivalences. Rejection of the slimy feeling of a frog may delay the categorizing into the class of amphibian and reptile. The teacher can inadvertently introduce a "noisy" attribute of this kind by an offhand remark or a show of feeling on his own part. Exploration of categorical possibilities, on the other hand, is a challenge to teacher and children.

Noncategorical Thinking

Logical, rational thinking can be developed in many ways, but such thinking must not be developed to the exclusion of the nonrational modes of thought. In his *Essays for the Left Hand*, Bruner describes the artistic and aesthetic modes of thinking as different from the logical, step-by-step process of concept formation and attainment, which he calls "right-handed thinking."

[8] Bruner, Goodnow, and Austin, p. 14.

The elegant rationality of science and the metaphoric non-rationality of art operate with deeply different grammars; perhaps they even represent a profound complementarity. One is at the center of awareness as desire: it is directed toward achieving an end and is specialized to the tasks of finding means. The other is at the fingers of awareness, a flow of rich and surprising fantasy, a tangled reticle of associations that gives fleeting glimpses of past occasions, of disappointments and triumphs, of pleasures and unpleasures. It is the stuff of which James' stream of consciousness was made.[9]

Left-handed thinking has been either neglected in formal education or taught inadequately under the guise of "appreciation" of art, music, and literature. These aesthetic modes of thinking are discussed in other sections of this book as presentational symbols. Their inclusion in the curriculum should be founded upon their value as ways of thinking about the world. Today's students need to practice both "left-handed" and "right-handed" ways of thinking if they are to experience the whole of life and not just the scientific-technological aspect of it.

section 2

The Disciplines of Study: The Sciences, Social Sciences, Humanities, and Mathematics

The words of Piaget, Vygotsky, Allport, Bruner, and others describe kinds of structures in individual thinking: operational structures, symbolic structures, and language structures in various combinations. Piaget and Vygotsky find that children structure their experiences into thought in different ways at different stages of their development. Allport and Bruner observe that the adult formulates structures of thought into categories and thematic formations. Harvey, Hunt, Schroder, and George Kelly[10] view the personality as an integrated cluster of concepts, or *personal constructs* or systems of life interpretation, that predispose an individual to act and talk in a certain way. People together cluster and structure ideas into aggregate knowing.

Aggregate Knowing

The launching of Sputnik I, the moon walks, and the pollution–energy crisis of the Seventies are examples of those rare moments when whole populations have to come to terms with new discoveries in their environment.

[9] Reprinted by permission of the publishers from Jerome S. Bruner, *On Knowing: Essays for the Left Hand* (Cambridge, Mass.: The Belknap Press of Harvard University Press), copyright 1962 by the President and Fellows of Harvard College.

[10] George Kelly, *A Theory of Personality: A Psychology of Personal Constructs* (New York: Norton, 1963).

The modern speedup of communication caused people around the globe to be confronted almost instantaneously by the arrival of Sputnik. Another similar event in recent times was the announcement of the exploding of the first atomic bomb. It is significant that although government scientists had already done their symbolizing much earlier at the firing of the first atomic device at Alamogordo, the public could not begin to respond until the secret events were revealed several years later.

In earlier times the symbolic reaction to new discoveries took generations as the symbolic process filtered down from scholars and scientists to the people. The delayed reactions to the genetic theory and the theory of relativity are impressive examples. The Copernican theories took even longer to disturb the public into rethinking the relationship of the earth to the sun and universe.

Sometimes the public is slow to incorporate a new phenomenon into its conceptual scheme for reasons other than slowness of communication. Darwin's theory of evolution, for example, was widely (and violently) discussed in newspapers and magazines shortly after he published it. However, negative emotion (*"He* may have descended from an ape, but *we* didn't") and misconception delayed assimilation of the theory as a public concept.

Today, the theory of relativity in relation to time, space, and speed is becoming a more comprehensible concept to the public as we have more experience with satellites, manned space flights, and lunar vehicle launchings. Eventually, most people will have a reasonably accurate conception of this theory as more experience is interpreted and symbolized in light of the theory and through science fiction as well as scientific accounts. They will possess a language for coping with incidents involving relativity.

Evolving Fields of Knowledge

The great minds are the first conceivers, and they develop the first new conceptions of the universe and the interrelationships within it. Scholars in a burst of language activity reorganize, restate, and reformulate these theories in terms of the particular and in relation to other bodies of knowledge. As each aspect of knowledge becomes more specialized, a new field is developed. It all began as philosophy. Originally, *science* was simply another word for knowing, the activity of philosophy. But beginning with Aristotle, perhaps before, the special categories of knowledge began to be developed.

As new discoveries were made by perceptive leaders, disciples followed them by conceptualizing the material into schools of thought; that is, clinical psychology grew out of medicine and philosophy under the leadership of Freud and others as they developed new concepts of man and his emotions. Anthropology stemmed from biology and philosophy as new concepts under the leadership of Boas and others were developed from evolutionary theory and from the study of primitive cultures. New ways of exploring and studying man in his world were devised with each new discovery. A way of thinking, of looking at things, developed with each field. Although there have emerged some agreements and interrelationships, each field is a little different, depending not only on the style and attitudes of the scholars attracted to the field but also the differentiated content.

Today, these special fields are seen in any university catalogue, each with its own conceptual structures, approach to the life-situation, and ways of studying and working. These are called the disciplines, and each has been created in a sublanguage of its own.

The Disciplines of Knowledge

The disciplines encompass all the personal knowings of individual scholars. They are the established knowledge of the world at a given time, but inquiry goes on more rapidly now than ever before. New concepts overthrow old ones, and new investigations begin. The earth was conceived only a few years ago as a somewhat flattened sphere. Now it is conceived as pear-shaped. The satellites were able to gather vast amounts of data quickly, and computers were able to process the new information within hours. A few closeup color TV pictures with accompanying descriptions by astronauts on the moon have swiftly changed concepts of that celestial body.

Each discipline views the world from a different vantage point, and, therefore, a special set of concepts is derived by a particular type of investigation. There are perhaps three major ways of looking at the world, and these are reflected in the great division of academic studies: (1) the natural sciences, (2) the social sciences, and (3) the arts and humanities. Within each of these broad fields there are individual disciplines whose scholars investigate particular classes of phenomena.

A discipline is made up of the concepts, generalizations, and procedures of investigation that scholars and creative artists, looking at the world in a certain way, develop as they study a piece of the universe. It is the structure of the knowledge gained from their reflective examination of experience. Disciplines are made in a search for truth. The scholar is the curious child grown up. While retaining the childhood zest for inquiry, he develops complex skills for quantifying and qualifying the world about him and for assessing the work of previous scholars. He builds a language by which phenomena can be studied, explained, and reflected upon. The curious child does the same, but with less sophisticated tools of investigation and more modest language means.

No single adult today, much less a young person, could possibly know all that is presently gathered in any one of the disciplines, although in Renaissance times this was thought possible. A student must come to know how to use a discipline to solve a problem or understand a phenomenon. He cannot know all the content of the discipline, but he can learn how to work in a discipline and use its findings. He can begin to gain what Schwab calls the "syntax" of a discipline, the "pattern" of its procedure, "its method: how it goes about using its conceptions to attain its goals."[11]

Structures of the Disciplines

Scholars of the world have structured knowledge of reality into disciplines of study that are broadly divided into the subject areas of the physical and biological sciences, the social sciences, the humanities, and the arts. Generally, scholars studying these areas view the world from a given position and explore new phenomena with methods appropriate to the discipline's viewpoint. Each discipline has its own language structures that developed with the formulation of the symbolic and operational structures.[12]

NATURAL SCIENCES The natural sciences are usually divided into two main branches of study: the physical sciences that incorporate the disciplines of physics and chemistry, and the life sciences that study plant and animal life through the various subdisciplines of biology. Scientists speak of matter, forces, and energy, or of cells, genes, and antibodies. Their language strives for universality through new uses of Latin or the generation of new international terms. The natural scientist's approach is always experimental, objective, and tentative. Whether he is looking at inanimate objects or animate ones or at the relationships between the two, he is mainly interested in describing, classifying, analyzing, and attempting to explain the phenomena he observes. Through precise observation and analysis of a phenomenon in the natural world he derives hypotheses to be tested in carefully controlled experimental situations. From these tentative generalizations he may create a model of interactions and interrelationships; this model guides him in further investigations. Discrepancies that do not fit his tentative generalizations and model suggest new searches that may in time overturn the generalizations and model that had been his original guide. This way of studying phenomena is called the scientific method. It has been responsible for the development of such theoretical propositions as Newtonian mechanics, atomic structure, relativity of time, and the evolution of species.

SOCIAL SCIENCES The social scientist views the world as a set of interactions of people with people and of people with environment. He is concerned with the concept labeled *behavior*; his investigations, based on the

---

[11] Joseph Schwab, *The Concept of Structure in the Subject Fields,* mimeographed material from the author, 1961.

[12] Two books are recommended for discussion of the disciplines in relation to curriculum development: Arthur King and John Brownell, *The Curriculum and the Disciplines of Knowledge* (New York: Wiley, 1966); Philip Phenix, *Realms of Meaning* (New York: McGraw-Hill, 1964).

assumption that behavior is caused, attempt to explain actions and reactions. The procedure of organized observation, measurement, and classification of behaviors is customarily used. Because ethical considerations prevent his using the strictly controlled laboratory experiment in many studies of man, the social scientist has developed highly sophisticated methods of statistical measurement. Each discipline within the social sciences has main concerns that are different from those of the others. At the same time, there is much overlapping among many of the disciplines in interest and methods, and with the disciplines of the natural sciences as well. Thus, there are physical anthropologists and medical statisticians and ecologists, all concerned with the interaction of man and his physical-biological environment. They talk of societies with cultures and subcultures, of ethnicity and class status, and of man in ecosystems.

HUMANITIES Under the classification of the humanities fall the disciplines sometimes referred to as "Arts and Letters." Their view of the world is sensuously rich and charged with personal immediacy. There is minimal psychic distance between the scholars of these disciplines and the things they study. The languages of literature, art, music, and dance are means for investigating the condition of man and of making interpretations of it. Emotion is a valid component of these disciplines, and the "what" and "how" of scientific method are joined here by the "why" gained from insightful imagination. *War and Peace* tells as much about the impact of war on people as a documented, historical study might do. Martha Graham, choreographer of "Appalachian Spring," conveys the essence of the Shaker experience in pioneer America as no sociological study of the same phenomenon ever could.

Although the historian sometimes uses the findings and methods of social science, his primary purpose is to locate the great themes that seem to explain the emerging pattern of events in man's existence. One example is Beard's interpretation of the American Revolution, based on the significance of economic themes in generating events. Philosophy is a discipline within the humanities, but it holds a special position because of its attempt to synthesize all of knowledge and because it grapples with the ultimate question of the purpose of the universe and of man in it. The cave metaphor in Plato's *Republic* memorably summarizes the "ideal" life possibility.

APPLIED DISCIPLINES The applied disciplines make use of findings from basic research and study. Engineering is an example of an application of the natural sciences. Social work is an application of the social sciences. Journalism gains its basic knowledge from the humanities, as does architecture from the arts. Education takes its basic concepts from the social sciences, the humanities, and the arts. Problems of learning and teaching involve human interaction and the artful use of various media of communication.

Studies in education are also dependent upon answers to questions raised in philosophy ("learning for what?").

Mathematics is a unique discipline that allows man to quantify and measure his universe in a shorthand symbol system which can also be used for developing pure theoretical constructs in abstraction—it was an equation that played a key part in the discovery of atomic energy. Mathematics is one paradigm for structure in the sciences and is most useful in the engineering aspects of many applied sciences.

Language of the Disciplines

There are languages of physics and geology and biology, of psychology and sociology and geography, of economics and government, of history and philosophy, of art and literary criticism, and of such applied disciplines as engineering and education. The expertise of these disciplines is merely a language effort to embrace ideas that attempt to describe the world from different vantage points. The chemist describes and explores a world made up of a myriad of combinations of particles of matter. Each particle and compound is given a chemical name and relationships between particles and compounds are described in shorthand sentences called formulas and equations. Knowing something of the chemist's view helps the layman to appreciate the awesome natural phenomenon of chemical change and aids him in making everyday decisions about cooking, health care, and home repair. A child can learn to know his way around the world much better after seeing the universe of matter and force through the eyes of the chemist and the physicist. Viewing the world as a biologist can help him explain environmental pollution and the need for a personal health program. He can also learn to make wiser judgments about practical matters impinging on his life and that of his fellows.

The language of psychology is interesting in that a most influential branch of it, psychoanalysis, was constructed by one man. The language and idea structures of Freud are fascinating metaphors, which when put together into his great scheme reveal a profound myth of the battle for survival of the self "ego," caught between the devil "id" and the archangel "superego." Freud's life and the lives of his followers were devoted to describing the odyssey of the "ego." This magnificent schema has helped reveal to man the ways of the personality; with continuing investigations of the formation and operation of personality, psychologists continue to alter and expand its concepts and language.

In music, too, there is a language that describes its processes and results. Music cannot be known entirely without knowledge of the musician's terms and of ways of talking about the art. The world of artful sound gains meaning as melody, counterpoint, harmony, color, and rhythm are understood in the context of musicmaking. To teach children to "enjoy" or "appreciate" music, as educators usually say, can hardly be accomplished with any significance unless children know what music is and how it is created. Understanding of the structure of music must not only be experienced but talked about. The dialogue with the teacher will not be concerned with the "pictures" children are sometimes asked to see as they listen to music but should be about the happenings in the musical structure and the means the composer used to create them. Art has created a magnificent language of line, color, and form, while dance has created one of bodily movement and gesture in spatial designs.

Schwab has referred to the pattern of a discipline, its procedures, its methodology, and the language of its conceptions as the "syntax of a discipline."[13] These syntactical structures are reorganized from time to time as concept revisions are forced by evaluation of new data. Students need to understand that the syntax of the disciplines is constantly changing and being renewed. *The language of tentativeness in propositions and of playfulness in investigations, if used in the classroom, will impress upon children the dynamic quality of structuring thought that makes a discipline.*

section 3

Structures for Teaching from the Disciplines, Including Mathematics

The structures of the disciplines are man's attempts over time through the processes of experimentation, deliberation, contemplation, and generalization to describe, explain, and imagine his universe. Each child makes the same attempt. The scholar's search for meaning in the world differs from the child's quest only in quality and in sophistication of tools. Once a child has reached the level of abstract thinking, thought and language structures are developed in essentially the same way as those of the scientist and artist. The difference is in degree, and indeed some of the children will become the next generation of scholars and artists. The man-made structures of the disciplines are used by teachers to order the world for themselves before they try to help children do it.

The conceptual framework does change as scholars discover new views. The world was conceived as being flat with a sky dome overhead, then as a sphere with vast space about it. Most recently it has been seen as pear-shaped, and the old dome concept has returned as the ionosphere. Teachers need to keep abreast of major conceptual revisions in the fields they refer to in their teaching. They need to know how to study in those fields and respect the scholar's constant tentativeness about knowledge.

Children must not be led simply to copy and parrot the aggregate

---

[13] Schwab, mimeographed material.

thought and language structures of scholars of the disciplines; Piaget stresses
that children should be permitted to find their own structures and that teachers
should refrain from presenting the adult structures, particularly those in
language, until the child has made some formulation of his own.[14] The
teacher, of course, will know the adult structures and will set the environment,
limit it, and rearrange it to facilitate discovery of significant factors. Given
the importance of language in thinking postulated by Vygotsky, Langer, and
Cassirer, discovery of environmental cues is only the beginning of learning.
The child needs not only to talk about his discovery with his peers, as Piaget
suggests, but also to tally his thinking with the adult thoughts, as Vygotsky
recommends. In his theory of interaction Thelen calls this the "dialogue"
between "personal knowledge" and "established knowledge."

> Teaching is the facilitative reorganization of thoughts and feelings, and its
> essence is the control and direction of consciousness in planned and selected
> experiences. First, there is the stimulation of personal knowledge in a situa-
> tion selected or sanctioned by the teacher.
>   I will call this *discovery*. It would be possible to raise students to be primarily
> discoverers. The successful adult result would be the "self made" man—a man
> who knows a great deal about many things and has opinions about the rest, but
> does not know which of his ideas are acceptable, valuable and demonstrable.
> Becoming a discoverer, wonderful as that would look when compared to present
> outcomes, is not enough.
>   *Discovered knowledge* has to be reflected against *established knowledge*: this
> is how the experience of the human race helps the individual. The activities
> through which this interplay is accomplished will be referred to as *dialogue*.
> Teaching method produces an alternation between these two activities of ex-
> periencing or interacting. In one, the individual is making discoveries. In the
> other his discoveries and those of other individuals are confronted by established
> knowledge in such a way that personal knowledge is assessed, corrected, ex-
> tended; and in such a way that new tensions generate new questions for
> investigation.[15]

Sample disciplinary study is one instructional means for accomplishing
the interaction of personal and established knowledge in planning curricula.
Educators with the aid of scientists prepare a thematic series of investigations
for youngsters with simplified materials so that they may live through the
same type of investigatory experiences that the scientist originally had. There
have been nationally developed programs, for example, in geography, economics, anthropology, and physics. Some educators have referred to this
approach as a *pre-science* curricula, since the young investigators do not have
the sophistication of the adult scientist. However, students do experience the
ways of the scientist and gain his satisfactions in discovering new relation-

---

14 Duckworth, p. 4.

15 Herbert Thelen, "Insights for Teaching from a Theory of Interaction," *The
Nature of Teaching* (Milwaukee, Wisc.: The School of Education, University of Wis-
consin–Milwaukee, 1962), p. 27. Reprinted with the permission of the School of
Education, University of Wisconsin–Milwaukee. Italics added.

ships between environmental phenomena and the human condition. Cultural anthropology, for example, might be the disciplinary base for multiethnic studies in school.

Interdisciplinary study is another way of applying the disciplines in developing school curricula. Several disciplines are drawn upon as teachers focus classroom studies around conceptual themes or life problems, issues, and questions. "Man's Dependence on the Sun" is a suitable theme for studying man's energy and production problems. The disciplines of astronomy, physics, economics, agronomy, and geography might be employed and inter-related in such a study. Educators have also referred to such curricula as *integrated studies*, also stipulating that such studies need to be integrated with the learner's experience and personal thinking style. The focus then becomes the learner's conceptual scheme about such matters and how that scheme can be enhanced through dialogue with the relevant concepts developed in pertinent disciplines. The concept of the *emerging curriculum* suits this "integration" need best. The teacher picks up an idea, concern, interest, or question that youngsters express in an open-ended, idea-sharing session like "show and tell" or the "classroom meeting." The teacher then draws upon his own resources and those of the school and community to develop a brief curricular plan that will permit further investigation of the thoughts raised. Many teachers collect their own resource materials and cluster them thematically for just such an occasion. The *open-inquiry approach* to education is structured around perennial child interests and is characterized by preplanned studies on the part of the teacher. The interdisciplinary conceptual themes are set down, appropriate manipulative and reading materials are organized and informally packaged for availability to students. Inquiry-type work cards are attached, allowing youngsters to work through their own selection at their own rate. These compact studies or units can be described as small-scale individual delivery systems for bringing personal conceptions into interaction with scientific concepts.

Sequencing Thought Structures for Teaching

The conventional way to structure the major disciplinary concepts for teaching is to borrow from the pattern of most textbooks. A topic is posed and concepts of equal complexity often drawn from several disciplines will be clustered around the topic, an approach that often results in a mere array of loosely connected facts. Through the work of David Ausubel and others who have studied high-school and adult learners, it has become clear that conventional sequencing is not similar to the way learners actually construct their own thought patterns. A "subsumption process" takes place as learners incorporate or discard new ideas. "As new material enters the cognitive field," Ausubel writes, "it interacts with and is appropriately subsumed under a relevant and more inclusive conceptual system."

> The very fact that it is subsumable (relatable to stable elements in cognitive structure) accounts for its meaningfulness and makes possible the perception of insightful *relationships*. If it were not subsumable, it would constitute rote material and form discrete and isolated traces.[16]

Clarity, generalizing ability, cohesiveness, and stability are some of the factors weighed as the new concepts are considered in relation to the existing ideational structure. "Furthermore," he writes "subsumption of the traces of the learning task by an established ideational system provides anchorage for the new material and thus constitutes the most orderly, efficient and stable way of retaining it for future availability."[17] This system is not unlike the structuring of the manmade disciplines. Therefore it seems advisable to structure ideas for teaching in the same manner by identifying the basic *organizing concepts* for a study from the disciplines and then by developing the "organization of presentation and sequential arrangements of component units."[18] In completing his instructional plan the teacher needs to be sure that the students have some previously developed ideational structures under which the new can be subsumed to further the differentiating process. Ties of an integrative nature need to be planned in an effort to aid the student in perceiving overlapping ideas, similar or related concepts, and ways in which the new can be subsumed under previous organizers or slightly altered ones. The use of *advance organizers* for this purpose has advantages. They can be in the form of verbal or multimedia presentations, designed to show the principal similarities and differences between the ideas in the new material and the known structure. Such an activity would begin the subsuming process in an oriented fashion rather than by hit-or-miss.

AN EXAMPLE: TEACHING MATHEMATICS AS STRUCTURE[19] Nowhere are symbolic thought structures (categories) more apparent than in mathematics. Mathematicians study their subject as to its nature and its uses, its possibilities and its limitations. Users of mathematics are especially concerned with its role in the solution of human problems and its contribution to a better understanding of their own fields. The result of these activities has been a contemporary organization of mathematics *unified* by basic concepts (sets, relations, mappings), by fundamental structures (groups,

[16] David Ausubel, "Cognitive Structure and the Facilitation of Meaningful Verbal Learning," *Journal of Teacher Education, XIV*, No. 2 (June 1963), 219.

[17] Ausubel, p. 219.

[18] Ausubel, p. 219.

[19] This section has been prepared by John Camp, Mathematics Education, Wayne State University, Detroit, Michigan.

rings, fields, vector spaces), and by the interrelations of its topics. This mathematical achievement, beyond its theoretical value, has valuable applications in all fields of knowledge. Piaget speaks of their tremendous importance:

> A critical account of structuralism must begin with a consideration of mathematical structures, not only for logical but even for historical reasons. True, when structuralism first made its appearance in linguistics and psychology, the formative influences were not directly mathematical. . . . But the structural models of Lévi-Strauss, the acknowledged master of present-day social and cultural anthropology, are a direct adaptation of general algebra.[20]

In recent years there have been extensive changes in the goals, methods, and content of school mathematics. Basically, the changes reflect the tremendous recent (since 1860) increase in the amount of mathematical knowledge and the way that mathematics is used in the real world. Educators now recognize that students can no longer be presented with a myriad of unrelated mathematical facts and be expected to absorb them in some mystical way. Instead, at the elementary and secondary levels, structures are playing an important organizational role in the mathematics education of our youth.

Contemporary goals for the teaching of elementary school mathematics include the following needs: (1) to emphasize the unity of the subject; (2) to embed the *important* classical skills and concepts in a structural framework; (3) to prepare students for subsequent study of mathematics and fields that rely heavily on mathematics; and (4) to prepare *mathematically literate* students. Thus the objectives of instruction in school mathematics relate to knowledge about mathematics, development of skills, and literacy for the future.

Especially important today is mathematical literacy, as students leave our schools and enter a rapidly changing scientific world.

> The mathematics we teach to our students today should be relevant to their needs in the society of tomorrow in which they will live. . . . To this end we must first of all be concerned with the formation of the intellect—the ability to do cognitive thinking. What we teach must develop the human mind in the capacity to understand and interpret numerical, spatial, and logical situations occurring in the physical universe and life within it, and to approach problems with a scientific, questioning and analytic attitude.[21]

Along with the preceding contemporary goals, which are mostly content and attitude oriented, there are new ways for presenting mathematics within the intellectual stages of development. Due mostly to Piaget's theory teachers are providing opportunity for students to be actively involved in the

[20] Jean Piaget, *Structuralism* (New York: Harper & Row, 1970), p. 18.
[21] Information Bulletin 7. SSMCIS: Teachers College, Columbia University (Spring 1973), pp. 4–5.

learning process by using concrete materials like multibase blocks, cuisenaire rods (simulating mathematical units), geometric models, and operational machines. Students experiment to discover patterns and regularities, and do suggest explanations for mathematical ideas. Skill and proficiency thus come from understanding. In fact, by presenting mathematics from a structural point of view, with its unifying concepts and elements, teachers are easily able to develop topics *spirally* and thus conform to the "learning stages."

The concern for a mathematically literate society also has influenced the content of school mathematics programs. Although the content question is still being debated, most mathematics educators agree that students should graduate from elementary schools with a conceptual understanding of rational numbers and operations on rational numbers (including the four fundamental operations of arithmetic) and, at a concrete level, should be introduced to topics from geometry, probability, statistics, and topology. In large part, computational skills should be developed by doing problems in the areas that require use of the skills.

Implementing the mathematical goals, methods, and content of contemporary school programs requires that there be materials based on the symbolic structure and that the teachers themselves be mathematically literate. Mathematics uses a special language and in many cases uses language in a special way, and teachers need to be able to help students read this language.

Learning To Learn:
A Disciplined Process

The implications of the theory of thought and language structure for teaching can be summarized in the modern dictum, "education is learning to learn." As the child discovers structures of knowing that help him give meaning to one instance in the environment and move him toward generalities, he can cope with other similar instances and learn about them on his own. The school cannot possibly teach all there is to know about any subject. The teacher can only show the way to learn, but he should do so effectively.

The school curriculum might best be constituted of sample investigations made in terms of the structure of the disciplines that explore contexts meaningful to children. Aspects of geography, agronomy, economics, astronomy, and entomology, and of literature and the arts are pertinent examples; philosophy and theology are examples of disciplines that would be less appropriate for school study. The development of thinking processes of various kinds would become the main goal of the curriculum. General strategies might be devised for fostering these processes at the different levels of the child's development of thinking capabilities. Some goals that should be considered and some possible general pedagogical strategies for their realization are listed:

THINKING-PROCESS GOALS	PEDAGOGICAL STRATEGIES
Learning to classify objects and events according to various critical attributes.	Question games with selected arrays of pictures or objects.
Searching for exemplars and testing the criticality of defining attributes.	Field work with observation and collection guides.
Validating categories by several means.	Dialogue with experts and/or source materials, interviewing.
Hypothesizing about relationships between concepts of objects and events.	Open-ended experimentation, problem finding and solving.
Developing generalizations by interrelating concepts.	Prepared environment with cues for finding relationships.
Incorporating generalizations and concepts into larger thematic structures.	Experimental "setup" for checking out previously derived generalizations in new contexts.

Orchestrating Personal Knowings with Knowns

Bruner calls the function of instruction that will bring together personal and established knowledge "orchestration."[22] He distills the processes of thinking used by adults into three forms of representation, three ways that man represents experience. These forms also probably appear sequentially in the child's development of thinking processes. As formulated by Bruner, they involve some of the same characteristics as Piaget's main stages of intellectual development.

1. *Enactive representation* by a set of actions appropriate for achieving a certain result. (A demonstration of athletic skills or manipulation of objects to show a mathematical concept, a sensorimotor memory)
2. *Ikonic representation* by a set of summary images or graphics that stand for a concept without defining it fully. (A diagram or picture, for example, a climate and product chart, an image in the mind)
3. *Symbolic representation* by a set of symbolic or logical propositions drawn from a symbolic system that is governed by rules or laws for forming and transforming propositions. (Language of propositions or expositions of ideas in the mind, spoken or written)[23]

In concrete terms, the stages are quite easy to pinpoint. Young children experiencing the same event—a country fair, for example—probably would not advance in their thinking beyond the enactive or ikonic representations of riding ponies or seeing tractors pull equipment. Older children, on the

[22] Jerome Bruner, "Needed: A Theory of Instruction," *Educational Leadership* (May 1963), p. 530.

[23] Jerome Bruner, "Some Theories on Instruction Illustrated with Reference to Mathematics," *Theories of Learning and Instruction*, NSSE Yearbook (Chicago: University of Chicago Press, 1964), p. 310. A full discussion of "representation" can be found in Bruner, Oliver, and Greenfield, Chaps. 1, 2.

other hand, are more likely to have built their own symbolic representations regarding the products being displayed, where they come from, and how they are made.

Bruner writes of the importance of language in bridging the gap between the concreteness of reality and the abstraction of thought:

> Once language becomes a medium for the translation of experience, there is a progressive release from immediacy. For language . . . has the new and powerful features of remoteness and arbitrariness: It permits productive combinatorial operations in the absence of what is represented.[24]

The teacher "orchestrates" the structured or disciplined representations that he presents to children with the probable representational modes of the children. An "economy" in the child's learning can be accomplished as concepts are clustered and generalizations are drawn that give him "power" to apply them in new but similar situations.[25] School can then be the beginning of a venture in thinking.

Testing Ideas against Reality

The following sample activities are suggested for assisting teachers in relating ideas about the "knowing" process to their own experience and those of their students in "coming to know."

Select a concept that has recently become a part of your thought system, such as "fusion" or "women's liberation" or "open education," and trace back your personal history with it. Why do you know much or little about it? What occasions brought it to your attention? Explain it to someone else and note in your formulation of it the cognitive, affective, and imagistic aspects. Ask youngsters to do the same regarding one or two of their recent concept acquisitions. Have a group sharing period on when and how they think they learned these concepts. Pick up a misconception stated in the classroom and probe to find out how and why it got established.

Construct a Piaget-type conservation-of-thinking experiment for children four- to eight-years-old, using different shapes of the same amount of modeling clay or the same amount of water poured into different glass shapes. Ask whether there is the same amount and why. Ask them to do the manipulations. Record

---

[24] Jerome Bruner, "Course of Cognitive Growth," *American Psychologist, 19*, No. 1 (January 1964), 14.

[25] For a discussion of "economy" and "power" in learning see the article by Bruner referred to above.

observations of behavior and language. Compare the results from students of different ages.

Play a game of "categories" with a circle of adults or youngsters in which each player in turn gives an example of a labeled category such as "fruit." Those who cannot think of another example are eliminated unless they can think of a legitimately related new category such as "trees"; the game continues until the examples of new group labels are exhausted within that family of categories. The last one to give a legitimate answer is the winner, and he gets to introduce a new category family.

With a group of adult students make a chart of all the disciplines of study under the labels Natural Sciences, Social Sciences, Humanities, and Applied Arts and Sciences. Note how scholars study in the different disciplines; use these descriptions as your criteria for deciding where those disciplines not readily categorized should go or if additional categorical labels are needed.

Turning Ideas into Practice

All of Part Two deals with application of language and thinking theory to curriculum development and teaching strategy. A few teaching examples are presented here to illustrate how the notions presented can be applied in the classroom.

Bring a novel object into class such as a new gadget, an unusual plant, a picture with incongruities in it, or an illustration of persons with enigmatic expressions in a social conflict situation. Set up an open-ended discussion and note the different perceptions and interests. From these decide what might be pursued further. Develop several activities that would involve youngsters in expanding the concepts. Then provide guidelines for ways that the learners might "present" their expanded ideas in different media or combinations of presentational forms.

Pose a problem such as one of the following, and ask youngsters to speculate on ways to find a solution and criteria for judging it. Two samples for discussion follow. (1) Tommy had cramps in his stomach one morning at school. When the teacher asked him what he had eaten recently he replied that for breakfast he had eaten two sausages and a bowl of cereal with strawberries and milk, and, the night before, some leftover fish and french-fried potatoes. What do you think caused Tommy's illness and why? What do you think the teacher should do and why? (2) The custodian has not been able to get grass to grow on a particular part of the school grounds. Ask the youngsters to list all possible reasons, and specu-late on which ones may be most significant and why.

In planning a social studies and/or science project think of all the disciplines of study that might be brought to bear on a study of the topics, issues, or questions. As you choose each discipline, state a generalization and the concepts in it that would need to be understood. Devise learning strategies to help youngsters reach the concepts and draw the generalizations. For example, take a study of "the school" as a societal institution, and describe its social structure and cultural milieu as a sociologist would; then view the school as an economist would in terms of input and output. After viewing it from the perspective of other possible disciplines, focus on developing an instructional plan that would involve those disciplines that would be most appropriate to the learners' backgrounds and capabilities.

GRAMMAR
IN
PERSPECTIVE

Language is perhaps the ideal example of one such powerful technology, with its power not only for communication but for coding "reality," for representing matters remote as well as immediate, and for doing all these things according to rules that permit us both to represent "reality" and to transform it by conventional yet appropriate rules. All of this depends on the external resources of a grammar, a lexicon and (likely as not) a supporting cast of speakers constituting the linguistic community.

JEROME BRUNER, Toward an Instructional Theory (Cambridge, Mass.: Harvard University Press, 1966). Cited in SATURDAY REVIEW, February 19, 1966, p. 71.

The important question is: What are the initial assumptions concerning the nature of language that the child brings to language learning, and how detailed and specific is the innate schema (the general definition of "grammar") that gradually becomes more explicit and differentiated as the child learns the language?

NOAM CHOMSKY, Aspects of the Theory of Syntax (Cambridge, Mass.: M.I.T. Press, 1965), p. 27.

TEACHING FOCUS

What are the rapidly changing views of English grammar? What different insights into language and language learning come from application of these views?

Does knowledge of grammar help the pupil in achieving language effectiveness? How does the teacher use such knowledge in fostering pupil growth in language effectiveness?

9

Which Grammar: Three Views

Traditional School Grammar: Grammar As Received

Over the centuries a tradition has grown to regard grammar, the structure and system of language, as *received*. A set of fixed rules was assumed to exist independently of actual linguistic behavior. Taught as prescriptive dogma in school, these rules were to be followed at all costs—language that deviated from such rules was labeled wrong, and teachers worked diligently to stamp it out.

The language ability that children developed before they came to school was largely ignored; it was deemed of little importance compared with the ability they would acquire in school through diligent study of correct, proper, prescriptive grammar.

This traditional *school* grammar (a curriculum) should not be confused with traditional grammar (old language scholarship). School grammar derived not from contemporary language study by grammarians but was borrowed from Latin School grammar in England at the time when the English language was introduced into the school curriculum. Previously, all learning had been in Latin and Greek, and English was assumed to be unworthy as a medium of learning and learned discourse; it was a "decayed" language to be fitted into the mold of Latin.

The major difficulty with the application of Latin grammar to English has been that Latin is an inflected language (one that depends heavily on word endings) and Modern English is no longer an inflected language, although Old English (Anglo-Saxon) was. The transfer of Latin grammar to English was made under the illusion that English is an inflected language. In fact, inflectional forms in Modern English are vestigial, the remnants of a long-lost central pattern. Most of the grammatical function formerly supplied by case endings has been supplanted by positional indication. In "the man killed the bear" the subject and object are made known by position in the sentence; put the man in the bear's place and you have another story. In an inflected language like Anglo-Saxon or Latin, you can put *the man* or *the bear* almost anywhere in the sentence, and the endings of the words make clear what the grammatical relationship is. There are many variations on the basic patterns of English sentences, but there is no doubt that Modern English grammar is different in kind, not only from Latin but also from its own inflected ancestor Old English. The subject, verb, object pattern is central and pervasive in Modern English. The imposition of Latin grammar on English preserved not only distorted views of English, but also the philosophical assumption that rules may exist even though they are not consistent with the realities of language use. These two facts had the effect of causing generations of teachers to persist in teaching generations of youth rules that were neither verifiable in language use nor productive of more effective language. "Thou shalt not end a sentence with a preposition" is one such rule; this particular dictum results in awkward sentences like: "That's the box in which it came" in place of more natural ones, such as "That's the box it came in."

Traditional school grammar requires elegant, clever, and intricately tenuous connections to be made between its system and the actual language. Perhaps the cause of reluctance to give it up is man's craving for authority and his need for definition of language in terms of where it came from rather than in terms of what it is. Strangely enough, the sole source is assumed to be Latin, and Latin grammar is accepted as universal grammar, despite the fact that English is a Germanic language and is a cousin of Latin rather than a descendant of it.

Language is like an organism in many ways; it changes and grows and is dependent on the human organism in society for its life—a kind of symbiosis. This is particularly true of the spoken, the sounded, language, which modern scholars have come to see as *the* language. The written form of a language is a limited and somewhat distorted representation of a much more extensive system. It is anchored securely to the page and is more conservative than the spoken language, but it departs from the sounded form at its own risk. When the two part company, we have the development of two or more languages, or we get a moribund stylized literature. Literature is geared to the living moment, and when language leaves behind psychological and sensuous embodiment in the human organism, it is not literature, as Dante well knew when he turned away from Latin to the vernacular.

section 2

Descriptive Linguistics: Grammar As Product

Out of a new scientific tradition in language study came a simple, prag-matic view of grammar. In this view language, as it is spoken, is subjected to careful empirical study. No preconceptions are allowed to interfere with this study. Grammar is the structure that the scientist finds as he describes language, a cultural product of human society. Rules, patterns, and systems do not exist independently of language behavior but in fact are attributes of that behavior. If a grammatical argument is to be decided, it is settled not by citing a rule but by studying language as it is spoken. Descriptive linguistics does not directly produce a school grammar. It produces, instead, a view of language as a human social product from which new curriculums can evolve.

It is important for educators to understand the descriptive linguist's viewpoint because the structure of language is pertinent, not only to the study of grammar but also to reading, writing, and general classroom dialogue. In the following section, some key concepts from descriptive linguistics are discussed. As these are used in subsequent chapters, some attempt will be made to redefine them.

Linguistic Assumptions

Descriptive linguists have devoted most of their study to oral language. Putting the emphasis on living, spoken language brings into sharp focus several facts of language:

Language is a code, using significant sounds as symbols. It has no meaning per se but is a means of transmitting meaning.
Language is systematic and orderly.
Language is dynamic and ever changing.

Viewed thus, language should and can be studied descriptively. Careful scientific description is the linguist's basic methodology. Concepts not derived directly from description must be tested against real language as it is spoken.

Phonemes: The Significant Sound Symbols

An important concept of descriptive linguistics is that the unitary symbols of language are not single sounds but are bundles of sounds per-ceived by the native user of the language as equivalent. The sounds have some key features in common and some differences that are not significant to users of the language. Any characteristic of sound variation can be significant or insignificant.

Out of the full range of available sounds that people can produce, each language develops a limited set of *phonemes, bundles of sounds perceived by language users as the same*, to use as symbols. Morse code is a very simple analogy to language. It uses variations in the duration of sounds and in the duration of silences between bursts of sound as unitary symbols. Linguists have developed a set of symbols to represent the phonemes of English. A symbol between two slash lines as /□/ is always a symbol for a phoneme, not for a letter. Phonemes are perceptual rather than real language units. Thus the language user learns to pay attention to significant contrasting features of sounds (those that matter in his language) and to ignore others. In studying perception in listening and reading it is important to remember that a language user learns what to pay attention to but equally important he learns what *not* to pay attention to. Through highly selective attention to only those sound features which are significant the language user functions efficiently.

Morphemes: The Meaning-Bearing Language Molecules

The phonemes of language have no meaning. But when they are combined in certain recurrent sequences they acquire the power to represent meaning. /b/, /æ/, and /t/ have no meanings, but together they form the *morpheme* /bæt/ (bat). This morpheme carries meaning that can be indicated in a dictionary. But the precise meaning will depend on its occurrence in the flow of language. Morphemes outside of context carry *lexical* meaning; full meaning must include *contextual* meaning. (The boy can *bat* very well. He uses a hickory *bat*. He is *bat* boy for the Tigers. His mother is an old *bat*. She has *bats* in her belfry.) In this example, at least two different homophones are represented by one morpheme. But even within one the precise meaning can be obtained only from the whole sentence.

There are two types of morphemes: free forms and combining forms. /bæt/ (bat) is a free form. /s/ is a combining form; with /bæt/ it adds an element of the meaning. *Bats* is different in meaning from *bat*. I *bat*, he *bats*, or I have one *bat*, he has two *bats*.

Syntax: The Systems of Language

Only when phonemes are combined into morphemes that are, in turn, formed into recurrent patterns and sequences does language become fully capable of transmitting meaning. The study of the system and structure of language is *syntax*. In English there are four important systems that operate.

PATTERN AND SENTENCE ORDER The most important system in English is that of pattern or word order. The following list of words can only be arranged in a limited number of ways: *horse, man, the, carried. The man carried the horse* or *The horse carried the man*. The first meaning is less likely but equally permissible. Any other arrangement would sound strange to a native speaker and would not be understood. The only way that the reader (or listener) can know whether man carried horse or horse carried man is by word order. As earlier indicated, some sentence patterns—subject-verb-object, for example—are very common. There is some disagreement among descriptive linguists about how many basic sentence patterns exist in English, but all the linguists agree the number is small, certainly less than ten.[1]

WORD CLASSES AND FUNCTIONS Descriptive linguists have not found the many parts of speech of traditional grammar in their description of English. They generally recognize four word classes that are defined by the positions in patterns that they can occupy. Some linguists do not mind using traditional terms: *noun, verb, adjective,* and *adverb* for these classes; others prefer new terms. Charles Fries merely numbers *1, 2, 3,* and *4.*[2]

Class 1 words fit into the slots represented by the blanks in this pattern: *The _____ carried the _____.*

Class 2 words fit into this slot: *The horse _____ the man,* or into this slot: *The horse _____ brown.*

Class 3 words fit into these slots: *The _____ horse carried the _____ man.* Class 3 words pattern with Class 1 words.

Class 4 words are more movable. They fit this slot: *The horse _____ carried the man.* But they may also be moved to other positions. That is, the pattern could be: *The horse easily carried the man,* or Easily, *the horse carried the man,* or *The horse carried the man easily.* Class 4 words pattern with Class 2 words.

In most cases groups of words may replace single words in these four pattern slots. *The white horse I have in mind could very easily carry the heaviest man you could find.* English is quite a flexible language; many words cannot be assigned to a class because their class depends on the slot in which they are found. *I have a bat. I bat right-handed. He is the bat boy.*

Descriptive linguists are perhaps more concerned with functions than with parts of speech. If the word or phrase performs a particular function—sentence subject, for example—that is what is significant.

INFLECTIONAL CHANGES Inflection is the system of changes in words to achieve changes in function or meaning. These changes in English are relatively infrequent as compared with other languages. However, some verb endings and auxiliaries that denote changes in tense and mood are still extant as are the plural and possessive endings in nouns. Most pronouns still retain inflectional forms. The changes can be internal as *mouse* to *mice*; or

[1] See Walter Loban, *The Language of Elementary School Children* (Champaign, Ill.: NCTE, 1963) for one delineation of basic patterns.
[2] Charles C. Fries, *The Structure of English* (New York: Harcourt, 1952).

they can be made by addition of suffixes, as *book* to *books, jump* to *jumping*. Nevertheless, formal inflections in English are minimal in contrast with most Indo-European languages.

FUNCTION OR STRUCTURE WORDS A fourth system consists *of a s*mall set *of* words *with* little *or no* lexical meaning *that* serve *as* syntactical signals. *Although* few *in* number, *these* words recur frequently *and* make *up a* large part *of the* volume *of* language. *The* words *in* italics *in this* paragraph *are* function words. Function words *may be* divided *into* operationally defined groups, *just as the* form classes *were* operationally defined. Here are some of the groups of function words, named according to function. The approximate number of words in each group (according to Fries) is also indicated.

NAME	EXAMPLE	NUMBER
Noun markers	*The* man came. (This group also includes possessives and cardinal numbers used in this slot. It is thus the only open-ended group of function words.)	
Verb markers	He *is* coming.	About 15
Negative	He is *not* coming.	1
Intensifier	He may be *very* tired.	25
Conjunctions	The man *and* woman are singing *and* dancing.	9
Phrase markers	They will come *into* the house.	12
Question markers	*When* will they come?	7
Clause markers	They will call *before* they come.	12

The names assigned these groups are perhaps self-explanatory. Each group of words is a category of structural signals that define and mark off the language structure. "*The* blobble *of* garfia *was* arkpuling *and* heboling *when his* wibfrid norped." The sentence doesn't make sense, but it has a ring of sensibility because the structure is all laid out by the function words. *Blobble* is unmistakably a noun just as *arkpul* and *hebol* are unmistakably verbs. The markers make it clear.

Intonation: The Melody and Rhythm of Language

Intonation is the system of "signals of pitch, stress, and juncture that clot the utterance into word groups that are meaning groups."[3] Speakers of English use very subtle variations in relative stress, pitch, and pausing or spacing between sounds to convey important variations in meaning. Is a certain toothpaste "proved (pause) effective" or "proved defective"? Why do rebels rebel? Is a blackboard always a black board? As an adult highly proficient in both oral and written language, you supply intonation in these

[3] Donald J. Lloyd and Harry Warfel, *American English in Its Cultural Setting* (New York: Knopf, 1956).

written sentences as you determine the grammatical structures and move to the meaning, although you may be hard pressed to pinpoint without considerable effort precisely *how* you comprehend. Similarly, you know when a person addressing you wants you to continue listening to him, to respond to a question, or to act on an instruction, although few of you who are not students of intonation could explain the patterns of pitch and stress that you subconsciously interpret and respond to.

Dialect: Language Variant of a Particular Speech Community

Every language is a family of variant forms—dialects of the language—each different in some consistent ways from all other variations but sufficiently alike so that they all may be considered one language. Everyone speaks a dialect; that is, there is no correct English that some speak while others speak inferior forms. If one dialect has more status in a wide language community than all others, this is entirely a social phenomenon and is not due to any intrinsic linguistic superiority. The equality of dialects is not a value judgment but is a fact of linguistic reality.

Every person develops his own language pattern (his idiolect) within the framework of a native language and a dialect. Although it falls within the dialect norms, the variance of it from the language of his community makes it uniquely his.

It is strange indeed that native speakers of any language are so little aware of the realities and complexities of the language they speak. Stranger still is their long acceptance of language rules and descriptions from traditional grammar books, which correspond very little to the language as it rolls off their lips and as they hear it spoken. The study of formal grammar has contributed somewhat to scholarly knowledge about language and to rhetoric, but it is also surprising that grammarians and philologists have been so unaware of the living world of language.

section 3

Transformational-Generative Linguistics: Grammar As Process

The descriptive linguist's work begins with a transcription of language as he finds it. He seeks system within the linguistic product. In recent years another major school of linguists has devoted itself to the study of the process by which the linguistic product is generated.

Every speaker of a language can generate an almost infinite number of sentences in his language, many of which he has neither heard nor uttered before. Yet he and other speakers of the language can easily differentiate sentences that are acceptable in the language from sentences that are not acceptable. These linguists reason that while the number of acceptable sentences in a language is very large, the speaker's generative process must be governed by a much smaller number of rules.

Transformations

The rules that the speaker masters enable him to produce novel sentences that will be understood by other speakers because they also are able to use the rules. The generative grammarian claims that the descriptive linguist is concerned only with the surface structure of language, the end-product of the linguistic process, while he considers that each utterance also has a deep or underlying structure. From this deep structure the surface structure is derived through a series of transformations that result from the application of obligatory and optional transformational rules. The process is illustrated in this example:

> Tom was hit by the ball.
> The ball hit Tom.

These sentences, although they differ in the surface structure, have the same deep structure. When the passive transformation rule is applied to the deep structure (*The ball hit Tom*), it results after several changes in the passive surface structure. *Tom* moves to the position of the sentence subject, the verb *hit* takes the auxiliary *was,* and *ball* becomes the agent that *by* introduces. A further transformation could produce the surface structure *Tom was hit*. Although an agent is not present in this surface structure (a deletion transformation has removed it), it is present in the deep structure: (*Something*) *hit Tom*. This, by passive transformation, becomes *Tom was hit by something* and then by deletion becomes *Tom was hit*. A question transformation could produce another surface structure: *Was Tom hit?* This still has the deep structure: (*Something*) *hit Tom*.

Transformation often results in compact, economical surface structures from multiple deep structures. *Mary saw the boy who hit Tom* is a surface structure that combines two deep structure sentences: *Mary saw the boy* and *The boy hit Tom*. A relative clause transformation transforms the latter sentence into a relative clause and embeds it in the surface structure noun phrase *the boy who hit Tom.*

Adjectives are regarded by transformational grammarians as derived from deep structure sentences. In *The little boy hit Tom*, a deep structure sentence, *The boy is little* is embedded in the noun phrase *The little boy*. A relative clause transformation could have produced *The boy who is little hit Tom.* A further transformation, the adjective transformation, deletes *who is* and places the adjective before the noun.

Meaning is more significant to the work of the generative-transformational linguist than it is to the descriptive linguist. Transformational grammar adds introspection and inference to the tools of the linguist. He is not satisfied to work with what he can observe; he seeks to go beyond linguistic *performance* to *competence*. He is interested not only in what a speaker does but also in what he knows that makes it possible for him to do what he does.

Value of Linguistics

It should be clear that looking at language as a product and looking at it as a process are not intrinsically conflicting views. The information and insight gained can be complementary and not contradictory. Further, each may be useful for specific purposes and applications. It may be quite useful to look at differences between dialects descriptively, because breakdowns in communication may occur because of differences in phonemes, intonation, and inflectional suffixes (or lack of them), as well as rule differences. On the other hand, a generative view may be very useful in dealing with comprehension problems in reading that result from the grammatical complexity of a noun phrase involving adjectives.

Generative semanticists have moved beyond concern for grammar to concern for meaning itself as it underlies language use. Nevertheless, there has been considerable controversy over these two schools of linguistics and over the knowledge they have produced. Coupling either of them with psychological schools of thought tends to increase the controversy. Descriptive linguistics, because it concerns itself with observed behavior, is often combined with behavioral psychology in research and applications to learning. Cognitive psychologists, themselves concerned with the process by which knowledge is acquired, have frequently moved toward a generative-transformational theory. Other combinations are also possible. At present, transformational linguistics is in the most dynamic state. Its theory is constantly evolving. For example, Noam Chomsky, the leading spokesman for this school, published a book in 1965[4] that made many statements in his pace-setting 1957 book[5] obsolete.

Much of what modern linguists produce, as they move toward a more perfect understanding of how language works, will be of limited direct utility to education. The theory, however, will form the bases for the content of instructional sequences that deal with how language works. The greatest contribution that linguistics will make, particularly as it is linked with psy-

[4] Noam Chomsky, *Aspects of the Theory of Syntax* (Cambridge, Mass.: M.I.T. Press, 1965).
[5] Noam Chomsky, *Syntactic Structures* (The Hague: Mouton, 1957).

chology, is in the insights it will provide into the developing child as a user of language. In this important area *language as process* will be most relevant, and language as the product of this process will be of lesser importance. As teachers seek to help learners become more effective users of language, their success will be contingent to a great degree on the extent to which they understand language processes. The generative-transformational view of language would seem to be the most useful for teachers to take, because the child is constantly generating new transformations as he attempts to describe and come to terms with his world. Both idiolect and dialect will expand and become more effective language tools as teachers and parents see the generative possibilities of a child's language. In designing curriculums it will be most useful to move beyond attempts to change linguistic behavior to changes in the basic underlying language competence of developing learners.

In teaching reading and listening, teachers seek to help the learner get from a surface representation through an underlying structure to meaning. In teaching speaking and writing, teachers strive to help the learner formulate his thoughts, generate underlying language structure, and then produce a surface representation which will express the message clearly enough that it will be comprehensible to his readers or listeners. In all this the teacher must focus on the process while the learner concerns himself primarily with communication.

10

Why Study Grammar?

By what means can communication skills be taught? I agree . . . that it is extremely improbable that they should be affected at all by instruction in explicit grammar, whether that grammar be traditional or transformational circa 1958, or transformational circa 1965, or on the transformational frontier. Study of the theory of language is probably irrelevant to the development of skill in the use of the language.[1]

Traditionally language instruction has had three broad goals, all of which have become intertwined in the school curriculum: (1) To help children become more effective language users; (2) to influence children to speak in socially preferred ways; and (3) to provide children with knowledge and terminology so that they may understand and discuss how language works.

The relationship of grammar study to the last set of purposes is the most obvious and the least open to debate. Language, like any other aspect of human interest and activity, is worthy of and amendable to study. The study of language structure can be a fascinating part of any curriculum, particularly because learners can regard themselves as the resources. They have learned to speak the language. They can gain much insight into how language works by carefully observing and examining their own use of language.

[1] Roger Brown in James Moffett, *Teaching the Universe of Discourse* (Boston: Houghton Mifflin, 1968), p. vii.

185

It is also obvious that the schools are obligated to make available to learners the most modern and up-to-date insights, concepts, and information about language. In such a dynamic period of language study as this one, it is not conceivable that schools can be content to present a closed and static system, whether that system is a received one or one that views language as a product or a process. Even young children cannot be offered misconceptions in the name of simplicity.

The proportionate amount of time and effort devoted to the study of language for its own sake is a good deal more open to question. Here, several considerations are important, including:

> the importance of this set of purposes as compared to the other language goals of the school;
> the ease of acquisition of the knowledge;
> the general need for such knowledge among elementary-school age children;
> the degree to which the knowledge achieved will relate to or bring about the achievement of the other goals.

The building of more effective language is a much greater concern in the competition for time and energy in the school day. Further, a year's intensive study of grammar in junior high school would probably be more productive than several years of time spent in earlier grades. Such terminology as is needed in discussing compositions and other forms of language activity can be introduced in the elementary school as they are needed.

A few basic grammatical concepts should be the goal in the elementary grades. Here are some examples:

> Language is systematic.
> Language change is continuous and inevitable.
> There are many forms of English in current use.
> Speakers of a language use its rules as they speak.

A speaker can study his own language to discover the rules he is using. Consideration of the last item requires more careful discussion. It seems so logical to say that learning about grammar will influence the effectiveness of language use and will produce more socially preferred language; but we must clearly separate what is effective language from what carries high social status. Effective language is language that can be used most successfully in expression and communication. It needs to be flexible, rich, and variable so that the user may adjust it easily to the demands of particular situations. The language that is frequently called proper language tends to be inflexible, narrowly correct, and particularly confining for a language user whose native dialect is divergent from it. Even for the fortunate child whose dialect comes close to the preferred form, it will be necessary for him to achieve a flexible ease in using his language if he is to be fully effective in the varied communicative situations of modern life.

Grammar Study As a Means of
Achieving More Effective Language

Previously, the lack of a substantive base for prescriptive grammar was explored; also considered was the failure of received grammar as presented in standard school texts to explain adequately the language as it really exists. Interestingly, it was not the advent of scientific linguistics or the realization of the inaccuracy of traditional school grammar that caused educators to be dissatisfied with direct instruction in grammar. What bothered teachers was that this instruction did not work. It did not achieve any of its significant objectives. Children simply did not apply what they had been taught.

Teachers became aware that many pupils, confronted in each grade with nouns, verbs, and other elements of grammar, were often unable to learn anything they could retain from grade to grade. Whether grammar was taught directly or by controlled induction, it was necessary to start over again for most pupils in each successive grade in elementary school. Then, in junior high school, and again in senior high school, the curriculum started from the beginning. Unhappily, it could not be assumed, for most children, that any grammar had been learned in prior education. Teachers also noted that some students, after repeated exposure, had indeed mastered the grammar as measured by achievement tests, but this mastery had no noticeable effect on the everyday language of the children. Undaunted, the children persisted in using their "quaint" personal grammar in their routine communications with each other in and out of the classroom. Teachers painfully realized that by emphasizing grammar instruction, they failed to improve oral language and written composition and, in fact, they were actually interfering with its improvement. Some children became frustrated and intimidated; for them the best solution was to say and write as little as possible. Others learned to substitute stiffly correct phrases and constructions for colorful natural ones.

Research on Teaching Grammar

Dissatisfaction with the results of instruction in school grammar was reinforced by the findings of grammar research, which had finally begun to investigate the cherished beliefs of educators about the reasons for such instruction. The research corroborated what teachers had suspected. Here is a catalogue of beliefs about the value of instruction in standard grammar and usage that were questioned by substantial research findings:

Belief: The study of grammar is good for the mental discipline of the pupil. In 1913, Briggs tested nine typical claims for mental discipline value of grammar instruction and found no improvement.[2]

---

[2] John R. Searles and G. Robert Carlsen, "English," *Encyclopedia of Educational Research* (New York: Macmillan, 1960), p. 459.

Belief: Grammar study produces transfer of learning to other subjects. Studies by Rice in 1903, Boreas in 1917, and Bender in 1935 showed no evidence to support this belief.[3]

Belief: Knowledge of traditional grammar improves the ability of children to interpret literature. Studies by Hoyt in 1906 and Rapeer in 1913 found no transfer at all.[4]

Belief: When school grammar is learned well, it remains a useful tool. Macauley tested seniors in Scottish schools who had passed stiff tests on grammar as part of the 11 plus examinations that they took when they entered the schools. He found that their knowledge of school grammar had virtually evaporated.[5]

Belief: Knowledge of school grammar aids in reading comprehension. Greene found no important relationship between the amount of grammatical information possessed and the ability to read and comprehend sentences.[6]

Belief: Ability to cite grammatical rules improves grammar in written expression. The research of Bender in 1935 and Catherwood in 1932 says no.[7]

Belief: Grammar instruction is the best approach to teaching sentence structure. In 1934, Ellen Frogner demonstrated that children taught sentence structure by thoughtful analysis of their own writing rather than by direct grammar instruction learned better. The time spent on grammar instruction could have been better used in letting children write, she concluded. It was wasted time as far as improving sentence structure was concerned.[8]

Belief: School grammar is the best approach to teaching punctuation. Evans showed in 1939 that it was far more effective to teach punctuation by example as an aid to comprehension than to teach rules of grammar first.[9]

Belief: When children can cite grammatical rules, they apply them. Segal and Barr demonstrated in 1923 that there is no more correlation between formal and applied than between two unrelated topics.[10]

Belief: Knowledge of school grammar reduces errors in usage. In 1916, Diebel and Sears showed that eighth-graders, after years of grammar instruction, made more errors in using pronouns than children in lower grades.[11]

Belief: Grammarians agree on what is and what is not standard English. Perhaps the cruelest blow of all was dealt by the 1938 research of Marckwardt and Walcott. They found great disagreement about what is correct

---

[3] J. J. DeBoer, "Grammar in Language Teaching," *Elementary English, 36,* No. 6 (October 1959).

[4] Searles and Carlsen, p. 460.

[5] Searles and Carlsen, p. 460.

[6] Harry Greene, "Direct versus Formal Methods in Elementary English," *Elementary English Review, 24* (1947), 273–285.

[7] DeBoer, p. 415.

[8] Ellen Frogner, "Grammar Approach versus Thought Approach in Teaching Sentence Struceure," *English Journal, 28* (1934), p. 578.

[9] DeBoer, p. 418.

[10] DeBoer, p. 414.

[11] Searles and Carlsen, p. 460.

and incorrect among a group of experts on English grammar and usage. Further, these researchers found that many usages considered substandard by a majority of these experts were labeled correct by authorities such as the Oxford Dictionary.[12]

School grammar instruction is ineffective. Many children have learned to write effectively while being taught by grammar, but probably more have learned in spite of it rather than because of it.

Language use may have been improved by a study of school grammar in some instances because the grammatical question points to the rhetorical and semantic problem in language. However, this is an exercise more for language scholars than for students.

The Value of Teaching Linguistically Valid Grammar

An important question, as yet unanswered, is whether the content of prescriptive grammar instruction alone was at fault, or whether the type of grammar and the teaching strategy was also to blame. Was traditional school grammar instruction a failure because it was inaccurate, or did it fail also because children do not learn how to use language through formal instruction in its grammar? Loban states flatly, "Since formal instruction in grammar, whether linguistic or traditional, seems to be an ineffective method of improving expression at this level of development, *one can conclude that elementary pupils need many opportunities to grapple with their own thought in situations where they have someone to whom they wish to communicate successfully* [emphasis added]."[13]

Little evidence exists of the value of grammar instruction based on linguistics. Material appropriate to use in school has only recently become available, and careful studies have yet to be conducted that compare the value of formal instruction in traditional and linguistically accurate grammar but vary only the content.

Theoretically, a new *prescriptive* grammar could be evolved based on descriptive linguistic studies or on generative rules. A new prescriptive grammar would be superior to traditional grammar in that it would be based on English rather than on Greek and Latin. It would, however, still share several faults with traditional grammar:

1. Because language is constantly changing, any prescriptive grammar will lag behind and be somewhat out of step with linguistic reality.
2. Unless a separate grammar is developed for every major dialect, any

[12] Albert Marckwardt and Fred Walcott, *Facts about Current English Usage*, Monograph No. 7, NCTE, 1938.

[13] Walter Loban, *The Language of Elementary School Children* (Champaign, Ill.: NCTE, 1963), p. 88.

standard grammar will be inconsistent to some degree with the language of many people. (This is a problem evident in new linguistically based English text series.)

3. The new grammar would still need to deal with the anomalies of language, instances where the rules do not work or where they become complex. It is possible that no system can completely explain the structure of living language. At any rate no current system does.

Most proposals for teaching modern linguistic grammar have stressed the use of controlled induction, a system in which rules are discovered in highly controlled situations. One elementary text workbook series presents the structure of language, sentence patterns, and spelling patterns. A group of parallel sentences is presented.

It is a <u>cat</u>.
It is a <u>man</u>.
It is a <u>chair</u>.[14]

Function is emphasized. The underlined words are color-cued. The child is encouraged to notice the words that have the same function. Later he is asked to select words from a group of words that can fit a position in a pattern. In early grades no labels are attached to such functions. Later, however, terms are introduced, and generalizations are stated after they presumably have been *discovered* by the children. Spelling and grammar are linked in the program because both are regarded as aids to effective written expression.

Another contemporary English program is almost entirely devoted to the deductive teaching of transformational grammar.[15] Paul Roberts, author of the Roberts series, indicates that the knowledge presented will make the students who use it better writers. Yet no evidence exists from research to support that claim. Its approach is based on the use of literary selections, notably poetry, as a source of examples, but its primary format involves the presentation of a grammatical rule or definition and the presentation of examples to illustrate it. More examples are presented as exercises for the students to use in demonstrating their knowledge of the rule. Perhaps because of the complexity of definitions in transformational terms, the definitions used in the Roberts series are either traditional—"Particular names of persons are proper nouns" (Book 4, p. 70) and "Tense is a word that means time" (p. 188)—or they are based on examples—"Words like these (everyone or somebody or nothing) are called indefinite pronouns."

Despite the tentativeness of any contemporary grammar, there is a need for children to understand how their language system works, as there is a need to know how their number system works. If the school can establish

[14] Morton Botel, *Spelling and Writing Patterns* (Chicago: Follett, 1964), p. 10.
[15] Paul Roberts, *The Roberts English Series* (New York: Harcourt, 1966).

a real purpose for grammar instruction, it could then either choose one of the three following strategies to bring about the learning it seeks or develop a program mixing all three.

1. *The Deductive Strategy.* A list of rules is taught to each child. These are the grammatical generalizations of the language. The methods may vary, but the basic assumption is that learning is a matter of being told something.

2. *The Controlled Inductive Strategy.* The child is exposed to many examples that apply each grammatical generalization. These examples are carefully selected and grouped. Exceptions may be presented as contrasts. The child is led to arrive at the rules and generalizations of grammar inductively through the controlled language experiences.

3. *The Uncontrolled Inductive Strategy.* No attempt is made to teach rules or to control the language experiences of the children. It is assumed that the process of self-induction of the structure of language that took place in preschool language learning will continue in school. No special time, materials, or exercises are provided to assist in the self-induction. There are many opportunities to use language, both oral and written. At times, children may be encouraged to discuss and formulate what they have discovered about the structure of language.

In mixing strategies, for example, some rules may be taught (deductive method), while others are developed through controlled induction. This is, in fact, the approach to teaching grammar and usage that has become most common in the last half century.

When the deductive strategy is used, after rules are taught exercises are provided so that the child may have practice in the application of the rule and may demonstrate his ability to apply the rule. When an error is detected in exercises or in the oral or written expression of the child, the rule is cited as an explanation of what is wrong.

In the controlled induction strategy, the child is provided with selected examples of exercises designed to lead him to the conclusion. Borderline or confusing examples are avoided, so that the child is led, for example, to form the generalization that double negatives are unacceptable. After the generalization is achieved, additional exercises are provided to confirm the generalization and to provide opportunity for the learner to demonstrate his attainment.

In the deductive strategy exceptions to the rule are taught as subrules with suitable lists of items that illustrate each exception. In controlled induction the learner is led, probably after the main generalization is acquired, to arrive at the parameters of application and the areas in which the rule is not applicable.

Programmed learning utilizes controlled induction for the most part. A series of generalizations is arranged in a sequence. Then a series of exercises is provided, so that the learner is carefully led to arrive at each generalization. By being continually required to choose correct answers in preference to incorrect ones, the learner uncovers the full extent of applicability of each generalization. Of course, in programmed learning there is only *one* right answer at any time.

Uncontrolled induction in a pure form utilizes no selection of examples or exercises. In fact, one could not expect a child to discover the latent structure of language on his own unless he had wide experience with a full range of language experience. Any tampering with language, or simplification of language, might cause the learner to adopt generalizations that are not applicable except in the limited sphere.

The deductive, controlled inductive, and mixed strategies, require some absolutes, because the rules are either taught directly or carefully induced. The absolutes of prescriptive grammar lend themselves well to these strategies, in the sense that one can present a neat curricular package of prescriptive grammar.

Research evidence exists that controlled induction is more effective in teaching grammar than the deductive approach, but there is no evidence yet that such knowledge, however accurate it may be, actually improves the effectiveness of the child's language. This objective can be achieved more surely if primary emphasis in the school program is on *expanding the language of learners to better serve their communicative needs.*

Inquiry: Letting the Questions Control the Inductive Process

Inquiry is an approach to learning that organizes around key questions that the learners seek to answer through experimentation and through whatever techniques are available. It has been advocated in science and social studies because it not only offers a highly motivating way of organizing the content but also lets the learners operate like scientists and scholars do in investigating questions in their disciplines. The learner acquires not only concepts but also a sense of the structure of the discipline and an understanding of its methods.

Language study, particularly grammar, is an excellent subject for the use of inquiry methods. Because every learner has already acquired control over at least one dialect of one language, he is his own resource. He can, as linguists do, collect his data from within his own language groups, family, friends, and class. He can examine his own language, hitherto the least used resource in school grammar study. He can compare and contrast language forms heard in his class, in the community, on trips, in the mass media, in business, and in forms used in "old fashioned" literature. Although language varies, the universal characteristics of language (for example, that it has system) are present in all language, including his own. Further, what he learns provides him with insight into how language works in general, but it also helps him see specifically how *his* language works.

Inquiry starts not with rules or sets of preselected sentences but with questions. At the simplest level is a "how come" question, which even a six-year-old can formulate. "How come we say 'new, red car,' but we never say 'red new car'?". In such inquiry, the pupils may ask themselves what other sequences are possible. They may discover that strings of words in front of words like *car* say something about *car*. They may categorize these describing words (if the term *adjective* is needed it will be introduced after the concept is already shaped by inquiry) as those that show age, color, size, condition, and so on. In the process of deciding what rules are used by class members in ordering adjectives, they begin to get the more general proposition that users of language are following rules that they have learned. They continually discover that language has order to it. They find that words and phrases are often interchangeable in recurrent language patterns. The specific knowledge gained is, of course, never as important as the generalizations it leads to; and, therefore, any language inquiry is a useful base for building these generalizations.

Upper elementary or junior high school pupils might well undertake the construction of a descriptive grammar for their own dialects or undertake an inquiry into the comparative use of verb forms in their community. Inquiry need not be confined to grammar, of course; in fact, language inquiry is likely to touch numerous dimensions of language because it stems from questions that are not always neatly classified. Youngsters might become curious about the use of idioms or slang by themselves, their parents, and their grandparents. In the course of their investigation, they may find changing forms in phonology, vocabulary, and grammar.

Inquiry has some drawbacks that sometimes discourage teachers. Its direction is often neither predictable nor controllable. Examples in language data are likely to be found that contradict the concepts that the teacher holds or that do not easily fit the rules he knows. In many cases the inquiry will lead into unsettled areas where even the most modern, authoritative references disagree or offer no help. So much incidental learning may take place that it is difficult for the teacher to measure and evaluate it. And the teacher must trade the role of language judge for that of co-researcher. *Teachers who have used inquiry, on the other hand, find that their pupils no longer regard language study as dull and uninteresting, because they are dealing with their own living language.*

Testing Ideas against Reality

Leave a tape recorder running as a group of teachers or college students enter a room. Listen to the tape and make a list of grammatical structures and usage which don't fit traditional grammatical beliefs.

Ask a junior high school group of pupils to put two words, one for color and one for age, in these slots: I bought a _____ _____ car. Have each one decide whether color comes before age (red new) or age before color (old blue). Then try other pairs (age–type) (type–name) or triads (old red Ford), (blue Ford convertible), and so on. Derive a rule for adjective order.

Say to a three- to five-year-old child, "When I stop, tell me what comes next." Then say: "I walked down the _____." Try a series of such sentence beginnings and note ability of children to supply gramatically appropriate completions.

Turning Ideas into Practice

Conduct a study of how questions are formed in English. Teams might gather data as to how questions begin, end, and so on, from several different sources and report their findings to the class. Some data sources: questions in science, math, and social-studies textbooks.

Tape a dialogue between two pupils standing back to back who must get a description of each other by asking questions.

Keep a list of questions teachers ask during a day.

Pupils should be able to conclude that among other things, questions often begin with who, what, when, where, how, why, and which. They are likely to discover that a form of be or other auxiliary verb often starts a question and that the question "Is he going?" corresponds to the statement "He is going." The special use of DO in such questions may also turn up.

Take a paragraph from a book and ask pupils to think of other ways to say the same thing using, in turn, more sentences, fewer sentences, more words, and then fewer words.

Have pupils rewrite the dialogue from a play scene as a narrative using direct and indirect quotes.

For an alternative exercise, take the dialogue from a story and turn it into a comic strip with balloons for each character's statements.

ORAL
AND WRITTEN
COMMUNICATION

[The educative problem] is to direct pupils' oral
and written speech, used primarily for practical
and social ends, so that gradually it shall become
a conscious tool of conveying knowledge and
assisting thought.

JOHN DEWEY, How We Think
(Boston: Heath, 1933), p. 239.

We know very little about the origin of human
speech but it is probably safe to assume that men
found pleasure as well as use in it from the very
beginning. Like other means to make life
increasingly bearable in a practical way, it was
adapted also to aesthetic satisfactions. Pitch and
stress, qualities of vowel and consonant, tempo
and dynamics were present in spoken sentences
and offered the raw materials for artistic creation.
We may assume that as long as men have been
human they have been aware that one way

of saying a thing might be more pleasing
than another. . . .

MARGARET SCHLAUCH, The Gift of Language
(New York: Dover, 1955), p. 227.

Words have in great part been responsible for
the increase in man's control over the things
about him. But man is frequently overcome by
his words. This is because not one of us
is completely free from the error of looking
on words as if they had a separate existence,
with strange powers of acting by themselves.
We are in far less danger of making this error
if we keep clearly before our minds the order
of the three parts of this chain: Referent—Thought—
Symbol.

HUGH WALPOLE, Semantics
(New York: Norton, 1941), p. 104.

TEACHING FOCUS

What does artistry in communication imply, and how can
young people be led toward it in the various forms of oral
and written language?

Given the differences between speech-thought and written
thought, what can teachers do to aid youngsters in transforming their inner speech-thoughts to written communication
patterns?

How can a teacher tie his writing activities into the psychic
and imaginative world of young people?

What practices for developing power in literacy skills can
teachers use that are consistent with knowledge of how
language actually works?

11

Language and Meaning
in Composition

Language and Reality

The structure of a particular language causes speakers of it to perceive and conceptualize their total environment in a certain way. Language is a conventional system for representing reality. There is no necessary connection between language and reality, the word and the thing; the object English-speakers call table is just as well called *la mesa* and *der Tisch*. This is not to say that a connection between the object and some conventional means of symbolizing and manipulating it is not necessary. A name, obviously, is necessary. Even so, the name is not one of the actual properties of the object. Language represents a system parallel to reality, and organizes its own relationships to represent those of reality, but language and reality never touch. Taken as a whole, the one corresponds to the other and tries to keep its internal system in harmony with it.

Language and Magic

Because originally there were no name tags on things, man had to invent names, and he built an elaborate structure that required a complex plan. In the beginning, man thought of words and word patterns as magic for controlling nature and events. One of the fundamental assumptions of the myth-making consciousness itself is the notion that name and essence bear a necessary and internal relation to each other, that the name does not merely denote but actually *is* the essence of its object, that the potency of the real thing is contained in the name.[1] A later age called this superstitious and misguided. Today, we see it as figuratively true. Although man could not make the rains come with chants or drive his enemies away with verbal spells, his language did provide a means for controlling more and more of nature.

Reference in Language

It is possible to view an object and a word as two sides of a triangle, the third side of which is the mind of man, which joins the word and the object (referent). Man experiences the object (a tree, for example) in many contexts. At some point he gets a concept in which many percepts participate. At some stage the process seems to reverse itself. The name of a thing (concept label) gains a force that makes it seem governing and all-powerful. It can turn out as many "trees" as it likes.

Endless arguments can go on as to whether a window-hanging is a curtain or a drape. A more fruitful discussion might begin with the statement that it is simply some thing, and then reasons for using one word or another in reference to it could be discussed historically, socially, psychologically, statistically, or in some other useful way.

Semantics

Semantics is a systematic study of the meaning in language. It attempts to explain the relationship between a symbol and its particular referent in the environment of things and happenings. Definitions according to context (physical, psychological, and symbolic) and the effects of metaphorical expansions (for example, *hot* to *hothead*) are among the concerns of the semanticist. Semantics is interested in the *senses* of words and is of value because it gives a better knowledge of what one is doing every time one makes use of language.[2]

Semantics tends to be analytical, but language does not always lend itself to analysis. Sometimes it is synthetic; at other times it operates on assumptions that cannot be dispensed with, without some adequate substitute. Semantics represents a way of looking at language, a valuable way of keeping it in check when it wanders in a detrimental way, but it is not the final court of appeal in all cases.

[1] Ernst Cassirer, *Language and Myth* (New York: Dover, 1946), p. 3.
[2] Hugh Walpole, *Semantics: The Nature of Words and Their Meanings* (New York: Norton, 1941), p. 34.

The Range of Language

Ogden and Richards, in *The Meaning of Meaning*,[3] did general language a service by making discourse more precise; however, in that work and particularly in *Principles of Literary Criticism*[4] and *Science and Poetry*,[5] Richards unnecessarily restricted the range of language. In refining the use of discourse, he neglected other linguistic modes and set them apart from the patterns of intelligibility. Poetry, for example, was to be considered psychologically soothing but not a carrier of signification other than its incidental discursive content. Richards assumed that language was polarized into two forms, either emotive or referential, and that it moved in either one direction or the other.

Emotive: ◄————————————————————► *Referential:*
Poetry, oratory,   Scientific statements, legal
cries of anger or joy   documents, giving directions

Recently, linguists have said this kind of system, which imposes opposites on reality, is a specific culture-bound manifestation of the Western world and its languages. In our language (and thinking) there are endless pairs of opposites: good, bad; hot, cold; fast, slow; short, tall. People tend to impose an either-or pattern that is sometimes more psychological than "logical." It is not that this sort of system is wrong but that it just one possible way of looking at things.

Philip Wheelwright in an extremely interesting book[6] has rebutted this thesis of Richards (and others) most effectively. He says the opposite of *referential* is not *emotive* but *nonreferential* and that two dimensions are involved, as represented in Figure 1 (p. 200).

The most significant thing about Figure 1 is that it adequately represents the literary use of language and catches the quality of the central human experience, whereas a purely discursive approach denies the possibility of a qualitative appraisal, through language, of the most significant things in life. At least two variables are brought into play to represent a very complex thread of definition. That the emotive in language should not violate the patterns of intelligibility is important, but it is also important that the strictly referential should not be used to explain away the emotive. The emotive has a life of its own, and if the purely referential is used as the final and absolute basis of linguistic analysis, then the separation of the last

[3] Charles K. Ogden and Ivor A. Richards, *The Meaning of Meaning* (New York: Harcourt, 1948).

[4] Ivor A. Richards, *Principles of Literary Criticism* (New York: Harcourt, 1966).

[5] Ivor A. Richards, *Science and Poetry* (New York: Norton, 1926).

[6] Philip Wheelwright, *The Burning Fountain* (Bloomington, Ind.: Indiana University Press, 1954).

FIGURE 1   Language representation.

element that reveals total structure will reveal also that life itself has quietly slipped away and evaded the search for the life-principle.

Wheelwright's diagram in Figure 1 indicates that literary language lies in the quadrant formed between the referential and emotive lines. Things do not exist in isolation in life, and in certain areas a reductive process produces distortion. Organic patterns must be caught in context (although analysis can be helpful, as long as it is realized that what is taken apart must be put together again). A precise, one-at-a-time reference is not appropriate in many areas, even in reference to the concrete. Individual threads in the web of words with which man tries to catch the world catch nothing when taken singly. Literary language must not be merely emotive, nor purely referential, for stress of one at the expense of the other results in distortion.

It is important, of course, to consider the aims of the language in any situation. The purpose of literature is to represent emotional knowledge and to represent intelligible patterns of being. In a great novel such as *Moby Dick*, for example, both sense about life and feeling for life are manifested. An intellectual analysis of man's relation to powerful emotional forces is combined with strong affective responses to them. Among the classics the Greek tragedies present compressed and highly emotional statements of man's tragic predicament that attempt to both explain and evoke.

One needs to be aware of the effects of emotive language in matters of thinking and argument. It can persuade, can even distort an idea beyond its reference in reality, as can be seen in propaganda. The language of reasoning must be referential. The language of judgment involves expression of values and attitudes that require emotive statement in addition to facts.

COMMUNICATION. The difficulty with a linear approach to language in communication is that it seems to describe language as lacking in psycho-sensuous substructure. It also makes language a matter of duration without consideration of simultaneity and instantaneous feedback. A basic consideration of the nature of language indicates that the message is made up of language *before* it is encoded. The encoding can only be a process of formalizing or projecting what is already shaped into words, even at the preconscious level. The conventional concept of "noise" as disruption in communication leaves much to be desired in terms of overall communication. It makes sense only in a "telephone wire" concept of communication. "Noise" should be seen as a part of context, which is not merely the sentence or linear communication in which a word appears, but the total linguistic milieu, including paralanguage and the kinesthetic participation of the human organism.

Perhaps the biggest problem in accepting a narrow concept of communication is that of explaining communication with yourself (reflective thinking) and the vocative projection of self (speaking out to the world whether or not an answer comes back). If we accept communication theory as an attempt to schematize for purposes of clarification, with the understanding that what is taken apart must be put back together, then it can be helpful. An alternative is to make the concept of communication inclusive enough to encompass self-communication and communication with the world at large. Even so, we must have something to communicate, and what we have is made of words and shaped with syntax; reality itself is grasped through the symbolic process of language.

Language Brings Meaning to One's World

The vigorous application of semantics or communication theory to language as a discipline is extremely valuable; to employ it indiscriminately and as a dialectic system for reducing areas of signification outside its province, or for chopping down the necessary *a priori* of language—that is another matter. *Language tenders meaning when it is both referential and emotive.* In a consideration of thinking, both these possibilities need to be remembered. It is the thinking that is engendered between referent, sign, and symbol that is crucial to the educational process.

> The two central skills, ability to name instances and ability to react to the name as a sign of an instance, are both created by experience of the name in association with instances of the referent category. This is an experience that comes early to all children and these are skills that adults everywhere look for as evidence of the comprehension of linguistic forms. The reference-making procedure and the two abilities it creates are central to the language game.[7]

By evoking both affective and intellectual reactions, language can carry full and rich response to the world, and be more than mere description. This

---

[7] Roger Brown, *Words and Things: An Introduction to Language* (New York: Free Press, 1958), p. 107.

remarkable human potential for composing in language, however, is hardly touched upon in school, considering the wide range of possibilities.

Composing in Language

Although few people compose full-fledged literary works, everyone uses literary language and literary techniques constantly. Literary composition is essentially an act of discovery, often preceded by a chance suggestion from the total context in which man moves. From the germ, a poem or story or novel may grow. The writer must make himself receptive, open and ready for this gift of discovery when it comes. What he wants is not to impose his order on the world, but for the world to make its order known. Man must try to attune himself to things outside his own ego; he must conceive of the *other* that helps him to become a fully realized person. Language composition can not only help promote such an abstract growth, but also may serve a more practical purpose committing thoughts to paper is often the only way to organize one's ideas to arrive at some synthesis.

Discovery and Surprise
Energize Composition

The writer should not know too well where he is going when he begins his writing. If he does, the work becomes merely an illustration of the preconceived. He must discover in the act of composition where the story is going. The outcome of the creative act must be a surprise and a discovery for the writer. Something that had not existed in the world has come to be; some new harmonious combination or pattern has been arrived at. The writer "discovers" in the older sense of the word, to reveal or make known, as well as the common modern sense of the word, to find. When the writer has discovered something and delighted in the surprise of it, the chances are that his readers will also do so. That the delight is not terminal is indicated by the fact that great literary works can be read again and again with the same—or even increased—joy.

Putting characters into a situation and letting them work out their destiny is a kind of play matched only by the play of the creative mathematician who catches the elements of a problem and lets them come together into a new pattern.

Every writer shares much of the literary artist's activity. He starts to write without knowing quite where he is going. He may have a good sense of his general direction, but even when he is dealing directly with problems, he finds new solutions to those problems on the way. He did not know what he thought until he extended himself in writing; he did not know what he felt until he gave a sharper focus to his feelings. New concepts arise out of the work that were not "put into it."

Expository Writing

What has been said is applicable in some degree to all kinds of writing. Straight exposition requires a free act of creation, the lack of which causes it to become wooden and unreadable. Students often strain to write what might have been done easily with much greater success. Writing should be a natural act, and it can be when done freely—and frequently.

In the main, literary language is much closer to the total range of language, whereas expository, strictly logical, rational language represents a later and more restricted development. A specialized and highly canalized form, it succeeds best when the writer is fully aware of the resources of the language he is *not* using.

Vocabulary in Composition

At this point, a word about vocabulary is appropriate. From the point of view of composition, it is much better to use a small vocabulary precisely than a large vocabulary imprecisely. Almost anything can be said by the manipulation of a limited core of words without resort to exotic and interesting, but outlandish, words. The use of words selected honestly, so that they fit into the total pattern of language, is much more effective. Students certainly should be encouraged to increase their vocabularies and use a word with precision regardless of its length or origin, and they should be encouraged to play around with words, as a means of making them their own. They should *not* be encouraged to sprinkle new and impressive-sounding words into their writing or to learn lists of words that they are asked to use in compositions. The choice of words should come from within; words should not be applied externally. Of course, the words must first be learned, but once they have been represented to an individual, he must be allowed to handle them in his own way, to give them a multiplicity of meanings and shades of meaning that, when developed, can be handled with assurance and accuracy. Words acquired otherwise make for shallow writing, which never quite comes into focus. Working toward more effective and exact writing by changing words in the context of the whole can be very valuable, but as often as not this means making the language simpler rather than dressing it up.

Speaking in Relation to Writing

In writing, it is most important to impress on students the similarity (and differences) between written and spoken English. Writing should catch the flow and continuity of potentially spoken language. Obviously, there is a great range in spoken English, but all writing should be geared to the oral language of the individual; it should have the quality and continuity of speech but not be an exact copy of it.

The matter of the use of *potentially* spoken language is very important. In other words, the writer can push to its limit what *speech* has in it to say. Because writing may be artistically organized or more carefully put together, the critics may say that no one actually talks like that (as in a Hemingway dialogue), but in such cases the living, moving language is artistically organized. This is much better than trying to build a piece of writing out of the literary remains of the past, out of a dead and dissected language. A lively piece of writing must be made with lively material. The living language should be the starting point and should infuse all that comes thereafter.

A boy's eloquence on the playground can be caught in his compositions if the teacher and his instruction do not stand in the way. Once the eloquence is caught (and the possibilities for arousing it are unlimited) the individual can extend it into many areas of the curriculum, including composition.

12

Letters to the World:
Children Composing in
Oral and Written Language

This is my letter to the world,
    That never wrote to me,—
The simple news that Nature told,
    With tender majesty.[1]

Emily Dickinson's "letters to the world" were touchingly conceived, and their artistry finely honed. Few people, even artists, have been able to communicate their reflections and reactions to the life about them so exquisitely, but all men present their thoughts and feelings about the happenings of life in one way or another. The child, like the artist, explodes with delight in the world and with wonder at its mysteries. Given an opportunity, he will tell it to the world, making his own presentations.

They are behind you.
They are holes,
Holes in the snow,
Holes in the sand,
Holes in the mud.
Your feet make the holes, lots of holes,
So your mother can find you.[2]

[1] Emily Dickinson (Frontispiece in the first edition of her poems). (Boston: Little, Brown, 1944, p. 2.)
[2] "Footprints," dictated by a five-year-old child to his teacher.

The beach is peaceful in the winter.
I often go when I'm disturbed.
I can sit on the rocks lining the shore.
I sit and throw bread to the friendly sea gulls.
I watch the crashing waves tumble in.
Pretty soon the waves hit my feet.
The tide is in, so I get on my bike and ride home.
I feel much better now.
I sure hate to see the summer come.[3]

The first thing I noticed when I walked outside in the early morning was a big red-tailed hawk that would send shivers down your back. When I walked farther out into the wet field with the diamond-like sparkle of the dew, I saw a baby red fox go across the field eating the fresh strawberries wet with dew. I followed it past an old barb-wire fence and down an old cow pasture and I stopped at the edge and didn't follow him into the woods because I was looking at a big patch of succulent strawberries and they made me stoop down and I ate them.

In about ten minutes I stopped eating them because I heard the jangle of a cow bell. I got up to see the cows. There were five cows in this pasture.

It was funny when the cows first came to this pasture from another. They were jumping around and butting each other and running up and down the field. They were young calves just getting their horns.

All of a sudden I heard a screen door bang. I thought it was the farmer who owns our cottage. I was wrong. I knew the second I heard a bark. It was my dog, Ginger, She was chasing a chimpmunk down a stone wall in front of our house.

The screen door banged again. It was my mother calling me in for breakfast.

That's what happens in the early morning in the country.[4]

Like Emily Dickinson's, these letters to the world are addressed as much to the self as to others. Still, children's messages find their way out to others, in conversation, in the dialogue of play, in reverie committed to writing, in debates with themselves and in argument set down, and sometimes in the literary forms of stories and poetry or in descriptions and explanations of events.

Modes of Presenting

Language is not the only, and not always the most appropriate, medium for presenting one's ideas and feelings about one's world. The expressive relationships of line and mass in painting or drawing, the form of a piece of sculpture, the telling movements of dance, or the harmonious flow of notes in music may be the means that best present a particular letter to the world. That marvelous combination of the arts called "theater" when

[3] "Winter Beach," by David Mullis (12 years old).
[4] "At Five Forty-Five in the Country," by Jon Smith (10 years old).

presented for adults and called "creative dramatics" when presented by children is one of the most communicative of the modes of presentation because it uses several modes simultaneously.

All such means of presenting one's own symbolic formulation should be cultivated. Few children will be artists, but many will find these modes useful and enjoyable and all will learn, through experimenting with each, to "read" them in their own forms. What a pity when an adult cannot "read" in the artist's terms the playfulness of a painting by Miró, the passions in a drama of O'Neill, the serenity of a Bach fugue, the inner conflicts of Martha Graham's choreography.

Artistry in Communications

Communication is a two-way process of output and input, of speaking and listening, of writing and reading, of presenting and receiving. The more artistry, the more effective is the communication, and this is where teaching comes in. First, the teacher must be sure not to thwart the child's natural tendency to present his symbolic formulations for testing against those of others and for expressing ideas to others in search of reflection and refinement. The teacher creates a classroom situation that encourages free discourse within the limitations of group operation. These limitations, however, should be only for insuring the kind of orderly working environment that will permit a maximum of individual expression and a minimum of willful self-indulgence. Gaining artistry in presentational modes requires the calm of reflection and the rigor of discipline as well as the excitement of sharing ideas in discourse with others.

Composing in Speech and Writing

Although one needs to keep constantly in mind the possibilities of the strictly nonlingual modes of presenting and communicating, the main concern of the ensuing discussion will be speech and writing. At the outset it is important to state two postulates with regard to writing and its relationship to speech. Although an expression of a notion, an idea, or even a fact in speech is never quite the same in writing, writing is founded in inner speech. They are alike in that the key morphemes (idea units) are essentially the same. It is the syntax that is a little different. Hand written, typed, or printed matter does not have the benefit of intonation, gesture, or pauses to develop meaningful flow.

Anyone can follow spoken narrative or discourse, but if it is written down exactly as said, it is hard to read. This is why dictated letters have to be rewritten from the rough draft until the author has, through practice, learned to speak in written terms. This is why good dramatic dialogue is so hard to write and so difficult to read. Being oral language, it needs the stage or an imaginative reader to make it live. The great Shakespearean actor is the one who really "reads" the lines as speech, for there is little helpful punctuation in the old Shakespearean texts, and the meter was made for speaking, not for reading. Shakespeare evidently did not make any attempt on his own to prepare the texts to be read.

The matrix of written language is speech. The concepts, ideas, and relationships being prepared for written expression are generally worked out in a shorthand of inner speech. Then they are tried on paper, read over, given to someone else to read, and revised to make sure that they "say" what was thought. Although the differences between speech and writing are important, their interdependence is even more significant. Lyric poetry, for example, is often written to be read aloud.

For the teacher of children, the argument just given is a crucial reminder that he can neglect neither speech nor writing; he must develop both modes in relation to each other because the normal child enters school with a large speech repertoire but without the ability to write. While his speech patterns are continuing to grow in sophistication, the child must learn to move from speech patterns to simple written patterns. The disparity, which is wide at the beginning and slowly narrows over a four-to six-year period, can cause great frustration.

Vygotsky's Position on the Difference between Speech and Writing

Vygotsky, in reporting his investigations of the relationship between school instruction in language and child development of language, states clearly the difference between speaking and writing.

> Written speech is a separate linguistic function, differing from oral speech in both structure and mode of functioning. . . . It is speech in thought and image only, lacking the musical, expressive, intonational qualities of oral speech.[5]

Vygotsky then goes on to suggest the reasons why young children do not find conventional writing and composition an acceptable task, even though oral speech is the basis for such composition.

> In learning to write, the child must disengage himself from the sensory aspect of speech and replace words by images of words. . . . Our studies show that it is the abstract quality of written language that is the main stumbling block, not the underdevelopment of small muscles or any other mechanical obstacles.[6]

[5] Reprinted from *Thought and Language* (trans. E. Hanfmann and G. Vakar) by L. S. Vygotsky by permission of The M.I.T. Press, Cambridge, Massachusetts. Copyright 1934 by The M.I.T. Press. P. 18.

[6] Vygotsky, pp. 98–99.

Vygotsky continues his discussion with two other reasons for the reluctance of the child to begin writing. "Writing," he says, "is also speech without an interlocutor, addressed to an absent or an imaginary person or to no one in particular—a situation new and strange to the child."[7] Children do not recognize the need for writing when communication by conversation is sufficient for their immediate needs. The writer, on the other hand, is required to make up his approach and point of view. In Piaget's terms, writing is a decentering, objectifying process that requires some maturity beyond the egocentricity of the young child. Related to the writer's problem is the fact that writing is a conscious art requiring objective analysis of what he is doing while he is doing it. Writing hardly ever becomes as spontaneous as speaking. When speaking, the school-age child produces the sounds naturally without effort, but in his first writing he must deliberately form statements. He cannot let ideas tumble out as they do in talk, although this is where he will begin.

If one admits an "inner speech" as Vygotsky does, the problem becomes a relationship between it and oral speech on the one hand and written speech on the other.

Written language demands conscious work because its relationship to inner speech is different from that of oral speech. The latter precedes inner speech in the course of development, while written speech follows inner speech and presupposes its existence [the act of writing implying a translation from inner speech]. . . . Inner speech is condensed, abbreviated speech. Written speech is deployed to its fullest extent, more complete than oral speech. Inner speech is almost entirely predicative because the situation, the subject of thought, is always known to the thinker. Written speech, on the contrary, must explain the situation fully in order to be intelligible.[8]

The Primacy of Developing Speech-Thought

Even though written language is quite different from speech language, it is founded upon speech development and derived from inner speech. The cultivation of speech is a primary task, for on it all else is built. Neither "elocution" nor "speech improvement" is the concern. They are special problems, but the development of *speech-thought* is a matter of general import. The student will have nothing of significance to write down or communicate, nor will he understand sophisticated reading unless his speech-thought is constantly nurtured in ever widening circles of sophistication.

The child often has no one to talk with except his unsophisticated peers. He may have no one to talk with at home who is much more sophisticated, and often working adults have little time for extended conversation.

[7] Vygotsky, p. 99.
[8] Vygotsky, p. 100.

Adult–child dialogue about the world could be encouraged in the school (although the skill of reading cannot be learned without it), but many teachers also say there is no time for such dialogue because of societal pressure for reading-skill achievement. Skill workbooks or even programmed skill exercises with computer-assisted instruction are no substitute for daily practice in talking, reading, and writing about relevant and important ideas. Persistent low reading scores from most schools in slum areas, despite great drill efforts, may be caused by the overemphasis on sounding and teaching word-attack skills to the neglect of significant and total language development within the curriculum. Many children from suburban homes are equally disadvantaged. They are often left alone or with teen-age sitters. They are shunted from one afternoon activity to another with no time to ask questions of their parents or to talk about the multitude of experiences they have. Uninterpreted and unused experience teaches nothing except survival by trial and error. Many of these children, if failing, are often subjected to hours of ineffectual remedial reading-skill instruction instead of being given the rich language experience they need.

In the past, the farmhouse and the craftsman's house were centers of learning, not only about the day's work but about life as well. Adults and children were in regular dialogue about the events happening to them all. Even though children were supposed to be seen and not heard, they heard the important adult talk and they had their questions answered at proper times. The children of the wealthy were tutored individually or in small groups by a governess or a young university scholar. At a certain age the children were admitted to the dinner table and its discourse. Even in so-called preliterate tribes the young are in constant communication with the adults. In many instances the fathers take on the training of the boys by having them accompany them on food-gathering expeditions. The young hear their elders' discussions and begin to participate in them. The younger children are always in close social contact with the women and they join in the large tribal festivities.

Only in social environments where the young are included in the talk and have opportunities to ask questions and participate in the dialogue of inquiry with adults can they develop their speech-thoughts adequately. Otherwise, thinking as well as speech becomes retarded. The conceptualizing process never develops sufficiently. The grammar of reasoning is never heard. The "because," the "if-then," and the "unless" never develop beyond the instinctual level. Unless concepts of the environment become clear through describing, defining, classifying, categorizing, interrelating, and eventually hypothesizing, the thought process remains dormant. If the child has never been encouraged in his questions and has never been shown, at least by model behavior, how one goes about seeking answers, his mind may not develop very far beyond that of feral children who have been isolated completely from intercourse with people and things. A stimulating environment of objects is necessary, but it is not enough. *There must also be a stimulating and varied interactive human environment if children are to achieve in the uses of language.*

Fostering Speech-Thought

Scientific investigation substantiates the common-sense view that the development of speech-thought requires adults to interact with children, with lots of "good" talk. Yet in our "quiet" classrooms—even in some kindergartens—this activity is discouraged, is considered to be a waste of time, or at best is operative at a minimal level of "yes-or-no" questioning. The level of classroom language improves when elementary school teachers know their subjects thoroughly. Even more important, the teacher must be aware of the significance of this whole process of speech-thought and the importance of taking time to nurture it. Less curriculum content to be covered and more thinking out loud about it with children will advance learning rather than retard it as many of the routine written exercises and "busy work" do.

The following example shows speech-thought from an interview with a boy in the fifth grade. He is talking about the insulating quality of fur after he had experimented in class with tin cans of hot and cold water wrapped in fur. This episode occurred on a very hot summer day in an environment that also has very cold winters.

Q. Tell me what you did with the cans and the fur.
R. Took a big can, filled it up; and a small can, filled up. The big—I mean the small one cooled faster. Then two small cans, one with fur. Fur one cooled slower. Fur insulated. Wouldn't let cold go in.
Q. Could you say the same thing differently, not using "cold"?
R. Can with fur won't let air come in to cool it. Then we took two small cold cans, one with fur and one without. The one without fur warmed faster.
Q. For the same reason?
R. The fur wouldn't let the heat come in.
Q. True to say, fur warms animals?
R. If animal is warm, then the fur won't harm it but keeps it warm. But I understand with cold water it would be colder, still gets colder: cans with fur. The animal with fur would get colder. Then when hot weather begins fur keeps hot in . . .
Q. In the winter?
R. About 10 degrees cooler.
Q. Animal's temperature?
R. Body inside.
Q. What warms animals which haven't any fur, like us?
R. Our blood.
Q. How?
R. Going so fast.
Q. Think about this. How different are we from cans?
R. But cans don't move around as much and won't get so hot.
Q. Animals move much in winter?

R. They hibernate. But in jungle it doesn't matter in the winter.
Q. What about furry animals in hot places?
R. Keeps hot out.
Q. Cut fur off?
R. Heat would go in.[9]

Students in an earlier class discussion suggested the previously mentioned experiment of wearing a fur coat on a hot summer day to see what would happen.

Except for the church in its special field, the school is the only social institution that can make up to some children what they are missing in cultural participation with adults. Even if there were no remedial demand, the school should be the agency that extends the speech-thought activities of the community. However, schools should encourage parents to participate with their children in general cognitive activities growing out of school programs as well as home experiences, rather than discourage them by throwing up fences of educational expertise. Parents should be encouraged to participate in the school program as invited participants in the classroom when they have particular knowledge or skills to contribute. These occasions can be planned by the teacher with the parents. In some inner-city situations, mothers have been encouraged to go on trips with the children and to return to the classroom to join in a discussion of the experience. This procedure shows the mothers how to talk more constructively with their children. As "good talk" takes over in home and school, the excitement of learning is conveyed and communication is enhanced.

Relation of Reading
to Speaking and Writing

Teaching to write is a challenge as great as that of teaching to read; yet, unfortunately, it has never been given the same prominence and consideration as its sister skill. Probably for this reason there is even more failure in writing than in reading. Some educators have seen the inter-relationship of reading and writing, but they are few. Despite the obvious fact that the printed word is the same as the written word, reading and writing are taught as separate tasks, and reading always receives the greater emphasis—despite the label "language arts." Because both tasks depend on a speech base, speaking, writing, and reading should be handmaids to each other in the school program. They are the main modes for the everyday presentations of an individual's symbolic life and his only means of encountering the day-to-day symbolic presentations of others. The way to learn to "read," in the sense of understanding the presentations of others, is to prepare one's

[9] Margaret Donaldson, interviewer, from "Fifth Grade Interviews" (Cambridge, Mass.: Elementary Science Study, summer 1964, mimeograph).

own presentations so that they can be more easily "read" by others and to learn to "listen" to what other people are "saying." Obviously, both presenter and receiver should deal with things of concern to both. Relevant reading, talking, and writing need to be a vital part of every child's school day, especially writing since it is so often neglected.

Some experts feel that learning to read one's own spoken language should be one of the first steps. The dictated story or "experience chart" can be used to advantage as reading material. One of the few advantages of the Initial Teaching Alphabet (ITA) approach to reading is that children can write their own little stories without much of a spelling problem as soon as they can form letters with some ease. Mass production of typewriters that print out spoken language will be a boon to teachers of the early grades for the purpose of tying speech sounds to written symbols. However, the children would learn about the processes of language and, in turn, about reading if the teacher helped them reformulate their spoken language into written language for the purpose of reading it.

Worn-out, dull, pedestrian stories contrived for reading lessons will not do. Nor will sentimental social studies units about "our helper friends" set the fire for discussions. Substantial matters of concern to children is the only matrix in which significant presentation and communication can occur. When school life is a challenge and full of exciting explorations, children will have need to speak and write "letters to the world."

Fostering Written Thought

The use of encoded and decoded messages is important not merely for human beings but for other living organisms, and for machines used by human beings. Birds communicate with one another, monkeys communicate with one another, insects communicate with one another, and in all this communication some use is made of signals and symbols which can be understood only by being privy to the system of codes involved.[10]

From the nursery school through elementary and secondary school programs this phenomenon of communication, with its interplay of oral, inner, and written speech, means that there must be much lively practice of speaking as the more formal language of reading and writing is slowly introduced. Children present their stories orally and make comments about happenings and ideas. These are then transposed by the teacher without content change to the written form and are read back to young children or are prepared for the older children to read to themselves. In turn, books are read to the children who then talk about what has been read. They react to the story, relating it to their experiences, reflecting upon it, extending it with their

[10] Norbert Wiener, *The Human Use of Human Beings: Cybernetics and Society* (2d ed.; New York: Doubleday Anchor Books, 1954), p. 74.

ideas. In addition to talking among themselves, they talk with the teacher. He presents his ideas and frames questions that will encourage the children to think more deeply about what they have read. He must confront the children with new experiences and happenings that will warrant talking, reading, and writing about. A cycle of language activities causes one to reinforce the other.

Writing can be scheduled as one of several independent activities to choose from, or at times everybody can work on some kind of writing activity: dictating a first draft into a tape recorder or dictaphone, going over a first draft by reading it aloud with the teacher or another student, or copying a second draft for display or for submitting to a school paper. Some children, during this activity, can be reading material written by classmates or members of other classes. Reports on social studies or science topics can be in preparation. This type of classroom period might well be labeled "The Young Writer's Workshop," and be a valid replacement for repetitious language-usage skill periods.

As children grow older, the same general procedures should be continued, as reading and writing emerge to replace in part the oral-aural process. And so the school world wags from speaking to listening to writing to reading and back again.

The Teacher As Guiding Critic

All strategies for teaching the arts of communication must emphasize the transposing of speech-thought into written language and back again. If from the beginning the child is made aware of the different syntaxes and is encouraged to strive for meaning in each form, he should find it natural to punctuate and properly phrase for communication as the time comes. If children are preparing something significant to them that they wish to be read by others, they will try to put in the punctuation that will make it readable.

Students of composition will wish to be helped with the phrasing that will transpose their speech-thoughts to the written page. In this spirit, the teacher can safely raise questions and offer suggestions much as the friendly critic operates in support of a writer. Most authors ask some friend to go over their manuscripts for just this purpose. Sometimes teachers are overly precious about the child's first words and let the raw language stand rather than offer help. However, the act of criticizing does not mean interference or adult rewriting. Helping a child rephrase a spoken story for reading need not be an infringement of his right to express himself nor an infraction against the postulates of child development. It is education. Eventually, the older child becomes able to rewrite his own first drafts for reading. The child must make the decisions to transpose, while the teacher bases his critical advice on meaning and language convention broadly conceived.

In order to assist in this way, the teacher must know what he is doing; he must have a broad view of the language system of English and know of its infinite variety; otherwise, he may not recognize the situation when the child in his fresh approach has written more effectively than if he had used the convention. For example, in the story "At Five Forty-Five in the Country" (see p. 206) the teacher insisted on an alteration in the passage about stooping down to eat the succulent wild strawberries that deprived the original of its power. The original was: ". . . I was looking at a big patch of succulent strawberries and they made me stoop down and I ate them." The teacher's correction was: ". . . I was looking at a big patch of succulent strawberries, so I stooped down to eat them." By invoking the rule that inanimate objects should not be given human attributes, the teacher denied the child the use of exception to the rule when the meaning called for it. The teacher must not be a purist, but at the same time he must know what is possible and what is not. However, in this case, if the child continued to animate everything in his writing, the teacher would raise the question and discuss it with the child.

In order to accomplish the role of guiding critic, the teacher needs to promote an atmosphere in which there is a disposition to write. He must set up a permissive and flexible situation in order that children will not feel pressured and become blocked, while at the same time he must establish the need to write things down. He must also provide an atmosphere in which disciplined work can be carried on.

In these ways children will write their "letters to the world."

13

Strategies for Teaching the Art of Communication

Developing Speech-Thought

Many classroom strategies for furthering the development of speech-thought were developed during the progressive movement as means for involving children in "experiences." They were part of a recommended "activities program" that emphasized "doing." Too often, however, the activity was carried on for its own sake, and the next step of language interpretation was not taken with sufficient resolve. In a modern, language-centered view of teaching, these strategies are recommended mainly for their potential in extending language and thinking through relevant language practice.

Child Talk in Creative Play

All children aged three to twelve years employ speech-thought during periods of concentrated play. These periods are rehearsals, with the play objects simulating the world situation of the child.[1] Past learnings and de-

---

[1] The term *rehearsals* appears in discussions of this subject by Lawrence K. Frank in *The School as Agent for Cultural Renewal* (Cambridge, Mass.: Harvard University Press, 1960).

veloping concepts, with associated language, are paraded before the other child or children as each contributes to the emerging drama. Creative play can happen in a housekeeping corner with dress-up clothes, in a pile of building blocks representing an airplane, in a playground sandbox, in a dirt hole under the back porch with little fire engines and police cars, in a pup tent in the woods with Father's discarded camping equipment, or in a cellar space preempted for electric trains. No better empirical proof is needed than the fact of play to show that children are natural learners, busy at making discoveries and testing what they know against simulated reality. If more play were permitted in school throughout the period of childhood, the teacher would have more opportunities to observe the child's level of operation with ideas and language under somewhat natural circumstances. Children playing with toys create *analogues* of reality—it could almost be said that play is reality for children. It certainly is their self-imposed work.

GUIDING PLAY TALK Without forcing play into a contrived educational mold the teacher can, through the introduction of playthings, miniature toys, and simple paraphernalia pertinent to a classroom study, provide a means for concept rehearsal and concept testing. It is not unusual for children to ask adults to enter a play episode in an adult role or as an adviser on the accuracy of their life projections. If an argument develops over a matter of fact, a parent may be invited to discuss it or provide a needed fact. The teacher can make himself available for this kind of supportive role, provided he does not begin to dominate the situation. He can judiciously make suggestions or inject a novel object that will cause the children to reconsider or reorganize their thinking in relation to a slightly different situation.

Substantive Play at Different Levels

The author has observed two boys playing in the same sand hole with practically the same miniature tractors and trucks during the same time of year at ages five, nine, and eleven. As expected, the activities, the accompanying language, and the attention span advanced markedly in sophistication over the years. At five years of age the two boys talked about playing with their tractors in the sand under the porch, but they were distracted by a number of extraneous things before each began to build a road on which they planned to have their respective farmhouses. Although the following dialogue, along with the appropriate action, reveals some concepts of dirt roads and tractor use, the episode is inconclusive, brief, and ends with the throwing of sand.

Jon: Here's a road.
Jim: It won't make a road. This is a dead end.
Jon: No, this is a farmhouse—right over here is a tall, high farm.
Jim: Now, here is a dead-end road.

Jon: No, the house.
Jim: I'll make it over here.
Jon: Hey, Jimmy, stop messing up this road.
Jim: I'll make it over here.
Jon: I'll flatten all the roads.
Jim: I'm flattening the roads.
Jon: Oh, Ginger (*the dog*), you're in the road. You're under arrest.
Jim: Here's sand. Hit her right between the eyes.
Jon: Come here, Gingy.
Jim: Now open your mouth.
Jon: You're a bad dog. (*Humming rhythmically.*) Hey, Jim, help me, I got stuck (*meaning his tractor*). Help, help, look at the big hole I dug. Anyway, I'm a tractor, err, err, err, err, kach, kach, kach. I'm getting stuck.
Jim: Why are you getting stuck?
Jon: Addy, pladdy—hey, it's a sand and dust storm raging across the earth.

At nine years of age the boys assumed the roles of two farmers, Roy and Joe. They helped each other with the building of their roads and farmhouses as if they were neighbors. They had a much better concept of how a road is built and of the give-and-take that occurs when men are working together with different kinds of equipment on different aspects of a job.

As the observer took his position, the two children were carrying on independent play, one on each side of a clump of birch trees, each developing his own dirt project with trucks and bulldozers.

Jon: Hey, Joe (*imaginary character*), if you want to work on one side you could make a sand pit with your project. I've made one with all my leftover.
Jim: Can I have the thing that scrapes the roads?
Jon: Why?
Jim: To make a driveway.
Jon: When you're finished with the yellow thing (*road scraper*) leave it right there. (*An array of road equipment has been placed carefully in a row and is ready for use when needed. Jim is developing a similar project with industriousness, building miniature walks and special areas for the road equipment. It is beginning to look like Jon's. At least three minutes of silence pass here.*)
Jon: Hey, Joe, anytime you need the dump truck just call.
Jim: O. K. Any rocks in here? I'll dig up the whole row. Wow! See this rock in the way.
Jon: Wow!
Jim: No wonder I couldn't plow. (*Long silence, and much work.*)
Jon: Now why don't you come over and see my plan?
Jim: We need clearance here so I can get mine out. These tractors are all ready. Those would be out working.
Jon: They use that on different kinds of farms (*constructing a part between them together for mutual improvement*). Where are you going to go?
Jim: Up to your farm. We are helpful farmers. Hey, Roy, can we use some of the excess dirt?
Jon: Sure, I'll help you load it up. I'll bring down the bulldozer.

Jim: Say, this is a phone. I'll call you. Is this Roy? I need some more dirt.
Jon: O.K. I'll bring it over. Guess it can only be half a load because of this truck. (*Silence for a minute while truck is filled.*) Beep, beep.

At eleven years of age the two boys worked diligently in parallel play, not because they were in a less mature social stage, but because they each had such big ideas for the development of their prospective farms. The farm setting was quickly constructed; the play then became the rehearsal of the highly complex agricultural procedure of preparing the fields for a crop, including sowing, cultivating, and harvesting. There was much less talk; the running commentary was no longer needed. No fictitious role names were used, but they both adopted a "country" accent when they did converse.

It is not unusual to find older children playing in this manner, yet in most schools creative play is last used as an educational method in the kindergarten. Play should be continued in more sophisticated forms at least through the primary grades as a means for developing speech-thought. From the play situation it is an easy step to *informal dramatics* in which children create roles based on stories or incidents they have experienced or can imagine. Mock telephone conversations and television interviews often suggested in "using English" textbooks can be more than an exercise in courteous usage; they can be rehearsals of ideating language. Telling the class about a story that one group has read is sometimes best done in dramatic form. *Role-playing* social conflict situations taken from classroom life or from big picture sets suggesting social problems between adult and child worlds can be expanded into informal dramatics. Modeling adult roles and creating dramatic situations among adults and children are enjoyable activities which are psychologically sound.

Creative Dramatics

Creative dramatics is another natural form of play popular among older children that can be used effectively by teachers for speech-thought development. The enthusiasm with which children plan a show to be given in the back yard or basement can be linked to educative purposes if the teacher permits children plenty of time, space, and freedom for exploration in composing. To cut off creativity prematurely, forcing the dramatic play to gel before children have been able to verify their ideas, will leave only the stiff and awkward shell of a drama.

The educational purpose of creative dramatics in relation to social studies units is to rehearse ideas developed in the study. Most of the children should have an opportunity to play and talk them out. Otherwise, the value of the exercise is lost, even though the production might be more presentable at an assembly with only the born actors taking part. A judicious combination of oral and written composition is necessary before the final working-out in action. The following extract of a fourth-grade play shows the possibilities when a composite of the class's ideas is used. It was composed from group discussions and composites of individual writing after the Homeric hymn to Persephone had been read to the class during a study of the early Greeks. The written text was not memorized but became the agreed-upon base for improvisation. It never played quite the same way at rehearsals. Music and choreography were composed by the youngsters. A group-painted mural of expressionistic designs suggested by possible happenings in the "underworld" formed the backdrop for Hades' throne, which was placed in the middle of the playing area.

In the central scene the children envision the shades in Hades awaiting the return of their lord with Persephone:

Narrator: This scene takes place in the lower world. King Hades has not yet returned with Persephone. The ugly ones, Death, Night, and Dreams, are dancing around the empty throne. The ghosts of Tantalus and Sisyphus join them in their dance. They finish dancing and sit down in a circle, except for Tantalus and Sisyphus, who continue their punishments.

Tantalus: Oh, how I wish I could get this water (*bending over to try to scoop it up, then reaching for some fruit*). How I want that fruit! Now it's gone again. I think I'll stop and take a rest as long as King Hades isn't here.

Sisyphus: I think I'll stop rolling this boulder. I'm very tired and there's no use working while Hades is away. He's the one who makes me do this.

Night: Where could Hades be? It has been a night and a day and he has not returned.

Sleep: I'll go up to Earth and see if I can find him. Who will go with me? Do you want to go with me, Tantalus?

Tantalus: No. I'm afraid I couldn't get out. I'm only a ghost, and besides I'm still trying to get some water and fruit. I'd better stay here.

Night: I'll be glad to go with you when my time comes around after sunset, but now day is still up there and I can't go yet.

Death: There's no use bothering. He'll be back and all too soon. I wish he'd never come back; then I'd be ruler of the lower world.

Sleep: Why did he go up to Earth? He doesn't usually go for so long.

Death: He went to get a queen. He said he wanted something beautiful down here to keep him company. He said we were ugly and he was tired of us.

Night: And this queen, she'll be more important than you, won't she, Death?

Death: That's what I don't like. Maybe we shouldn't ever let her sit on this throne. I shall put an end to her. I shall stain my knives with her blood. Perhaps we should attack King Hades as well; then I would be ruler of the dead for sure.

Tantalus: Yes, let us kill Hades, then perhaps I could get some water and eat some fruit at last. It is he that punishes me forever.

Sisyphus: I too want him dead, for then the boulder would stay at the top of the hill and I wouldn't push it ever again. I'll help to kill him. Maybe I could crush him with this boulder.

Death: We can't really kill him, so what's the use? After all, he's an immortal god. He might make us work all the harder if he found out our plot. But as for the new queen—

Night: Here they come—I can hear the opening of the gates.

Death: .Quickly to your places!

(They line up on either side of the throne to welcome the king.)

Hades: *(Calling from off stage)* Get another throne ready. I have brought my beautiful queen.

(The shades plot ways to persuade Persephone to eat the pomegranate to keep her in the Lower World, while still planning to do away with Hades.)

Hades: Now, Persephone, sit down and you shall be my queen.

Persephone: I will not. I don't want to be your queen. I'm already the queen of the garden of spring.

Hades: Not any longer! You are to be my queen and rule one third of the universe with me, and this is your palace. Don't you like it?

Persephone: I don't like it. I want to go back to my mother, the rich-haired Demeter. I'm lonely and frightened here by all these ugly people.

Hades: *(Whispering to Death)* Bring me five hundred glasses of nectar. That will surely tempt her to stay.

Death: *(Whispering back)* That's a good idea.

Persephone: I overheard you, Hades; I'm not going to drink anything.

Death: *(Whispering to Hades very softly)* Perhaps you can persuade her to eat. If she does she'll have to stay here forever.

Hades: But you will *eat* something, my dear, won't you? You must be very hungry I have the most luscious pomegranates!

Persephone: Well, I might taste of a pomegranate, but nothing more.

(Persephone eats as they all stare at her, for now she is theirs.)

Hades: And now you are truly dark Queen of the Lower World.

(The ugly ones chant a hymn to the King and Queen and resume the dance around the thrones which they were doing at the beginning of the scene.)

Chorus: Once she was the queen of spring.

Now she is the queen of Hades.

Death instead of flowers she will bring,

Now she plays with ghosts instead of ladies.

Other myths, folk-tales, or heroic stories from Asia or Africa or from American-Indian collections can be the inspiration for creative dramas. In social studies the struggle for life on the frontier, or the adventures of fleeing slaves in the Underground Railroad, or imagined life in the first moon-colony are thematic possibilities for *rehearsing* conceptual learnings through creative dramatics.

Classroom Conversation

Originally, "show and tell" was introduced as a practice to help the young child bridge the gap between home and school by permitting him to bring an article of attachment from home into the new, strange environment of school. It was felt that if he talked about something of his own, he would become relaxed in speaking before his peers. The practice can easily be abused by overstructuring it into a routine for speech drill and making it into an opener for the day, giving the teacher time to attend to milk money and other accounting tasks while a child chairman calls on some of his classmates to talk and on others to criticize.

On the other hand, an informal period of class discussion with the teacher about happenings inside and outside the school is a productive practice that could replace the old "show and tell." The teacher can be in the center of the conversation, raising questions of interpretation, of evaluation, and of relation to matters learned before. When class conversation is well done, it can be one of the most fruitful exercises for developing speech-thought, because the concern is usually one the children have brought in and has immediacy, which heightens curiosity. In this way the teacher can keep abreast of what is on the children's minds, provided he is truly permissive in allowing the children to talk about what *is* on their minds. Very often, clues for later study or for extensions of what the class is already working on are presented. Glasser's proposed technique of *classroom meetings* is a permissive yet organized approach to informal discussion that has proved productive in encouraging children to respond to what is happening to them in and out of school. Frequently these meetings become the jumping-off point for classroom studies of substance based on child concerns and interests. An extensive body-health project was proposed by a sixth-grade group discussing the offensive odor of a classroom member. Such "talk-about-anything" periods need not be held every day, but they should be regular enough for children to expect such a time.

With older children, a topic presented by one of them can be discussed in small groups, and opinions can be collected from each group for consideration by the class. The teacher can sit in with different groups and lead a summary discussion. Snack time and lunch time afford opportunities for informal discussion if arrangements are made for conversation on designated topics. Parents can assist as talk hosts. In those situations, teachers have tended to sit back and let the children lead and comment, the teachers thinking that they need the experience, but perhaps it is as important that the children are challenged by a teacher's questions and some adult thinking about a subject of their choice. The dialogue between teacher and pupils will foster improved speech-thought much faster than when students tell each other what they already know.

A good example of appropriate exploitation of "table talk" is a practice carried on for a number of years by the athletic director of the Shady Hill School:

> "The Luncheon Club" was held once a week at a special large table set up in the dining room. Anyone from the fifth through ninth grades was invited, provided he was willing to present a brief program about some hobby or interest of his at least once during the year. There was a child chairman who introduced the speaker of the day and organized a question period following each talk. The children rose to this new procedure and participated with

enthusiasm partly because it was theirs and partly because it was a role-playing of the adult world of their fathers. Teachers were invited from time to time as members who participated in the discussion.[2]

Classroom Dialogue: Exposition, Discourse, and Argument

Organized discussion should be used regularly in classroom programs for the social sciences, the humanities, the arts, and science. The teacher consciously plans a logical outline for the discussion to make sure that various kinds of thinking processes and their accompanying language structures are exercised within the milieu of meaningful content. There is a lively debate among psycholinguists[3] as to whether all children, including those who live in slum ghettos, develop the language of logical structures as a matter of course or whether these are learned only in culturally sophisticated families. Most children can gain the rudiments of logic in language, albeit in their own dialects, and can, with practice, develop thinking by analysis, synthesis, and hypothesis.

A study of concept understanding on science was done with children of the same grade levels in suburban and slum schools. The same manipulative materials and Piaget-type interviews were given to each group. Concept understanding was the same; only language style differed. The black city children described the science phenomena in a folksy, informal style, while the suburban children used a formal, text-book style of expression.[4]

These tactics of argumentation and formal discussion may sound old-fashioned, a return to the formal disputations of the Roman school, but they need not be. They can be the newest fashion of "learning to learn." These discussion sessions should be moments of inquiry and times for the integration of ideas.

Although modern investigators of thinking would question Dewey's all-inclusive dictum that the "scientific method is the method of mind itself,"[5] there are legitimate situations in which the use of his five phases for *reflective thinking* would be most advantageous as a general tactic for problem solving:

1. *Suggestions,* in which the mind leaps forward to a possible solution
2. An intellectualization of the difficulty or perplexity that has been *felt* (directly experienced) into a *problem* to be solved
3. The use of one suggestion after another as a leading idea, or *hypothesis,*

---

[2] Shady Hill School, Cambridge, Mass. Description by the authors of this regular event led by Helen Hayes, athletic director.

[3] From discussions with Henry Olds, Harvard Graduate School, 1966–1967.

[4] Donald Protheroe, doctoral dissertation, Wayne State University, 1968.

[5] John Dewey, *The Relation of Theory to Practice in Education* (Cedar Falls, Iowa: Association for Student Teaching, 1962), p. 15.

to initiate and guide observation and other operations in collection of factual material
4. The *mental elaboration* of the idea or supposition as an idea or supposition (reasoning, in the sense in which reasoning is a part, not the whole, of inference)
5. *Testing the hypothesis* by overt or imaginative action.[6]

All these phases involve *talking from* or *talking through an experience*. When educators adopted the "doing" aspect of Dewey's recommendations, they forgot or ignored his emphasis on "reflective thinking" during and following an "experience."

Discussions Used as an Invitation to Inquiry

To Joseph Schwab[7] the older problem-solving methodology advanced by Dewey and dogmatized by his followers is too limiting for the kind of investigation today's children should be practicing. He calls the old method a "rhetoric of conclusions," which takes children through experimental steps and brings them to conclusions already attained by predecessors. Instead, Schwab makes an eloquent plea for advancing the *narrative of inquiry*, in order to exhibit the *course of inquiry*.[8] The teacher will aid the children in finding the *syntax* and the English *style* that will carry the burden of meanings[9] as the course of fluid, open-ended classroom discussion progresses. A problem is described. The data, focused by a scientist, are given or shown, and his interpretation of the event is described. A further problem is made visible by the outcome of the previous research. "The second enquiry is seen to elicit new data requiring revision of the earlier formulation and so on. . . ."[10] Schwab goes on to say, "Care should be taken to emphasize the doubtful aspects of each research, the limitations in scope or adequacy of its conclusions, the questions and problems it leaves unanswered."[11]

The teacher, with the children, adopts the attitude of the inquiring, questioning, and always doubting scientist. Schwab suggests a classroom strategy of *invitations to enquiry*[12] that could be adapted for use with children at different levels in school, provided the teacher sets the expectations within the limits of background and thinking capacity of the children. For example, younger children could be asked to make a narrative description for the following question: If we assume that all pets are animals that live with

[6] John Dewey, *How We Think* (Boston: Heath, 1933), p. 107.
[7] Joseph Schwab, *The Teaching of Science as Enquiry* (Cambridge, Mass.: Harvard University Press, 1962).
[8] Schwab, p. 88.
[9] Schwab, p. 80.
[10] Schwab, p. 88.
[11] Schwab, p. 93.
[12] Schwab, p. 96.

people, are fed by people, given a home by people, and trained by people, then, is a cow a pet? This question would require the marshaling of descriptions of different kinds of pets in order to check the hypothetical classifications. Surely, other criteria would be discovered and checked out against the exemplars of pets named in the beginning. The differentiating attributes would be located for cows, horses, goldfish, and so on. The process of inquiry, which describes and classifies the phenomena of our universe in a special language style, would thus be experienced by the children. *Young children are capable of descriptive and categorizing inquiries, and older children can cope with propositional and hypothetical forms of inquiry. All children can be "invited to inquire."*

USING NOVEL OBJECTS The "invitation" strategy is only one of many that could be devised to give children guidance in the development of speech-thought. Useful would be a statement of observed fact, followed by a program of provocative questions leading the child into new considerations. A novel object or two can be placed for the children to manipulate freely while raising their own questions and propositions. The teacher, as he observes the playful investigations of the children, can phrase questions growing out of their comments, which will lead them to further description and analysis of previous attempts as the narrative of inquiry unfolds. Scientists are always saying that the questions are at least as important as the answers, so that educating children to frame questions is one way to the exercise of logical thinking. The "twenty questions" technique can be adapted for use with science or social science phenomena, especially in the area of framing questions.

With children in the middle grades and above, such activities can be in small groups under child direction (team learning) so long as the teacher keeps in touch with the ideational movement of the group and guides their questioning. Social science questions and matters of judgment in viewing human situations can be explored in a fashion similar to that of scientific discovery as different kinds of evidence are considered. A parable or a short story that involves problematic situations of questionable morality may provoke as much reflective discourse as a question of space science if presented as a matter for inquiry.

ENLIGHTENED OPPORTUNISM The Elementary Science Study had as its guiding motto, "enlightened opportunism."[13] All their suggested unit plans encourage the teacher to seize opportunities presented by children to explore phenomena in an enlightening manner. The teacher, being well versed in the science of the phenomenon, intelligently arranges the environment

---

[13] Elementary Science Study, publications upon order (Watertown, Mass.: Educational Servics, Inc., 1962–1964).

and guides the questioning, while listening to the children's open-ended investigation for clues to be explored.

The following is an account of several episodes involving first-graders in an exploration of shadows at the Elementary Science Study summer school.[14]

Upon reaching a sunny, broad expanse of sidewalk, the teacher began to play with her shadow. All joined the game.

T. What can you make *your* shadow do? (Shadows jumped, hopped, skipped, grew short, etc. Shadow-makers talked about their shadows.)

Ch. My shadow can do anything I can do.

T. I can step on your shadow (shadow-chasing).

T. Can you get away from your shadow? How could you make your shadow disappear? (Jumping and stooping.)

T. Hold out your hand. Look carefully at your hand and at the shadow of your hand. What do you think is causing the shadow?

Ch. My hand. I am.

T. What do we have to have in order to have a shadow?

Ch. (Tentatively) Well, the sun.

T. Could anyone tell how the sun might be causing the shadow?

Ch. (Children appeared unable to think further about this question.)

T. Can you catch your shadow? Can you pick up your shadow?

Ch. (Many children stooped to pick up their shadows; others did not respond to this. Two boys began to talk about the cement and one expressed the idea which both seemed to share: Well, if I could pick up the cement I could pick up my shadow.)

T. Well, I know one way you can catch your shadow and pick it up, too!

The teacher showed the children how they might trace around each other's shadows. All the children were eager to do this. . . . Although undoubtedly tired and restless either from work or waiting, the children were full of talk about these caught shadows and wondering about what might follow. . . . The class wrote a story about shadows. . . .

Another day the teacher planned to probe a remark made by one child which suggested that he had been thinking of his shadow as occupying space.

T. Yesterday someone said something very interesting about his shadow. He said it was a funny thing it was there on the ground but it also came up to meet him and touch him (moving her hands up her body as the child had done). Let's go out into the sunshine and look at that person's shadow.

Ch. It will look the same as any shadow. The shadow touches all over the front of me. (The teacher put her hand into the shadow in different places. Children began to fish for the shadow.)

T. Is this body blocking off the sun? (Many yeses. Does there seem to be shadow in the air here?

[14] Reprinted from *HIGHLIGHTS of the 1963 Elementary Science Study Summer Conference*, pp. 5–9, with the permission of the Elementary Science Study of Educational Services Incorporated, from work done under a grant from the National Science Foundation. Copyright 1964 by Educational Services Incorporated, 55 Chapel Street, Newton, Mass. 02160.

Ch.   Yes, yes, yes (from those fishing).

T.   (Walking back under the tree.) Do you think there is shadow in the air under the leaves? (A few positive yeses as though these were silly questions to be asking.) Could the shadow reach from the leaves to the ground?

Ch.   (Children looked up and down and seemed to be considering this idea.)

T.   (Walking out into the sunshine while opening one of two umbrellas she had brought.) Do you suppose there would be shadow in the air under this umbrella? (The teacher raised it high over her head, then lowered it so that her head and shoulders were in the shadow.)

Ch.   I've seen ladies use umbrellas to keep off the sun.

Ch.   We used beach umbrellas at our beach.

Each child took a turn with one of the umbrellas in a purposeful way not really anticipated by the teacher. The teacher asked from time to time if they could feel or see the shadow coming down around them. Some children "tested" by raising and lowering the umbrella several times. Many mentioned that it was "darker under here." One child said *she did not see any shadow in the air anywhere.*

QUESTION CARDS Another tactic for encouraging children to think out and report their own hypotheses and solutions is the question card, presented in the following account of work on light and shadow with sixth-graders.[15]

This lesson started with discussion of x-ray shadows, light shadows, and paint spray shadows. Then each pupil was given a set of cards with different questions encouraging exploration of shadows and the straight-line nature of light:[16]

1. Suppose light moved in the way smoke travels, can you think of some way the world and the things in it might be very different?

2. Is the kind of shadow made by a clear bulb the same kind of shadow as that made by a frosted bulb? Can you predict before you try it out? Then tell us how you tried it out.

3. Can you make the shadow of a straight stick be a curved shadow? Can you make the shadow of a curved stick be straight?

4. Can you invent something to show why one cannot see around corners? How many things can you think of that will let you see around a corner? Tell us about some of these. Or show us one or several.

5. Make a shadow. How many ways can you find to hide the shadow now that you have made it? Can you think of one, two, three, four, five, six?

Each child was asked to read these cards one by one, and then choose one of the questions to explore, alone or in pairs. They were shown boxes and a shelf containing lamps, string, tape, tinker toys, flashlights, mirrors, styrofoam balls, candles, bulbs of various sorts, extension cords, and other materials which they could use to answer the questions themselves.

15 *HIGHLIGHTS*, pp. 10–13.

16 These are but a few examples out of seventeen question cards.

Mary chose to try to make a straight shadow bend and did it with a curved card. She also made a curved shadow straight, but said: "I can do it, but I don't quite know how I do this."

Janice, Gail, Roland and Anna ended up working together with the candle. Janice found out how to cancel the candle's shadow with a light; they all were very interested in the relationship between the movement of the shadow and the way the flame darted about.

Noel broke a shadow into two pieces with two lights.

Robert tried to make a shadow appear in an unusual place and did it using a mirror. . . .

After putting the equipment away, the pupils came back for . . . reporting. Robert reported on a second question he answered, "Why can you not see around corners?" He said, "I can see around a corner with a mirror, but I can not see around it without one, because the eye can not bend around the corner; It is like light." Ross had made the mirror train—a series of mirrors, like a periscope—to show the same thing.

The teacher pushed this question a little more and asked Robert to go further. He was not quite satisfied that it was his eye that did not "bend like light," but he was sure that whatever it was, it did not bend.

PICTURE SETS In the social sciences, similar tactics can be used for advancing inquiry. Joseph Grannis[17] has experimented successfully with primary-grade children in using pairs and sets of pictures for developing and extending categorical thinking. The children talk together first in pairs and then as a group about the likenesses and differences in a set of pictures that suggest categories. A class observed by the author conversed about sets of pictures showing the same jobs done by farmers, fishermen, and so on, in different environmental settings. An imaginative teacher who knows the concepts and language of a subject discipline can devise similar discussion games through which children can experience the speech-thought of reasoning.

Sound and Word Play

If a scale has rational scientific discourse at one end, at the other end will be the purely playful and emotive language of the rhyme, the limerick, the joke, the pun, and light verse of all kinds. Poetry, however, is the most intense concentration of both the ideation of prose discourse and the emotive language of verbal play. It is rooted in as intense an observation of the world as is science. It grows from the very core of language energy. The way to poetry for children is through a close reflective look at the world and experimentation with the sounds, shapes, colors, and intonations of words and combinations of words in flow that can describe it. Poetry expresses "as ifs" about the cosmos and provides memorable metaphors for recog-

---

[17] Joseph Grannis, unpublished mimeographed material, Harvard Graduate School of Education, Cambridge, Mass., 1964.

nition. Once in a while, children reach poetry in their speech and writing, as do some adults. Although few of them will become poets, children should come to know poetry and experience its possibilities as a grand vehicle for knowing and as a high form of symbolic presentation, a very special form of communication.

Practice in discursive thinking and speaking has been discussed, but there is left for consideration the practice of sounding the depths of the language through language play with sounds, timbres, and richness of meaning. The young child can be observed in the natural state of play exploring his language in all these dimensions. As will be noted in the following transcript of a play episode recorded by the author, children enjoy playing with the possibilities of sound—assonance, consonance, the onomatopoeic—the rhythm of phrasing, and metaphorical possibilities.

Jon (5.9) and Jim (5.10) are digging in the loose dirt under a birch tree and in a nearby abandoned flower bed.

Jim: I'm going to dig with this shovel. Are you going to dig with that one? I'm not going to dig with this fork. I'll dig with this one. I'll dig with *this* one. I'll dig—da-dee-da—dee-da (*rhythmical singing*). Can I dig with this one?

Jon: I'm taking clovers out. (*Continues rhythmic singing.*)

Jim: I'm putting good soil in the holes. Can I put your good soil in the holes?

Jon: I'm just taking the grass and clover out. Aren't I a good boy?

Jim: Aren't I a good boy. (*He looks at a moth that had been captured in a glass jar not long before.*) Look, his wings are sticking.

Jon: Hey, give me the moth, please.

Jim: Please, sneeze, bees.

Jon and Jim: (Alternating) Peas, dees, see saws, bee-uh-for-you, gee-oh-for-you.

Jon: Why did the gee any say ay for you? (*They pick up two cartons, put them on their heads, and march around.*)

Jim: Bum-tee-bum-ah-bum.

Jim: Where is the wash basket?

Jon: There's the bay basket.

Jim: That's the bake basket.

Jon: This is the real bake basket. Rake basket. (*They both play on the vowel and consonant sounds in a rhythmical chatter.*)

With this kind of language activity so much a part of the child's own development, it would seem only common sense to encourage language play in the school setting. Opportunities for sound play should always be available for younger children. For practical reasons, language play is useful in helping children differentiate the sounds of the language in preparation for more sophisticated use in reading and writing. For aesthetic reasons, such play is the gateway to the feel of language that will contribute to their understanding and love of poetry. This natural tendency can be blocked by strait-jacketed exercises in "making" poetry that rhymes in regular meter or force-feeding the "old chestnuts" of grownups' verse to reluctant children.

Extending Play Talk into Verse Talk

The teacher may pick up interesting chants that emerge while young children are playing and may encourage their extension. On the other hand, he may interject into the classroom some words he knows from his experience with children and thus prompt extemporaneous sound play. The teacher need not be afraid of permitting presentation of group chants and individual variations at the same time, because this is the way language play develops. A child picks up an idea from another and plays with it in much the same way jazz musicians improvise on a musical phrase they hear. Children will not become undisciplined in such a session if the teacher gives them a feeling that language play is a constructive enterprise. The following example comes from a home setting, but it is not unlike the kind of activity that should be happening from nursery school through the second grade:

A father is sitting in a rocking chair in front of the fire; his son is climbing on his knees, hoping for some roughhouse. The five-year-old boy begins:

> Do it with me on your knees.
> Do it with me on your knees.
>
> Clap, clap, clap on your lap.
> Lapity lap lap lap.
>
> Do it with Pete on your feet.
> Do it with Ted on your head.
> Do it with Hans on your hands.
>
> Clap, clap, clap on your lap.
> Lapity lap lap lap.

Traditional nursery rhymes will, of course, stimulate extensions. Children will chant them in unison and make up variations.

A related form of language play is making up word pictures or definitions. As children develop their ability to classify and categorize, they enjoy creating similes or operational definitions. The following examples of simile making come from a fifth-grade class:

Jane: Snow is like feathers.
Robert: Yes, like feathers from a flock of geese flying north.
Lucy: Like icy feathers that melt and leave their shape in your hand.
Jimmy: Freezing with a special shape you can remember later in a warm house or even next summer.

Ruth Krauss's book *A Hole Is to Dig* reflects the delight children have in defining things by their use, an expression of the "operational" way they think about the world. Five-year-olds completed "A meadow is . . ." by saying, "where cows eat grass," "where horses are," and "it's an animal place." A seven-year-old responded to "spring" by saying, "Crocuses are a sign of spring. Why? Because they can put up through the ground and when the ground gets soft that is a sign that spring is here."

Rhyming will come naturally to youngsters because of their delight in word-sound play; but the wise teacher may wish to de-emphasize it at first in order to break through to their basic poetic resources. A better pathway to the creation of poetry by children is to start with a joke poem, like and dislike poems or a comparison—whatever brings forth honest feelings.[18]

The oral-aural method is the precursor to written expression and is the father to it when the skill of handwriting is achieved. The teacher can begin a story that the children complete as a game, somewhat in the way folktales have emerged. A trip to nearby woods or a studied look out the window as a storm gathers can be the subject of delightful verbal interchange. Sometimes these "stories," "reactions," "definitions," "or poems" are worth writing down and saving or preparing to share with another class or with parents. This is when writing begins for the young, when the teacher writes down their "stories" to be read; older children, of course, will write down their own. With older children, there will be less talk and more writing at such a time, but talking must not always be replaced by writing. Some subjects are too complex to write about at a certain stage, but they can be thought about out loud.

section 2

Developing Written Thought

The child's written thought is being cultivated simultaneously with speech from the moment he first recognizes the importance of printed language as he "reads along" while being read to. Little children should be encouraged to dictate stories and letters to their parents or teachers and should be read to from books when information or enjoyment is sought. These are the first lessons in writing.

Although writing is based on speech-thought, it is not exactly like it. As previously mentioned, speech-thought is abbreviated and casual in its grammar and is punctuated with pauses, inflection, and gesture; writing must be more complete and more carefully designed for communication with the reader. The writer must always keep him in mind and, therefore, he constructs his ideas and develops them for readability. It is important for children, even when they are dictating stories, to become accustomed to assuming the objective role of author.

[18] Kenneth Koch and Students of P.S. 61 in New York City, *Lies and Dreams: Teaching Children to Write Poetry* (New York: Vintage Books, 1970). Also *Rose, Where Did You Get That Red: Teaching Great Poetry to Children* (New York: Random House, 1973).

Creativity in Writing: Tactics
for Teaching Creative Writing

Often the word *creative* is loosely applied to all children's writing. Although all discursive writing (for example, social studies reports, business letters, and scientific explanations) should be creatively composed, the label "creative writing" is best applied to imaginative compositions drawn from experience or fancy or both. Guilford's proposition, setting up the dual typology of *convergent* and *divergent* thinking, is applicable to the writing situation. The *convergent* mode of thinking "tends toward retaining the known, learning the predetermined, and conserving what is"; the *divergent* mode "tends toward revising the known, exploring the undetermined, and constructing what might be."[19] Investigators further clarify these classifications: "A person for whom [convergent thinking] is primary tends toward the usual and the expected. A person for whom [divergent thinking] is primary tends toward the novel and speculative."[20]

The mode of divergent thinking is most related to what is currently called creative thinking and writing. Getzels and Jackson point out that although one of the modes may be dominant in a certain personality complex, both modes are "found in all persons, but in varying proportions."[21] The divergent element, then, needs to be exploited for the children who already possess the ability and to be developed in the children who have not yet had the opportunity to expand their thinking in divergent ways. Creative writing is one of the best means for enhancing the thinking processes of imagination and divergency.

Types of Creative Writing

Two types of creative writing can be described by categorizing the sources of imaginative thinking: the experiental and the fanciful. Although these two types overlap as one contributes to the other, most children's stories are dominated either by inspiration from reactions to life experiences or by such psychic forces as wish-fulfilment and identification with heroes. If teachers recognize these wellsprings of the imagination, they can initiate cues that will motivate creative writing of both types.

Experiential Stories

A child's stories may begin in reality and conclude in fantasy, but quite often a child wishes to record things experienced, because they are new and

[19] See Jacob Getzels and Philip Jackson, *Creativity and Intelligence* (New York: Wiley, 1962), p. 14.
[20] Getzels and Jackson, p. 14.
[21] Getzels and Jackson, p. 14.

exciting and he wishes to tell the world about them. Accounts may record immediate events, or they may—especially with older children—tell of several related experiences that set a mood or relate a story. The following examples are all by the same child "writing" under the guidance of different teachers.

IMMEDIATE EXPERIENCE RECALLED The first story was dictated by the child at the age of 6.9, on the day after his visit to the county fair. It was taken down during several sittings, with short breaks in between. The sentencing and paragraphing were done by the recorder as the dictation proceeded. It was agreed that the story was to be written so that it could be read by others.

> I like Granddaddy because Granddaddy takes me to the fair. He promised me two whole months before the fair began that he would take me, just Granddaddy and me. Daddy would stay home, Mommy would stay home. And I decided not to ask Jimmy, just Grandaddy and me would go.
>
> Granddaddy is big and tall and has no hair. He needs to wear a hat to keep from sunburning his head. Granddaddy takes rests every day the way I do, only he falls asleep and snores sometimes even when he is reading to me; but I like Granddaddy's snore because it is like a purr. When Granddaddy takes me to the fair, he buys me tractor models when it isn't even my birthday. . . .
>
> [The story continues about the boy's seeing tractors and their attachments, sitting on one and steering it, getting separated from his Granddaddy but being found in time to be given a surprise ride on a tractor, sitting in the lap of one of the salesmen.]
>
> When I got back from my ride Granddaddy had a little model tractor for me and he gave it to me.
>
> When I got home I showed the tractor to my Daddy and Mommy. And when I went to bed I took it with me. Granddaddy came and said goodnight and we talked about the tractor ride and the fair until I went to sleep.

Younger children do not usually have the concentration to sustain a story of this length and complexity. However, when an event is as exciting and important as that trip to the fair, there is much to tell if the recorder will be patient, allowing for interruptions but bringing the child back to the thread of the story by asking, "What happened next?" The cumulative tale based on experience and then embroidered is a form popular with children. Sometimes older children once they are underway can write for days as they present an adventure story that spins a web of narrative around a kernel of personal experience and becomes a story of wish-fulfillment.

MEMORIES OF EARLIER EXPERIENCE RECALLED This genre of children's writing has probably developed because of the frequent first assignment in the fall, "Write about your summer vacation." This strategy, although somewhat threadbare from overuse, can be enlivened. Children do want to tell about the events of a vacation, of a weekend, or of a family trip, but not as the fulfilment of a routine assignment. The results rarely exceed "I went there and I did so and so." Preparing little lectures with pictures or setting up groups to write scripts for television or news reports about different kinds of vacation experiences could stimulate more thoughtful presentation of vacation memories. Perhaps a class could set up and document a museum with the inevitable rocks, shells, and other treasures children bring home from trips.

The following is a dictated story by the same six-year-old boy about his experiences as a four-year-old in response to the questions, "What do you most remember about the place where you last lived? What happened to you there?"

> I remember my little army jeep. Once I was just driving along looking up in the air and I was driving along the sidewalk. Then crack, boom, my jeep ran into a bush. Then I honked the horn twice and it went toot toot.
> I remember when it was Halloween. I was a fireman with a little red fire hat and I went to my next door neighbor and I had a little hose and she answered the door. Then she said, "You can't come in if the hose is too long."

Typical Child's Writing Style

Both these stories dictated in the late sixth year of age reveal typical characteristics of the written-thought style of the child in the primary grades. Children use the rhetoric of repetition effectively. The frequent use of *and* in the run-on sentence is another popular device at this age level. *And* signals that more is coming. It creates an easy grammar to follow and express, as no other sentence form does, the fast-moving activity of the child from one event directly into another. Often tenses are switched quickly from past to present when an event is so vivid in the memory that it is as if it were happening now. Simple time clauses appear, but it is unusual to find complex grammatical structures that hold one idea while another related idea is developed. The simplicity of grammatical structure is congruent with the stage in thinking development. Some teachers make the mistake of trying to dissuade children from repetition and run-on sentences, pushing them into using the complex syntactical forms of the adult before they have fully explored the simple but highly effective ones for their own kind of narratives. One result may be the peculiar type of composition in which each sentence is exactly one line long.

By ages nine and ten, advanced thinking ability and a more detached view of events have developed to the point where the chain of activities become more objectified and where situations become more interrelated. Mood and theme emerge as the events are recorded for a purpose and formed into ideas. "At Five Forty-Five in the Morning," quoted in Chapter 12 reflects the development of language and thinking in children's writing that comes during the preadolescent period.

The following example comes from the writing of the boy who went to the fair and recalled dressing up as a fireman on Halloween; he is now age eleven. The style is very different, but the delight in telling is the same. These later stories were written by him. Speech-thought has developed into written thought. The phrases are molded, one after the other, as they are put down on paper, and have the effect of being addressed to a reader. One reason for this is that they were written for exhibition in a school festival of arts. A classroom book of stories, the publication of a literary mimeographed magazine, or just the wish to share each of these stories may be sufficient motivation to set the stage for writing to an audience.

MY FIRST CAMPING TRIP

It was the first camping trip of the season and what an awful month to have it. I know better now to go in August, when there aren't so many bothersome bugs. We did have some fun too.

I had all my things together and Jim, my friend and camping companion, had his. We got the canoe and started off but his father said it was much too tippy, even if I did know how to handle it. So we took the rowboat across the still pond and started making camp.

Jim and I started making bough beds. I tried it out and thought it felt good and soft.

When it was about six we started a fire for supper. We each had a hot dog and a hamburger and about half our weight in marshmallows, after.

We went to bed about nine. (The bed still felt good.) We woke up about eleven in the night and got our flashlights and went feeling around for wood in the underbrush. Then we saw something black, with a big stripe of white on his back and that's all we needed to know to get the heck out of there. We ran in our bare feet over blackberry bushes, rocks and everything else, jumped in the boat and rowed like a devil was after us, 'til we were about fifty feet from shore and rowed over to Jim's house, got some cookies and milk. We went back in about fifteen minutes and built a huge bonfire. . . . Then went to bed, but the bed didn't feel good, so we went fishing at one in the morning.

The Fanciful Story

Stories of fancy are built from direct experience, but they have incorporated elements of make-believe that may be psychological in source. The frightful, the mysterious, the awesome, and the wondrous are embodied symbolically in folk tale, myth, and ritual. The ancient symbolic meanings of Halloween and Christmas, once folk celebrations of the mysteries of death and life, live on in children. The myths and rituals of these occasions have survived in the oral tradition and in the fancy of children. The fanciful is not simply the weird; rather, it conveys truths about the human situation that cannot be embraced by the discursive, rational, and logical language of statement.

Children's efforts in telling or writing fanciful stories usually reflect such psychic matter as wish fulfillment or hero worship, as well as wonder about the unknown. At five years of age the same boy who wrote the experiential stories quoted earlier devised an extra-world of Cuckoo Bunnies. He became so enchanted with the possibilities of life in a society of Cuckoo Bunnies that he spent considerable time one summer dictating stories about them to his father and drawing pictures of their activities. Some dictated excerpts follow to demonstrate the psychic qualities of this kind of fantasy that undoubtedly influence the symbolic content and language of a child's life during the preschool and early school years. The presentation of such symbols should be encouraged.

> Cuckoo Bunny Land is a wonderful place. I go whenever I want to. You can go, too, if you want to. All you have to do is get silly and off you go.
>
> Cuckoo Bunny Land is a wonderful place where you can eat lollipops without asking your mother. As a matter of fact, you don't have mothers there. You can have desserts for breakfast, desserts for lunch, and desserts for supper.
>
> Whenever my father says, "Come now it's time to go to bed," I go to Cuckoo Bunny Land, because in that place there is no bedtime, because there is no nighttime, because it's always day and time to play.
>
> Cuckoo Bunnies are grown up when they are five. They don't get any bigger but they are twenty or thirty years old. . . . They are never lonesome even though there are no daddies and mommies because there are hundreds and thousands and millions and trillions of Cuckoo Bunnies.
>
> Uncle Ted is an honorary Cuckoo Bunny but Daddy is only half. The Golden Rule is to do what Jesus says: to do to other people what you want them to do to you. The Silver Rule is not to catch cold.
>
> In Cuckoo Bunny Land you are boss of the family like when Daddy is away. You can boss anybody anytime. You can tell your baby sitter to stop nagging you. You are boss of all the children. I like this place because you can have all the toys all the time and I don't have to share. Sometimes I share with a friend but I know that there is a place where I don't even have to do that. It feels like you are on a mountain and it is even better than summer vacation.
>
> But if I were there all the time I know I would want to be back in Mommy-and-Daddy Land, just for a little while because some time I might get tired and want to go to bed and if I did, I'd want my daddy to carry me piggy-back up the stairs.

Wish fulfillment and secondary identification with Uncle Ted are obvious psychic elements in this fantasy, which has been constructed for telling to an audience. Child syntax is strongly in evidence. The run-on sentences, especially the long "because" series, convey meaning swiftly and directly. The repetition of rhetorical phrases gives emphasis when the child wants it and adds to the rhythmic flow of the language. Even though the child author switches from the general to the egocentric "I" within the same thought–word grouping, his meaning is clear.

Child grammar is effective in its own way. If it is ineffective because it confuses meaning, then the teacher or parent raises a question, "I don't understand what you have said. Say it again." The child needs many opportunities to tell and write in his own way, because the connections are building and the schemata are developing in Piaget's sense as the child practices and rehearses his own way of relating to the world and symbolizing it. Teachers can pick up cues about wish-fulfillment and encourage children to spin their stories from them. They can also tap this source directly by the tactic of using open-ended questions.

If you had your own way what sort of place would you want to live in?
Do you have a Never-Never Land? What is it like?
If you and your friend could do anything you wanted, what would you do?
Suppose there were witches or fairies. What could they do for you?

The suggestive opening phrase might also be a fill-in tactic, for example, "If I were a spaceman . . ."

Writing in the genre of fantasy should not be restricted to young children. The more sophisticated fairy story or space adventure is legitimate material for older children's written thought. The following verse by an eleven-year-old girl demonstrates continued interest by modern youngsters in an old-time subject. It also shows how her compulsion to make the fourth line rhyme with the second thwarts her imagination.

> The fairies dance on rainbows,
> Their houses are the stars,
>
> Their mirror is the moon,
> But they've never heard of Mars.
>
> They slide to Earth on moonbeams
> Their playground is the sky.
>
> They play all night and sleep all day
> Though I know why.

When children are introduced only to conventional patterns of versification tritely used, they are bound to make up senseless last lines to their stanzas or foolish rhymes along the way. Story form and free verse are more appropriate unless the child has an unusual language sense and an ability to build with formal poetic structures. Fantasy writing in verse can easily fall into patter if the child is not accustomed to good poetry and if he is not permitted freedom to write outside the conventions of regularized rhymes and meter.

Parody

It is perhaps more plausible for children to write parodies of common verse forms because the wrenched line can be part of the parody. By the time he is eight or nine years old, the child is able to place experience into perspective and not believe everything he hears. The strength-through-cereals kind of television advertising becomes a joke, and the children can devise all kinds of advertising parodies when they write script for simulated television programs. The parody is a kind of fanciful writing that is an expression of the child's break from egocentric subjectivity to a degree of sophisticated objectivity. He begins to stand off from events and to take a look at them in perspective. This breakaway stage is one to be encouraged and explored fully. The following is an eight-year-old's parody of the "Night before Christmas."

> The night *after* Christmas, all through the house
> Pop guns were popping and so was the mouse.
> The rifles were banging and the cymbals were clanging
> And the electric train whistled toot toot.

Older children delight in writing parodies of stories, movies, and television programs that they enjoyed as younger children. This is one way to cast off old skins in growing up.

Psychic Fantasy

The clever teacher knows how to exploit natural psychic tendencies in each period of growth by stimulating their expression through discussion and questioning at the appropriate times. The hero-worshiping or model-identifying story is one type that can be written as serious fantasy at the time of identification and parodied at the time when it has been replaced by another. Boys writing about cowboys and astronauts, and girls writing about nurses are common examples. A listening teacher may locate other heroes as cowboys give way to baseball players and nurses give way to TV and recording stars.

Certain other fantasies are sources of symbolic expression. In this culture there is a horse-loving period for many girls and a war-games phase for many boys when every story and every picture has to be about horses or jet fighters. Again, it is important that these fantasies be given legitimate expression and artful structure in order that the emerging psychic and cognitive development be realized at the proper time and not thwarted, only to erupt in unattractive immaturity in later life. Fantasy continues through adult life, but in adult forms that should not be throwbacks to unexpressed childishness. In child writing these expressions can have charm; in adult writing childish fantasy becomes foolish.

The imaginative and the experiential come together in the best of creative writing. Given opportunities to be expressive in both, children come to combine them in their best works at any age. The author, child or adult, imagines as he focuses and intensifies experience in terms of his life-view.

The following poem by a fourth-grader was taken from a collection of children's writing quoted in a helpful book for teachers:

> There are four blue eggs in the brown nest;
> The mother robin gentles her red feathers
> Down over them
> And never makes a sound.
> Then suddenly there are four baby birds
> Squawking with surprise
> To see the great brown world of the nest.
> And the mother bird
> Stands on the edge of the nest
> And sings to everyone,
> Look, look,
> The world is full of baby birds.[22]

All of these forms are appropriate at secondary and higher levels. Older students can work with literary forms (especially the short story) and can also become deeply involved in the many journalistic forms of writing through simulations of newspaper and magazine writing. Participation in actual school publications is also invaluable. Practical writing of individual and team-study reports and of career-related compositions should be common fare in most courses. Every secondary-level teacher should be capable of teaching writing and reading as well as a single subject.

The curriculum strategies and the classroom tactics for encouraging youngsters to present their symbolic structures require planning that is sensitive to the personal worlds of young people and has respect for the possibilities of their language. As youngsters gain in the practice of presenting their speech-thought and written thought, the art of "of everyday writing" may be advanced; we shall have more and better "letters to the world."

[22] From *They All Want To Write: Written English in the Elementary School,* Third Edition, by Alvina T. Burrows, Doris C. Jackson, and Dorothy O. Saunders. Copyright 1939, 1952, © 1964 by Holt, Rinehart and Winston, Inc. Reprinted by permission of Holt, Rinehart and Winston.

14

Writing: Spelling, Handwriting, and Mechanics

Written thought becomes written communication only when the language conveys effectively and persuasively the ideas intended. An important element of communication, personal writing style develops with many experiences of refining expression to convey thoughts effectively. Various literacy skills aid writers in meeting this task.

Much of the language teaching in schools, particularly elementary schools, focuses on aspects of written language. These aspects are spelling, handwriting or penmanship, and the mechanics of written composition.[1] Often, these are treated as skills that are taught in exercises isolated from the written thought expression that the development of the skills is intended to facilitate.

Expression through written language is a process of encoding meaning and using a system of graphic symbols for the purpose of self-expression and communication. Writing is the productive, generative counterpart of speech in written language. Isolating the skills from the communicative and expressive use of language makes them abstract exercises unrelated to the encoding process. Some children may be able to learn specific skills in isolation, for example, how to spell *dog*, how to form a cursive *b*, how to indent for a paragraph. But for many children the gap between isolated skills and

[1] Other aspects of literacy are discussed fully in this book in the chapters on reading and language structure.

written thought may never be fully bridged. The assumption in isolated drill on skills is that a "transfer of training" will occur. It is assumed that skills or rules learned in isolation will be transferred to the writing of compositions, essays, letters, notes, and other real uses of written language. Repeated research studies, however, have failed to support such an assumption.

Many teachers still have the seemingly logical view that children cannot express written thought until they have mastered basic literacy skills. "I can't let them write yet," said one second-grade teacher, "they don't know how to spell."

Such a view if applied to speech-thought would mean that children could not be permitted to express themselves in oral language until they had fully mastered all the phonology of adult speech as well as all the intricacies of its structure; they would be confined to a vocabulary that accorded with adult meanings. This view, of course, is absurd. The child's need to express his thoughts and feelings furnishes his motivation for developing oral language. As he strives for more effective communication, he is pushed toward the norms of adult language. The same force operates as he develops written language. He tends to move toward adult norms in handwriting, spelling, and form if the written language activities he engages in involve an expressive or communicative purpose. He wants his written thought to be understood, just as he wants his speech-thought to be understood. This force would tend to make many learners adequate in penmanship and spelling even if they had no formal periods devoted to these subjects and had no special exercises. The developmental process of acquiring one's own written language would be in force as each child strove to make himself understood in the written form.

Keeping Writing in a Communicative Context

A major problem in teaching effective writing is that there seldom is provision made for what is written to be read. Language exists for communication. When children are learning to speak, the responses of their listeners play a vital role since they can judge whether they have successfully communicated by the responses. In listening and reading, language learners can judge their success on the basis of whether they comprehend what the speakers or writers have said. But in writing activities in school the teacher often evaluates, assigning grades without responding to the message. Comments on papers by teachers are often sweeping negative condemnations: "Sloppy"; "You can do better"; "Be more careful."

Even when comments are specific they tend to focus on spelling, handwriting, punctuation, and mechanics without relating them to the writer's success in communicating their messages. Teachers appear to be comparing the draft to a writing model rather than considering how well the writer has expressed his meaning. Skills become ends in themselves, and pupils come to regard writing activities in school as empty exercises unlike language in real use.

The solution is to provide real purposes for every writing activity which will insure that there are readers whose concern is the message. This is not so hard as it may seem, but it does require a careful reorientation on the part of teachers. Pupils can write notices, letters, reports, stories that are part of activities that involve others and which have communicative purposes other than the practice of written language skills. *Writing is not writing if it isn't read.* The teacher's purpose may be more effective writing, but the pupils' purpose is to express their ideas and be understood in real communication.

There is a vital part–whole relationship and an ends–means relationship that must be in the teacher's mind in planning all language activities. Written language is *not* a matter of stringing together a series of pretty and efficiently formed letters into a series of correctly spelled words that are properly spaced on the page with correct headings, margins, punctuation, and paragraphing. The whole is much more than the sum of its parts, and it is only in relationship to the message that the value of legible handwriting, correct spelling, suitable punctuation, and form becomes clear.

It may help to visualize a classroom bulletin board labeled "Our Best Work," a common sight in many schools. What is displayed on the board exemplifies the teacher's criteria for judging pupil success in writing. Is it a set of neatly written, perfectly spelled but identical papers? Then the teacher has isolated the aspects of written language from their use and made them ends in themselves. Is the board filled with papers which vary somewhat in wording but which all are informal letters addressed to an imaginary Aunt Sally inviting her to an imaginary class program? Then the teacher has lost sight of the essential need for language: a real communicative purpose.

What should the bulletin board display? First, its name should be changed. "Our Best Work" is not a title that relates to the purpose of using written language. Instead, call it "Our Class Magazine" or "Our Letters to the World" or "In My Opinion . . ." or "Dear Reader." But make sure that what is posted is for reading, not just admiring.

We should make sure that *all* pupils can be represented on the board if they have something to communicate. Regarding material to be submitted, criteria for inclusion should be (1) Appropriateness of topic to the theme of the board (which can be specific and changed regularly, or general and more permanent); (2) clarity of message (it has been thought through and expressed relatively completely); (3) evidence of suitable editing, proofreading, and rereading (to make it as legible and interesting as possible). These criteria must be applied with concern for individual differences among pupils in interest, development, and coordination. It should be possible for interesting papers to appear which contain misspelled words and clumsy or immature writing. The board in an early primary room should reflect the characteristics of the age group just as one in a junior high school should. Neither should show attempts to imitate adult writing. *Skills will develop if the teacher stimulates the learners to write frequently and confidently, but neither skills nor effective writing will develop if the focus is on isolated skills.*

The Special Characteristics of Written Language

In order to understand the problems inherent in the acquisition of literacy skills, it is necessary to examine some of the special characteristics of written language that are involved in teaching composition, spelling, and handwriting.

Written language, first of all, makes use of *graphic* symbols rather than the *sound* symbols of speech. In English orthography these symbols are alphabetic in nature; that is, they correspond to sounds in speech rather than to syllables or to meanings. Our numerals *1, 2,* and so on are examples of the type of symbol corresponding to meaning. They represent the same numerical concept to speakers of English, French, German, Russian, and other languages, although the names the languages give to the concepts may be very different.

The alphabet, as we suggest in later chapters on reading, is more a convenience of writers than readers. Readers have no more trouble with pictographs or logographs or syllabaries than with alphabetic writing. But writers are greatly convenienced by a system that uses a small stock of easily formed letters roughly corresponding in number to the number of phonemes the oral language uses.

Oral language, unless it is recorded electronically, is perishable. Once uttered, it is gone. Written language, on the other hand, is more permanent. It can preserve thought for some later decoding, perhaps long after the writer is dead or at a place far distant from the place of writing. Written language is also perfectible. It can be reworked and revised until the author is satisfied that he has used it in the most effective manner to express his thought. Perhaps for this reason more precision is expected of written expression. For the same reason, written language tends, except in the hands of the very confident user, to be somewhat more stiff, more formal, and less natural and spontaneous than oral language.

Written language as it is being created has a space–time sequence, whereas oral language has only a time sequence; that is, the symbols of writing are usually produced sequentially and in a spatial direction (left to right in English orthography), whereas the sounds of oral language need only be produced sequentially. This may explain why writers are more aware of the sequence of letter production than speakers are of the sequence of sounds in speech production. As proficiency in the skills of literacy increases, however, this letter-sequence awareness tends to diminish. Many adults find it necessary to write a word out fully, perhaps in several alternate spellings, so that they can see it as a whole and decide which spelling "looks" right. Written language is often ambiguous where oral language is not. The intonation of oral language may make clear the underlying structure and meaning of language, which is ambiguous in written form. For example: *The store is closed at 8* P.M. This could mean that the time of closing is 8 P.M. or that it's closed at some earlier time and is not open at 8 P.M. Intonation would avoid the oral ambiguity. Punctuation does not provide the ranges of cues to the underlying structure in writing that intonation does in speech. An author proofreading his own written work is aware only of the structures and meaning he had in mind at the time of composition; a second person however may be able to uncover an unintended ambiguity, a possible alternate meaning or syntax which is equally plausible. In some instances written language may be less ambiguous than speech. Homophones, words that sound alike, may be spelled differently, for example.

Written language has the advantage of permanence but that is also one of its disadvantages. It becomes, over time, a fossil that preserves thought encoded in language at the time of writing. It is more resistent to change and therefore tends to lose touch with sociocultural reality and become out of phase with the changing oral language. Perhaps the greatest difference between oral and written language is that speech is very likely to occur in a situational context in which there is much to support the language, while writing is most often far from the reality it deals with. Speakers can point or motion to things that are visible to their listeners as they speak. The face-to-face character of most oral language communication is even more facilitating. Writers must more fully express their meanings through language because it is removed from any supporting situational context. This difference is of course a continuum. Written language in the form of signs, labels, illustrated texts may be embedded in a situational context while oral language may be dealing with abstract ideas or involve media, such as radio or telephone, which transcend time and space. The use usually made of oral and written language, though, imposes some basic differences on the ways they work and the factors necessary for their use in successful communication.

section 1

Spelling

Some time ago, a child in a familiar comic strip announced proudly to his friend, "I got an A in spelling. When I grow up I'm going to be a speller." This illustrates well the way in which spelling has been lifted out of its proper place as a means to effective written communication and been made an end in itself. There are some historical reasons for this. A hundred years ago it was thought that before a child could read, he had to memorize the correct spellings of a stock of words. Spelling instruction thus preceded reading instruction in that day, and the first book a child encountered in school was a speller, not a primer or reader. Another reason why spelling is so much stressed in schools is that poor spelling is equated in folk humor and popular belief with ignorance and lack of education. From the one-room rural schools, the spelling bee became a national pastime, a source of family entertainment, and a means through which children received recognition. Parents competed through their children with other parents, not unlike modern Little League baseball competition.

The spelling bee, as a competitive activity, was possible because spelling English is something of an art. There is enough variability from consistent one-to-one relationships between letters and sounds that the spelling of a particular word is not highly predictable from a set of simple rules. As a matter of fact, the child who acquires a set of phonic generalizations for spelling, on his own or in school, often becomes a phonic misspeller: *Hee spelz wurdz ukording tu thu roolz, az this sentinz iz speld.*

English Spelling

English spelling is neither as chaotic and capricious as is popularly believed nor as simple and straightforward as some teachers have believed who felt that a small set of rules could be taught to students which would make them accurate spellers. Part of the complexity of English spelling reflects its multiple sources in Latin, French, Germanic, and other languages. Words like *know, knee,* and *knob* clearly reflect their Scandinavian origin, for example. Much of the system of prefixes and suffixes in English (apart from Germanic inflections) are Latin based though they largely came into English through the Norman-French influence. Later borrowings from French are more likely to retain French spellings as they also are given more French-like pronunciations: *chef, chauffeur, recipe, rendezvous,* for example.

Printers are responsible for standardizing English spelling. They felt the need for uniformity in spelling probably both because of their concern for making their products readable, and because consistency is an attribute of a professional looking product. In moving toward standardization the printers, in a sense, "locked in" the writing system. This is an advantage since variability could be a source of confusion. It also makes spelling uniform across dialects, which is important for a language medium intended for use across larger spans of time and space than oral language. But in holding spelling constant the printers assured that there could not be a close letter to sound match for the range of dialects in English. Further, as oral language is continuously changing, the mismatch increases as time passes. This is exemplified by common pronunciations of words like *comfortable, interest-*

ing, toward, walk, night, colonel. This does not make the spelling system a bad one. A choice must be made between universal spelling or close letter–sound correspondence. The spelling system chooses universality.

One goal of spelling reformers is to bring spelling up-to-date eliminating outmoded spellings. But such a goal could be achieved only in the cases where *all* dialects have shifted. Likely examples often cited are *gh* words: *night, light, cough, hiccough,* and soon. But in some Scottish dialects, at least some of these *gh* words seem quite rationally spelled. Perhaps the *k* in *kn* words could be dropped, but that would eliminate one way of distinguishing some homophones such as *knew/new, knight/night, knot/not.*

English spelling, recent research has revealed, is considerably more regular than it was presumed to be.[2] It also shows, however, that complexity and regularity must not be confused. In the Cronnell study 166 rules were found to account for the spelling of about 90 percent of 9000 selected one-or two-syllable words. *Sure, sugar,* and *insure* are regularly spelled words. $<s>$ represents /š/, which is more commonly spelled $<sh>$ before the sound /ʊ/. Those *su* words are regularly spelled. There just are not very many such words in English.

The relationships between English speech and spelling are not simply between letters and sounds. They are between spelling patterns and sound patterns. The sound system of English dialects are not simple either. Complex shifts take place as sounds precede each other. The spelling system reflects these shifts at some times but not at others. For example *bomb* has what appears to be a nonfunctional $<b>$ at the end. In *bombing* it still seems superfluous. But in *bombard* its function becomes apparent. Similar patterns are found in *damn/damnation* and *hymn/hymnal.*

Vowels in unstressed positions are pronounced identically as /ə/, as in: *contain, defeat, certain, rapid,* and *capable.* In these cases the spelling is the same as it would be in a stressed syllable in a related or derived word: *rapidity, ascertain, capacity.*

The spelling is unchanged when affixes produce other sound shifts; *rite* and *ritual* are both spelled with a $<t>$ though the sound becomes /č/ which is sometimes spelled $<ch>$. *Repress, repression, press,* and *pressure* all have the $<ss>$. The meaning relationship is preserved though the apparent inconsistency in spelling results. This departure from letter–sound regularity is a basic feature of English spelling. It facilitates reading because the reader is not distracted from meaning relationships, and it does not appear to interfere with spelling or make it more difficult as long as young spellers are not taught misconceptions about close letter–sound correspondences.

Some of the most common spelling patterns are used to contrast similar

[2] Bruce Cronnell, *Annotated Spelling-to-Sound Correspondence Rules,* Technical Report 32, Southwest Regional Laboratory, June 1971. Ruth Weir and Richard Venezky, "Spelling to Sound Correspondences," in K. Goodman (ed.), *The Psycholinguistic Nature of the Reading Process* (Detroit: Wayne State University Press, 1968).

sounding words. Consonants are usually double after "short" vowels: *diner/dinner*; *super/supper*; and *later/latter*. A final *e* marks the ends of "long" vowel consonant patterns *at/ate*; and *bit/bite*.

Three key principles have emerged from modern research on English spelling:[3]

1. Alphabetical systems don't simply operate on a *letter to sound basis*. They involve complex pattern relationships.
2. English spelling is, in general, regular (rule-governed) but the rule system is very complex.
3. Spelling is fixed and standard across dialects.

PREDICTING ENGLISH SPELLING Can a literate user of English predict the spelling of English words from the way the words are pronounced? This is a crucial question because its answer or supposed answer is the basis for the spelling instruction to be provided in school. Teaching should help a speller produce accurate spellings of all words. The SWRL study cited above suggests that one can use one of the 166 rules they have identified to decide how a word is spelled. So large a set of rules itself poses a problem, but their use in deciding how to spell words is more complicated than that.

Here are two common English patterns, for example:

ea/ee			*a–e/ai*	
eat			ale	ail
beat	beet		bale	bail
feat	feet		dale	
	greet	(great)		fail
heat			gale	Gail
meat	meet		hale	hail
				jail
			male	mail
				nail
			pale	pail
				rail
			sale	sail
			tale	tail
			vale	avail
			whale	wail

Nothing in the *sound* of the words can tell a listener that a word is spelled *meet* or *meat*. Knowing something about correspondence of English sound patterns to English spelling patterns will help the listener to know what alternatives exist but not which alternative is the right one. The listener must know which *mail* gets postage, which *tale* is told, which *sail* is on a boat.

[3] Kenneth S. Goodman, "Orthography in a Theory of Reading Instruction," *Elementary English*, 49, No. 8 (December 1972).

Vowel patterns, particularly those using two or more letters to spell the vowel phonemes are very hard to predict. Vowel phonemes are highly variable from dialect to dialect as well. Add the fact that any word with an unaccented syllable will have a schwa /ə/ sound, which may be spelled by any vowel, and the situation is complex indeed.

So the answer to the crucial question is "maybe." *Maybe* the listener can predict the spelling of a word from hearing it if he knows the complex rules that relate sound patterns and spelling patterns. But he will need to hear it in a *meaningful context*, and he will need to appreciate its morphemic structure (the base, affixes, and their relationship to syntax and meaning). In many cases he will simply need to know which of several possible patterns a word fits. If he doesn't know, his set of alternatives will help him to know where to begin a dictionary search.

The problems of writers and readers in using the spelling system are not identical, but they are related. An alphabetic system is a convenience for a writer in that it reduces the number of forms he must produce. The reader is less convenienced since he can handle a range of forms without apparent trouble. A key difference is that a reader samples the print (*see* chapter 15), while a writer must produce a full, complete representation. But no learned set of rules can generate all English spellings; the writer must either specifically know individual spellings or ultimately be able to resort to authority—the dictionary. As we have said earlier, the dictionary does not establish meanings, it reports them. But spelling is, by common agreement standardized so the dictionary may record the standard spellings. Meaning is in motion; spelling stands still.

Accuracy in Spelling

Another question that must be answered in setting up spelling instruction is just how accurate spelling must be. British and American standards vary, but within each system there is (with rare exception) a standard spelling. But how much will misspelling interfere with the readibility of written communication?

Interestingly, a good deal of misspelling can occur before it interferes with readability. How much is tolerable depends on how closely reader and writer know each other, how familiar the reader is with the topic, and how different misspellings are from the standard spellings. Misspelling, in fact, is as much a problem to the writer because of the attitudes of his readers toward his misspelling as is the difficulty it causes in their reading of his writing. Readers will judge character, education—even intelligence—on the basis of misspelling. Such judgments are clearly unwarranted, but they indicate a reality that must be dealt with.

The worst manifestation of intolerance of error is among teachers. The ability to use standard spelling is an ultimate goal of education but demanding *only* accurate spelling at all stages, in all written work, no matter what its purpose, is both unreasonable and self-defeating. It is unreasonable because there are many informal uses of written language in which total accuracy is quite unnecessary for effective writing. It is also unreasonable because no aspect of any language process is learned perfectly at all stages of development. Language learners move toward adult norms in phonology, grammar, and meaning. They also move toward adult spelling. But a good deal of misspelling is to be expected on the way to this goal, and here is where intolerance of error is self-defeating. The greatest contribution to progress toward adult spelling norms comes from writing. As youngsters use a wider and wider range of vocabulary in their writing their spelling continually improves. But if teachers insist pupils must spell every word correctly they discourage risk taking. The pupils use only those words they are sure they can spell correctly. Consequently, both their writing and their spelling suffer.

LEARNING TO SPELL THROUGH READING In writing one must use spelling, so the role of writing in the development of competent spelling is an obvious one. Reading also contributes to spelling. Through reading pupils encounter written words in meaningful contexts. They develop a sense of the "look" of a word which is not so much a memory of the individual letters as an image of the whole pattern. Frequently, literate adults find it useful to write a word in one or more spellings to see which "looks right."

During reading, generalizations are formed about the relationships of speech patterns to sound patterns. These are formed whether there is direct instruction in them or not. Young learners are constantly looking for patterns in their experience; they are always building structures to organize their experiences. In turn, the developing readers use these generalizations to produce spellings for words whose spellings they do not know as they begin to write.

Goodman and Goodman[4] studied the spelling ability of a six-year-old who had learned to read on her own before coming to school. They found that, on a dictation test in which each word was said by the examiner in a sentence, she was able to spell 60 percent of the words correctly. She spelled many words correctly without hesitation. On some words, however, she would tell the examiner that she did not know how to spell them. Those words she would either spell correctly or misspell. In both cases, however, she seemed to be making use of generalizations resembling the rules we discussed earlier. She only resorted to these rules when she doubted her ability to spell the word. Following that, she was given another spelling test on the words she had misspelled. This time she was asked to pick out the correct

[4] Y. M. Goodman and K. Goodman, "Spelling Ability of a Self-Taught Reader," *Elementary School Journal* (December 1963).

spelling of the word from a list of four possible spellings including her own misspelling. Together with the results of the first test this raised her score of correctly spelled or recognized correct spellings to over 90 percent. Clearly, she had learned to spell a number of words through her reading. Clearly, also, she could recognize the correct spelling of words when she saw them in print that she could not yet spell herself. This appears to underscore the role that reading played in her spelling development. As might be predicted her misspelled words were almost entirely words in which multiple vowel letters represented vowel sounds. In the study cited there is no doubt that reading influences spelling development. It seems to play a variable role, however, for different learners. Not all strong readers are strong spellers.

SPELLING INSTRUCTION Two basic approaches have dominated spelling instruction. In one the curriculum is designed to teach a set of rules for spelling words. The goal, as was suggested above, is to make it possible for a writer to determine the spelling of words by analyzing their sound patterns and applying the speech to print rules. The alternate focus has been on learning words as individual units. This trend in spelling paralleled the whole word focus in reading instruction. Words were selected on the basis of their frequency and grouped into lessons around central topics; a group of common words relating to animals might make up a lesson. Combinations of these two alternatives have also been used in spelling programs. Rules are taught, but individual word spellings are taught too.

In teaching word spellings, study patterns have been common which used sight, sound, and feel. Pupils looked at words, shut their eyes and tried to recall the image, said the word, and traced the word in the air or wrote it to get its kinesthetic "feel." A variation on rule-centered spelling instruction involves the organization of lessons in which contrasting patterns are presented, such as the *at/ate* contrast, and pupils are led to form their own generalizations.

Spelling programs that focus on learning individual words are limited in the number of words that can be taught. Usually a program presents 15–20 words in a week. Over a six- to seven-year span the total number of words which can be presented is something under 4000. This number is considerably smaller than the conservative estimates of children's vocabularies at age six. It has already been noted, however, that there are severe limits on the utility of rules in generating standard spellings, even when the rules are accurate. And many spelling programs present rules that are not accurate, particularly as they apply to low-status dialects and polysyllabic words.

A basic fault with spelling instruction is the assumption that all children can profit from the same spelling program. Some teachers, using a word focus, vary the spelling program on their own initiative. They may group for spelling instruction, requiring the poorer spellers to learn half or less each week. They may give pretests and excuse children from studying words they already know. They may encourage children to keep word boxes or lists of words they find they need to spell in their written work. All these steps, of course, are designed to adapt the spelling program to the individual children in their classes.

INSTRUCTIONAL PROBLEMS It has been mentioned that although there are many different dialects and pronunciations of words in English, there is, in most cases, only one accepted spelling. Spelling programs designed for use in all parts of the country, however, do not allow for the differences in pronunciation that characterize various American dialects. Phonic misspellers will tend to misspell according to the way they speak in their own dialect. Furthermore, spelling programs focus on the word isolation from language. In isolation, words are often pronounced in uncommon ways. *Have, to, desert,* and *the* do not sound the same in isolation as they do in *You have to go to the desert to find cactus.* Even if the child learns to spell these words, will he know that he knows them when he needs them in his written communications? Will he recognize that /hæftə/ (haftuh) is graphically *have to?*

Perhaps the most significant problem in designing school programs for teaching spelling is the very large oral-language vocabulary the child has available to him and that he wishes to use in written composition. No program of teaching lists of words could possibly enable even a six-year-old to express his written thought in the vocabulary he chooses with all words spelled correctly. Neither could a simple set of rules taught deductively or by controlled induction generate enough "spelling power" to enable a child to spell correctly the large numbers of words he needs.

NEW VIEW Perhaps schools and teachers need to take a new view of spelling. If the demand for absolute perfection in spelling at all stages in all written expression were abandoned in favor of a developmental approach—that is, movement *toward* correct spelling—then children would eventually become more effective spellers. Spelling should facilitate communication of written thought, not limit it. Rather than being limited to writing with words they can spell correctly, children should be encouraged to use their language in as rich a form as possible. They will tend to learn to spell the words they use.

Children, of course, will always need to know how to check the spelling of a word through a dictionary or glossary; they will always need to realize that correct spelling is an aid to effective written communication. But spelling should be taught as a subsidiary skill rather than as an end in itself. *Children should not learn to spell words for some future use. They should learn to spell words as they need them and use them.* The plain fact is that much of the time spent on spelling lessons in school is wasted. It could be better spent on more extensive and meaningful reading and writing.

section 2

Handwriting

There was a time when a significant objective of instruction in hand-writing (or as it was more commonly called, penmanship) was beauty, conceived as something quite apart from function. Perfection in form. embellished by ornate flourishes, was the desired end. It was actually considered more important to have a beautiful handwriting than a legible one. Children not only practiced forming letters but also spent endless hours in the "push-pulls" and spirals of the penmanship books. For the placid, well-coordinated child these exercises were tolerable and a source of some satisfaction, because they won praise and penmanship awards. But for others they were at best dull and meaningless and at worst pure torture. Many children were endlessly rehearsed in tasks for which they were physically not ready. As adults, these unfortunate victims may find consolation in the fact that there is no correlation between handwriting and intelligence or achievement in other fields.

Fortunately, educators have become aware that handwriting is not an end in itself, but a means to effective communication. In rank order the objectives of a modern handwriting program are legibility, efficiency, and attractiveness.

An analogy to speech further clarifies handwriting's goals. As speech develops it becomes intelligible as it moves within the range of adult speech. It may vary considerably, however, as long as it avoids ambiguity which would make doubtful which phoneme of the language is intended in a sequence. Similarly, handwriting is intelligible to the extent that it falls in the range of variation that avoids ambiguity.

LEGIBILITY If language is considered a code, it can be seen that illegibility is in a sense a kind of noise on the communication channel. When an *o* begins to look like an *a* in cursive writing, then a perceptual problem that may interfere with effective communication is created. The forms of letters, particularly in combination with other letters, must be perceived by the reader as the writer intended. There are limits, therefore, on the variability of letter form. These become the norms of acceptability if legibility is to be achieved. To some extent, the task of staying within these acceptable limits is influenced by the complexity of the letter forms. There has been, therefore, a tendency to eliminate unneeded parts of letters and to achieve a maximum simplicity.

Writing requires a great deal of coordination and small-muscle control, perhaps more than many six and seven-year-olds possess. Two measures have been used with great success to minimize this problem. First of all, manuscript writing, a system of unjoined letters composed of circles, part circles, and straight lines, is now almost universally used as the initial medium for writing in school. Combined with the second simple measure of providing paper with large spaces between the lines (often with a light guideline between the two heavy lines), the early task of writing is transformed to one that requires less small-muscle coordination and more large-muscle movement. Beginners are permitted to write with large strokes. They may use crayons instead of pencils. Gradually, a succession of more finely ruled papers is used as the child's coordination and skill increases, until eventually his writing is down to adult size.

These reforms in handwriting instruction came about in the 1930s and were so effective that schools found it possible to deemphasize the teaching of handwriting. School handwriting coordinators were no longer needed and the proportion of time in the school day spent on direct handwriting instruction reached a sensible minimum. As often happens, however, school administrators and teachers have not always been aware of the background for the use of manuscript writing and special paper. Ignorance has sometimes brought back the earlier practice as well as its related problems.

Perhaps more important than the reforms just discussed, however, is the attitude of the teacher toward the children and the writing task. It is vital that the teacher remember the great variability among learners and keep ends and means in proper perspective. Children vary greatly in coordination, and their handwriting will reflect these differences. The teacher, in working toward the goal of *legibility,* must be satisfied with progress and not demand perfection. The teacher must also know what the key elements in legibility are and keep these separate from other demands made on the child. Neatness is no doubt an important virtue, but messy papers can be legible; in fact, some of the messiness may reflect a child's progress toward legibility; his awkward erasures may result from trying to make his initial attempt at a letter-form come closer to his view of the norm.

When a teacher offers help to children it should be specific and easily related by them to greater legibility. The teacher can help the learner to see that he can evaluate his own handwriting by asking himself if it can be read and understood.

EFFICIENCY Like any physical skill, the skill of forming letters rapidly and accurately can be performed with varying degrees of efficiency. Generally, people who use a skill continuously over a long period will tend to become more efficient on their own. However, they may take a long time to arrive at a high degree of efficiency and may still preserve some inefficient movements or procedures.

It is obvious that teachers can eliminate a good deal of trial and error and, in many cases, head off the formation of inefficient writing habits by presenting a systematic set of procedures in letter formation that have been tested and proven efficient for most people. Showing the child efficient ways of placing his paper, holding his pencil, and seating himself will no doubt be helpful to him. It will also probably help him to learn an efficient step-by-step procedure for forming each letter. Some teachers may become confused over the apparent variety of commercially published handwriting program, which provide differing guidelines. Some of the differences between systems exist literally for their own sakes, however. To copyright a handwriting system it must have a number of points of difference from all other systems. Therefore, every system contains many arbitrary elements, things that can be done as efficiently one way as another. Teachers must keep in mind, that the goal is efficiency and not slavish imitation. All studies of different handwriting systems have indicated that while some systems are more efficient than others for most people, there are always some people who are more efficient with systems that are less widely effective.

The teacher should present a system of writing and concentrate on efficient ways of letter formation and use. From the beginning, however, the teacher must be willing to accept deviance. Forcing youngsters who have learned another system to change for the sake of conformity should particularly be avoided.

ATTRACTIVENESS Although beauty in handwriting is clearly not requisite to its effectiveness as a medium of written thought, it does condition the receptiveness of the reader. It is well known to college students that messy, unattractive handwriting on an essay question will probably result in a lower grade than would a similar response in a more attractive handwriting. To some extent, then, children must be encouraged to develop handwriting that is attractive as well as legible and efficient. This will be most likely when the child is writing something he wants to have well received. Each person varies his handwriting, depending on the occasion. A scribble is adequate in a reminder to oneself or in composing the first draft of a story during the heat of imagining. A clean style is necessary in a letter of application or a note of condolence. Typewriters are used for many written language activities and, where not available (as in the filling out of forms and applications), writers are often urged to print. Perhaps cursive handwriting as we now know it has outlived its utility and is obsolescent, at least for many requirements.

HANDEDNESS Left-handed pupils have been at a great disadvantage in many schools. Right-handed readers of this book may assume that the horror stories of mistreatment of left-handed learners are all from the dim past. But virtually every left-handed person reading this book will have some personal experiences to recall which show that such rejection and misunderstanding of differences still exist. Although few teachers try to force children to become right-handed as in days past, many teachers teach them styles and techniques that may result in writing that looks right-handed, but which are awkward and inefficient for left-handed people. There is no justification for demanding writing that looks right-handed from left-handed people, who could more easily achieve a distinct but equally legible style.

People who are left-handed are different and in the minority. How teachers treat their difference will have a strong impact not only on their writing but on their self-images, their treatment by other pupils, and their general attitudes toward school.

VARIETY It is a remarkable fact that follow-up studies of people taught to form letters according to a common system invariably show that a great deal of variety has entered their individual writing style by the time they are adults. This may come about because they have discovered alternate techniques that are personally more effective. Or it may be because they are consciously or unconsciously seeking to make their handwriting more personal and individualized. Preteen and teen-age girls frequently experiment with highly stylized handwriting, whose end result in any case, is not undesirable. People communicate effectively with an infinite variety of voices. Why can there not be effective communication with an infinite variety of forms of handwriting? *The teacher again needs to encourage not conformity but legibility.*

It may be apparent in this discussion of the teaching of handwriting that though an attempt has been made to present a positive position, a good deal of attention has been given to what *not* to do. That is because so many problems are created for pupils and teachers by ill-considered, inappropriate, and insensitive instruction.

At the risk of some oversimplification we present a list of do's and don'ts that may help to avoid some unnecessary anguish.

DO:

Keep the focus on legibility in teaching handwriting. Efficiency and beauty are minor goals.

Keep handwriting in its place—a *means* to written expression.

Accept difference and allow for it in teaching handwriting.

Make left-handed pupils feel normal and accepted. Be sensitive to their difference and provide for it.

Teach a system but be open to variation. Accept another system already learned.

Keep in mind that maturation and differences in coordination are factors in developing handwriting skill.

Teach handwriting as a whole process with components in normal relationship to each other.

DON'T:

Judge all handwriting by an adult model and insist on conformity to that model.

Use drills on isolated letters. Don't make children do line upon line of single letters or word parts.

Teach handwriting apart from its use in communication.

Make children feel inadequate, abnormal, or defeated because their efforts are not very effective. Don't make major issues out of minor deviations.

Let handwriting problems interfere with the need for the learners to express themselves.

Require pupils to copy papers over and over in the quest for perfection.

Make children move too quickly to adult paper, pencils, pen, and ink.

Surround handwriting with a set of fetishes. Handwriting must be kept in realistic perspective.

section 3

The Mechanics of Written Composition

The arbitrary nature of the various conventions regarding the mechanics of written composition is attested to by the fact that there never has been agreement among authorities or among the public on any single element. Basically, of course, form is important in written expression of all kinds to assure favorable reception by the reader and, therefore, better communication. Some aspects of mechanics have practical bases; margins must be provided to allow binding or for marginal notations and comments, for example. And, of course, there are things we do in writing that are really social traditions, such as opening a letter with *Dear* _____, signing minutes with *Respectfully Submitted*, and so on.

Perhaps the reason why children have difficulty with the mechanics of composition is that they are not placed in proper perspective. If there is need for a set of conventions within a classroom concerning the form of written work, the teacher should discuss the reasons and the limits in which decisions must be made and then allow the children to participate in making the decisions. Is there a need for the learner to identify himself on his written work? What other information is necessary: date, subject, time, assignment, teacher's name? Is this all necessary, all the time? Is there reason (or reasons) why this information should always appear in the same place on every pupil's work? Where could that place be? Are there conventional forms for business letters? What variations are possible? Are there advantages, social or practical, in using one form or another? What about personal letters; how important are traditional forms there?

It is important for the teacher to get straight in his own mind when these arbitrary decisions are made for practical reasons, when they involve traditions, and when they are made because a decision must be made although one decision is as good as another. Form in footnotes is an example of this last. There are a number of conventional forms for footnotes and several different ways they may be numbered and placed. It is generally agreed that consistency in form and placement of footnotes and completeness and accuracy of content are important, but beyond that, it matters little which choice is made.

Again, it must be emphasized: The focus should always be on written thought, particularly in the creative stages of composition. *If a child has something he wants to say, let him say it. Then he will want and need to know about the form that will make his written-thought most effective.*

Learning from the Miscues of Learners

Kenneth Goodman and his associates have developed an approach to the study of reading which treats unexpected behavior, *miscues*, as sources of information on how the learner is using language processes and the extent to which he controls them. Instead of regarding deviations as errors that must be avoided or eliminated, they are seen as resulting from the same process that produces the expected responses. They reflect both the strength and the weakness of the learner and, thus, when understood by the teacher, offer powerful insights in planning instruction (see discussion on miscue analysis in Chapter 16).

The key question a teacher must ask is not, "How well are my pupils doing in conforming to a model of behavior?" but "What are my pupils doing and why are they doing it?"

It has been traditional, for example, to compare handwriting to a model and assign an evaluative rating. Points of possible difference (error) include degree and angle of slant, and openness of loops. All that does not conform is error to be stamped out. If we treat such differences as miscues, then we ask what is the learner doing that is "unexpected." We may then find that the writer shows a left slant, or does not stay within the lines, or forms certain letters and letter combinations (such as $\mathcal{U}$ and $\mathcal{U}$) ambiguously.

Next we ask why is he producing these miscues. We may find in connection with his slant that (1) he is left-handed; (2) he is deliberately experimenting to achieve a distinctive handwriting; or (3) he places his paper at an odd angle when he writes. Each of these gives different significance to the behavior. In the last case, detection may lead to some instruction on useful ways to place paper when writing. In the first two cases, however, it may well be that the teacher will stop considering the left slant a miscue and understand that it is expected behavior for such learners. The teacher would, of course, in reaching this decision consider whether the unusual slant interferes with the legibility, efficiency, or attractiveness of the writing.

In the situation where a writer is not staying within the lines the teacher must consider both maturity and coordination. Does the writing reflect ignorance of the relationship of the lines to legibility and attractiveness? Again, answers to these questions and others will lead to different instructional planning by the teacher. If immaturity is involved, patience is called for. Demanding perfection before the pupil is ready produces frustration and hostility, and is a waste of energy since time will itself help to solve the problem. Instruction will help, however, if he does not realize why the lines are important. If inappropriate instruction has triggered the problem then a change in instruction will certainly help.

In the last example, the teacher needs to attend to the general problem and not be distracted by particular miscues. *Telling the pupil your "d" looks like "cl," at best, handles one problem. But using this example to develop the insight that one way to avoid illegible writing is to avoid letting letters look like other letters gives the writer a powerful strategy for self-checking to improve legibility.*

In *punctuation* the miscue approach is also useful. When a writer does not supply quotation marks where needed, it may be due to (1) forgetfulness (checking the rest of his writing should answer this question); (2) ignorance of conventional use of quotation marks (his miscues will then be either consistently wrong or notably erratic); (3) the lack of a concept of direct quotation (instruction should then center on building the concept, for no amount of instruction in the use of quotation marks will help if the pupil doesn't know what a quotation is); or (4) similarity in the reader's dialect between direct and indirect quotes ("*I asked him was he going*" rather than "I asked him if he was going"). In both dialects the direct quote is "I asked him, 'Are you going?'" If the writer's miscue reflects this dialect factor the teacher will need to help the learner to identify direct quotes as *he* uses them. Another typical punctuation problem involves the fact that young writers have been told to always end a sentence with a period, exclamation point, or question mark. If they knew what sentences were they would have little difficulty following such an instruction.

The miscue approach helps to look beyond superficial, unexpected behavior to the underlying process. It can be applied in teaching *spelling* too, stimulating such questions as the following. How does the pupil misspell? Are his miscues near-misses? Do they usually involve vowels? Does he do well on tests but not in written work? Does his misspelling show up in his writing because he is using language boldly and not staying with safe words he is sure he can spell? What kinds of words does he misspell: nouns, verbs, function words? Does he overuse phonics and produce phonic misspellings? Is he better at spelling words in context than isolation?

Perhaps what makes the concept of miscues most useful is simply that it is neutral; it allows the teacher to work with the learners rather than spend valuable time constantly correcting them and punishing them for being wrong. The learner is given credit for what he knows rather than abuse for what he does not know. The approach is much more constructive, then, for it involves expansion on a base of strength rather than attack on the weakest point.

TEACHING LITERACY Because composition is a process that involves thought translated into written language, the practice of literacy skills must go hand in hand with composing. First, the child should be permitted to jot down the speech-thoughts in the best way he can. He will use his own orthography, written reminders of what he has said. If he cannot spell a word, he can put down a few clues and move on, thereby not waylaying the train of thought. He can punctuate as he feels the caesura, a pause in the rhythmic pattern of intoned oral language. He can write quickly in a scribble (which perhaps only he can read) to catch the speech-thoughts as they tumble out. This will be the *first draft*.

PUNCTUATION Some teachers during this period of critical composing will at the request of the child, write on the blackboard or on a slip of paper the spelling of a word that the child wants to use. They can also be available to hear parts of the story read to them for discussion of punctuation requirements. One exercise for preparing children to become sensitive to the positioning of commas, periods, and question marks is to write down oral language as it is spoken and see if it can be read without punctuation and without filling out the abbreviated structure of oral patterns. Given the period, comma, and question mark as tools, children can explore the possibilities of transforming the speech-thought into readable, written thought. The old techniques of dictation may be useful in this new context of language learning if the teacher dictates in a conversational tone. Tapes of brief conversations can be devised in such a way that the child can go back and hear them several times to get the oral pattern fixed in his head before trying to write them out. Handwriting practice exercises might follow this same pattern once the letter shapes and ties have been accomplished.

FINAL COPY The best practice for both punctuating and handwriting is preparation of final copy of original stories first made in rough draft. There are many valid reasons for children's preparing final copy. Stories can be prepared for reading by other class members. If a class newspaper or storybook is being prepared, a clean, clear copy of each individual's story must be made available to the editors. In addition, a permanent bulletin board or colorful folder of final copies of stories can keep interest alive in composition. In a *writing conference* the teacher can encourage reading the script aloud both to help children hear the flow or lack of it in their rough draft and to help raise questions of how to deal with problems of communication that arise. The dictionary becomes a handy tool at this stage, and clear, legible handwriting becomes as much a necessity for preparing a script for reading as is proper punctuation. Children can be paired in a *team-*

learning situation to help each other work out the fine points of final copy by practicing decoding and encoding on their own works. *In brief, the best way to learn the literacy skills is to be given frequent opportunities to use them in writing projects that satisfy the desire to communicate one's ideas to other people.*

Testing Ideas against Reality

Creative language combinations in English are myriad because of the richness and flexibility of English. Because it has been and is a common language of so many diverse cultures in so many parts of the world. English has a unique potential for creative expression. Even today a new literature in black English is enlivening the language. With such incentive, understanding the language's possibilities and gaining practice in realizing them should be two desirable, as well as necessary goals for teacher and student alike. The following sample suggestions are offered.

Select a piece of lyric poetry such as Hopkins's PIED BEAUTY, "Glory be to God for dappled things," and try to put its ideas into prose. Note that which can be conveyed and that which is missing from the account. Read several Haiku and create several of your own. Take an occasion of high emotionality in your experience, and describe it in writing to yourself as if you were writing in a diary.

Record place names, local expressions, and special word-uses that are indigenous to your own area. Trace sources to Indian and early-settlement language. Bring these to the attention of youngsters. If youngsters have come from another part of the country or from other English-speaking countries, ask them to interview their parents regarding different expressions. Read Lorenz Graham's DAVID HE NO FEAR to youngsters and point out how powerful even a pidgin form of English can be. Read the King James Bible version of DAVID AND GOLIATH, and compare and contrast the two styles for particular strengths in composition.

Videotape your retelling of a good, short, short story. Make a script of it as well as a typed copy of the original story. Then play back the tape while following the two scripts. Note the differences including gesture, and propose reasons for the differences. Repeat this little experiment with youngsters and ask them also to write a summary of the story after the oral retelling. Compare and contrast the three documents in terms of the differences between speech-thought, written thought, and literary style.

Take an original document from the Elizabethan or Jacobean periods with many diverse spellings in it. Put it alongside a statement using some newly proposed, consistent spelling system for English (a passage using the ITA alphabet will do, even though that was not proposed as a replacement for conventional spelling). Compare and contrast these documents with a passage using similar words conventionally spelled. Note the attempts at new or old conventions. Introduce some words and sounds in some languages that are more phonetically consistent than English.

Turning Ideas into Practice

Although many teaching strategies are proposed in the text, the following activities are presented as examples of oral and written composition activities that can be developed as self-selected suggestions on "work cards" in a "writing corner."

OPEN-ENDED and INCOMPLETE TOPIC SENTENCES can encourage personalized telling or writing. For example:

My feet or hands would like to do, go _____.
If I were a nurse, a space explorer, a movie star, I would like to _____.
The fun things in life are _____.
I was frightened, sad, or happy when _____.

SIMULATION of newspaper reporting, magazine writing, crime-detection reporting, and so on can set the stage for imaginative composition.

EXAMPLES of riddles, jokes, or nonsense rhymes can spark the composing of individual ones or variations of traditional ones.

RESPONSES to happenings in nature or confrontations with people can be elicited by open-ended topics such as:

When I was surprised. . . .
The time I was scared. . . .
The place I like to go to be alone. . . .
Where the best things are. . . .
If I had my choice. . . .
A time of trouble. . . .
With my best friend I would like to go and do. . . .
Adventuring on a bike, on a motorcycle. . . .

ENCOUNTERS with provocative words such as the following can be effective: Winners, Losers, A Fight, Remembrances, Caught, Roam, Escape, Dream, Cry, Hate, Love.

SPELLING Youngsters can set up their own "spelling banks" from their writing and reading activities. The teacher can add a few basic words every week to each "bank" and prepare a variety of spelling "activity cards" from which pupil study-pairs can select.

PUNCTUATION can be better understood if learners occasionally "take dictation," as it were, from a person speaking on a videotape. The intonations, stops, lifts, and gestures reveal the places where punctuation is needed for reading the transcript later.

READING

Bright is the ring of words
   When the right man rings them,
Fair the fall of songs
   When the singer sings them
Still they are carolled and said—
   On wings they are carried
Often the singer is dead
   And the marker buried.

ROBERT LOUIS STEVENSON,
from Songs of Travel.

Methods for learning to read come and go
across the educational arena like the march of
super-numeraries upon the stage. Each is
heralded as the final solution of the problem
of learning to read; but each in turn gives way
to some later discovery. The simple fact is, that
they all lack the essential of any well grounded
method, namely relevance to the child's mental
needs. No scheme for learning can supply this want.

Only a new motive—putting the child in a vital relation
to the things to be read—can be of service here.

JOHN DEWEY, quoted in Emmett Betts,
Foundations of Reading Instruction.
(New York: American Book Company, 1957), p. 8.

TEACHING FOCUS

How does reading work in the relatively proficient reader?
What does a reader do as he moves from print to meaning?
How does it help in understanding what happens if reading
is considered as a psycholinguistic process in which thought
and language interact?

In considering reading instruction answers to these questions
may be sought:

What alternative approaches to reading instruction are possible?

How do popular methods relate to new understandings of what
the developing reader must learn to do?

What are the essentials of an approach to reading instruction
which can make learning to read an extension of natural
language learning?

15

The Reading Process:
A Psycholinguistic View

Reading is the active process of constructing meaning from language represented by graphic symbols (letters) systematically arranged, just as listening is the active process of constructing meaning from the sound symbols (phonemes) of oral language. Reading programs in the past were built on principles of psychology, child growth and development, physiology, and, to some extent, sociology, but not on any systematic knowledge of language. This chapter will present a total-language, psycholinguistic view of reading. The entire process of reading can be best understood when consideration is given to the devices within language that convey meaning and the ways readers interpret and react to these devices.

Phonics Approach: Its Limitations

A reading program based on phonics teaches children to associate sounds with letters. The reasoning in this phonics approach (sometimes mistakenly called phonetics)[1] is that if the child learns to associate sounds with letters, he can then sound out words and thus read. In one kind of phonics, children are taught to read *dog* by saying the sound of each letter: *duh, aw, guh.* Phonics techniques are included in many current reading programs,

[1] Phonetics is the study of the sounds of language. Because all languages are sound languages, all languages are phonetic.

but its *method* of teaching reading has fallen into disfavor for several reasons:

> Each letter in written English does not regularly represent a specific sound. Some sounds may be spelled a number of different ways. For example, consider this group of rhyming words: *go, know, though, hoe, sew.* Equally confusing, some letters may represent a number of different sounds as the *o* does in *do, so, won, women,* and *not.*
>
> Many successful readers do not appear to go through this letter-by-letter analysis but seem to get to meaning.
>
> The generalizations contained in most old phonics programs are unscientific. Rules not only have many exceptions, but they are often based on erroneous understandings of the language. Division of English vowels into two classes, long and short, is an example of an inaccurate view that confuses the learner and does not on any way describe the English vowel system. So-called vowels are not single vowels at all but are compound vowels. The speaker glides from one to the other. As a person says these words, he can feel this glide: *I, bone, came, tube, extreme.*
>
> Dialect differences mitigate against any attempts at standard sounding (phonics) systems.

Word-Recognition Approach: Its Limitations

For many decades reading programs have put the main emphasis on words. The central task of early reading teaching in these programs was to develop a vocabulary of words that the young reader recognizes at sight. Those who prepare materials for teaching children to read by this word-recognition approach[2] must answer the question, "Which words should be taught first?" Two answers have been used singly or in combination. The words children actually use can be listed in order of frequency from those most commonly used to those rarely occurring. Alternately, a count can be made of the words used in adult speech or literature to determine the frequency and, by implication, the order of importance for early learning.

By means of these lists, basal readers are constructed on the principle of vocabulary control. At the peak of their importance preprimers contained only 10 to 20 of the most frequently occurring words plus a minimum number of proper nouns. Each successive volume in the series repeated these words and added a few. The teacher's manual listed each new word so that it might be taught to the learners. Word-attack skills, including phonics and use of contextual clues, were taught in this word-centered method so that the child would be able to "attack" new words.

Many teachers highly skilled in phonics or word-recognition methods have been successful—to a point—in teaching children to read. Enthusiastic learners with dedicated teachers can probably learn to read regardless of

---

[2] Referred to by phonics advocates as the "look–say" approach.

method—and most children *do* learn to read. But what is missing from most reading instruction is an understanding of *how* the reader reconstructs meaning from written language. Linguistics and related fields have produced new knowledge about language. To apply these new insights to reading, teachers must let go of their preoccupation with letters and words and take a broad look at reading as one phase of communication.

The child learning to read who is a native speaker of English—any dialect of English—has acquired skill in getting meaning from oral language. He responds quickly and accurately to many cues in language. Only a small fraction of this power over language, however, is put to work through phonics or word-recognition approaches to reading.

Possibilities of a Psycholinguistic Approach

In one sense, readers can be regarded as decoders trying to reconstruct a message that has been coded. Written language has symbols, like the dots and dashes of Morse code, and complex systems of signals involved in the arrangement of the symbols.

To understand how readers utilize signal systems in language to reconstruct meaning, consider this list of nonsense words:

Gloopy	klums	poved	jonfy	klorpy
borp	Blit	Ril	rom	lofs
lof	floms	lo	bofd	

We might assume that the three words with capital letters, *Gloopy, Blit,* and *Ril,* are proper nouns; otherwise, we have no sense of meaning. But now consider this primer story in which nonsense words have been substituted for all the meaning-bearing words, with everything else left intact.

GLOOPY AND BLIT
Gloopy is a borp.
Blit is a lof.
Gloopy klums like Blit.
Gloopy and Blit are floms.

Ril had poved Blit to a jonfy.
But lo had not poved Gloopy.
"The jonfy is for lofs,"
Blit bofd to Gloopy.
"Rom are a borp."
Gloopy was not klorpy.
Then Blit was not klorpy.

This story presents, in extreme, the problem of the reader's meeting words he has never seen before. Yet, there seems to be some sense to it. In fact, there are many cues to the meanings of the unknown words, and if we apply our knowledge of English, we can come close to understanding the whole story.

The title presents two nonsense words joined by *and*, so the words must be of the same class (nouns or verbs, for example); that is, *town* and *country* can be joined by *and*, as can *red* and *green*, *run* and *play*, *quickly* and *quietly*, but not *town* and *green*, *red* and *play*.

The first sentence provides more cues. By its position in a familiar pattern, we know that *Gloopy* is a noun, probably a singular name, because it is not preceded by a noun marker like *a*, *the*, or *one*. *Gloopy* is singular because *is* goes with singular nouns. *Borp* is a noun, we can see, because it follows *a*, a noun marker, and because it occupies a particular position in the equation-like sentence. Similarly, we know that *Blit* is most likely a name and *lof* is a noun, perhaps a category contrasting with *borp*.

Three cues tell us that *klums* is a verb: (1) its position in the sentence, (2) the inflectional ending *s* marks it as a singular verb confirming that *Gloopy* is a singular noun, and (3) it patterns with *like*.

Floms is a plural noun, we know from the plural left side of the equation, the verb *are*, and the *s* ending. We learn also that *borps* and *lofs* can be *floms*. Notice that this little story is lavish in the cues it provides. Seldom are we given only one. Note also that we are not just guessing as we decode this message. We are responding to cues.

Ril is another name. We can see that *poved* is a verb from the verb marker *had*, the inflectional ending *ed* that sets the whole sentence in the past, and again its position between two nouns, which here must be actor and object. By their positions in this sentence we know that *Ril* is the actor and *Blit* the object: it was *Ril* that poved *Blit*; *Blit* didn't pove *Ril*.

Lo appears to be a noun, but not the printed symbols do not show intonation. The addition of appropriate intonations that cannot be represented by the graphic symbols reveals *lo* to be a pronoun with *Ril* as its antecedent. We know then that whatever *Ril* did to *Blit*, *Ril* did not do to *Gloopy*.

The reason for this becomes apparent in the next paragraph. *Blit* is addressing *Gloopy* here, we know from the quotation marks that enable us to supply proper phrasing and intonation. The reason *Gloopy* was not *poved*, *Blit* *bofs*, is that the *jonfy* is for *lofs* and *Gloopy* is a *borp*. *Rom* can have only one meaning, since *you* is the only singular subject that can pattern with *are*.

Finally, we learn that as a result of not being *poved*, *Gloopy* was not *klorpy* and this lead to *Blit* also being *unklorpy*. If only *Gloopy* had been a *lof* instead of a *borp*! Then *Gloopy* would have been *poved* to the *jonfy*, too. We can come very close to understanding the whole little story even though the important words are all nonsense. When these were presented in list form, they meant nothing to us at all.

Adult readers can use generalizations they have acquired about letters and sounds to say the words in the list, but that is not reading, because no meaning is involved. *Reading is not reading unless it involves some level of comprehension.*

Readers, even beginners, engage in the same kind of process we have just gone through, although not often on so conscious a level. By the time they start school, children have internalized responses to systems of language cues.

There are really three kinds of cue systems that operate in reading to cue meaning. These are (1) cue systems within words, (2) cue systems in the flow of language, (3) cue systems within the reader.

section 1

Cue Systems within Words

To understand how cue systems within words function, consider the case of a first-grader encountering *monkey* for the first time in his reading. In a phonics approach, under his teacher's urging, he would try to recall sounds he had learned to associate with the letters in the word: *m-mm, ah, nnn, ka, eh, ye* (or *ee*). He would attempt to string these sound–letter associations to make a word. Hopefully, the word would be *monkey*. Is the *ey* the same as the one in *key* or is it like the one in *they*? Aside from the problems of undependable correspondence between letters and sounds in English, this approach is quite limited. It is indeed only one of several word-attack skills.

If a child has been taught with a word-recognition method to use word-attack skills, he is basically using cues within words. He can use phonic generalizations, as just mentioned, or he can use phonics in a modified sense, concentrating on important letters like initial and final consonants, the *m* for example.

The child may notice and remember the shape of this new word. It's high in the middle and drops down at the end: monkey

The young reader may pick small words which he knows out of the new word and words he knows that are spelled similarly and rhyme. In this case, the only word that might help is *donkey*, which rhymes with *monkey* in some American English dialects but not in others. Children may also learn to see affixes in words and may use their recurrent meanings as cues. Ultimately, the child will rely on remembering whole words.

To recapitulate, *within words* there are these cue systems:

Letter–sound relationships (phonic generalizations)
Shape, or word configuration
Known little words in new words
Affixes
Recurrent spelling patterns
Whole known words

Language is learned from whole to part. In fact, children can get the meaning of a sentence long before they can recognize each word in isolation. Similarly, all proficient readers have acquired the ability to use cue systems within words. Overreliance on these cues in words in the early stages of learning to read leads the child away from meaning and away from the extensive knowledge of the language he brings with him to school. He focuses on minute detail and must subsequently build back toward language. Reading, with the emphasis on words, may become a continuous series of words to attack with meanings lost or neglected. The child and the teacher may be so concerned with word-attack skills that the child may not even be aware that there *is* any meaning or that he is supposed to look for it. In fact, few children who become remedial readers lack the ability to attack words. Many just can't get to meaning.

WORDS At this point, it might be well to say a few words about words. Many teachers have been amused by children's asking how to spell *hafta* (as in *I hafta go now*). Adults think of words as entities, islands surrounded by pauses or white space, but words are not nearly so distinct. *Hafta*, for example, behaves very much like a two-syllable word. It even has one-word synonyms such as *must* that can be neatly substituted for it in many cases.

The concept of language as composed of words is a useful and ancient invention. Ancient scholars no doubt noticed the perceptible pause in language that marked off recurrent patterns from each other. They noticed that these marked-off patterns had relationships consistent with meaning. The invention of written language must have predated the invention of the word concept because early written language offered no spaces to separate words. Now, however, our written language is neatly subdivided.

Teachers have tended to treat words as self-evident. They have expected children to know what words are, although it took mankind a good long time to think up the idea. With all due reverence it must be stated that in the beginning was not the word but the utterance—a glob of language. Children perceive these utterances as wholes long before they begin to notice the constituent elements. Only after a child has learned many utterances does he begin to sort out elements. And only after he has acquired a modicum of literacy does he begin to know and use the norms for recognizing where one word leaves off and another begins.

The truth is that words do not really exist. It is useful and convenient to think about language as made up of words, but words have no reality extracted from language. They cannot be defined, pronounced, or classified out of the stream of language. Let us take for example the word, *white*.

Can *white* be defined in isolation? Most likely it is a color. But it could be part of a chicken egg. It could be a man's name, a substitute for *Caucasian*, black's foe in chess, or red's foe in politics.

Can *white* be pronounced in isolation? Most speakers would read *white* in a list with similar intonation. But what about this sentence: *In Washington, D.C., there is a white house called the White House but the White family doesn't live there. White* has three different intonations in that sentence that must be precise. Any variation in the way *white* is stressed would change the meaning of the sentence completely.

Can *white* be classified in isolation? It is an adjective: *They waved a white flag.* But it is also a noun: *Add the white of an egg.* It can be inflected like a verb (*He will whiten his shoes*) or compared as an adverb (*Cheer washes whiter*). *White* can be classified, but only as it occurs in language.

If words cannot be defined, pronounced, or classified, they cannot be recognized. Children can learn to call their names from lists, but word recognition is a much harder task than reading language.

The assumed controversy between phonics and whole-word approaches to reading in reality turns out to be two sides to the same coin. Both treat words as ends in themselves. With phonics, words are assaulted letter by letter, whereas whole-word approaches take them in bite-size pieces. But reading in both cases is assumed to be naming words.

section 2

Cue Systems in the Flow of Language

Another set of cue systems is contained *in language* as it flows in actual speech or writing and not in the words alone. This second set of cue systems consists of:

1. Patterns of word or function order
2. Inflection and inflectional agreement
3. Function words
4. Intonation (stress, pitch, and juncture)
5. Contextual meaning
6. Redundancy in language cues

If the young reader encounters the new word *monkey* embedded in a story he is reading, he will have all the cues that exist within the word plus many cues outside the word itself but within language. Suppose he finds the unfamiliar word in this story fragment:

Tom saw a *monkey*. A man played some music. The little *monkey* clapped his hands. Tom gave the *monkey* a penny.

The child responds as we did with *Gloopy* and *Blit* to features that are peculiar to the English language. He began learning these responses in his infancy. Scientific linguistics has described the vital features of language to which the child responds. Psycholinguistics is providing insights into how his responses are learned and generated.

PATTERNS OF WORD OR FUNCTION ORDER The first set of cues consists of a limited number of common patterns by which the elements in an utterance may be arranged. *Tom saw a monkey* is an example of the most common sentence structure in the English language. In formal grammar we might call it subject-verb-object or noun-verb-noun. Recent studies have demonstrated that when children come to school they have mastered all the basic patterns of the language; this is true even of children with quite meager language development. Children will know by its position in the sentence that *monkey* is something that Tom saw. In some other languages, even in Old English, *Tom saw the monkey* could mean *the monkey saw Tom* if *Tom* had an objective case ending and *monkey* had a nominative one. In the English of today we rely much more on position than on case or inflectional endings. So there would be no doubt that *Tom* did the seeing; the positions of *monkey* and *Tom* in the pattern make this clear even to a six-year-old.

In the brief story just given *monkey* is used in three different positions in the same basic pattern: as subject (*The little monkey clapped his hands*), as object (*Tom saw a monkey*), and as inner or indirect object (*Tom gave the monkey a penny*). The reader sees the unfamiliar word from three angles with three sets of cues.

INFLECTION AND INFLECTIONAL AGREEMENT A second set of cues includes inflectional endings. Not as important as they once were in English, these endings where they exist, play an important role in cueing meaning. Certain sounds usually represented in writing by *d* or *ed* are added to many verbs as a signal that the action or event took place in the past. Similarly, *s* or *es* represents in written language a group of sounds added to many nouns to indicate plurality and to many verbs to indicate singularity. There is pattern in the use of these inflectional endings; that is, they must be consistent. *The boy sees the monkey* is acceptable; *The boys see the monkey* is equally good. But *The boys sees the monkey* would not be consistent in most dialects of English.

Children are basically aware not only of these inflectional cues but also of the need for them to be consistent. If a child reads *The boys sees . . .* it just does not sound right to him.[3]

FUNCTION WORDS The third set of cues consist of the function words—a small number of words in English that have little or no meaning but perform key functions as structure cues. In a major language study,[4] Fries found that 154 structure words made up fully a third of the total volume of language.

---

[3] Of course, in dialects with no *s* forms, *He see* will sound consistent to a reader.
[4] Charles C. Fries, *The Structure of English* (New York: Harcourt, 1952).

Linguists have called these words *structure words* or *function words*. Le Fevre calls them "empty words," referring to their lack of referential meaning as compared to "full words"—nouns, verbs, adjectives, and adverbs.[5] Function words are the articles, auxiliary verbs, prepositions, and conjunctions of traditional grammar. Often they have only two or three letters. Here is a verse from Lewis Carroll's "Jabberwocky" with only the function words shown to illustrate how function words serve as cues to structural meaning.

> 'Twas _____ and the _____ _____
> Did _____ and _____ in the _____,
> All _____ were the _____
> And the _____ _____.

In the sentence "Tom saw a monkey," *monkey* is literally marked as a noun by a noun marker, *a*. If the reader mistakes *monkey* for *money*, he would be likely to realize he had made an error, because *a* does not precede a noun such as *money*. This would not be a conscious, reasoned decision but, nonetheless, it would be a sure one because the reader would be relying on his knowledge of the language.

Other function words can be verb markers (*is*, *has*, and *will* are examples) that cue the reader that a verb follows as in *Ril had poved Gloopy*.

The question marker serves much more surely as a signal that the sentence that follows is a question than does the question mark (which, lamentably, comes at the end in English writing). Words that serve as question markers include *who, what, did*, as in *Did Ril pove Gloopy?* or *Where is the jonfy?*

Some of these same words and others (for example, *because, that*, and *if*) can be clause markers as in *Gloopy was not poved* because *Gloopy is a borp*. Function words like *in, on, of, for, by*, and *to* can serve as phrase markers. For example, *Blit was poved* to *a jonfy* by *Ril*.

Some vital function words are literally in classes by themselves, as *Gloopy was* not *poved*. Not has no meaning of its own, but it signals that the whole statement is negative.

These function words must be present in the very simplest language passages, but their lack of meaning makes them difficult for children to learn and remember in reading. When they are presented in isolation, they are even more difficult for young readers. Many teachers have been perplexed because children could remember such words as *something*, but not *the, on, or*, or *was*. Many of the function words are also irregularly spelled; that is, they are likely to contradict phonics rules that children are taught. Some examples of function words that do not obey phonics rules are *of, for, to*,

[5] Carl Le Fevre, *Linguistics and the Teaching of Reading* (New York: McGraw-Hill, 1964), p. 80.

do, from, was, what, can (a homophone of *kin* when used as a function word in many dialects), *the*, and *a*, to mention just a few. Again, remember that the reading beginner is not a language beginner; he has learned to interpret these function word cues automatically in oral speech.

INTONATION Intonation is a fourth system of cues in the flow of language. It is, in a sense, the tune to which the language is sung. Intonation is only partially represented in the written language, but in speech all three parts of intonation (stress, pitch, and juncture) play a vital role in signaling the underlying grammatical structure and meaning. To a large extent, the reader must learn to supply his own intonation. He does this by setting what he reads to a familiar tune—a common intonation pattern of English— as he forms a hunch about the pattern he is dealing with.

Stress is one constituent of intonation, and it plays an important part in English utterance. Shifting these stresses from one word to another can indicate different structure and completely change the meaning. For instance, in *Tom saw a monkey*, if unusual stress is placed on *Tom*, the reader knows that *Tom*, not Jim or Bill, saw a monkey. Shift this heavy stress to *saw* and the sentence means there is no doubt he saw it. Shift the heavy stress to the noun marker *a* and the singularity is stressed, not monkeys but *a* monkey. Stress *monkey* and the sentence means he saw not a dog, cat, or kangaroo, but a *monkey*. This kind of special stress can be signaled in writing by under-lining, italics, or bold face type, but the regular, important, subtle stress differences among the words of an utterance are not represented in any way in written English.

Many words are spelled the same when used as verbs or nouns, but the stress is shifted from the first syllable for the noun to the second syllable for the verb. *Contract* and *progress* are such words. Compounds such as *blackboard* are stressed differently from the way the same two words are said when used together but not compounded. *Not all black boards are blackboards.* To understand the sense of this sentence the reader must supply appropriate stress. When a teacher says to a child, "Read that the way you would say it to a friend," he is asking the child to supply natural intonations.

Pitch is a second constituent of intonation, whose rises, falls, and steadi-ness are also used to cue meaning in English. Few speakers can describe how pitch works, but all use it to get structure and meaning. By varying the pitch pattern of the single word *what*, we can make it mean, "Go ahead, I'm listening," "I didn't hear you," or "I didn't understand you," "You're kid-ding," "I can't believe what you just said," and many other things.

Juncture, the third constituent, refers to the ways we mark off groups of sounds with pauses of variable length to produce words, phrases, or com-munication units. In written language the spaces between words and punctuation such as commas and periods provide graphic cues to the reader that correspond with juncture in speech. However, this correspondence is incomplete and somewhat capricious. Our division of written language into words does not accurately reflect the oral language as children know it. *Look at the monkey* has four words, but the child normally hears no separation between *look* and *at* because there is none.

Pitch and juncture are the cues that tell a listener that an utterance is concluded or continuing, that he is expected to continue listening to a series of statements, respond to a question, or act on a request. Readers must learn to associate punctuation with familiar pitch and stress patterns in oral language and vice versa, for the intonation they use is a direct reflection of the grammar they are processing.

All three aspects of intonation—stress, pitch, and juncture—work together in oral language. When words are read from lists, the intonation is quite different from when they are read in stories. To hear this difference, read this list of words: *peaches, pears, plums.* Now read this sentence: *He bought peaches, pears, and plums.* In the list, each word has the same intonation—the same stress and pitch pattern as the last word in the sentence. Some children are word-callers who read as if they were reading lists of words: *Tom, saw, the* (probably pronounced *thee*), *monkey.* Punctuation cues are of little help to these readers, because every word is the first, last, and only word in a one-word sentence.

Word-callers are so busy recognizing words by using cues within words that they make little or no use of cues within the flow of language. They may call the names of the words correctly, but they cannot get the meaning from a story without using cues that are not contained in words. They can see the trees, but they are lost in the forest.

CONTEXTUAL MEANING The fifth-system of cues lies in the contextual meaning of prior and subsequent words and whole utterances. Earlier, full and empty words were mentioned. Full words have dictionary (lexical) definitions with some substance, but everyone knows that a series of lexical definitions cannot be put together if one is to understand a sentence without awkward, comical, and misleading results. How could one get the sense of this sentence from dictionary definitions of the individual words: *He got up, took a dip, and split.*

The lexical meaning must have added to it a contextual one. This is supplied partly by nearby function words, inflectional endings, the position of the word in a language pattern, intonations, and the lexical meaning of nearby words. Actually, only larger units of language, sentences or groups of sentences, convey meaning, and this meaning is always more than the sum of its parts. As was apparent with "Gloopy and Blit," adults who are good readers often meet unfamiliar words in their reading that they can understand because of the numerous cues that surround them. Children learn to read new words in similar fashion.

REDUNDANCY IN LANGUAGE CUES The last cue system involves another important aspect of language—its *redundancy*. In the story "Gloopy and Blit," the generous number of cues available was noted. Communications theorists use the word *redundancy* in a special sense to describe a tendency of languages to restrict the sequences in which language symbols can occur, to provide several cues to the same bit of information, and thus to be less than 100 percent efficient in the amount of information transmitted per unit of language.

Our language, like all other natural languages, is not very economical in the way that it transmits information. To be completely efficient (that is, to transmit the maximum amount of information per unit of language), every sound or letter would have to occur with equal frequency after every other. Likewise, every word would need to follow every other word with equal frequency. But a word like *ngopr* could not exist in English because the sequence of sounds in it is not used in our language. A sequence of words such as *To ran elephant the him not* is also not a permissible sequence in English.

Some sequences seldom occur in our language. Some never occur. This inefficiency or *redundancy* has two important effects on reading. First, it provides the reader with the repetitious cues we noted earlier. In the sentence that follows there are no less than four cues to the fact that the subject is plural: *At noon, the boys eat their lunches.*

Second, redundancy provides a narrowing of elements in the language that can fill certain slots. Only certain sounds can occur after /t/ in *Tom*. Only certain words can occur after *Tom*. After *Tom saw*, still fewer words are possible. After *Tom saw a*, possible correct words are more restricted. Furthermore, the unknown word *monkey* must fit equally well into a number of such restricted settings.

The process by which the child immediately or eventually knows this word is *monkey* is a kind of tentative "zeroing in." Successive sets of redundant cues narrow the number of possible words in the language that can fit. As he responds to these redundant cues, the child is guessing, but he is an enlightened guesser. He is using his knowledge of language, his past experience, and his developed concepts. If he makes a mistake, there are almost always abundant additional cues to tell him that he is wrong and to tell him what is right.

Children do not need to know all the words before they can read stories. In a study by Goodman,[6] first-grade children were able to read two thirds of

[6] Kenneth S. Goodman, "Cues and Miscues in Reading: A Linguistic Study," *Elementary English, 42*, No. 6 (1965), 640.

the words that they had missed on a list when these same words occurred in a story. Second-graders read three fourths of their list errors correctly in a story context. Third-graders got more than four out of five right in the stories. They were able to do this because of the cue systems that exist in the flow of language but not in words.

section 3

Cues within the Reader

Obviously, learning to read depends to a very great extent on the individual characteristics of the learner. What the reader brings to the language he is reading is as important as the cues in the language itself. The message does not exist in the language. Language carries the message from the writer, but it must be re-created by the reader out of raw material within himself. A good writer always has his audience in mind. The reader must have certain associations with the language symbols in common with the writer. But he must also have some experiences in common with the writer and must have reached a level of concept development that makes communication possible.

Consider the absurd example of a six-year-old English-speaking American child trying to read an ancient Chinese philosophical tract written in archaic Chinese characters. The task is patently ridiculous, but why?

First, the child does not understand Chinese. Even if he did, the dialect he understands would be one of many modern dialects; it would be very much changed from the ancient dialect of the Chinese philosopher who wrote the tract. Communication depends on a common language. If the young reader did overcome this handicap, he would be confronted by a system of writing he does not know. He would not have learned responses to the symbols of the written language that the writer expected to evoke in his readers. But even if he did learn the symbols, he could not read the philosophical tract because he would not have had the experiences or have developed the philosophical concepts to know what the writer intended him to know. Further, his American culture would be so different from the culture of the ancient Chinese that many of the philosophical thoughts would be literally unthinkable, even for adult Americans. The six-year-old American child learning to read English is confronted with problems that differ in degree but not in kind from this absurd example.

As within words and within the flow of language, there are several systems of cues and responses to cues that are within or must develop *within the reader*. These are:

Language facility (the internalization of a dialect)
Physiology (as it affects perception and expression)

Learned responses and strategies
Experiential background of the reader
Reader's conceptual background and ability

LANGUAGE FACILITY The first important chacacteristic of the reader is language facility. Success in any communicative transaction, including reading, depends to a great degree on the ability of the two parties, the speaker-writer and the listener-reader, to communicate. Close agreement on language between these two parties is important. Even though both may speak English, there may be large or small differencies between the English of one and the other.

Differences in use of a single language are generally termed *dialects*. Groups of users separated by time, space, social or economic class, interest, political barriers, or age may develop dialect differences. Further, each user of the language develops his own *idiolect*, different in some respects from those of all other users.

Every child starting the first grade has mastered, for all practical language purposes, the language of his subculture—his family, friends, and community. This dialect is deeply internalized in the child; it has become a part of his personality.

When a child is learning to read, he may have problems if the school and teacher reject his dialect.[7] If he does not speak a standard Midwestern dialect, he may be confused, because what sounds right to him when he reads is labeled wrong by the teacher.

Most people develop the ability to understand a wide range of dialects that differ somewhat from their own. Children in New England, New York, Chicago, and the deep South all "savvy" the lingo of the television cowpoke. In reading, the fact of dialect is reflected in a tendency on the part of the reader to translate the text language into his own dialect. Not only are the phonemes those of the oral language of the reader, but grammar, usage, even vocabulary are unconsciously shifted into the more familiar dialect. *There were a lot of pumpkins* might be read by some children as *They was a lot o' punkins*. This translation is not error, pure and simple; the child is making a linguistic leap. He is reading his own dialect from the printed page. If his teacher rejects his attempt at bridging the gap between the book dialect and his own by treating it as an error, he may be bewildered. If what he reads sounds right to him, how can it be wrong? *This is not the time to be concerned about changing dialects, when reading is the goal.*

Beginners, including those who speak standard dialects, are confused if basal readers use language that does not occur in anybody's speech. Older children find it difficult to read classics that employ archaic dialects. Not only have meanings changed, but structural patterns, usage, and other vital

---

[7] Kenneth S. Goodman and Catherine Buck, "Dialect Barriers to Reading Comprehension Revisited," *Reading Teacher* (October 1973).

elements are different. Perhaps most difficult is that children are asked to reconstruct a dialect they have never heard spoken. This is not to suggest that all classics should be abandoned, but that special problems are involved in reading them, and teachers need to help students develop special skills to deal with these problems.

PHYSIOLOGY Physical factors, a second important consideration, may interfere with effective communication. Writing may be illegible because of physical disability or lack of coordination of the writer. Visual factors may interfere with the reader's ability to discern language units clearly. Hearing problems may make it difficult for children to hear sounds in language and to associate these sounds with graphic symbols. General factors of physical and mental health affect all learning, including the ability to read. These factors are of course intertwined with the total well-being of the learner—economic, social and emotional, as well as physical.

Some medical authorities have sought to identify a pattern of physiological factors that would cause the child to fail to learn to read. This has been labeled by some *constitutional dyslexia.* Children seem to have some ability to overcome physical and perceptual disabilities, however. Interestingly enough, many of the factors that researchers have sought to link to constitutional dyslexia have been found among readers as well as nonreaders. Research has failed to find any substantial cause for reading failure in physical, mental or perceptual difficulties.

LEARNED RESPONSES TO GRAPHIC CUES The third set of cues affecting the reader are learned responses. Letters, singly or in groups, do not have sounds or meanings; they just lie there on the page. But they may evoke responses in people. Thus, people may see letters in isolation and call their names, *A, B, C,* and so forth. Or they may see letters in isolated words and call the names of the words: *peaches, pears, plums.* These responses are all learned. The important thing is that they must evoke the same general responses in all who use them.

The reading beginner has not learned these responses to graphic cues, but he has learned to respond rapidly to groups of sounds as language symbols. In reading he must become at least as facile in responding to graphic symbols. He may acquire this ability to interpret print in a "natural" manner, deriving his own generalizations just as he learned to talk and understand oral language. Or he may learn systems of reading attacks, skills, or learning strategies, which he applies in a synthetic manner[8] (phonics is such a synthetic learning strategy).

In either case, he must transfer his existing knowledge of language to

[8] Frank Smith, *Understanding Reading* (New York: Holt, Rinehart and Winston, 1972).

the task of reading. He can only do this effectively if what he reads is real language, which differs only from oral language in its use of graphic symbols rather than sound symbols.

Code and Meaning

If language is viewed as a code, a system for communicating meaning, then reading may be seen as a process of *decoding*. The reader uses a printed code and decodes from it the meaning that the writer had encoded.

It is also possible to go from one code to another without decoding for meaning. Such a process can be called *recoding*. For example, a telegraph operator takes a written message and sends it out on his key in Morse code, having recoded the alphabetic code as dots and dashes. He need have no understanding of what he is reading to successfully recode; in fact, the original may be in a secret code that he does not know.

In oral reading, beginners and others who are not very proficient may, in fact, be recoding graphic code (print) as oral code (speech) without decoding for meaning.

Eventually, though, in proficient reading, the process becomes parallel to listening. There is no necessary resort to recoding print as oral language. Rather, the reader goes directly from print to meaning in the same manner that he goes from speech to meaning as a listener. This direct process[9] may be illustrated as follows:

In the beginner's model, the recoding and decoding cannot be separated because the reason for reading is to reconstruct meaning. If children develop skills for recoding in school while using exercises and materials that are not in real, meaningful language, they will not be able to use the available cues within the language but will be confined to working with cues that lead only to words. Even there they have no check on whether they have selected the right word because they cannot check their choices against cues within the flow of language.

The controversy over code-emphasis versus meaning-emphasis programs in reading instruction stems from the erroneous assumption that language is simply a collection of words, and that all that is necessary for reading is to identify (or recognize) words. But the code that is language is a *system* of symbols and not merely a collection of symbols. To decode one must

---

[9] Kenneth S. Goodman, *The Psycholinguistic Nature of the Reading Process* (Detroit: Wayne State University Press, 1967), p. 18.

respond not simply to symbols with other symbols: One must respond to the system (which in linguistic codes is called grammar) as well as to the symbols in order to arrive at the meaning. The research summarized by Chall[10] and others that purports to show that code-emphasis programs are superior to meaning-emphasis programs for teaching reading is in reality a comparison of two kinds of programs for teaching children to recode. The phonics programs focus on letter-to-sound recoding. (Chall labels this *code emphasis.*) The sight–word programs focus on word-shape–word-name recoding. (Chall calls this *meaning emphasis.*) The only sense in which the latter are more involved in meaning is that words have dictionary, lexical, definitions. But in none of these programs are all of the cues within language emphasized. They are not really decoding systems.

In addition to the previously mentioned systems of cues and responses within the reader there are two other factors significant for reading ability: (1) the experiential background of the learner, and (2) conceptual background.

THE EXPERIENTIAL BACKGROUND OF THE LEARNER The reader depends heavily on his experiential background to decode what he is reading. If the events, places, people, and objects the reader encounters are unrelated to any experiences he has had, he will have great difficulty reading about them, even though the language elements may all be familiar.

Communication depends on some base of shared experience between the sending and receiving parties. This base may be the common experience of all those who share the culture or the subculture, or may be the intimate experience shared by a small in-group or even by just two. The more intimate the base of experience, of course, the less complete must the language be, so that between close friends or family members a nod or a single word may be sufficient to communicate whole thoughts.

The following passage illustrates the kind of language composed of familiar elements that can be understood only by those who share the common experiences of the group: "If you're running a big bad AA fuelie, man, it costs dough every time you're just tripping the lights to get the tires ready. Some slicks take ten or twelve runs to be right."[11] Teachers of adolescents sometimes despair that their pupils can handle, with ease, passages like that above but that they bog down hopelessly in *Silas Marner* or a tenth-grade world-geography text.

Of course, reading itself is experience. This experience can be built layer upon layer, so that the armchair traveler, armchair detective, armchair scientist can come to be almost as much an initiate as his real-life counterpart. But this is all vicarious experience. Language is symbolic. It can only

---

[10] Jean Chall, *Reading: The Great Debate* (New York: McGraw-Hill, 1967).
[11] LeRoi Smith, "New Drag Slick!" *Hot Rod* (July 1964), pp. 46–47.

evoke images, feelings, thoughts, visions, which have some base in the real experience of the reader.

Recently a seventh-grade boy was observed[12] attempting to read a work sheet in a junior high school print shop. The sheet provided directions for printing personal stationery. The boy read with difficulty but paused every time he came to the word *stationery*. Each time his teacher supplied the word, but the next time the boy was stumped again. When he had finished reading the sheet, the boy could describe the technical details involved in setting three lines of type for the job, but he had no idea what the purpose of the project was. The simple truth is that the boy had had no experience with stationery. The writer of the work sheet had assumed that all the boys had seen stationery in use and would appreciate the value of personalized stationery. This type of unwarranted assumption is frequently reflected in text material for all subjects at all levels and penalizes children whose experiences are different. Teachers who know their children and preread text material carefully can soften this effect somewhat by providing experiences that are needed to make text material understandable.

CONCEPTUAL BACKGROUND AND ABILITY OF THE LEARNER Just as reading is limited by the experience of the learner, so is it limited by conceptual development. A reader cannot read written language that expresses concepts that are far beyond his developed ability to understand. Concepts may be attained through reading, but they must be broadly within the grasp of the reader. Beyond this point, a learner must have help in understanding concepts before he can read. Indeed, teachers would be unneeded if this were not true.

When a teacher thinks that language alone conveys concepts and simply assigns textbook reading, learners flounder. Concepts are communicated from person to person through language, the symbolic medium individuals use to manipulate their experiences and ideas in order to develop concepts. But language can be manipulated by children without their understanding the concepts involved. A child may state correctly that Michigan is a peninsula and that so is Florida, without grasping the basic significance of peninsularity. He may just be repeating, appropriately, statements he has heard. Similarly, he may read from a text and even supply correct answers to questions at the end of each chapter without in any way understanding the concepts. *Question:* What is Gloopy? *Answer:* Gloopy is a borp.

Some teachers naïvely assume that if a child can translate the written symbols in a text into oral speech, he is capable of dealing with the concepts being presented. If he cannot read a particular word, the teacher con-

---

[12] Kenneth S. Goodman, "Decoding: From Code to What," *Journal of Reading* (April 1971).

siders this a vocabulary problem. But what is labeled a "reading vocabulary problem" may involve problems on four very different levels. Here are four cases to illustrate these levels of vocabulary difficulty:

1. The reader understands a word or phrase—*monkey* or *stationery*, for example—and uses it in his oral speech, but does not recognize its graphic representation.
2. The reader does not know or use the word or phrase in his oral language but can grasp the meaning, particularly in familiar natural language. His previous experience and conceptual development have made this easy addition to his vocabulary possible.
3. The reader does not know or use the word or phrase in his oral language and cannot understand the meaning because it depends on experiences and a level of concept development that he has not attained.
4. The reader can tell the name of the word or phrase, using cues within words, but he does not know, use or understand what he is reading. Because he does not understand, he is not reading.

Research on the reading process among readers from low-proficiency second-graders to highly proficient adults[13] has demonstrated that the major difference between weak and strong readers is in how well they have the process together. Regardless of level of proficiency, all readers are users of language. They attempt to use graphic, syntactic, and semantic cues to get meaning from written language, and all readers use all types of cues. Proficient readers are both efficient and effective. As *effective* readers they get the most meaning out of the task. As *efficient* readers they do it with the least amount of effort and energy. They are highly selective, using only enough cues to get to the meaning.

The more that is understood about reading the more complex it appears. And yet it is no more complex than listening, a processing that most children master without school help.

Understanding how reading works and how children learn language may turn out to be the key to universal literacy.

[13] Kenneth S. Goodman and Carolyn L. Burke, "Theoretically Based Studies of Patterns of Miscues in Oral Reading Performance," U.S. Office of Education, Final Report, Project No. 9–0375 (April 1973).

16

Teaching Reading: Developing Strategies for Comprehension

Much of reading material, reading curriculum theory, and reading teaching has suffered from a lack of accurate knowledge of how language works. Generalizations in teaching of reading from psychological, sociological, physiological and pedagogical sources are not inaccurate, but they are incomplete. Old knowledge and new knowledge must be integrated to produce better methods and materials for teaching reading. Fortunately, a good beginning has been made on building a new productive methodology in reading.

Old and New

There is a tendency in education to throw out the old and substitute the new. This would be a grievous error in the field of reading instruction. Valid, tried, and accepted principles of reading instruction must not be abandoned without examination. The processes of reading and of learning to read are complex indeed, but reading teachers have frequently been beset by persons or groups peddling panaceas, returns to simple "commonsense." and sure-fire methods like phonics. Invariably, the panaceas claim to teach all children, no matter how young, to read in an unbelievably short time. They also make unrealistic promises to bring all retarded readers up to grade level in a few short months and to teach illiterate adults to read overnight.

Once mastered, any learning task seems simple. Adults who read have long since forgotten the problems they encountered while learning. They have repressed memories of classmates who never learned, of unhappy oversized youngsters at adjacent desks who left school, still illiterate, as soon as laws and circumstances permitted. Suddenly these adults discover, perhaps through experiences with their own children, that present methods and materials are not teaching all children to read well and quickly. They seek the simple panacea just as the sufferer from an as-yet incurable physical affliction runs from quack to quack seeking quick and simple cures.

Children have so much going for them when it comes to learning to read that most can overcome deficiencies in instruction and learn anyway. Although misconceptions abound, no method yet developed has worked with all children. There has been no golden age in American education when all children learned. Nor is it true that reading problems exist only in America or in English-speaking countries—in many countries, poor readers simply drop out of school at early ages. As compulsory education is becoming more universal, however, reading problems are getting more attention all over the world.

Most of the simple panaceas in reading instruction are not methods but sets of tactics that emphasize the learner's use of one set of cues or a group of related cues. Phonics, for example, is a set of tactics for handling letter cues. These tactics, if they are based on a sound understanding of letter–sound relationships, can be fitted into a method of reading instruction. But phonics is not a complete method of reading instruction.

Understanding of reading and learning to read is now making it possible for educators to explain, predict, diagnose, and prevent or remedy reading difficulties. But this involves not only highly sophisticated application of knowledge from many disciplines, but also teachers who thoroughly understand language, language learning, and the learners themselves. *Any strategy of reading instruction based on a single principle or tactic is incomplete, no matter how valid the principle. Reading methods must be based on a complete understanding of the complex reading process.* Children do not learn in the same way linguists study language. Nor do they learn synthetically, one small piece at a time, as do psychologists' pigeons. They learn as children. Reading methodology must reflect an understanding of language, of learning, of children, and of children learning language. Just as important as the proper concepts and tools are enlightened teachers, without which the goal of universal literacy will never be accomplished. In this chapter, a view of the teaching of reading based on these important considerations will be presented.

section 1

The Reading Curriculum

Every curriculum has a point of departure and objectives. There must be criteria for selecting learning opportunities and for deciding on the sequence of their presentation. Reader interest must also be a consideration. This section will discuss these themes.

THE BASE The reading beginner is not a language beginner. The reading curriculum must be based on the prior language experience of the learners. Because all children do not start from the same point, the reading curriculum must be flexible *from the very beginning*, allowing for wide differences in dialect, experience, conceptual development, motivation, and interest. Learning to read must become an extension of children's natural language learning.

OBJECTIVE Reading instruction has one central goal. The learner must become able, to some degree, to understand written language—to construct a message from print which substantially matches that of the writer. All other goals are subsidiary to this one. Some of these secondary goals are:

1. To develop strategies for sampling and selecting graphic, syntactic, and semantic cues;
2. To develop prediction strategies to anticipate meaning, syntactic patterns, and graphic features not yet seen;
3. To develop confirmation strategies to check predictions against subsequent cues;
4. To develop correction strategies when miscues occur which interfere with comprehension;
5. To develop flexible strategies for dealing with a wide variety of materials:
   (a)   Literature
   (b)   Nonfiction
   (c)   Instructions and directions
   (d)   Content area material
   (e)   Other materials
6. To develop critical strategies for judging validity of information in reading;
7. To develop flexibility in use of the reading process for different purposes:
   (a)   Pleasure
   (b)   Quick review
   (c)   Specific information seeking
   (d)   Other purposes.

Notice that these goals do not imply that reading can be treated as a sequenced set of minute steps, each a separate skill, to be learned one at a time. Technologists are bombarding educators now with such "systematized" "skill mastery" programs. Each letter–sound relationship is pulled out for separate instruction, each word is taught as an isolatable unit. These sequenced lists, sometimes hundreds of objectives long, have the appearance of logic, order, and tangibility to them. But they are not in fact based on any scientific research. Usually they are simply culled from old reading texts. Sometimes they are conjured out of their author's heads. But language isn't learned piece by piece. Fractured, it becomes a set of abstractions hard for kids to learn. Whole and in proper relationship to relevent meaning it is easy to learn.

The goals of the reading curriculum cannot be separated from those of all language instruction, of course. Prime among these is that the learner expand his ability to communicate effectively.

SELECTION AND ORGANIZATION OF LEARNING OPPORTUNITIES Every curriculum must proceed along some lines of sequence, such as simple to complex, near to far, then to now. Sometimes the internal logic of the subject or the internal psychologic of learner motivations and capabilities can furnish sequence. Most people developing reading curricula have sought to utilize reading materials that move from the simple to the complex. Most materials designed for reading instruction attempt to control readability. Word count is the most common criterion; the number of uncommon words is also controlled. In addition, there is some concern for the length of sentences. Conceptual complexity and interest level are considered, too.

Critics of basal reading materials and advocates of simple panaceas frequently poke fun at those silly little primers, the implication being that an alternate approach will not produce such silly material. This is an irrelevant and specious argument if it is used by anyone who advocates a sequence of reading materials simplified according to any criterion. Whether the criterion for simplification is word count, phonic consistency, spelling patterns, or sentence structure, the result is artificial language.

The problem with most beginning reading materials is not that they are silly, but that they are not language. Any system for simplifying reading material must stop short of creating language that is like none the child has ever heard. The child must be able to use his language knowledge right from the beginning. This is only possible when written language contains the same patterns and behaves much the same as oral language.

Nothing—even at the very beginning of reading instruction—should be included in the reading curriculum that is not real language. This is not to say that there should be no simplification. But the simplification should be in the direction of the most common, most expected, most predictable language patterns and sequences. As much as possible, the frequency with which language phenomena occur in oral language should be considered in constructing materials. Fries found that about 7 percent of all utterances are requests in the pattern: *Give me the book.*[1] *Father! See Susan!* is not just silly, but it is a pattern too uncommon to use so frequently in early materials.

[1] Charles C. Fries, *The Structure of English* (New York: Harcourt, 1952), p. 51.

Even if a child used this pattern he would be more likely to say, "Look at Susan, Daddy."

It is not merely the length that makes the latter sentence more difficult to read. There are complex interrelationships between the clauses that would tax the ability of a beginning reader. He would have great difficulty processing all the cues involved, for too many complex interrelationships can hamper comprehension. Bormuth[2] has found a fairly high correlation between difficulty of comprehension and average word depth (the number of syntactic relationships of a word in a sentence).

Sometimes highly complex syntactical structures can be made up of a few simple words. A sentence such as *See Spot run* is very unusual and complex. The form is that of a request, with the subject abstract and missing. There are two verbs, and in this unusual construction the verb that follows the singular noun is not the *s* form, *eats,* that occurs much more commonly after such singular nouns. *Do you see Spot* and *Spot is running* are easier to read than *See Spot run* because the patterns are common, and the cues lead the reader in expected rather than unexpected directions.

Materials for teaching reading should avoid ambiguity as well as undue complexity. Ambiguity in written language comes from an insufficient number of cues; sometimes the same sentence in oral language would not be ambiguous, because intonation would make the meaning clear. *"Tom," said Mother* must be read with a particular intonational pattern to differentiate it from the more common, *Tom said, "Mother."* Such ambiguity in early reading material can be avoided by using alternate forms.

Ambiguity can also be avoided in the contextual settings of easily confused words. In *Mary was a girl* and *Mary saw a girl, was* and *saw* are equally sensible. But in *Tom saw a girl* the reader would know he was wrong if he said *Tom was a girl.* Common, persistent word confusions might be eliminated altogether if structural and contextual ambiguity were avoided and children were taught to look for sense in what they are reading. Redundant cues can be intentionally included to avoid ambiguity (for example, *Sally saw a girl named Mary*).

Recent research evidence indicated that *was* is sometimes substituted for *saw* in reading by nonproficient readers, but *saw* is rarely substituted for *was.* This demonstrates that even weak readers are using their knowledge of what is most likely to occur in making their predictions. They substitute *was* because it is so much more likely than *saw.* An unambiguous context will help them detect their miscues and correct them.[3]

---

[2] John R. Bormuth, "Recently Developed Syntactic Variables in the Prediction of the Comprehension Difficulty of Written Language," paper read at California Education Research Association meeting, Los Angeles, March 1964.

[3] K. S. Goodman and C. Burke, "Theoretically Based Studies of Patterns of Miscues in Oral Reading Performance," U.S. Office of Education, *Final Report,* Project No. 9–0375 (April 1973).

Certainly there is some validity in the concern for vocabulary as a means of simplifying reading. Repetition is an important aid to learning, and controlled repetition of words and phrases will, in general, help children learn them. But the selection of words must be based on more than their frequency in language. Furthermore, the way a word is used is as important as how often it is used. The word *circus* is harder to read in *He is a circus clown* than it is in *The clown is in the circus.* Common words used as proper names become very difficult for beginning readers (Mrs. White, Miss Park, Mr. Town).[4]

Actually language controls its own word frequency in a natural way. In any text there will be two kinds of very common words. One kind consists of those very frequent function words common in all language. The second kind includes those most central to the theme of the particular selection.

Function words, despite their prevalence, are hard to retain, probably because of their lack of meaning. Function words should be introduced in reading early and with great care. Noun markers such as *the* should accompany nouns as they are introduced.

Question markers can be introduced to make question patterns out of statement patterns that have already been introduced. *I have one* becomes *Do I have one?* When the question marker *do* is added.

Verb markers, when used, will call forth from the language storehouse of the child's mind correct accompanying verb forms: *Spot is eating. Puff has eaten. Sally will eat.* Words that are uncommon but used frequently in a story build their own meaning through repeated contexts.

INTEREST The interests of readers are also important in planning the reading curriculum. Studies have shown some common interests among boys and girls of various ages, but all such studies have also turned up children whose interests are decidedly atypical. The only way a reading curriculum can interest all children is by providing choice and variety. Writers who have attempted to define levels of readability have agreed that children can read material that is very difficult for them if their interest is intense.

Reading material must also be conceptually suitable for children. It is more important that the conceptual difficulty of reading material be controlled than that vocabulary be controlled. Words are more easily learned than ideas; on the other hand, neither words nor ideas will be retained if the ideas are not understood.

To sum up, materials providing opportunities for children to learn to read should be selected with the following criteria in mind:

[4] Yetta M. Goodman, *A Psycholinguistic Description of Observed Oral Reading Phenomena in Selected Young Beginning Readers*, unpublished doctoral dissertation, Wayne State University, Detroit, Michigan, 1967.

They must contain real language as close as possible to the language the child already knows.

They must emphasize the most common patterns and sequences of oral language. The most expected phenomena should occur with the greatest frequency.

Undue complexity should be avoided.

Ambiguity should be avoided.

Vocabulary control can not be the sole means of sequencing materials.

Children's interests must be considered and choice offered to them.

Conceptual difficulty should be controlled.

section 2

Reading Readiness and Motivation

The admonition, which has become a cliché in education, that *teaching must start where the child is*, is a most significant principle to apply to reading readiness. The child has learned language before he begins the task of acquiring literacy in the language. The child's pride in his mother tongue, the dialect of his home and community, and his confidence in his ability to communicate effectively through his language must be firmly established if he is to be successful in learning to read. If his language is rejected by the teacher and the school, if he is constantly told he has said something wrong every time he attempts communication, the learner becomes confused about his language knowledge and doubtful of his ability to learn to read. Learning cannot be built on a foundation of shame, confusion, and doubt.

Any reading-readiness program must begin with the child's own language. Opportunities must be present from the first day of kindergarten for the child to use language so that his language will expand and grow and his confidence and effectiveness will constantly increase. There is a story about a kindergartner who comes home the first day from school and announces he is not going back. "I can't read and write," he explains. "And they won't let me talk, so there's nothing to do!" The language knowledge the child brings to school with him is his greatest asset in learning to read. The school must nurture the child's language and cause it to grow—not frustrate and choke it off. *The child needs to be talked to, listened to, understood. He needs opportunities to communicate his wishes, feelings, emotions, and ideas. The teacher makes communication a vital program element daily.*

Confident, effective use of oral language is the basis for learning to read. Consider the problem of teaching a deaf child to read. It is really a different task, more akin to the original acquisition of language than to learning to read a language the learner already speaks.

Because reading is a counterpart of listening in language, children can use their ability to respond rapidly to cues they hear in language in learning to respond to these cues in graphic form. Learning experiences that help each child utilize the aural cue systems in the language so that he will comprehend more fully will make it possible for him to utilize the graphic counterpart of these cues.

Children will profit from listening to rich and varied language. Not only will their own language grow, but the range of language they understand will increase. This is important for all children, not just those who speak a divergent dialect of English.

Experience is also important in making children feel a need to learn to read. Some children have an enriched home life, which is advantageous in school; others have varied experiences but of the type not valued there. Children with few parental restrictions, who roam through the noisy and crowded central areas of great cities, have no lack of experience. But they have not found these experiences in their early reading material; nor have they talked or written about them in school.

A reading-readiness program can involve expanding experiences for children through such things as trips, walks, and activity programs. At the same time, with an attitude of acceptance and understanding, bridges must be built from the experiences of the child to the common experiences of the general culture. He must come to see more, not just *differently*.

The child must always hear and use language in conjunction with his experiences—to express himself to others, to use as a medium in which to think reflectively about his experiences, and to form concepts and generalizations.

CONCEPTS Particular attention must be given to concept development. Teachers need to assure themselves that children have sufficient background to deal with the new concepts that they will encounter in reading. Opportunities need to be provided for learners to verbalize the concepts they are acquiring, not just by answering questions on paper, but through the give-and-take of discussion. This not only establishes the concept, but makes it possible to move on to other more complex or abstract ideas. The learner must acquire the concept as he acquires the language to express and manipulate it.

Conceptual development unaccompanied by language development is possible, although people who have concepts to communicate will invent language if none exists. This is true of the scientists on the frontiers of knowledge who develop a new concept, and of the teenagers tinkering with a hot-rod engine who discover an old concept but who do not know the existing language to express it. Each will devise language to express new thoughts.

But teachers need to beware of mistaking the ability to manipulate language for conceptual development. Emphasis on isolated language skills and use of meaningless language drills and exercises may produce a wide gulf between language skill and the ability to use the skill communicatively. Children may learn to give the expected language responses to questions in oral or written form, without at all understanding the concepts involved. Questions that require children to manipulate language, but not ideas, will not prepare the child for dealing with ever more difficult concepts. Take a common example: The child is required to answer in writing the question *What were the chief products of the Middle Colonies?* He runs his eyes over the preceding chapter until he spies the title "Middle Colonies." He then scans that section until he finds a line that begins, "*The chief products of the Middle Colonies were.*" Then he reproduces the section in writing, taking care to rephrase it slightly, because a rule of the game, he has learned, is that he must not copy exactly. But he can carry out the entire task without any reflective thinking. In his answer he can use words and phrases that he does not in any way associate with meaning. He can even memorize whole language sequences that convey no message to him and can reproduce these in response to cues in test questions. *Preparing a child to read must involve preparing him to understand, because there is no reading without comprehension.* The traditional concerns of reading-readiness programs formed into concepts are not so important as the firm base in language and experience that the learner must bring to reading.

Motivation in Learning To Read

Children learn language because they need to communicate. Their oral language is continually polished and improved to make it more like the language of their family and subculture, because the closer it comes to the language of those around them, the more effective it is in meeting their

Communicative need is the most important motivation in reading as communicative needs.

well as in speech. In our society the nonreader is seriously handicapped because there is so much graphic communication. Streets and buses are labeled, letters are written, packages are printed on. Most children quickly become aware that all around them is language that can only be understood by readers. For some children, the need to learn to read is so great that they virtually teach themselves.

Children from highly literate homes have the additional stimulation of large numbers of books of all kinds and the frequent example of adults and siblings spending time reading. Children who are read to frequently become aware of the pleasure and entertainment reading may provide. A highly motivated child from a literate home may be able to carry his enthusiasms through an extended learning period during which little communication is involved; the materials he is reading may have little or no message or literary quality; the hours spent drilling on skill exercises may be unrelated to any communicative goal the child can discern. But he is sustained through all this by the knowledge that at the end of the process he will be a member of the prestigious society—he will be a reader.

For many children, however, the relationship between reading and previous language experience may be temporarily or permanently forgotten unless reading has an early and continuing communicative function. A basic difference between oral and written language is in their use. Written language is removed from the situations with which it deals. Oral language tends to be here and now, face-to-face, with its referents present. Written language is between a writer and reader remote from each other and the real referents of the language in time, space, or both.

This may explain why all children learn oral language and appear to be ready for learning written language and yet some do not learn.

Perhaps their need for written language has not yet been established. They live in a here-and-now world without need for a language to communicate over time and space. For such children, readiness may largely be a matter of establishing a need, a motivation for literacy.

Advocates of many approaches to teaching reading have claimed that the learner's success at each stage is motivation for the next stage. Reading teachers know from experience, however, that this kind of motivation involves only a small number of children and that their motivation is not to learn to read but to be successful, that is, get the grades, or smiles, or gold stars that the teacher awards to those who succeed. Reading then can become a contest or a school chore, a daily ritual unrelated to language, communication, or life.

To sustain the motivation of all children, then, reading materials at all ages must be worth reading; they must be real language with a real story or message that is interesting to the child and that is broadly within his realm of experience. Until such motivation is established some children may not learn to read.

Starting with Experience

A good way to insure that the beginning reader is reading language that he understands is to let the child, group, or class dictate a story to the teacher about a real experience. Here is an example of an experience story created by a group of first-grade children:

WENDY'S DUCKLINGS
Wendy's got two cute ducklings.
We saw Wendy's ducklings.
The yellow one is Salt.
The black one is Pepper.
They like each other.
They peeped and peeped until Salt found Pepper.

The *experience story* has several virtues: (1) The children see that oral language can be written down, that it is not a special language, for even their own speech can be written down; (2) the content of the story is a real event that happened to them; and (3) the language in the story is their language as they use it.

Many teachers begin the use of experience stories by having each child draw a picture of an experience and then by letting the child dictate something the teacher writes on the picture. In this way, each child has a brief experience story of his own to share with his classmates.

Teachers need to be careful about how they tamper with language as they write it down. There is some tendency to make it approach the language of preprimers so that the form and vocabulary of the preprimer will be introduced. "Wendy's Ducklings" might become something quite foreign to the children like this:

> PEEP! PEEP!
> Look, look.
> See the little ducks.
> Oh, look.
> See little Salt.
> See little Pepper.
> See Salt and Pepper
> Peep, peep Salt.
> Peep, peep, Pepper.
> Oh, see Salt and Pepper.

What should the teacher do, however, when the language of the children is distinctly divergent? The teacher should use the language of the children as much as possible. *Since spelling is constant for all dialects, standard spelling should be used in transcribing, but the teacher should not insist on the child's reading the way the teacher would.*

If the children had said *We seen Wendy's duckses*, the teacher might first ask *What do we call baby ducks?* When the children had supplied the term *ducklings*, the teacher would then write *We seen Wendy's ducklings*. But the children would be permitted to read it the way it sounds best to them. The teacher must recognize that *seen* is standard in the dialect of some children; it is what their parents might say, whereas *duckses* is immature. Similarly, if a child said *We helded them*, the teacher would know that this was not an example of the dialect or mother tongue of the child but a vestige of immature usage. The teacher would use his own dialect but would not insist on the children's doing so.

It is particularly important in transcribing children's stories not to change the grammar or vocabulary. If the child says *Me and James was chunking the ball around*, the teacher's changing it to *James and I were throwing the ball around* will confuse the child and the issue. *The goal is literacy in reading instruction, not changed speech.*

section 3

Reading Practices

Oral Reading

Through the years of reading authorities have argued the merits of oral reading. Strong arguments have been advanced against oral reading as a part of reading instruction.

It is slower than silent reading and may cause children to develop into slow readers.

Oral reading has limited social utility. Most adults seldom find it necessary to read aloud.

Studies have shown that children tend to comprehend better when they read silently than when they read orally.

Oral reading in round-robin style with each child reading in turn while the others follow in their own books is dull and tedious.

While valid, these criticisms are of the traditional form of oral reading. To avoid such negative effects the experience should take on a more communicative function. Children should be encouraged to select stories or sections of books that they have particularly enjoyed and that they think will interest their classmates. The teacher should then arrange time for the children to read while others listen. For the reader, the objective should be to entertain or enlighten his listeners. For his audience, this will be a listening activity. They should not be asked to follow in their own books, but should be encouraged to listen effectively. Discussion should follow and should focus mainly on the story or information provided. The reader should play a leading role in this discussion, with the teacher functioning as a guide. The reader's skill should be discussed only in relationship to his effectiveness in arousing interest and conveying information. Children should also be encouraged to read interesting parts of stories and books to their teachers or to a classmate. Teachers may find it useful to have pupils read to a tape recorder for later miscue analysis and discussion. *It is important that they be encouraged to use their knowledge of language cues to correct their own errors in oral reading. Listener prompting and correcting is unnecessary and should be avoided.*

Skill and Strategy Instruction

Skills and strategies in reading are means to an end; the end is fuller comprehension. Most skills necessary to reading will develop gradually in most children as they learn to read, provided the material they are reading meets the criteria we have discussed. Teachers can assist children in developing strategies by calling important cues and cue systems to their attention as they occur in the children's reading. They can also encourage children to discover and discuss generalizations about language and how it works.

A strategy is a general approach to a recurrent problem. Because reading requires the reader to deal continually with complex kinds of information— graphic, phonic, phonemic, syntactic, semantic—in order to construct meaning from print, the reader must develop information-processing strategies. He will need, for example, strategies for deciding which letters are most useful (initial, medial, final). He will need scanning strategies (indeed, moving his eyes from left-to-right is a basic reading strategy).

The reader will need general sampling strategies to select the most productive cues from all those available to him. He will need prediction strategies to help him anticipate what is coming and to help him predict grammatical patterns.

He will need strategies for dealing with special kinds of reading materials: textbooks, works of fiction, recipes, maps, charts, and mathematical symbols.

All of these may develop in a natural way as children gain proficiency in reading. Some children will, however, need specific instruction in specific strategies. The important thing is that it be offered to the right child at the right time. The specific child or children must show a definite need. The patterns and rates of learning of children differ so greatly that it is highly unlikely that all or even a substantial number of a class would have the same need at the same time. As a matter of fact, some children might suffer from the same kind of instruction that others might profit from. Suppose, for instance, that a whole class is drilled on initial consonants. This may be very helpful to some children who have not learned to use these cues. But it may only intensify the problem of children who are already using initial consonant cues but are ignoring other important cues—function words, for example.

The common practice of giving a class, or group, instruction in a specific reading skill is analogous to a doctor's lining up all his nine-year-old patients and giving them all penicillin shots because some need it now and some may in the future. The only way for a teacher to know when children need specific skill instruction is for him to give each child's reading close diagnostic attention.

MISCUE ANALYSIS The best way for the teacher to diagnose the strengths and weaknesses of children is to listen carefully to the *quality* of their reading errors.[5] Actually, these are not errors but miscues, since they reveal the child's cue system as a reader. Each unexpected response is

[5] Yetta M. Goodman and Carolyn Burke, *Reading Miscue Inventory* (New York: Macmillan, 1972).

caused by the same interaction between the reader and printed language as the reader's expected responses. The reader shows the strengths he has as well as his weaknesses. This places a considerable responsibility on the teacher, who will then need to devise or obtain materials to build on strengths in children's reading. Not all children will require special help from the teacher, however. Some will need only a little guidance and encouragement.

As the teacher examines the child's miscues he should note the following:

Which miscues does the reader recognize and correct?
Do his miscues change the meaning? Do they make sense?
Do they change the grammar?
Are they grammatically acceptable?
Is his dialect involved?[6]

From early infancy, children love to play and experiment with language. Skill instruction must be placed within this language-play context. *As much as possible, attention to specific skills should be a kind of game of taking language apart, seeing how it works, and making it work for us.* Even when the concern is for cues within words, these words should always be in the context of larger language units (sentences and sequences of sentences).

Classroom Organization

GROUPING Grouping for instruction is common in the teaching of reading. Many teachers divide their classes into two or three groups according to results on standardized tests; sometimes the teacher's own judgment is used to adjust membership. When children are placed in classes according to ability, reading achievement ranks second only to intelligence as a criterion of ability. Plans such as the Joplin Plan have children with the same reading ability leaving their regular classes and reassembling for reading instruction. One form of nongraded system places children in classes according to reading levels, so that in place of three grades or six half-grades there are nine to twelve reading levels.

The basic purpose of grouping is to provide instruction at the level of the child. It is reasoned that having three groups will make instruction possible on three levels and that children can be sorted into three relatively homogeneous groups. The second purpose of grouping is to provide an instructional structure that can be effectively managed. Three instruction groups require more planning and are harder to administer than a class instructed as a whole, but are easier to manage than an individualized program.

[6] K. S. Goodman (ed.), *Miscue Analysis: Application to Instruction* (National Council of Teachers of English, Educational Resources Information Center, 1973).

Some problems are involved in grouping for reading instruction, however. Present reading tests measure a variety of things; only one of them is comprehension. A score on a standardized reading test is an average of a number of factors. Several pupils may have the same scores on a reading test but present very different profiles of strengths and weaknesses. These pupils will also be developing at different rates. Although their scores are the same at the time of testing, they may be far apart a month or two months later. Reading scores may, to some extent, reflect differences in background, but they do not really measure the wide divergence of experience, interests, conceptual development, and language development that exists among learners.

Within every ability grouping there will be a wide range of reading needs, growth patterns, and abilities; so-called "ability groups" are by no means homogeneous. No system of group instruction can provide instruction that is at the level of more than a small number of group members at any time. Moreover, when the teacher is working with the group on skills, all members of the group get the same instruction whether they need it or not, whether they are ready for it or not. If all members of the group are reading the same story at the same time, which is the usual case, they are forced to read at the same pace, and their individual tastes and interests are at least partially neglected. When the teacher is not working with the group, much of the time is spent on seat work and not on reading. In fact, it is common for children to spend less than ten minutes out of sixty-minute reading period actually reading. Whether the class is taught as one group, two groups, or three groups, the children are being forced into rigid patterns of growth and reading progress. The only advantage of three groups over one group is that there are three acceptable learning curves instead of one. *Only flexible grouping seems to be justifiable in teaching reading.* The teacher can profitably bring together several children who have demonstrated the same need or similar needs and can work with them until their needs are met or changed. Children remain in the group only as long as they need to, and the group exists only so long as there are children with a common need.

Other short-term groups could be formed on the basis of common interest. Children could come together to read books or stories on the same topic. They would not necessarily read the same material, but their common interest would be the basis of group activities and discussion. The benefits of group dynamics would thus be obtained without forcing a pattern on the group members.

INDIVIDUALIZING An individualized reading program that provides freedom of choice for the learner from a wide variety of well-written and interesting books and that includes provision for continuous supervision by a competent teacher seems a most suitable approach. In the individualized reading program, instruction would be used at the point where one or more children had demonstrated a distinct need. In the periods that the teacher provides for listening to each child read, the teacher would be careful to consider the psycholinguistic bases for the reading behavior the child demonstrates. For example, if the child is using cues within words (key consonants perhaps) or is sounding out letter by letter, to the extent that he is a word reader, the teacher would assist him to use the language cues outside words. The child would be encouraged always to ask himself, "Does what I'm reading make sense?" The child's attention would be directed away from letters and words and directed toward meaning. Instead of asking a child to repeat and correct a wrong word, the teacher would encourage him to reread a whole sequence, encouraging him to evaluate all the cues and to realize that his error is inconsistent with these cues. On the other hand, if a child seems to understand that what he reads is supposed to make sense but appears to have only vague associations between letters and sounds, the teacher assists him in paying closer attention to specific letter cues and in acquiring phonic generalizations within the context of his search for meaning.

Individualized reading programs should also make it possible for teachers to evaluate the reading development of each child in terms of his own idiolect and language background, so that each child may build his literacy skills on the language skills he has already acquired.

A natural transition from experience stories into an individualized reading program would avoid artificial language and synthetic methods and materials. Children would not be homogenized into the reading levels represented by the graded readers. They would proceed as rapidly as they were able while self-selecting reading material with the guidance of the teacher.

The teacher is very important in all reading programs, but in a program that uses no basal reader, the effectiveness of the teacher is the critical factor. It is his responsibility to select and make available stimulating and appropriate materials and books for all children. He also has to be able to diagnose reading difficulties and to take effective measures to eliminate them.

Improving the Basal Reader

Although the merits of a sound individualized reading program have been indicated, many teachers and schools prefer the security of a series of texts. There is no doubt that basal readers will play a prominent role in reading instruction for some time to come. Several improvements must be made in basal readers if they are to reflect current language knowledge.

1. Pictures should be illustrative. They should not cue meaning. Only language cues should be used to get meaning.
2. Vocabulary control should not be the primary criterion for simplicity in basal readers. Attention must be given to structure, introduction of func-

tion words, and avoidance of contextual ambiguity. The word lists must disappear from the backs of the readers.

3. Language information in basal readers and the accompanying manuals must be accurate. Common-sense and traditional views of language must be replaced by the most scientific and up-to-date language information. For example, it is insufficient to consider English vowels to be of two varieties, long and short. Vowel sounds can be much more accurately described and their interrelationship better understood.

4. Basal readers should be used flexibly, not as a device for locking children in step. There is no evidence to justify the expectation that all fourth-grade children can read, do read, or should read at the fourth-grade level. The range of abilities is already wide, and the more successful a reading teacher is, the wider this range will become. Some children will make satisfactory progress while others leap forward. Conformity is not an ideal, and teachers should be free to use any materials with any child who can profit from them regardless of grade.

Grade-level norms in reading are based on test results. Fourth-grade readibility is what the average fourth-grader reads. Because it is an average figure, half read better and half read worse. The norm is in no way an indication of what fourth-grade readers should achieve or are capable of achieving. Even in theory, then, a fourth-grade reading text is only suitable for the small group whose reading ability is right at the national average.

If a basal reading series is used, it must be a springboard to other reading material. It is a means to an end, not an end in itself. Thus, the basal reader can never be the total program. It must always be supplemented by a variety of materials to be read for information and enjoyment.

The Future of Reading Instruction

Knowledge is still incomplete on what is needed for schools to achieve total success. The point has not yet been reached where a guarantee can be made that every child will learn to read easily and well.

But enough is now known to see four key elements in the ultimate solution to reading problems. Teachers will learn:

to work *with* learners, to build on their existing language strengths, to help them use their uniquely human language-learning ability;

to stop putting barriers in the way of learners in our attempts to help them; to stop fracturing language into abstract letters, sounds, words, and skills; and to help readers build strategies to find meaning in relevant, interesting, whole, real, and natural written language;

to be well informed about language/reading and interested enough in their pupils as unique people; furthermore to be able to hear them read and know, through the miscues, how well they are progressing in becoming efficient, effective readers;

to make learning to read so useful and relevant that it will become as universal and painless as learning to talk and understand speech.

Testing Ideas against Reality

Tape-record a student at any age from six to sixteen reading a story relatively difficult for him. Pay close attention to his miscues, and their effect on meaning and grammaticality. Note which miscues are self-corrected. Do the miscues reflect dialect differences between reader and writer?

Find a newspaper article that contains typographical errors. Ask friends to read it, and observe what they do when they encounter the errors. Ask them to discuss what they thought about in dealing with the errors.

Ask readers at various ages to read Gloopy and Blit (p. 267). Ask them questions about the story such as: How do Gloopy and Blit differ? What do they have in common? Which one is a lof? What had Ril poved Blit to? Why hadn't Gloopy been poved? Why was Blit unklorpy? Then ask your readers to translate the story into a meaningful one. Compare what different readers produce.

Look at the questions at the ends of chapters in an elementary- or secondary-school text in social studies or science. How many of them can be answered without comprehension from the text by treating them as grammatical nonsense: What is Gloopy? Gloopy is a borp. What are the names of the Great Lakes? The names of the Great Lakes are _____.

Pick a passage from a book or magazine that deals with a specialized interest or hobby of yours—photography, for example. Ask a student with no background in that area to read it and mark the parts that did not make sense. Then reverse the roles: you attempt to read something specially selected by that person, and mark your points of difficulty. Analyze the effect of strong or weak background interest on the comprehension of written language.

Turning Ideas into Practice

Have a group of students in any grade from four through eight read for thirty minutes from a book of their own choice. Ask them to insert a strip of paper at each point of difficulty and keep reading. At the end of thirty minutes ask them to go back and write the entire sentence they had trouble with on the strip. Have the class sort the problem sentences and make a list of problems noting how many students encountered examples of each problem: for example, unfamiliar names, foreign phrases, strange uses of familiar phrases, and so on. Develop a set of strategies with the students for dealing with each problem area. Example: In dealing with unfamiliar names use a place holder, abbreviate the name, and keep reading. Raskolnikov then becomes Mr. R. Students may be surprised at how common and easily dealt with many problems are.

Underline every tenth word or so in a text. Ask students to read, substituting another word that would make equally good sense. Work with them at being able to do this without hesitation. Such activities will build prediction strategies and confidence.

Select one particularly retarded reader in grades three to eight. Have the pupil dictate a paragraph to the teacher which will be put in a journal each day. Ask the pupil to read it to the teacher the next day. Concentrate on the sense of what is read and don't worry about word for word accuracy. Encourage the student to think of what would make sense whenever he is in doubt.

Analyze a chapter in a school text. Consider what concepts a reader would need to make sense out of it. Consider also special uses of language it involves for example, graphs, recipes, or map reading.

Before asking students to read a text, develop activities to build both background knowledge and special strategies for dealing with the special uses of language. A companion activity would be to have some pupils read the paragraph, note their miscues, and discuss their difficulties with them.

LITERATURE, MATHEMATICS, AND THE ARTS AS PRESENTATIONAL FORMS

. . . myth, art, language, and science appear as
symbols; not in the sense of mere figures which refer
to some given reality by means of suggestion
and allegorical renderings, but in the sense of forces
each of which produces and posits a world
of its own. . . . Thus the special symbolic forms
are not imitations, but ORGANS of reality, since it
is solely by their agency that anything real becomes
an object for intellectual apprehension. . . .

ERNST CASSIRER, Language and Myth
(New York: Dover, 1946), p 8.

What are the basic elements and stylistic aspects of literature that, when defined as quality criteria, need to be applied to selecting literature for young people in the several genre?

How can teachers use individualized reading instruction, class-room libraries, and book clubs to stimulate all youngsters to independent reading of literature?

What kinds of resources and methods are available for involving youngsters both in the "reading" of the presentational art forms themselves (art, music, dance, film), and in learning to express their ideas in these media or combinations of them?

What are the essentials in a mathematics education program that will carry youngsters into the "language" of that symbolic system?

17

Literary Language
and the Reading of It

> . . . poets love to "mess around" with words. I could argue that language is one of the profoundest and most singular of human activities, and that any man messing around with words is playing with one of our most essential tools of knowledge and one of our most essential human experiences. . . .[1]

Lack of consideration of the aesthetic, psychological, and sensuous aspects of language accounts for its often being considered mere exposition, the limited discourse that for its own ends de-emphasizes those elements not to its purpose. It must be pointed out again that language could not function even as discourse without the underlying support of the larger linguistic context, the symbolic representation of reality and the aesthetic-sensuous response of the human organism that makes language retention possible. Also, without the physical pleasure of manipulating language with lips, teeth, throat, tongue, and the total sounding board of flesh and bone, quite possibly it would slip into unretainable abstraction. This is not to say that man should be overwhelmed with the physical pleasure of his own speech, but it is ever present and is especially so when he is most eloquent. Literature is the ultimate refinement of the full range of language. It emphasizes the elements that appear in the most basic language, and it retains them (often intensifies them) in the highest artistic achievement.

[1] John Ciardi, "Poetry as Knowledge," *Saturday Review*, July 22, 1961, p. 7.

Literature and Knowing

Literature represents an attempt to use all the resources of language to give unified and integrated presentation of knowledge and pleasure; it should teach and delight, not by sugar-coating the bitter pill of knowledge but by harmonizing knowing and feeling. Knowledge and pleasure are inseparable in fact but may be talked about independently for purposes of clarification.

As Aristotle points out in *Poetics*, man practices *mimesis*, or imitation, naturally and delights in doing so. He re-creates reality to bring it more sharply into focus. Man is in his world and experiences it, but when he *knows* he is in it and experiencing it, he becomes truly human. Literature gives man perspective by the separation of the work from the world it represents. Delight in the *representation* of his own kind of world, his own kind of person, his own kind of people, is basic to all literary appreciation and permeates it at all levels.

In addition to giving him his world, literature acts as an ideal medium for the projection of problems and as a place for the postulation of solutions. The writer *creates*, but the reader *re-creates*. Actually, of course, the writer himself is a re-creator after the manner of nature. In this regard, one of the most significant aspects of literature as a cognitive means is that it can catch the patterns and movement of life with least distortion. Discourse (exposition and explanation) has to stop all action and life in order to dissect and analyze, whereas literary language does not have to go through this reductive process. Through sensuous patterns, its own movement and duration, it can catch the living quality, the felt pattern, the extension in time, with least distortion and with most of its immediately perceptual appurtenances still intact. The living truth is brought into the heart, the world is caught in context and not merely as a trophy snatched from resisting nature.

Literature in Culture

As has been said of language in general, the literature of a culture and the culture itself are inseparable. The literature embodies the culture, projects its ideals and values, and teaches individuals and subsequent generations how to belong to it. In other words, it teaches a society to be itself in a way that we have only recently seen attempted by public education in its role as agent of *cultural renewal*. Epics, such as the *Iliad, Beowulf*, and the Bible, show how one book largely served this role in earlier times.

Cultural intermingling today, coupled with the fragmented quality of modern life, makes this kind of monolithic representation impossible. But even in our age, a people sits at the feet of its literature. Kindergarten children do so quite literally when they sit listening together, learning aurally the cultural context they are growing into, bound to each other through the shared experience of oral literature. The children, like a preliterate people gathered around a tribal fire, are told, have chanted to them, are given their world, and give themselves to it; their community is articulated. Knowing that others are listening to what we hear or are reading what we read creates a community whose subtle borders are co-terminal with the culture embodied in the literature.

Literature and Experience

Every literary work represents an expanded metaphor (in Susanne Langer's terminology, a presentational symbol) in which literary language takes leave of discourse with its linear, one-directional, one-thing-at-a-time representation. Instead, literature reaches for a total projection that achieves simultaneity, although it has duration; it is a holistic presentation of which discourse is only one element. Literary language approaches the kind of communication and presentation of the other arts. A poem can have the plasticity of clay or oils, the orchestrated sensuousness of music and dance. Knowing and feeling intermingle in a harmonious whole of which a single line speaks no more for itself than a single gesture should in the dance.

The experience of literature can begin at an early age, through the great heritage of children's books and the fine modern literature for children. Paul Hazard has written about good children's books:

> I like books that remain faithful to the very essence of the art; namely those that offer to children an intuitive and direct way of knowledge . . . and books that awaken in them not maudlin sentimentality, but sensibility that enables them to share in great human emotions that give them respect for universal life.[2]

On Reading Literature

An important part of the experience of reading literature is being conscious of the organized quality of the literary work that can be gained sometimes only by rereading it and watching it unfold again in a way that is enhanced by foreknowledge of what will happen. *Literary language is never milked dry by one reading, nor is its cream removed by mere skimming; and the speed-reader races by without knowing what experience he has had and without having savored the landscape. The obverse is equally true; purely expository or informational language should not be read like literature. Attempts to make language one thing only run the usual risk of simplistic solutions to complex problems.* The reader who is aware of the full range and multiplicity of purpose of language is less likely to err in either direction —or in any direction for that matter.

---

[2] Paul Hazard, *Books, Children, and Men,* trans. Marguerite Mitchell (Boston: The Hornbook, 1944), p. 42.

Giving Oneself to Reading

The reader must give the literary work his total attention, suspending the operation of his challenging ego. The kind of negative capability Keats pointed out in the poet's approach to experience in general is appropriate for the reader of a poem or a story. He opens himself to total impression without rearranging the parts to suit his own pattern, without challenging before he knows what he is challenging, and without making the author an unwilling ally to his own preconceptions. The reader should interact with. what is going on at the moment (without distorting it, of course); he should react to the part, but while doing this he should always leave himself open to the whole for, at last, if the literary work is successful, everything should fit into a final harmony that is not contained in the parts. The harmonious whole will not be illogical or unintelligible, but it will no more submit to rational analysis, linguistic or logical, than will a musical composition or a painting.

It should be pointed out, however, that giving one's self to a literary work does not mean the resignation of personality and intellectual integrity or the suspension of critical judgment. The "resignation" is for the moment, and it should be an alert, perceptive suspension. Sensitivity and intelligence are, for greater efficiency, directed toward input rather than toward output. A kind of dialogue should be taking place between the reader and the work at one level, but the reader should not direct his main attention at head-on propositional refutation of what is being presented. He should not be affronted personally by the actions or ideas of fictional characters or of the author himself if the reader should be so cocksure as to think he has caught the author without his artistic mask.

Identification with characters should only go so far in order to do justice to the characters—and to oneself. This does not lessen the intensity of the artistic experience; it is the very essence of the artistic experience. Excessive identification causes the reader to drift away from the center of his own being, so there is no perspective for appreciation of the character. If the reader "lives" the role, the *fiction* is no longer a work of art but is merged with life. They parallel each other and reflect each other, but art is art and life is life. We talk about characters and situations in fiction as if they were real, but the "as if" is of vital importance. The man in the audience who was so carried away by the drama that he rushed on stage to rescue Liza in the dramatic version of *Uncle Tom's Cabin* is an extreme case of the breakdown of the all-important hiatus between life and art, but many people display a similar naïveté. Sometimes an individual cannot appreciate some fiction as art because it speaks too directly to his own life-situation. This however, is a personal variable apart from the general rule.

Literature does not offer an escape from life but offers a way of entering into it. Although it may convey metaphysical insights, it is on more certain ground when it gives us our world, sensuously realized and harmonized, and when it helps us be in the world and know we are in it.

The Language of Literature

Literature uses the same language as discourse, and this is a source of confusion for many readers. "Why doesn't the literary artist say what he means?" they ask. One answer is, "He does, exactly." One problem, of course, is the definition of meaning. Meanings may be patterns of intelligibility and perceived emotional patterns. These cannot be conveyed in "common-sense" terms or in expository language of the sort that explains mechanical processes. The "literature" of science and mathematics, treated in other sections, is mainly expository, refraining generally from personalized and subjective response. However, this literature need not be perfunctorily written. Scientific reports and mathematical explanations can be written in a clear and pertinent style. To convey complex mathematical and scientific ideas succinctly and persuasively is a great art.

Usually, at least in English, literary works are expected to aim at organization of perceptions and experience in terms of ideas and abstract thought. Some poems approach the manner of the other arts in deemphasizing the abstracting-ideational tendency of the language. The absence of this quality in Chinese has led to the observation that it is unsuited to scientific purposes without a great deal of adaptation. As a minimum requirement, literature calls for the *objective correlative*, the emotional and sensuous embodiment of the ideas presented.

Greater awareness of the artistic aspects of language may lead to more extensive exploration of that mode by writers, to literature even further removed from abstract thought. If so, a more sensitive, artistically oriented response will be required of readers. Children learn to read the potent language of literature by hearing it read to them from the earliest age and then by reading literature written for them. In these ways they become accustomed to the stylistics of the literary mode and come to delight in them as they learn to extract life-meaning from the page.

18

Children
and
Literature

section 1

Literature As Presentation

Literature is one of the chief modes by which men present their "knowings" about the world. There are the logical, analytical modes of scientific description, formulas, and diagrams and there are the aesthetic modes of written composition, art, dance, and music. Because language can describe both scientific events on the one hand and personal, emotional events on the other hand, the word *literature* is used for the description of both kinds of events, as in *scientific literature* or *English literature*. Children's literature involves both kinds: discursive, factual books and literary storybooks. Children need to learn how to read both. Discursive, factual writing can be carefully done and can have literary merit; however, most often "children's literature" refers to storybooks, poetry, and informational books.

> In literature, language is deliberately exploited for its expressive effect rather than to indicate, denote, or describe things for practical purposes. . . . A work of literature is not meant as a series of literal propositions, but as a construction to stimulate the imagination of the reader.[1]

[1] Philip Phenix, *Realms of Meaning* (New York: McGraw-Hill, 1964), p. 177.

Elements of Literary Structure

FICTIONS Literature is a fictional presentation of the stuff of life. The term *fiction* has been grossly misunderstood by many who use it as a synonym for *make believe*. A fiction is an "invention of the mind." Abstractions in the language such as "friendship" and "liberty" are fictions.[2] Invented narratives, essays, and poems are also *fictions* of the mind created to convey ideas and feelings about man's relationship to man and to the environment. They are the story of man based upon reality but interpreted by an author. The advantage of literature as a conveyor of knowledge over the more strictly expository forms is that fact and feeling are integrated. A literary statement about a world event tells more than the fact: It transforms the fact into meaning and significance and weighs the matter in the balance of values. While fiction, Hersey's *Hiroshima* tells something more about an atomic explosion than a scientific paper on nuclear physics.

SOUNDS IN RHYTHM Literature is possible because language possesses special qualities that permit presentation beyond the strictly referential. Language has a *rhythmic flow of sound* that can be heard in the mind when it is read. In this way it is like a line of music in which intonations and rhythms are conveyed. Churchillian oratory is best when heard, but even on the page it rises and falls like the sound of a great organ. Speeches in Shakespeare are only meaningful when the actor or reader has discovered the rhythmic pattern and has sounded intonations in the contour of each line. The intricate flow of a long Faulkner sentence captures the whole of an experience that a series of sentences could never reveal. In lyric poetry, rhythm and sound patterns such as rhyme and assonance intensify the literal meaning and give the poem an aesthetic lift.

FIGURES OF SPEECH The figurative use of language intensifies meaning in the literary mode. Images can specify and personalize meaning to the point in literary masterpieces of making the idea unforgettable:

> There's a certain slant of light,
> On winter afternoons,
> That oppresses, like the weight
> of cathedral tunes.[3]

The simile and the metaphor give an author the power to draw an analogy quickly and intensely. The great similes in *The Iliad* give vibrance and depth to heroic events. The intricate metaphorical conceit of a Shakespearean sonnet unfolds a world of understanding in its sparse fourteen lines. Fic-

[2] Hugh Walpole, *Semantics* (New York: Norton, 1941), pp. 159–177.
[3] Emily Dickinson, *The Poems of Emily Dickinson* (Boston: Little, Brown, 1944), p. 108.

tion, sound and rhythm, figures of speech make the literary mode the most versatile of all the forms of presentation. In effective literature these elements are combined and organized into language structures that have impact and aesthetic appeal. A poem is both meaningful and shapely. "Nothing is more powerfully of man," writes John Ciardi, "than the fact that he naturally gives off forms and is naturally enclosed by them. To acquire knowledge of esthetic form is to acquire knowledge of man."[4]

English, because of its richness of words from many sources and because of its flexible grammar, is one of the most pliable of the languages of man and is therefore one most suitable to the literary mode.

Youngsters Meeting Literature

A language is carried not only by conversation between the generations but also through oral transmission of folk literature and by the writing of individual authors. The richness of human experience is accumulated and reconstructed through literature. Children should meet some of the literary presentations from the past, from the folk tradition and the great authors, as well as the writings of their own time. This opportunity will help give them a feeling of continuity, of belonging to the family of man. The old language as well as the old universal ideas will penetrate the veneer of present times and will reveal a heritage. Folk literature is the common presentation of a culture, a distillation of a view of life, whereas literature by authors is an individual's intensified picture of his times.

Folk Literature and Children

Folk literature makes an especially suitable introduction to literature for children because in the main it was created and re-created in family and community settings that included children.

Folk songs are natural means for introducing the child to the ethnic dimension of his heritage. In them the delight and the sadness of simple living are conveyed through strong rhythm and colorful language. The melodies of the songs come also from the wellsprings of folk living.

> The folk art lives upon the lips of the multitude and is transmitted by the grapevine, surviving sometimes for centuries because it reflects . . . the deepest emotional convictions of the common man. This is truly democratic art, painting a portrait of the people, unmatched for honesty and validity in any other record.[5]

---

[4] John Ciardi, "Poetry as Knowledge," *Saturday Review*, July 22, 1961, p. 39.

[5] John A. Lomax and Alan Lomax, *Folk Song U.S.A.* (New York: Duell, Sloan & Pearce-Meredith Press, 1947), Preface, p. viii.

The exuberance and hardiness of pioneers is captured in "Old Dan Tucker," although it is an adaptation of a minstrel-show song and is, strictly speaking, not a folk song.

> Ol' Dan Tucker's a fine old man,
> Washed his face in a fryin' pan,
> Combed his head with a wagon wheel
> And died with a toothache in his heel.

The battle between people and machines is etched forever in memory by the ballad of "John Henry."

> John Henry told his old captain,
> Said, "A man ain't nothin' but a man;
> Before I let your steel gang down
> I will die with the hammer in my hand,
>   Oh Lordy,
> Die with the hammer in my hand."

During the depression of the 1930s the longing for comfort and three square meals was expressed in the hobo song "The Big Rock Candy Mountain."

> In the Big Rock Candy Mountain
> All the cops have wooden legs,
> And the bulldogs all have rubber teeth
> And the hens lay soft boiled eggs.
> The farmer's trees are full of fruit
> And the barns are full of hay.
> O' I'm bound to go, where there ain't no snow,
> Where the sleet don't fall and the wind don't blow
> In the Big Rock Candy Mountain.

The helplessness of a people is summed up in the simple and poignant Negro carol "Po' Little Jesus."

> Po little Jesus,
> Yes, yes,
> Child of Mary,
> Yes, yes,
> Didn't have no cradle,
> Yes, yes.
> Wasn't that a pity and a shame,
> Lawd, Lawd,
> Wasn't that a pity and a shame?

The *folk rhymes* that mothers say with their children are another introduction to the folk language and wisdom of the past. "Nimble" might well have left the language long ago had it not been for the nursery rhyme "Jack be nimble, Jack be quick, Jack jump over the candle stick." Even though Jack probably was originally a politician who was either too hasty or too sluggish in his decision making, the rhyme conveys the meaning of a fine old word and a suggestion to the young about keeping alert.

> Oral rhymes are the true waifs of our literature in that their original wordings, as well as their authors, are usually unknown . . . having to fend for themselves. . . . If Arden and Garret's definition of poetry, that is "memorable speech," contains no more than a tincture of truth, it is yet enough to dye the rhymes with the tints of poetry. They owe their existence to this one quality of memorability.[6]

The memorability of the language of folk rhymes is derived from their strong rhythmic patterns and tongue-tickling sound play of rhyme and assonance.

> Goosey, goosey gander,
>   Whither shall I wander?
> Upstairs and downstairs
>   And in my lady's chamber.

> Oranges and lemons
> Say the bells of St. Clements.
> You owe me five farthings
> Say the bells of St. Martins.

The fact that the themes and characters in certain *folk tales* are found in several cultures attests to their universality and wide appeal. Variants of the Cinderella wish are found all over the world. The folk-tale characters are archetypes that convey fundamental themes of human desires and feelings across the centuries and over the borders of nations. The uncluttered narrative style of the folk tale is as basic to the art of literature as is the primitive rhythm of the chant. These tales speak to children directly.

> Once upon a time there was an old man, and an old woman, and a little boy. One morning the old woman made a johnny-cake, and put it in the oven to bake. "You watch the johnny-cake," she said to the little boy, "while your father and I go out to work in the garden."
> The old man and the old woman went out and began to hoe potatoes, leaving the little boy to tend the oven. But he did not watch it all the time. Suddenly, when he was not watching, he heard a noise. He looked up and saw the oven door pop open. Out of the oven jumped Johnny-cake. He went rolling along end over end, toward the open door of the house.[7]

What child would not feel himself comfortable in this setting and eager to listen for the fate of the johnny-cake?

Myths are a special form of folk literature that convey cosmic themes of man's struggle with the elements, his battle with the forces of his passions,

---

[6] Iona Opie and Peter Opie, *The Puffin Book of Nursery Rhymes* (Baltimore: Penguin Books, 1963).

[7] From a modern presentation of the tale by Ruth Sawyer, *Johnny-Cake Ho* (New York: Viking, 1956).

and of man's relationship to powers beyond him. The Homeric "Hymn to Demeter" not only attempts to explain the mystery of the seasons through the saga of Persephone's capture by Hades, but also deals both with Demeter's passion of anger at the loss of her daughter and with the question of the judgment of Zeus. The very elements of human existence are at stake in the epic mythical narratives of Greece and Scandinavia. The same qualities abound in the newly discovered storehouse of myths from Africa, Asia, and The Indians of North and South America. Older children respond to their challenges as they themselves begin to ask the big "why" questions about the order of the universe.

From the roots of folk song and folk tale has sprung the world of literature. The writing down of the great epics constituted the first stable literature, and epics were steeped in myth and folklore. From the folk ballad and the lyric song came poetry. This folk tradition of oral transmission has continued, even as written literature has burgeoned, because of man's delight in telling a story or a joke.

Literature Composed by Individual Authors

Literature by individual authors, since the invention of the printing press has dominated the presentation of man's interpretation of his times. A little more than a century ago authors began writing expressly for children. There are, however, pieces of adult literature from the past and present that can be offered to children as introductions to earlier times and other cultures. At Halloween, children respond to a reading of the witches' scene from *Macbeth.* Some of the fast-moving stories about David in the King James version of the Bible can introduce children to good narrative style in the English of Elizabethan times. Edited sections of *Gulliver's Travels* and *Robinson Crusoe* from the eighteenth century and Dickens's *Christmas Carol* and *Oliver Twist* from the nineteenth century can give children some feeling for life in earlier times and other places. Much poetry speaks to all ages. Judiciously selected Psalms of the Old Testament, songs of Shakespeare and Blake, and the nature poems of Wordsworth all hold meaning for children. Poetry from other lands, such as Japanese haiku, although diminished by translation, can give the child a feeling for another culture more directly than any literal description of it.

> When spring is gone, none
> will so grumpily grumble
> as these chirping frogs.
>
> Snow fell until dawn.
> Now every twig in the grove
> glitters in the sunlight.[8]

[8] From *Cricket Songs: Japanese Haiku,* translated and © 1964 by Harry Behn. Reprinted by permission of Harcourt Brace Jovanovich, Inc. and Curtis Brown, Ltd.

The American child should become acquainted with the literature of his heritage. Because the child is of the culture, much of American literature can easily be adapted for his understanding. In *Pilgrim Courage* Smith and Meredith[9] have prepared for older children a text based on the first outstanding piece of American literature, Bradford's *Of Plimoth Plantation*. For younger children there is a picture book based on the same text, called *The Coming of the Pilgrims*. There are many other early narratives of adventure, exploration, and pioneering that teachers can edit and adapt for reading in their classrooms. *Exploring the Great River* is an adapted retranslation of original accounts of the Spanish and French expeditions into the Misissippi river basin. Youngsters can participate in these exciting journeys by canoe and overland, while finding out at first hand what Indians were like through the vivid and unusually accurate descriptions of their cultural life. Parts of autobiographies, letters, tracts, essays, and poetry from historical periods can be presented to children; for example, Franklin's own unprepossessing account of his arrival in Philadelphia;[10] Freneau's *To a Caty-Did*; parts of Joel Barlow's *Hasty Pudding*; and slaves' actual accounts of slavery in *To Be a Slave*, prepared by Julius Lester with moving illustrations by Tom Feelings.

The march westward and the industrial expansion of the new nation are well portrayed in documents from the Lewis and Clark expedition and some of the writings of Mark Twain, Whittier, Whitman, and Harte. James Daugherty, a vigorous illustrator and writer of children's books, has collected poems and prose writings on Whitman in a handsome book in which the words of Whitman and his own drawings capture the excitement and tragedy of the midcentury American struggle.[11] Many of the poems of Dickinson, Frost, and Sandburg can speak to children, especially those that demonstrate the American's relation to the land and to nature.

> The way a crow
> Shook down on me
> The dust of snow
> From a hemlock tree

[9] E. Brooks Smith and Robert Meredith, *Pilgrim Courage* (Boston: Little, Brown, 1962). Other firsthand accounts prepared for children: Robert Meredith and E. Brooks Smith, *Riding with Coronado* (Boston: Little, Brown, 1964); *The Quest of Columbus* (Boston: Little, Brown, 1966); and *Exploring the Great River* (Boston: Little, Brown, 1969). Esther Averill, *Cartier Sails the St. Lawrence* (New York: Harper & Row, 1956); George Sanderlin, *First around the World: A Journal of Magellan's Voyage* (New York: Harper & Row, 1965); Julius Lester, *To Be a Slave* (New York: Dial Press, 1968).

[10] Available in the "Founding Fathers" series, *Benjamin Franklin: A Biography in His Own Words* (New York: Newsweek Book Division, 1974), pp. 32, 33.

[11] James Daugherty, *Walt Whitman's America* (Cleveland: World Publishing, 1964).

Has given my heart
A change of mood
And saved some part
Of a day I had rued.[12]

Literature Expressly for Young People[13]

In the late nineteenth and early twentieth centuries some adult authors began to write books for children, stories that could be read to them and at the same time enjoyed by the adult reader at a different level of comprehension. Lewis Carroll's *Alice in Wonderland* was the forerunner. Kingsley's *Water Babies* was less successful, but the later *Winnie-the-Pooh*, by A. A. Milne, won the hearts of all. This genre has continued in popularity, with *Charlotte's Web* and *Stuart Little* as outstanding examples.

Beatrix Potter was the real innovator. She wrote her books expressly for children. They were stories that children could read to themselves. *The Tale of Peter Rabbit* soon became the possession of children alone. With this spectacular beginning, a new genre called "children's literature" was established. A virtual golden age of writing for children has emerged. Masterpieces like *Make Way for Ducklings, Mary Poppins, Madeline,* and *Henry Huggins* have been accepted. Publishing houses have vied with each other to produce the most handsome books. Nothing like the attention to beautiful illustration has been seen since the time of illuminated manuscripts. The result is a wonderful world of books of all kinds about all things for children to discover and explore.

Children need to be introduced to this wonderful world of children's literature not only for the sake of enjoyment and appreciation of the beauties of language, but also for learning about life. The literary presentation has many advantages over the factual and the diagrammatic, chief among which is the silent personal relationship that grows between a reader and a book. The child can learn by himself in a corner where he chooses to be and at a time that he designates. The totality of experience, its facts and its feelings, are presented to him. With a fine book in his lap, the child can experience a

---

[12] From *The Poetry of Robert Frost* edited by Edward Connery Lathem. Copyright 1923 by Holt, Rinehart and Winston, Inc. Copyright 1951 by Robert Frost. Reprinted by permission of Holt, Rinehart and Winston, Inc., and Jonathan Cape, Ltd., London.

[13] This brief presentation of modern children's literature can only tie this magnificent output to the themes of this book. Fuller discussion can be found in several excellent and comprehensive survey volumes: Virginia Haviland, *Children's Literature: Views and Reviews* (Glenview, Ill.: Scott, Foresman, 1973). May Hill Arbuthnot and Zena Sutherland, *Children and Books,* 4th ed. (Glenview, Ill.: Scott, Foresman, 1972). Charlotte Huck, *Children's Literature in the Elementary School,* 3d ed. (New York: Holt, Rinehart and Winston, 1975). For an anthology of modern poets see Stephen Dunning et al. (eds.), *Reflections on a Gift of Watermelon Pickle and Other Modern Verse* (New York: Lothrop, 1967).

sense of wonder within his own little world, and no one else needs to know about it.

Fine literature for children should have the same qualities as fine literature for adults, with some important additions. The literary and art presentations in children's books must take into account the general experiential background and the conceptualizing level of the children to which the book is addressed. This is not a matter of depriving children of opportunity for stretching their imaginations. That process must never be limited, but a child must be able to meet the book at least halfway. There are areas of life toward which children cannot be attuned because they lack the extensiveness of experience and the emotional wherewithal to meet them.

Most love poems are beyond the ken of the elementary school child, yet they are too often presented because the poems are old favorites of adults. On the other hand, Karl Shapiro's powerful adult poem *Auto Wreck* can reach today's youth at varying levels of meaning, depending on the conceptualizing potential of the individual youngster. Many poems and stories written for adults appeal to children because they deal with a subject universal enough to be included in the world of children. In such literature, adults appreciate more of the subtleties, but the presentation can be shared across age levels. Mark Twain's *Huckleberry Finn*, Robert Frost's *North of Boston*, or Jack London's *To Build a Fire* are examples of adult literature that can be read aloud in family groups or by teachers in classrooms after lunch or at the close of a day. Some books for children reach out to adults in their universality, and these may be shared. Elizabeth Enright's trilogy *The Melendy Family* and Eleanor Farjeon's poetry are examples of modern works for children that can capture the imagination of adults. Teachers and children can share many experiences in literature that have both aesthetic and informational qualities. Curricula in the humanities, social studies, and sciences can in good part be built around thematic collections of trade books.[14] Reading programs can be entirely built around children's literature.

Childhood Memories in Literature

Many areas of life explored in literature can have meaning for both children and adults, but there are some that belong exclusively to children, and adults can only respond to them through fond memory. Unfortunately, adult memories of childhood often are rose-colored and misrepresent the realities of child life. Authors who write from such memories do not make

---

[14] Some of the new "reading series" are based on a wide variety of children's literature selections giving each classroom an extensive reading library. Teachers can develop their own individualized reading programs around their own selection of children's books made with their students. The following book is helpful in giving teachers ideas of how to use children's literature in their instruction: Dewey Chambers, *Children's Literature in the Curriculum*.

successful books for children. Sentimental and "cute" stories may attract the book-buying adult and boost sales, but such books lie idle upon library shelves. To get inside children and view the world as they do is a feat accomplished by only the great authors of children's books. Usually Robert McCloskey captures the child's world and writes penetratingly about it, as in *Homer Price* and *One Morning in Maine*; but in *Burt Dow, Deep Water Man* the mark is missed because the boundary between fond memories and the child's view is not crossed. Joan Anglund's *Love Is a Special Way of Feeling* is another example of an adult point of view transferred in part to the child. Ruth Krauss usually finds the child's psychic pulse and is in tune with it as she presents her delightful imaginings, *A Very Special House, Backward Day,* and *The Bundle Book*. In these the illusion of "childlikeness" is kept.

To discover the child's world is the first task of an author of a child's book. *Teachers need to apply the same discipline as do the authors in putting aside the sentimental memories when they select books from which children will choose. If they have listened to children and watched them, they will surely have a sense of what is appropriate content.*

Writing Style for Children's Books

PLOTTING The structural treatment of the subject of a child's book should not be complex. Simple and straightforward plotting, short but potent description, and lifelike, swift-moving conversation will not tax the child's conceptual limits or deter him from comprehending the scope of a story. If there are too many intricacies to keep in mind as the story line unfolds, children will lose their train of thought, just as they cannot cope with scientific concepts that are too complex. One or two themes are all they can manage. McCloskey's story of Lentil, who could not blow his harmonica at the big homecoming because he saw a man sucking a lemon, is a good example of the extent of plotting and character development suitable for very young readers. Closely related illustrations can fill out the situation. Lynd Ward's *The Biggest Bear* is a masterpiece of direct plotting and telling for children of the late primary grades; *Homer Price* by McCloskey develops just enough complication for enjoyment by older children.

STYLE Language style needs to be straightforward but intensified by imaginative selection of words available to children in their oral communication. Too many unknown words on a page will so delay comprehension that the reading of the story will be tedious and the book will be abandoned. On the other hand, flat and commonplace language will also bore the youngster. A successful writer of children's books needs to have the same lingual imagination as the poet. Each word must count by carrying as much significance as possible. The flow of the simplified structures must have music as it develops contours of meaning. This does not mean that the prose will be flowery, but in its sparseness it should carry weight and color and have the rhythm of pleasant conversation. Marie Hall Ets and Margaret Wise Brown in their best works write with an ideal style for young children—lean and succinct yet lyrical; *Play with Me* by Ets and *The Dead Bird* by Brown have the power that comes from artful language selection on themes that have poignancy and significance for children. James Daugherty's rugged prose in *Daniel Boone* compliments the full-blooded quality of the illustrations, and together they convey the robustness of the frontier. Individual style is never compromised by these authors, yet the pallet of words is not too rich or varied for children's comprehension.

Style for children does not need to be drab because of the limitations on language. Margaret Wise Brown's setting of the scene in *A Pussy Cat's Christmas* is descriptive writing with an appeal to the senses.

> The little pussy cat knew that Christmas was coming. The ice tinkled when it broke on the frozen mud puddles. The cold air made her hair stand straight up in the air. And the air smelled just as it did last year.
> What did it smell like? Could she smell Christmas trees? Of course she could. And Tangerines? And Christmas greens? And holly? And could she hear the crackle and slip of white tissue paper. . . ?[15]

The opening page of Laura Ingalls Wilder's classic *Little House in the Big Woods* demonstrates the power of simple, direct, but highly selected language in writing for children. Echoes of the folk-tale style and of the "run-on" style of child language are blended into the author's own.

> Once upon a time, sixty years ago, a little girl lived in the Big Woods of Wisconsin, in a little gray house made of logs.
> The great, dark trees of the Big Woods stood all around the house, and beyond them were other trees and beyond them more trees. As far as a man could go to the north in a day, or a week, or a whole month, there was nothing but woods. There were no houses. There were no roads. There were no people. There were only trees and the wild animals who had their home among them.
> Wolves lived in the Big Woods, and bears and huge wild cats. Muskrats and mink and otter lived by the streams. Foxes had dens in the hills and deer roamed everywhere.
> To the east of the little log house, and to the west, there were miles upon miles of trees, and only a few little log houses scattered far apart in the edge of the Big Woods.
> So far as the little girl could see, there was only the one little house where she lived with her father and mother, her sister, Mary, and her baby sister, Carrie. A wagon trail ran before the house, turning and twisting out of sight in the woods where the wild animals lived, but the little girl did not know where it went, nor what might be at the end of it.[16]

[15] Margaret Wise Brown, *A Pussy Cat's Christmas* (New York: Thomas Y. Crowell, 1949).

[16] Excerpt from *Little House in the Big Woods* by Laura Ingalls Wilder. Copyright 1932 by Laura Ingalls Wilder. Reprinted with permisson of Harper & Row, Publishers, and Methuen & Co. Ltd.

The style of Laura Ingalls Wilder, as of all successful authors for children, talks directly to children and is never solicitous or presumptuous.

Ideas in Books for Children

Condescension in style or story is easily caught by children, and they will discard such matter. The "moral tag" is a sign of condescension and carries little weight with children. On the other hand, a story will appeal if it reflects children's life-situations in which moral decisions have to be made. In Ann Eaton's *The Cave*, the little Navajo sheep herder has to make some hard decisions about coming to terms with his fears. Lorenz Graham, a black author, in *North Town, South Town,* and *Who's Town,* confronts black and white youngsters realistically and powerfully with the social problems of race. An Aesop fable is accepted because the clever lesson is not hidden but is directly stated. Just as the incongruity of a riddle is expected, so is the moral of the fable anticipated as if it were a game.

Good children's books, like all good literature, must be authentic and valid in terms of the life-situation. Historical stories or biographies must be based on research. If an incident is not for children's ears, it should be left out or the story should be saved for later years, but a theme or a character must not be distorted. Sweetness and blandness must not be added to historical characters, for the misconception that results may last a lifetime. George Washington's character has suffered most among American heroes. Alice Dalgliesh has saved Charles Lindbergh from a similar fate by basing her biography *Ride the Wind* on Lindbergh's own humble account of the famous flight.

Validity in literary presentation requires that the life-situation, though compressed and highlighted for telling a story or illustrating a theme, must not be distorted by the story line, the theme, or the author's prejudices. The situation as told must have an authentic ring of life, of events that could have happened to the characters. Elizabeth Enright's realistic and touching description of the Fifth Saturday in *The Saturdays,* "Oliver's Saturday at the Circus," stands as an exemplar in writing realistic fiction for children. While at the circus by himself, Oliver forgets himself in the excitement of the occasion and when he starts for home he becomes the lost boy.

. . . For the first time the probable consequences of his adventure began to trouble him. It made him especially uncomfortable to think of Cuffy for some reason.

And now the streets kept turning out the wrong way and he found himself on Tenth Avenue instead of Fifth. The place looked strange, full of high dark buildings and big noisy boys who went bowling by him on roller skates, and shouted at him hoarsely to get out of the way. As if that weren't enough, he began to have a terrible ache. Though he was a calm and resourceful person, Oliver was only six years old after all. So the next move seemed to be to cry. He stumbled and banged along the street, sobbing quietly, wiping his nose on his sleeve, wishing with all his heart that he was home with Cuffy, and that he had never heard of hot dogs and candy.[17]

A ride home in the lap of a mounted policeman saves the day, but even so, Oliver is sad that he cannot truly appreciate this once-in-a-lifetime opportunity because he feels so sick and is concerned about what will happen to him when he gets home. When authors write as seriously and vitally as they do for adults, but in children's terms, the child readers are forever in in their debt; for them, literature has served its purpose of enriching life by commenting upon it.

Informational Books for Children

Outstanding informational books can also be literature. Some straightforward, factual books are designed simply to supplement textbooks, but some so describe the world and man's relation to it that they cause the child to contemplate with awe the phenomena of nature and to relate himself to them. Such books are fictions in the sense that although the details are factual, the author's skill intensifies the experience. Adult readers have this experience when they read such books as Rachel Carson's *The Sea Around Us*. C. Holling in *Paddle-to-the-Sea* and Alvin Tresselt and Leonard Weisgard in *Rain Drop Splash* have accomplished artistic presentations of the factual for children.

"Life cycle" stories about different animals have successfully integrated authentic scientific material with the drama of life and death in the animal world. One such example is the following story:

But Gray Squirrel stopped to nip a flower cluster off a twig. Turning the stem slowly in her paws, she nibbled off the flowers, one by one. Now and then she glanced below at the chattering squirrels. After every few hops or runs each one would stop, twitch its bushy tail, and look around, watching for enemies.

Gray Squirrel ran down the trunk a little way and stopped again, clinging headfirst to the bark. She saw a partly grown squirrel digging in a place where she had some acorns buried.

"Cherk, cherk, cherk!" she scolded. The young squirrel began to gnaw a nut.

Gray Squirrel suddenly flattened herself against the trunk. Her quick eyes had seen a strange movement down below.

It was not a twitch of a tail. But it *was* a tail—and a gray one. Not a squirrel's tail. It was a cat's. The cat lay behind a log, near the young squirrel gnawing the acorn. A loud danger cry rattle through the trees—fast like a machine gun: "Yak! yak! yak!— yak! yak! yak! yak!"

Instantly every squirrel stopped moving. The young squirrel sat like a statue, holding the acorn in its paws. It was Gray Squirrel that had given the cry. She rattled it again.

[17] Elizabeth Enright, *The Saturdays*, in the trilogy *The Melendy Family* (New York: Holt, Rinehart and Winston, 1944), pp. 112, 113.

The cat sprang at the young squirrel. Dropping the nut, it bounded to the oak tree. An older squirrel would have dodged around the trunk, but this one was too frightened. He started straight up. The cat climbed up behind and caught him. Then it walked off into the woods, holding the squirrel in its mouth.[18]

FANTASIES Even in animal fantasies such as Louise Fatio's *The Happy Lion* or in talking-beast stories like the adventures of Babar, the author makes clear that he is ascribing human nature to animals. In *The Littlest Bear* by Else Minarik the main character is like the littlest boy. The child needs to be clear about what the author is doing. If there is confusion as to whether this is true animal behavior or not, the characteristics of animals and human beings become blurred. The story deteriorates into cuteness or absurdity, and the fun is gone.

Realism in Literature

In recent years there has been a trend for writers of literature for children and youth to deal with subjects that were avoided by publishers of an earlier period because of the controversy surrounding the subject matter in the story. Called the "New Realism" by some authorities in the field, this movement is characterized by such authors as Maia Wajciechowska, Judy Bloome, S. E. Hinton, John Steptoe, and Louise Fitzhugh, who write books that deal with pregnancy, sexuality, drugs, urban life, the life of the migratory worker, and various counterculture life-styles. *My Darling, My Hamburger* by Paul Zindel reveals the novel's plot through the opening dialogue: "It was Marie Dazinski who asked how to stop a boy if he wants to go all the way! Maggie whispered."[19] Many of these authors are writing for the adolescent market, and seem to be concerned with "tell it like it is." Even books for the very young, however, have become concerned with controversial themes—Maurice Sendak, for example, explores the realistic dreams of children through his fantasies *Where the Wild Things Are* and *In the Night Kitchen* (the latter has received reactions from librarians and parents because Max, a preschooler, floats through his dreams sans clothes). Louise Fitzhugh deals with the problem of the onset of menses through the eyes of pre-adolescents in *The Long Secret*. Fitzhugh's main character in *Harriet the Spy* has great influence on her readers. A teacher reported that a thirteen-year-old girl reacted to Harriet by writing, "I always wrote in a diary but after reading about Harriet, I used her writing as a model and the way I wrote my diary changed."

---

[18] Copyright 1955 by Mary Adrian Venn. Reprinted from *Gray Squirrel* by permission of Holiday House, Inc.

[19] Paul Zindel, *My Darling, My Hamburger* (New York: Bantam Books, 1971), p. 3.

Not only do the plots, characters, concerns, and values take on a contemporary, realistic outlook with which young people identify, but also the language of the story itself reflects the speech used by people in an actual setting. In *Stevie* by John Steptoe, the narrator is Robert, whose dialect is, therefore, represented in the narration as well as the dialogue sequences in the story:

> And that time we was playin in the park under the bushes and we found these two dead rats and one was brown and one was black. And him and me and my friends used to cook mickies or marshmallows in the park. [20]

These books may pose a problem for some teachers in some communities, but they are very popular with young people. The students seem to relate to books that deal with the "now" generation. Teachers need to become aware of their existence, the impact they are having on readers, and the reasons students react with genuine interest to these books.

Humor in Literature for Youngsters

Humorous writing for children takes into account the special kinds of funny situations that tickle children at various stages in their reaction to people and things. Humor is a psychic release of tension in a burst of laughter at an incongruity or an absurdity. The little child delights in seeing the adult make mistakes, in seeing things fall apart that are supposed to be together, things upside down, backward, or otherwise out of tune with this world he is so conscientiously putting together. Falling down, falling off something, or being surprised suddenly are all fearful in life, but they can be coped with and enjoyed in fiction. The great writers of fun and silliness for children have an innate understanding of the incongruities in a child's life and of the suppressed wishes that, revealed in a story, give delight.

Ruth Krauss and Dr. Seuss have discovered children's funny bones. *A Very Special House* and *Horton Hatches the Egg* have deservedly found a place in children's hearts because these books recognize the fun of being silly. Much of the fun is in the language play and the jokes in words. Lewis Carroll, Edward Lear, and A. A. Milne discovered that delight for children in years past. John Ciardi's *As If* and David McCord's *Far and Few* present some finely wrought playful verses for children. William Jay Smith, also a modern children's poet, has been particularly successful in creating nonsense that makes sense to children.

> Dogs are quite a bit like people
> Or so it seems to me somehow.
> Like people, Dogs go anywhere,
> They swim in the sea, they leap through the air,

[20] John Steptoe, *Stevie* (New York: Harper & Row, 1969), p. 19.

They bark and growl, they sit and stare,
They even wear what people wear.
Look at the Poodle with a hat on its noodle,
Look at the Boxer in a long silver-fox fur,
Look at the Whippet in its calico tippet,
Look at that Sealyham in diamonds from Rotterdam,
Look at the Afghan wrapped in an afghan,
Look at the Chow down there in a dhow,
All decked out for some big pow-wow
With Pekinese waiting to come kow-tow.
Don't they all look like people?
People you've seen somewhere? Bow-wow?[21]

Lyric Poetry for Children

Lyric poetry for children is harder to come by. Some from the past is universal enough to speak to children still. Emily Dickinson's "Sunrise and Sunset," beginning, "I'll tell you how the sun rose,—/A ribbon at a time," is a good example. Fine anthologies like Adshead and Duff's *An Inheritance of Poetry*[22] and Walter de la Mare's *Come Hither* include appropriate selections carefully chosen by the editors for their appeal to children. Once in a great while, writers of renown have written poems addressed to children. Stevenson's *A Child's Garden of Verses* is perhaps the most famous of those from the past. Walter de la Mare in his poem "The Snowflake" enlivens an experience that delights children and is not forgotten by adults.

Before I melt,
Come, look at me!
This lovely filigree!
Of a great forest
In one night
I make a wilderness
Of white:

By Skyey cold
Of crystals made,
All softly, on
Your finger laid,
I pause, that you
My beauty see:

Breathe, and I vanish
Instantly.[23]

[21] "Dog," from *Boy Blue's Book of Beasts.* Copyright, © 1956, 1957 by William Jay Smith. Reprinted by permission of William Jay Smith.

[22] Gladys Adshead and Annis Duff (eds.), *An Inheritence of Poetry* (Cambridge, Mass.: Riverside Press, 1948).

[23] Walter de la Mare, *Rhymes and Verses* (New York: Holt, Rinehart and Winston, 1967), p. 185. Reprinted by courtesy of the Literary Trustees of Walter de la Mare, and The Society of Authors as their representative.

Eleanor Farjeon and Elizabeth Madox Roberts are modern poets who write lyrical poems of distinction for children. They are but part of the present golden age of children's literature. Teachers of today are fortunate to have these riches so readily available. There is no need for a text for learning to read beyond that period in a child's development when he becomes an independent reader. Some experts even doubt that a text is needed at all, claiming that the child can better learn to read from books of significance and import that from reading exercises. In any event, the modern elementary school teacher needs to know children's literature just as high school or college English teachers need to know adult literature. He should read in this literature and become acquainted with the best works. Unfortunately, not all the children's books published are desirable or effective presentations for children. *In selecting literature for children the teacher must have a set of criteria for choosing, of which the main criterion should be literary quality.*

Strategies for Using Children's Literature in School Classroom Libraries

Of course children's books should be read by children in school for enjoyment, and many of them—like riddle and joke books—just for sheer fun. One valid reason for reading at any age is to get a good laugh, giving release from the dreariness of the daily round. Another reason is to be thrilled, taken away from the pedestrian activities of regular living to mysterious, forbidden, romantic worlds. Enjoyment is also a synonym for a kind of "learning" that helps an individual enrich his life-understanding, bringing him flashes of insight into what he and this world are all about. If a person can not read he has to depend entirely on scheduled motion pictures or television shows for these "enjoyments" of living. Educational value is limited in these instances because once viewed, there is rarely the opportunity to go back to them for study as one can do with books.

Just as there exists a public library for adults there is one for children, and they need to learn the value of it and how to use it. One way to get used to sharing books with others is for the teacher to set up a *lending library in the classroom,* using books borrowed or donated by children from their home libraries. Some teachers set up a *library corner* permanently either in their rooms or in some hall space, or, where classrooms are clustered, in conjunction with other teachers. These collections can be supplemented monthly from local and school libraries. The reasonable cost of paperback books permits teachers to buy them for their classroom libraries, a few each year. In many British schools the child's feeling for possessing a book for awhile is very highly regarded—so much so, in fact, that the new and exciting "Ladybird" series of paperbacks,[24] written at several reading levels and abundantly

[24] This series of storybooks, designed for teaching independent reading, began in the 1960s and is still going strong. See *Ladybird* Books (Loughborough, Leicestershire, England: Wills and Hefrenarth Ltd.).

available in most classrooms, may be taken home if the child so wishes. They are considered in some schools to be expendable materials like paper or work sheets. The multi-book, paperback reading series now available in the United States could be used in the same expendable way to build classroom and home libraries. Parents could be asked to buy children books from time to time instead of other items, and to donate them to the school when the family has finished with them.

With the classroom library there needs to be a regular *library period* each day or every other day for individual and paired reading and for sharing times. Adults enjoy telling their friends about a new book they have read; children do also. Reporting and sharing of feelings about books can be varied through the use of panels of youngsters reading the same or similar books. Parts of books can be acted out or put into a visual form. If a book does not have illustrations students might present their understanding of key aspects of a story by making their own interpretive drawings. The formal book report, a stultifying assignment if done in the same manner book after book, does, however, have refreshing and enlivening alternatives. One enjoyment of reading is letting the ideas in books get one started on some new ideas of one's own. These can be presented and shared, in the ways mentioned above, and the classroom at such times can be transformed into an educational but fun-filled *library-reading club*.

Individualized Reading Programs

The proliferation of trade books in all kinds of subjects, especially accessible now in paperback form, presents teachers with a new opportunity for individualizing their reading programs. The possible plethora and wide variety of children's books at all reading levels allow for child self-selection of reading materials, always a desirable goal but not reachable in practical ways until recent years. Teachers and scholars of reading have known for a long time that learners of reading are more highly motivated to practice it when they have materials that interest them. When books are written by expert authors to be read not just be practiced in, the learning reader will become even more involved. The "interesting" materials can be the instructional materials in an individualized reading program. Some organization of the program is necessary if the teacher is to be sure that students are advancing in the various reading skills as they read in the books and magazines of their choice. The teacher needs to familiarize himself with the children's books by reading them and by maintaining a card file of the available books.

Sometimes individuals or groups of children having common difficulties with a particular aspect of reading (such as "unlocking" words they already know orally but cannot recognize in the printed form) can be instructed directly for as long as is needed while they continue the individualized program. Records of books read, difficulties surmounted, and comprehension checks need to be kept as the child's reading advancement is charted. The teacher needs to schedule reading conferences with each child at least once a week. In the meantime children can either work in pairs to help each other or get quick help with difficult words from a teacher, parent, or child aid. Most teachers have youngsters keep a private dictionary of the words causing difficulty along with a card file of the books they have read with a brief commentary on them. Some teachers organize their entire reading program on an individualized basis, while others combine it with a more formal program on alternate days. Such reading programs, geared to individual needs, should be part of a classroom library program to promote the sharing of reading experiences, trading of books, and reacting to them.

section 2

The Arts As Presentation

Language by itself as an idiom for knowing has limitations. Even when used to the fullest by the great poets it cannot present immediate *gestalten*. It cannot catch in an instant the whole horrible absurdity of modern war in the way Picasso's *Guernica* does. Nor can it convey the sublime repose of Michelangelo's *Pietà* nor the simple grandeur of Mozart's *Jupiter* Symphony. These works of art speak directly to the senses and are apprehended at once without the mediation of language. Indeed, an attempt to interpose language at the moment of apprehension is likely to distort the message of the painter, sculptor, or composer. This is not to say that the experiential impact of plastic or musical art is not to be talked about in the conceptualizing process but is to stress that visual and aural presentations can rarely be translated successfully into language.

> The meanings given through language are successively understood, and gathered into a whole by the process called *discourse*; the meanings of all other symbolic elements that compose a larger, articulate symbol are understood only through the meaning of the whole, through their relations within the total structure. Their very functioning as symbols depends on the fact that they are involved in a simultaneous integral presentation. This kind of semantic may be called "*presentational symbolism*" to characterize its essential distinction from discursive symbolism, or "language" proper.[25]

"Presentational symbolism" is structured, not with a syntax, but by the balance of sensuous forms in rhythm, in line, in color, and in space. Language, although usually used in a discursive manner, can be molded in this way in poetry. On the other hand, pictures can be discursive (literal exposition), for example, in a series of pictograms, graphs, hieroglyphics, or literal picture stories. The difference between the *discursive* idiom and the

[25] Susanne Langer, *Philosophy in a New Key*, 3d ed. (Cambridge, Mass.: Harvard University Press, 1956), p. 78. Italics are ours.

nondiscursive is that the latter speaks with directness and immediacy in its totality. The nondiscursive idiom, or *symbolic presentation*, can present concepts involving emotional overtones and significant particulars more effectively than can lines of discourse.

The fact that the arts are presentational symbols of ideas is the reason for their inclusion in the school program and especially for their integration into study of the content areas such as social studies. They are not just activities to be added to make classroom studies more fun or to teach appreciation of "classy" culture as was common, in their earlier introduction into the curriculum. The arts are substantive in themselves and they add substance to study in other areas. Along with humanistic and scientific literature they represent the highest ideations of man in all the world cultures and are as much a part of the heritage of knowledge as are the others.

Visual Presentation of Form:
The Literature of Pictures

Illustrations in children's books are visual presentations by which the discursive text is illuminated and extended in richness of meaning. They should not dominate a book and rob the text of its vitality, nor should they be so subsidiary to the words that they merely decorate. On the other hand, a neutral position wherein the picture literally repeats the text is wasteful. Such illustrations are pictograms and should stand alone as they do in a nontalking comic strip, or else they should be eliminated. In readers, pictures are placed on each page of text to give children clues for comprehension, even though their usefulness for that purpose is in question. Picture clues are a distraction from the main task of recognizing the printed form of the language. The pictures in the readers might better be true illustrations, bringing aesthetic extension to the text, rather than being dull repetitions of dull discourse.

There is an early stage in learning to read when the whole of a story cannot be read because the task of reading so much language is too long and tedious for the young child. At this stage, a fine mixture of word text and picture text should be concocted wherein the artist-writer judiciously selects the elements of his story that can best be told in words or in pictures. The pictures, then, must be artful illustrations to give substance to a fine story. The best picture books achieve distinction by successfully wedding picture and text, each making full use of its media of presentation to complement the other.

Marcia Brown's Caldecott winner, *Once a Mouse*, is a good example of a strong but lean folk-tale text enriched by illustrations that highlight in blocked greens and sepias the mystery and surprise in the telling of a good folk tale. In Robert McCloskey's *Time of Wonder* alliterative and fast-paced language join with active and colorful illustrations to project, among other Main coast happenings, a hurricane in all its terror and splendor. Lynd Ward's *The Biggest Bear* has become a classic among picture books because both reading text and illustrations are substantive and artistic. A child who is still learning to read is not overwhelmed by the text; the pictures fill out the story, the background, and the mood. *The Little House* by Virginia Lee Burton achieves the same complementarity in text and picture in its building of historical and social concepts through a story of sentiment.

For older children, picture essays such as *Life Magazine's History of the United States* present concepts of the ways of life in various epochs that, if left to words alone, would require volumes and might still miss the essence of an age. For example, George Caleb Bingham's paintings present the adventure and robustness of the frontier as only a sensitive participant in the experience could. Art photography has become in the twentieth century a highly expressive form that is as applicable as other media. The work of Ansel Adams in his Sierra Club posters has done much toward making Americans apprehend their wonderful natural surroundings and, incidentally, to feel deeply the need to preserve them. Silent film has become another effectively expressive medium that reached an artistic peak in the early part of the century but continues to have great influence upon cinema and television. Chaplin's *Modern Times* is as stunning a commentary on modern man's dilemmas as any social novel or tract, and the ideation is entirely conveyed through cinematic means.

The ancient Greeks' desire for the golden mean can be sensed in the sculpture and architecture of the time as well as in the writings of the philosophers. The Middle Ages are not understood until the massiveness and loftiness of the cathedrals and intricacies of the stone carvings are seen. Painters, sculptors, and architects around the world presently and in ages past have presented the ideas and the feelings of their cultures in intense and focused forms. Their works can be viewed and studied as reflections of man's relationship to the world about him.

Strategies for Teaching
Application of the Visual Arts

Teachers who believe that the visual arts are at least on a par with the language arts for the communication of ideas will make every possible use of them in their own right, not just as supplements to language work. However, use of the pictorial arts can encourage language uses and even be the stepping-stone to it. The author observed a most effective use of the picture essay with a group of nonreading junior high school youngsters from a black and Puerto Rican neighborhood school. They were given simple cameras and sent around their neighborhood to take pictures of the life of the people there. Then involved in learning how to print their pictures, they were next asked to make a story from selected ones if thy had not already conceived of a story when they took the pictures. The photographs were mounted in a thematic series. Although they told a story by themselves the teacher then asked the students to develop captions and a narrative to accompany the pictures. Similar activities can be done with 8mm film.

Youngsters are usually eager to illustrate stories that they have written. In such an activity the teacher can work with them in thinking through what kind of illustrations would complement the story and not merely repeat aspects of it. A painted mural or series of pictures, comic-book style, can be made by young people to summarize concepts learned in the social studies or science.

Teachers can use the folk art and fine arts from a culture to assist them in conveying the ideas and feelings that people had in times past or in differing cultures. It is also possible to study the arts themselves as symbolic representations of ideas, letting youngsters respond to them and try out the various media themselves as *conveyors of their ideas*. It is possible to have a small museum in the classroom as one of the learning centers where graphic arts in print form or in books are displayed and where different materials are available from time to time for expressive exploration. Instruction in the way to use them is often necessary, but copying adult works or presented patterns should be avoided. The variety of materials available and the wide range of art ideas, drawing upon the past, the present, and the world's many cultures make the possibilities myriad for presentations in art forms.

Musical Literature

Another direct idiom of presentation is music artfully made from the cacaphony of sound, in which the composer states his ideas about the world musically. Although much of music is linear in time, impressions are created by a piling up of notes and rhythms in harmony and in counterpoint. A Bach fugue conveys a religious sense of awe; a Schubert song can illuminate the concept of human love. Program music like Beethoven's *Pastoral Symphony*, Vivaldi's *the Seasons*, or Debussy's *La Mer* paints an aural picture; a Haydn symphony (*The Miracle*) or a Stravinsky chamber piece (for example, Dumbarton Oak's Concerto) presents abstractly man's delight in being alive.

Children respond directly to musical forms. Their ability to apprehend music has not yet been thwarted by cultural pressures for conformity that has labeled classical music as "highbrow." Music teaching of the past has abetted this conformity by placing an aura of difficulty and sophistication around classical music in contrast with the natural introduction to music that children of *the folk* were given in earlier times. Today's interpretation of music has almost become a cult open to only those who have had courses in so-called appreciation. The result of this approach to the teaching of music is the separation of the child's natural sensitivity to rhythm and harmonious sound from the messages of the musical composition. Some jazz and rock-and-roll forms are the folk music of today and can be the entry-way to musical understandings. Most music in the modern Western tradition was written for adults, and therefore much of the musical literature is no more accessible to children than the writings of modern literature. However, as with literature, some musical compositions such as Saint-Saëns' *Carnival of Animals*, for example, have universal appeal. Also, there have been some remarkable compositions written expressly for children, for example, Prokofiev's *A Summer Day* suite and Leopold Mozart's *A Toy Symphony*.

FOLK MUSIC Most folk music from the various culture groups of the world can become meaningful to children because it was composed in a family or total community setting. Children were as much a part of the rituals, festivities, and occasions where music was used as were the adults, except for special religious rites involving only the priests or elders. The best introductions to the musical idiom for children are the folk song and dance literature from family and community occasions. Negro jazz, Scottish and Irish airs, American-Indian ceremonial dances, African drum music, English folk carols, and Haitian carnival tunes are but a few examples.

Folk music has in it all the basic elements of the musical idiom; therefore, the step from the folk heritage to the more sophisticated composed music is not as difficult as some imagine, provided highly complex musical forms and overlong compositions are left for discovery in adulthood. Listening to Bach's "Air for the G String" can easily follow singing of the "Londonderry Air." The learning of a Hungarian folk song can be precursor to the hearing of Bartók's *Music for Children*. The dancing of a Russian folk dance can lead to some of the music of early Stravinsky or Prokofiev. Aaron Copland and Roy Harris in the United States have created music that can have meaning for American children because it has roots in the folk tradition of the frontier and of the age of jazz. Scott Joplin's ragtime music for piano or small band combines folk and classical qualities that have an appeal for children similar to that of the highly original Sousa marches; they both represent an American cultural age in musical form.

COMPOSED MUSIC A few of the great composers have written expressly for children. Bach wrote a substantial body of music for his many talented sons to use in practice and in the study of musical invention. Some of these were collected in the *Anna Magdalena Notebook* and the *Two and Three Part Inventions*. Schumann wrote four major piano works for the young, including *Children's Ball* and *Album for the Young*. In our time Bartók composed *Music for Children*. Almost all these pieces are suitable for children's listening and some for performing. Their particular advantage is that they introduce the child to the fundamentals of music, for usually each piece develops a musical idea with only one or two musical inventions, a particular rhythmic pattern, harmonic device, or a contrapuntal line. Didactics are not required as children experience directly the building blocks of the musical art. The mode of electronic music is perhaps closer in comprehension to the children of this generation than it is to adults.

MAKING MUSIC Modern musical education theory suggests that children can learn the art of music making by experiencing their own composition of musical ideas. They can create music just as they create written language composition or their own paintings. Children are quite capable of inventing melodies, rhythms, and even harmonies to present a feeling about some situation or experience. They can use their singing voices and various rhythmic and simple melody-carrying instruments to set forth their musical ideas. Children of the slums are seen in the alleys making very exciting music on oil drums, bottles, and tin cans, but this music is hardly ever brought into the school and made the base for further musical study and performance, as it should be.

> Experimentation and discovery are two of the most important aspects of creativity. This does not mean that the teacher should ignore the basic skills and tools of making music, but rather that he should present these elements in the context of creativity.[26]

Carl Orff, the modern German composer, has devised for children a structured program of activities for the creation of music. Benjamin Britten, the modern English composer, in addition to writing the most successful educational musical film for children, *The Young Person's Guide to the Orchestra*, has composed several works in which children can participate. Among them are *Let's Make an Opera* and *Noye's Fludde*. Prokofiev has, perhaps been the most successful composer for children. The popularity of *Peter and the Wolf* placed it in the "classic" category not long after its composition. He has also written a delightful suite of piano pieces for children. Children are surely deprived if they are not given the opportunity to learn how to "read" musical literature.

Dramatic and Dance Literature: The Mimetic and Terpsichorean Arts

The modes of drama and dance are among the first that the child uses and enjoys. The young child is a facemaker, and he delights in dancing about to a tune or some rhythmic beat, musical or otherwise. In the preschool

[26] R. Bernard Fitzgerald, "Creative Music Teaching in the Elementary School," *Journal of the National Education Association* (December 1964) pp. 43–44.

years, playing house and dressing up are natural diversions in which young children rehearse their concepts of adult societal roles. During the middle years of childhood, group theatricals are neighborhood entertainments studiously planned, although not always persuasively acted by adult standards. Their content usually expresses a child's view of adult happenings or fragments of the child's fantasy. Children respond readily to chants and tribal-like rhythms that are the essence of choral dancing and speaking.

Froebel, in his recommendations for childhood education, included eurhythmics as part of his proposal to present children with the unities of the world. Plato, in his curriculum for Athenian children, stressed the importance of music, by which he meant choral dance, for teaching balance and control to bring harmony to the emotions.

> The whole choral art is also in our view the whole of education; and in this art rhythm and harmonies form that part which has to do with the voice. . . . The movement of the body has rhythm in common with the movement of the voice. . . . The sound of the voice readies and educates the soul. [All these] we have ventured to call music.[27]

In modern times the dance and dramatic arts have been included in the school curriculum mainly as activities that would bring enjoyment and in time would permit release of the emotions in a "respectable" form. Their inclusion was based on a Freudian concept of sublimation of subconscious desires and wishes into acceptable outlets. Creative play was seen as an opportunity for appropriate expression of aggressions and untutored emotions. The child was permitted to express himself freely but within limits imposed upon him by dance and dramatic forms. This was a modern psychological rationale for accomplishing ends not too dissimilar from those proposed by Plato.

But dances and dramas are not composed just for fun or for psychic release. They are made for the presentation of ideas and archetypal patterns. They convey human knowledge as surely as do books.

The Modes of Dance and Drama

The forms of dance are made in space and time and by bodily movement. Choreography is the art of planning a dance presentation. Effects are created by the rhythmic movements of the dancer's limbs, torso, and head, alone or in concert with the patterned movements of other dancers. Gestures may be used to emphasize or highlight a meaning. In some cultures, particular gestures convey particular agreed-upon meanings, while in modern dance or ballet, although movements may be conventionalized to some

---

[27] B. Jowett (trans.), Plato's "The Laws," *Dialogues of Plato*, Vol. II (London: Oxford University Press, 1892), p. 672.

extent, the meanings depend more directly on the dynamics of tension and release expressible in the body as it moves.

The dramatic arts are extensions of miming that sometimes incorporate all the other presentational forms: the literary language of dialogue, the painting and sculpture of scenery, the visual effects of light and costume, music either as background or as an integral part of the performance, and sometimes elements of the dance. Children understand the theater's essential means of presentation when they watch a pantomime or when they enact one.

The child needs to learn how to "read" the presentations of dance and theater in order to gain meaning from them directly without a roundabout explanation of them through discursive means. He must become accustomed to their special cues for communication. One way he learns the syntax and rhetoric of these special arts is to create his own forms, much as children practice creative writing or painting. In "rhythms" young people can build whole dance forms from stories that deal with emotions. A third-grade teacher used the story of Joseph from the Old Testament as a base for a music-dance-drama presentation. After hearing the story read aloud and discussing its content, especially the relationship of the brothers, the children plotted several episodes to enact. For one of them, which featured the brothers working in the fields, the class composed a work song and a harvesting dance.

Youngsters should experience the aesthetic presentations of other persons. The folk-dance literature can convey directly the attitudes of other peoples toward certain aspects of life. An Indian rain dance or an African hunting dance tells of these peoples' dependence on the vagaries of nature far more immediately than verbal explanation. *The Second Shepherd's Play,* from one of the medieval cycles of religious plays, captures the rude humor of those times and the mystery of a people's religion. A dance from the Japanese Kabuki cycle gives a picture of medieval life and thought in a non-European culture.

THE MOTION PICTURE AND TELEVISION The motion picture and television are purely visual presentations when they deal with natural phenomena, but when they present human situations they use dialogue as well as movement and miming. It is possible for children to create crudely in the cinematic medium because costs of production with 8 mm film are not as high as they once were. The child learns early how to "read" movies roughly because of their availability on television and at local theaters. However, he rarely learns to understand their form with any discrimination or interpretation.

Films used in the school for social studies should, of course, be authentic, but they should also be artful. Just as good books are preferred over poor ones in teaching, so there should be the same discrimination regarding choice of films. Robert Flaherty's classic *Louisiana Story* not only pictures oilwell drilling on the Gulf coast, but also conveys the human drama of man against machine through the sensitive eyes of a curious boy—much in the vein of Walt Whitman's "Out of the Cradle Endlessly Rocking." The movements of the pumping shafts in the derricks are contrasted with the quiet shoreline; the sparse but pungent dialogue stands out against the mingling of harmonica music with sounds of the pumps and the softly lapping water. The total presentation is an artistic masterpiece. Movies of the caliber of *Louisiana Story* can tell children much about their world, and there are many more available since Flaherty showed the way.

Some informational films are very well made, and teachers need to search for them. The better the film, the better the message will be communicated. After seeing the powerful film on preserving wildlife, *Say Goodbye,* one class developed petitions to be signed and sent to local, state, and national officers.

It has even been said that the whole curriculum could simply be youngsters' responses to the television programs and movies that they see or could see every day. Ideas of all sorts including many misconceptions are conveyed to them in this manner. One regular topic for class meetings might be response to television programs of the night before. With the availability of portable television, teachers and young people can devise their own programs for presenting their ideas to others. When color-taping can be done the teacher will have the ultimate presentational instrument for his exploitation.

Multimedia presentations utilizing slides with two or three projectors and a synchronized sound tape can be very useful for presenting contrasting or complementary concepts and themes. Youngsters at the sixth-grade level have composed, for example, a slide–sound show called "Picture Our World," combining their own color slides of children and adults in nature settings of various kinds with a music tape of children singing the verses of the song. Pictures and music create an essay on ecology that is moving and significant.[28]

The dramatic forms of theater, movies, and television can at their best integrate the several symbolic forms (including language) and create a cognitive and emotional impact impossible in the separate forms. Some critics of our "wordbound" culture feel that the Guttenberg era is over and that mixed media will dominate communication in the near future. Written language will undoubtedly continue in usefulness, however, but children will increasingly need to learn how to use the visual, aural, and terpsichorean modes for coming to know about their world of the future.

[28] Douglas Cooper, Teacher, Brookside School, Bloomfield Hills, Michigan.

section 3

Mathematical Literacy: Reasoning in Language and Symbol[29]

When the term mathematical literacy is used, it usually refers both to the mathematical competencies that are a "must" for every citizen and to the language and the use of language in mathematics. The two interpretations of the term are related. Mathematics uses not only a special language, but language and symbols in a special way. For elementary school teachers, the fact is of particular importance because the K–6 school years are meant to serve as a foundation for the development of mathematics in subsequent grades. Figure 1 shows how *all* of mathematics can be thought of as arising from basic concepts and structures. Today, most school programs reflect this unified organization of mathematics by developing topics spirally and by emphasizing the concepts and properties of the structures that are represented in the trunk of the "tree."

A connection exists between language and mathematics in that each may convey ideas or facts. More importantly, both *seem* to convey certain facts when, in reality, they are expressing ideas that are quite different. For example, the youngster who says that he really does not care if he makes the team may or may not mean it. In arithmetic $8 + 8 = 10$ may or may not be true, depending on the underlying system of numeration.

Reasoning in mathematics, in law, or in science involves using accepted ways of *proving* what seems to be true. A prosecutor proves a defendant guilty by exhibiting motive, opportunity, and method. A chemist proves that hydrogen is lighter than air by comparing two like balloons, one filled with air, the other with hydrogen. A mathematician proves that the sum of two even numbers is even by using the language and rules that are a part of his subject. Some of these mathematical rules and ideas follow.

Statements

There are many kinds of statements that are used in everyday speech; for example:

> He was President of the United States.
> Go to bed!
> What is John doing?
> One-half is a rational number.

[29] This section prepared by John Camp, Mathematics Education, Wayne State University, Detroit, Michigan.

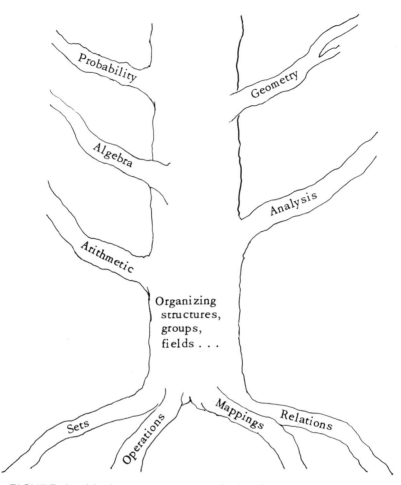

FIGURE 1   Mathematics as a unified subject.

These are either assertions, commands, or questions. Mathematics is primarily concerned with making statements that are assertions and then determining whether the assertions are true or false. The difference between everyday language and mathematics is that the mathematical assertion is either true or false, but it *cannot* be both. The following table illustrates some statements in mathematics.

Compound Statements

As in language, by combining two or more mathematical statements into compound statements, new statements are created. Depending on the truth or falsity of the simple statements, the compound statements are either true or false.

TABLE 1   Statements in Mathematics

statement	true	false
$5 + 3 = 8$	✓	
$4 - 2 > 2$		✓
Two congruent segments have the same length.	✓	
The diagonals of a parallelogram are congruent.		✓
$X + 3 = 11$	Not a mathematical statement—as written it is neither true nor false	

The four most common ways of combining statements in mathematics is by joining them with "and," "or," "if . . . then," or "if and only if." The following are examples of compound mathematical statements using the preceding connectives. Try to determine whether each simple statement of a compound is true or false, and then if the compound is true or false.

13 is a prime number *and* $4 \times 0 = 0$.
57 is not a prime number *or* 57 is evenly divisible by 7.
If 4 is a prime number, *then* 4 has only the factors 1 and 4.
$4 < 8$ *if and only if* $-2 > -4$.

At the elementary school level, the connectives "and" and "or" are introduced early in studying sets, in constructing mathematical statements, and in solving open sentences (for example, find numbers which when placed in the □ will make □ $+ 5 < 7$ a true statement). Implications (if . . . then) and bi-implications (if and only if) are usually not stressed.

The understanding of the meaning and truth values of a compound statement with "and" usually causes trouble. Another problem is that of the linguistic difficulty associated with the connective word "or" because in English it is used in two different ways—inclusively or exclusively. When we say "Paul or Jim will go to the game," we mean that Paul, or Jim, or *both* will go to the game (inclusive). In contrast, when we say "You may go to the movies or you may stay at home," we mean that you may do one but not the other (exclusive). Students need to understand that in mathematics we must adopt one interpretation for consistency, and so "or" is always used in the inclusive sense.

It is important that teachers understand the use of the vocabulary of mathematics. In addition to the special uses of "and" and "or," some other little words and phrases that have special meanings are: "at least," "at most," "for all," "there is," and "for some." Special language structures also exist for probabilities, time and rate questions, and for the mathematics of the financial system. At each stage of development, the vocabulary and ideas must be mathematically precise and correct if the spiral approach to developing mathematics is to work and if youngsters are to accomplish the reasoning language of the structural logic of mathematics.

Testing Ideas against Reality

Knowing the difference between literary and expository writing, along with the language features that make literature an apt combination of thought and feeling, gives teachers a basis from which to select books for youngsters and clues to using books in the learning process. Understanding the means for symbolic representation in the arts, music, and dance gives teachers background for using presentational symbols in teaching. Some validating activities follow.

Locate the original scientific journal report of a recent scientific experiment reported in a popular magazine. Compare and contrast the two reports for language style.

Compare and contrast the presentation of popular novels in the original and in their screen versions. Tolstoy's WAR AND PEACE has appeared in both Russian and American film versions, British television tape, and in the Prokofiev opera on records.

Get copies of reports of scientific experiments such as observation studies of animals of the area, edit them for older youngsters, and ask them to use them as models for observing and reporting animal observations or experiments that can be done in the classroom. Have older youngsters read literary models such as short stories, doggerel and nonsense rhymes, free verse on nature subjects, haiku, songs, and essays based on nature or people observations; ask them to try some of their own.

Mood music by impressionist or modern composers can be played from recordings or in piano transcriptions for suggesting interpretations into art, dance, or literary forms. (Ideas in art forms never can be transposed from one form to the other directly, but they often spur imagination for developing ideas in other media.)

Turning Ideas into Practice

The best way to learn how to comprehend and respond to literature and the arts is, of course, to read them, view them, and talk about them. Some suggested activities for fostering such practice follow:

BOOK CLUBS can be formed in a classroom for encouraging independent and paired reading by asking eight to twelve youngsters to form a club. From a suitable trade book collection, procured from the library or bought in paperbacks a teacher can, in time, help each club select 10 books, two copies of each. Two criteria would be set for selection: appropriateness of reading level, and wide range of interests with general appeal for the club members. Among the eight to ten members, readers should be paired according to their desires and reading rate. Each pair would select one of the books and read it together, reading independently and to each other from time to time during a regular daily library period or free reading time in an open schedule. Each pair would also prepare an appealing way of sharing their book with the rest of the club, which would give members an introduction to it. When everyone has read one of the books (probably only five or six of them would be completed by everyone before the youngsters would opt for some other means of reading and sharing together) the teacher should encourage a sharing panel discussion or presentation to the class. During the library period or free reading time the teacher would confer with each of the pairs once every week or two, asking them to summarize the story thus far, to read some passages aloud, and to discuss plans for presenting the book to club members. Club meetings for the sharing should also be held during this time when a pair has finished a book and is ready to present.[30] Interests or types of literature can form the basis for each group. The club approach can be used for gathering jokes, riddles, or scary stories to be shared, or for writing original stories or plays that can be typed, illustrated with photographs or drawings, and then used for reading practice. Discussing favorite tv programs and criticizing movies are also possible activities for the club format. A MINI ART MUSEUM can be one of the learning centers in a room or cluster of classes; art books and good reproductions and/or originals by local artists can be changed from time to time according to themes and space for exhibiting. Sculpture or carving that can be handled ought to be displayed from time to time as well. Response cards could be collected and used later for discussions of the works. A creative art program of exploring various media should accompany the development of a mini-museum along with art photography and 8mm movie-making clubs.

LISTENING CENTERS or posts can be devised for hearing cassettes of folk music, jazz, theater music, classical recordings, or recordings of poetry or drama. Associated with the center there should also be a program of creative rhythms, dance, and music making.

[30] This strategy was developed by Marion Risbrough, Crothers School, Centerline, Michigan.

7

LANGUAGE AND THOUGHT IN TEACHING

The cognitive need is as commanding and con-
straining, and at times as fulfilling, as any realization
of the more primitive organic needs. . . .

Does this mean that the teacher simply responds
to all which simply stirs response in the child? I
think not. It means, rather, that the interpersonal relations of teacher and pupil, and the pupil's potential
response to the reality waiting to be discovered, are
two aspects of one learning process. The irrational
and the rational are intimately blended in the teacher's
communications, as they are in the inter-communica-
tions between members of the group which is learning.
The clarifying merges into the electrifying.

GARDNER MURPHY, Freeing Intelligence through Teaching
(New York: Harper & Row, 1961), pp. 41–43.

TEACHING FOCUS

How can teachers, first, formulate curricular plans to produce higher levels of pupil language-use and thinking processes, and, second, adapt them to specific situations?

What specific classroom procedures are conducive to opening inquiry and heightening thinking powers?

How can the teacher's repertoire of questioning techniques be increased and enriched to induce improved language and thinking levels?

What means can teachers use to record, examine, and assess the impact of their teaching on pupil gains?

19

Language and Thinking
Strategies in the Art
of Teaching

The great teacher is an artist in presenting his view of the world to his students and in moving them to think and feel deeply about their existence and their relationship to the world about them. He creates in the media of language, mime, sound, and picture to effect a response to the world in other persons. As an artist, the teacher must master the crafts of his art. For him this means "mastery of language, of the visual arts, of stage setting, of movement and of the flow of events."[1]

Language is the prime vehicle of expression and exchange of thought in the classroom. It is the medium for that "mental play" that should distinguish the school from the natural play of the alley or of the backyard. Teachers, Dewey said, need to be able to "keep track of this mental play, to recognize the signs of its presence or absence, and to know how it is initiated and maintained."[2]

B. O. Smith, in his investigations of the teaching act, described seven major types of "didactic verbal behavior" in teaching performance: defining, classifying, explaining, conditional inferring, comparing and contrasting, valuating, and designating. Teaching is improved when the teacher is made

---

[1] Dwayne Huebner, "The Art of Teaching," an unpublished mimeographed manuscript (New York: Teachers College, Columbia University, 1961) pp. 14–18.

[2] John Dewey, *The Relation of Theory to Practice in Education.* Republished in 1964 by Association for Student Teaching, Washington, D.C.

345

aware of the actions he performs linguistically,[3] analyzes them for effectiveness, and changes them accordingly.

Teaching can be viewed logically as a "task word," and the action it describes as a "system" somewhat discrete from learning. To *learn* is seen as a "paralleling" and corresponding "achievement."[4] When this is the way teaching is conceived, then one of the actions in this system is the teacher's presentation of his own symbolic transformations of experience in a manner or method that will encourage students to develop their own conceptions and presentations in dialogue with his. The action (or as an Existentialist would describe it, this "engagement") requires artful strategies of presenting. These include the teacher's logical organization of his concepts around appropriate themes and their psychological reorganization for presentation to youngsters, the subtle framing of questions that will create dialogue, the careful preparation of resource materials, displays, and demonstrations to provoke questions and encourage self-study activities. Finally, he sets means for evaluating not only accomplishments by students, but also his own teaching effectiveness. These are the arts of teaching which, at their finest, create epiphanies, little revelations of life, for student and teacher alike.

When teaching is considered as both a presentational and communicative art, it seems evident that there are four phases involving the molding of language and thought:

1. Developing a general strategy for instruction
2. Organizing ideation for teaching, including cognitive-affective and psycomotor interrelationships
3. Devising pedagogical tactics for involving learners in instructional objectives and assessing ideational gains
4. Utilizing language strategies for expanding ideation
   a. Questioning in teaching
   b. Exposition in teaching

section 1

Developing a General Strategy for Instruction

Many general strategies for instruction could be developed, each based on a particular view of the educative process. For example, one of the instructional strategies developed from Dewey's emphasis on "experience" was Kilpatrick's "project method." When a personal knowing cycle of perceiving, ideating, and presenting is postulated, then there should be a similar cycle in the general teaching strategy for helping children to know;

[3] B. Othanel Smith, "A Concept of Teaching," in B. O. Smith and R. H. Ennis (eds.), *Language and Concepts in Education* (Skokie, Ill.: Rand McNally, 1961), pp. 94–97.
[4] Smith, p. 90.

Thelen, Woodruff, Taba, and others have projected possible process cycles.[5] The following discussion is freely adapted from their statements and incorporates additional ideas of the present authors.

Premise: An Interaction Theory of Education

A cycle of process can be built on a metatheory of interaction between the individual and his social environment; the organism sends messages into his environment through feelings toward it and actions in it, many of which are conveyed by language.[6] The environment sends back messages in the form of perceptions, which are then reorganized by the organism through assimilation and accommodation into ideations, and are then sent out again in new forms. The crucial factor is the reorganizing. If the individual merely reacts to his perceptions impulsively, nothing is learned; he simply protects himself as best he can. If he reacts in terms of the socially accepted manners, he becomes conditioned to the environment but does not know anything more about it than he did before. He adjusts and conforms. But if he stops to inquire with an open-minded value-orientation and then to reorganize the new perceptions in relation to previous knowledge, involving his ego in coming to terms with novelty, he is being educated.

Main Pedagogical Strategies for Phases of Coming To Know[7]

Perceiving Phase

CONFRONTING The attention of the learner is arrested by some novelty in the situation. Feelings are aroused; curiosity is engendered.

Students are confronted with new events, challenging questions, seemingly unusual occurrences that will cause bafflement and will stir speculation. Field trips, demonstrations, and audiovisual materials as well as excerpts from books or challenging questions can be used to produce confrontation. Students are encouraged to meet the new event with all senses open.

HEIGHTENING AWARENESS If the new event is not rejected because of lack of concern or suppressed because it stirs anxious feelings, the individual will let his preconscious reactions emerge. He will permit vague ideas, memories, speculations, and feelings to be expressed to himself. The mind wanders freely in and around the subject, sometimes holding an

[5] Herbert Thelen, "Insight for Teaching from a Theory of Interaction," *The Nature of Teaching* (Milwaukee, Wisc.: University of Wisconsin–Milwaukee, 1963), pp. 19–31. Asahel Woodruff, "The Use of Concepts in Teaching and Learning," *Journal of Teacher Education, 15*, No. 1 (March 1964), 81–99. Hilda Taba, *Curriculum Development* (New York: Harcourt, 1962), Chaps. 17–19.

[6] Thelen, pp. 20–26.

[7] The phases in coming to know are discussed in Chapter 5.

imaginary conversation with a friend or opponent. It is called in popular parlance "mulling over an idea." The language belonging to the idea is expressed.

This process of allowing the imagination full play should be encouraged in the classroom by permitting informal conversations and thinking out loud immediately after a confrontation. The child begins to get feedback from his peers that further stimulates his curiosity and his thinking mechanisms. Time for each pupil to ruminate should be permitted if the classroom talks suggest that imagining is taking place.

Ideating Phase

PROBLEM FINDING Learners begin to search their memories for principles or generalizations that might apply to the new event. They try out categories into which the new event might fit. Conflicting assumptions are brought to the fore as a problem, a question, or a hypothesis is developed. The goal of the search becomes clear.

Clarifying questions are raised by teachers as consideration of past experience is encouraged. Students present hunches regarding relationships to other ideas and hypotheses that might be tested.

BUILDING DIALOGUE BETWEEN PERSONAL KNOWLEDGE AND ESTABLISHED KNOWLEDGE The student is made aware of alternatives and of matters of value, truth, and justice as his personal views and ideas are pitted against those of educated adults who can interpret integrated and cumulative concepts from scholarship. Eternal questions are raised, and general principles are considered when the student's concepts are placed in dialogue with the common wisdom of man. The structure of the individual's knowing is placed in communication with the structures of the disciplines as a process of problem finding is further refined.

The teacher, by participating in class discussion, interjects his interpretation of established knowledge at the point when the student's concept can be related to and extended by the universal concept. Books, films, and programmed materials can be presented at the same time that the learner is gaining his own concepts from experience. Sometimes the process can be reversed by presenting the adult constructs first, followed by a student's finding his own experiential support. The dialogue between personal and established knowledge needs to be interspersed with questions that will define the issues, locate the significant problems or questions, and lead to the mutual forming of objectives for the search and application of findings.

PROBLEM SOLVING After finding and describing particular situations in which the issues or questions are present in the perceptual world, a procedure is adopted for finding solutions. The givens are stated and the criteria for solutions are set up. The paths to solutions or processes to be used may involve trial and error, analogy, hypothesizing, or inductive and deductive reasoning. Concepts become realized as they are put to work in actual situations.

Questions are raised that will focus attention on defining and limiting problems. The teacher challenges the assumptions and helps students clarify the givens. Problem instances have to be chosen in which feedback can be readily perceived by students, more or less instantaneously. As relationships are discovered tentative generalizations are drawn.

Presenting Phase

DEMONSTRATING AND REHEARSING The concepts and generalizations gained from the instances in problem solving are encoded into language. The original issues are reorganized in light of the experimentation, and language means are used to show the new results. Individual findings are pooled, and concepts are reorganized as different views are considered. The final and composite concepts and generalizations of this investigation are stated in summary.

Each student is given an opportunity to present his own reconstructed concepts in an appropriate manner. Writing down conclusions and summarizing the new ideas in oral or written reports with diagrams or pictograms for further illustration are encouraged. Group discussions and culminating activities, including creative dramatics, murals, mock television programs, and panels are planned and executed by the children and teacher.

ASSESSING AND APPLYING New issues and questions are raised as a result of the study and are set down for future consideration. Projections into future similar situations are surmised as an application of newly learned ideas is attempted in slightly different contexts. Procedures are critically analyzed, and recommendations are made for the next study as objectives are reviewed and reconsidered.

An evaluating session should begin with a look back to the initial question and issues while the class criticizes its own procedures, noting what was effective and what was inefficient. The teacher posits other situations in different contexts that would involve similar concepts and generalizations. The learners apply their knowledge in the new situations. As they confront the new context, new questions arise because the old learnings do not quite fit the new situations. *The cycle of perceiving/ideating/presenting/re-perceiving is pressed to completion in the classroom by a corresponding cycle of instructional strategies: confronting, building dialogue, rehearsing in new contexts, and then back to new confrontations.*

section 2

Organizing Ideation for Teaching: Focusing Themes, Process Objectives, Resource Studies, and Evaluation

The curriculum design most suitable for paralleling the knowing cycle is a *spiral curriculum* in which designated "focusing ideas" (related concepts and generalizations) are explored in different contexts and at different levels of perception. *Cognate increments* (ideations) are proposed for developing, enriching, and extending concepts and generalizations while more complex contexts are suggested for study. *Thought-process goals* are set with specifically designated intermediate levels that will encourage the cultivation of such scholarly processes of inquiry as classification, substantiation, verification, evaluation, and application. General teaching strategies appropriate to the selected contexts, to the chosen process goals, and to the general capabilities of an age group of learners are recommended. For example, the case-study method is especially appropriate for studying social interactions. Evaluated bibliographies of resource materials for the teacher and his students are offered.

Curriculum Making Process

In formulating *spiral curricula*, scholars from appropriate disciplines and educators with input from community and pupil representatives work in concert to prepare generalized *key themes* of knowledge that interrelate; they then suggest *contexts* in which the themes can best be developed and describe the general educational goals they would meet. These thematic clusters and possible contexts can be disciplinary or interdisciplinary in nature; in terms of scope for any schoolwide curriculum they must include themes from the sciences, social sciences, and humanities. Consideration of broad educational goals to be met by study raises the questions of relevance to the lives of young people and of significance in terms of the social and intellectual goals of the local and larger community. Citizens and student representatives can be appropriately involved at the goal-making and theme-generating stage of curriculum development. A most appropriate theme, for example, for study in America's sprawling, urban, and industrialized megalopolises would be the impact of a technological invention like the mass-produced automobile on the people and their environment. Educational goals involved would include career and work orientation, socioeconomic efficiency, and application of the rational process to sociopolitical judgment questions. The development and choice of themes and goals should be a constant and open inquiry, and school groups should have open options for both adapting curricular themes to their use and participating in the development of new themes and contexts. The British model of open-ended curriculum development through the widely representative Schools Council and its related field-testing activities in Teachers' Centers is preferable to any government dictated scheme. The "focusing theme" basis for curriculum planning replaces the old "subject covering" method which is inappropriate in this age of knowledge explosion.

Once public decisions have been made about the themes and goals, then the scholars, educational strategists, and representative practicing teachers prepare a series of sample Resource Studies around the themes. They follow a process of (1) refining the themes, by defining the concepts involved and proposing the generalizations from interrelating the concepts; (2) proposing general instructional objectives in both expressive and/or activity terms as appropriate; (3) exploring through field-testing sites the feasibility of various instructional strategies and materials development; (4) recommending general instructional strategies and preparing field-tested resource materials and advisories on means for preparing teacher-made materials; and (5) proposing evaluating mechanisms for assessment of the potential ideational gains in both expressive and action terms where appropriate.

The cooperating scholars make certain that themes are based on valid premises and that they may be logically expanded according to modern scholarship. They also recommend contexts that have been previously studied and about which there is sufficient information. In social studies, the recommended context may be an early society or, in biology, a species of butterflies that is well known because scholars have gathered data and tested hypotheses. The scholar will also know whether a particular context can be practically studied in school settings. For example, the life-cycle of certain butterflies is very difficult to follow within a reasonable school schedule, whereas that of other species may be so studied. Scholars can also recommend appropriate types of investigation, such as the grid-mapping procedures followed in an archeological dig, whether it be in a town dump or an ancient ruin.

Education specialists working on a curriculum-planning team contribute the psychological decisions about general instructional strategies; they answer the questions of what levels of generalization children can comprehend at various stages and the questions of which contexts will be most involving for learners. Teachers recommend possible educational tactics that will most likely engage the pupils in study. They also propose the instructional objectives and the means by which progress toward them will be evaluated. Together, the educators, scholars, and teachers screen the literature and available audiovisual presentations for accuracy and for educational soundness. They can prepare several ideational structures and sample contexts in the form of resource studies. The concept of irrigation, for example, can be studied in the context either of suburban lawn watering or of the agricultural output of the Sacramento Valley or the Nile River Basin. The individual classroom teacher or team of teachers can decide which context or contexts will carry the most meaning for a particular group of students and in which context relationships will be most easily made manifest to them. The teacher, then, prepares the tactical instructional plans, including operational objectives based upon the resource study he selects.

Sample Curricula Formed on Conceptual Schemes

Attempts have been made in recent years to develop curricula for social studies, science, and humanities based on *focusing themes*; such a method would structure the conceptual schemes that students need to derive in their own ways and in their own language.

COGNITIVE SCHEMES INTERACTING WITH VALUES THROUGH INTELLECTUAL PROCESSES Brandwein in his introduction to an elementary school curriculum says that concepts are not only effective in ordering a curriculum but also in being the basis for student understanding. "Concepts isolate the common attributes of social behavior and social events." "Values permeate a curriculum based on concepts. For understanding is basic to valuing." The "methods of intelligence" used by social scientists are the process goals of a curriculum that attempts to develop conceptual and valuative thinking.[8] The "cognitive schemes" of the curriculum for six levels of expansion and sophistication are built around five broad conceptual themes, each from a different discipline of the social sciences.[9]

1. Man is the product of heredity and environment (Anthropology);
2. Human behavior is shaped by the social environment (Sociology);
3. The geographic features of the earth affect man's behavior (Geography);
4. Economic behavior depends on the utilization of resources (Economics);
5. Political organization resolves conflicts and makes interaction easier among people (History, Government, Political Science).

Subsumed under the conceptual themes are six cognitive schemes of varying levels of expansion and sophistication, depending on age. Scheme A follows:[10] Beginning level, (1) Individuals resemble each other; (2) members of the family group are alike because of heredity and environment; (3) community groups adapt to the environment; (4) man inherits and learns patterns of behavior; (5) interaction of biological and cultural inheritance results in the adaptation of man to his environment; and (6) biological and

---

[8] Paul Brandwein, *Notes on Teaching the Social Sciences: Concepts and Values* (New York: Harcourt, 1970), pp. 2, 3.

[9] Center for the Study of Instruction, *The Social Sciences: Concepts and Values* (New York: Harcourt, 1970), brochure chart.

[10] *The Social Sciences*, see chart for beginning level.

cultural inheritance results in variation in the people of the Earth. The authors of this curriculum have developed a list of thought-provoking texts and supplementary materials originally piloted by selected teachers. The objectives of the program are to lead teachers and learners into direct interactions with the physical and social environment and to stress the acting out of concepts and values learned in behavior.

In another modern textbook series the content is also clustered around themes of related concepts; for example, one book is devoted to *Inquiry about Cities*.[11] The recommended teaching plans are built around three operations used in dealing with data.

1. *Data-gathering operations:* observing, counting and quantifying, interviewing, and experimenting;
2. *Data-organizing operations:* classifying, comparing–contrasting, mapping, modeling, graphing and charting statisitcs;
3. *Data-using operations:* inferring, deducing, generalizing, explaining, predicting, and hypothesizing.

Pictures as well as text and questions are used in interesting ways for setting the stage for the operations. One section, for example, deals with "City as Art" and includes reproductions of paintings by such renowned artist-recorders of city life as Ben Shahn, Raphael Soyer, John Sloan, and Fernand Leger; responses are then solicited.

A group of Canadian educators has developed a series of teacher advisory books, each focusing on a topic of importance in teaching the social sciences and sciences in the elementary and middle grades. An instructional approach gives basic design to this curriculum built loosely around the general theme *Examining Your Environment*. Each concept scheme that is needed for understanding such topics as *Pollution, Mini-climates*, and *Mapping Small Places* is stated, and then the authors describe specific learning activities that will involve the learners in deriving the concepts and putting them to work. The activities include simple construction of instruments and other means for gathering and assessing data gained from the environment; the exercises are presented in sequences that deal with: (1) raising questions, (2) digging deeper, and (3) branching out. Given the essentials with regard to concept and sample instructional activities the teacher is expected "to take it from there," depending on his situation. The topics may be set into any large school system curricular design, but the advantage of this approach is the directness of these teacher manuals in giving functional advice without hamstringing the teacher into some particular format.[12] The instruc-

11 W. Fielder (ed.), *Teachers Guide, Inquiry about Cities* (New York: Holt, Rinehart and Winston, 1971), pp. xiii, 11.

12 The series is called *Examining Your Environment*, by D. F. Wentworth, J. K. Couchman, J. C. MacBean, and A. Stecher; published by Holt, Rinehart and Winston of Canada, and, in the United States, by Winston Press, Minneapolis, Minn. Examples: *Mini-climates* (1971), *Pollution* (1971), and *Mapping Small Places* (1972).

tional ideas are highly imaginative, while being practical and soundly based in modern science and social science concepts. In *Mapping Small Places*, for example, the concept of contour mapping is presented and several activities for making such maps are demonstrated, beginning with the tracing of the edges of evaporating puddles on an uneven asphalt playground and leading to surveying hills and valleys.

Use of Focusing Ideas for Lifting Thinking

The social studies curriculum planned in Contra Costa County, California, under the guidance of the late Hilda Taba,[13] is an example of a curriculum planned around *focusing ideas*. These are developed and extended with children through comparative studies of different types of social communities, modern and early, in contrasting settings: African jungles, the Swiss Alps, or a Chinese river. The ways of living, the customs, and the traditions of a regional community are the contexts in which such ideas as the following are developed:

> Some people make their own homes and secure their food and clothing from the immediate environment. Some people live a very simple life even though they may be part of an ancient civilization from which came many things we use today. Many activities of primitive people are carried on through the family and/or tribe; a more modern community provides for these activities through organized institutions. All people teach their children the things they think are important for them to learn. They teach them in different ways.

Taba selected basic concepts (for example, cultural change, interdependence, cooperation, differences, and causality) essential to understanding all sociocultural phenomena as the foundation for the program's ideation structure.[14] They can be dealt with at different levels of complexity, abstraction, and generality, depending on the learner's levels of life-experience and thinking capabilities. *Interdependence* can be studied at the primary-school level in terms of relationships between community specialized workers and family members in terms of needs and services. Later it can be treated in terms of relationships between industries and government and between governments. The content to be studied can be selected in terms of opportunities to demonstrate the concepts at work, of availability of materials and of connections (relevance) to the learners. Old curricula need not be discarded but merely revised by developing some aspects in greater depth and by abandoning less relevant, thought-provoking parts. For example, old studies of South America can be revamped to focus on comparing and contrasting just two countries

---

[13] Hilda Taba, *Curriculum Development* (New York: Harcourt, 1962), Chap. 20, pp. 343–374. See also *A Study in Comparative Communities* (Pleasant Hill, Calif.: Contra Costa County Board of Education, 1961).

[14] This section summarizes ideas from Hilda Taba, *Teachers' Handbook for Elementary Social Studies* (Palo Alto, Calif.: Addison-Wesley, 1967), Chap. 4, pp. 13–26.

environmentally different but similar in racial and national backgrounds. When that comparative study is completed, two other countries could be selected that are opposite in setting and different in European national influences. *As teachers build such curricula in spirals based on increased sophistication of the "focusing ideas," they need to be concerned with the following criteria for selecting "main ideas"*:

Validity: Do they adequately represent ideas of the discipline(s) from which they are drawn?
Significance: Can they explain important segments of the world today?
Appropriateness: Are they suited to needs, interests, and maturational levels of students?
Durability: Are they of lasting importance?
Balance: Do they permit development in both scope and depth?

Specific facts change and eventually alter concepts and generalizations; therefore, it is more economical for teachers and learners to deal with concepts and generalizations provided that the teacher keeps abreast of conceptual changes through scholarship. At the second-grade level the *concept* of interdependence can be developed through the *main idea* that each worker provides a service someone else needs. The content can deal with the gas station, the supermarket, or drugstore until those "factual" agencies disappear or become transformed into some other community reality, such as the shopping center.

The "learning experiences" suggested by Taba for implementing each "main idea" are divided into three main instructional episodes: an opener, a development, and a conclusion. In the opener, students are confronted in a dramatic way with a novel situation, and new ideas or arrangement of ideas. In the development stage episodes focus around several means for "lifting the levels of thinking" about the idea from factual listing through classifying, categorizing, and labeling to inferring, hypothesizing, and generalizing. The last stage, conclusion, deals with generalizing and applying or testing the generalizations in new but similar situations (comparative study).

GENERALIZED THEMES ILLUSTRATED IN CONTEXTS Grannis, in the social studies curriculum for a team teaching project, constructed with teachers a trial curriculum that attempted to extend for children several basic generalizations and concepts in a variety of appropriate contexts.[15] There are three levels, within which generalizations cluster as themes in a logical order, each followed by suggested contexts:

[15] Joseph Grannis, mimeographed materials, Harvard Graduate School of Education, Cambridge, Mass., 1962. See also Judson Shaplin and Henry Olds (eds.), *Team Teaching* (New York: Harper & Row, 1964), Chap. 5; and "The Framework of the Social Studies Curriculum," *The National Elementary Principal, 62,* No. 5 (April 1961), D.E.S.P., Washington, D.C., p. 25. The authors have selected only a few examples and have made some adaptations.

LEVEL I

Theme: Man's natural environment varies significantly in different geographic regions of our country and the world.

Contexts: Emphasis will be on fundamental aspects of topography, climate and natural resources, especially as indicated in the lives of various preindustrial societies. Contextual topics: (1) Polar region (Copper Eskimos in Hudson Bay area); (2) hot dry land (Navahos); (3) temperate forest land (pioneer woodsmen of early America); (4) highland (Tibetans); (5) tropical grassland (Massai of Africa); and (6) volcanic islands (Indonesia).

LEVEL II

Theme: Man has found complex ways to improve his relationship to his natural environment.

Contexts: Six areas of human endeavor will be studied. In each area a modern approach will be contrasted with less advanced practices; the comparison will not belittle the efforts of any people to cope with their circumstances. The material lends itself to correlation with the science instruction, but the social studies emphasis is on man—the workers, the effects of these practices on men's lives, as well as the ingenuity of man. Contextual topics: (1) A water-control system (storage, irrigation, flood control, navigation of rivers); (2) A national park (forest preservation, wildlife protection, recreation); (3) A truck farm (mechanization, pest control, crop rotation); (4) A mineral mine or quarry (surface and subsurface mining, extraction, safety).

LEVEL III

Theme: The Industrial Revolution has widened the gap between advanced and underdeveloped areas and has increased the interdependence of men.

Contexts: The concern will be with the effects of certain factors on man's life, especially from the viewpoint of economic geography. Contextual topics: (1) Power and technology (hand, animal, water, steam, electrical, and atomic power with corresponding technology; productivity, human effort, cost); (2) Natural resources (selected animal, vegetable, and mineral resources, their uses, and distribution on the globe; comparison of the aggregate chief resources of several countries; strategic resources, relative natural wealth of areas, mineral survey); (3) Trade (Marco Polo, Massachusetts commerce with the Orient in the early 19th century, the trade of several interdependent countries today, a World's Fair; import-export balance, means of transport, tariff); (4) Economic development (by a colonial power, Operation Bootstrap in Puerto Rico, the American West, India; standard of living, exploitation, capital development).

Teams of teachers at each level prepare specific *context units of study.* One such team working at Level I prepared a unit on work with the contrasting contexts of Indonesia and America.[16] They choose Indonesia because of an abundance of pictorial material and because it offered a vivid contrast to the American scene with its mechanized work patterns.

This context unit was divided into three thematic phases: the need for work, how man meets those needs, and the different requirements of work. Each phase's theme was broken into a few key generalizations such as, "man

---

[16] *Work*, a unit of study prepared by Alpha Team, Franklin School, Lexington, Mass.; consultant: J. Grannis.

must extend himself in order to produce something," "man supplements local resources for production by trading, selling, and buying," and "most jobs require special training." Underneath each generalization the teachers outlined involvement-oriented activities, which included interviewing workers, reading about work in Indonesia, seeing films, categorizing pictures of people working in Indonesia and in the United States, building models of simple work tools like looms, and practicing with simple agricultural tools. A vocabulary list of terms was prepared along with an annotated bibliography of books and other printed and pictured materials for teachers and learners.

In order for the children to form these generalizations they must understand certain concepts. Grannis feels that the teacher must be secure in *his* full understanding of the concepts and the interrelationships that make the generalizations manifest in the context. For example, in a study of the Navaho Indian the following generalizations and concepts need to be clear:

> *Generalization:* Man, animals, plants—all living things need water.
> *Concepts:* Man, animals, plants, life, need, water, scarcity.

If the child does not have a fairly complete concept of what constitutes life or the sustenance of life, then he will have difficulty in drawing the proper conclusion. In the context of Navaho life, facts become pertinent for developing the generalization. Navaho Indians live apart when water and grass are scarce. They melt snow for their sheep to drink and they save water by using a sweathouse for cleaning their bodies.

The chart below shows the breakdown of the above generalization into its conceptual parts and combinations of subgeneralizations, including the applications in the context of Navaho Indian life. For completing the curriculum design further charts are developed in which each generalization stated as an hypothesis is explored in terms of suggested *learning activities* for the teacher to set up, major *questions* that need to be asked and answered, the work and *study skills* that need to be used and refined, actual *activities for evaluation*, the *equipment and materials* needed, and the printed references for teachers and learners.

In his strategic long-range planning and in his tactical daily planning of classroom activity, the teacher needs to have well in mind the concepts and generalizations derived from the structure of the pertinent disciplines. He needs also to choose contexts for study in which these concepts and generalizations will clearly apply. The chosen context should have the potential for relating to the student's personal experience. If the selected context is one with which the student is not acquainted, then ample concrete data must be made available. It should be an interesting context to explore, so that the child can transpose and extend ideas from his own situation.[17]

---

[17] Joseph Grannis from discussions with us regarding the social studies curriculum planning for the Harvard–Lexington Team Teaching Project at the Franklin School. See also Grannis, "Team Teaching and the Curriculum," in J. Shaplin and H. Olds (eds.), *Team Teaching* (New York: Harper & Row, 1964), Chap. 5.

Breakdown of a sample generalization into conceptual parts, subgeneralizations, and applications.

concepts ↓	man	animals	plants	life	need	water	scarcity
man	Maker of speech, tools, and art.	Navaho herd sheep, and goats.	Navaho grow corn.	Navaho life is relatively hard.	Navaho may have less food than is needed for survival.	Navaho save water by use of sweathouses.	Navaho separate households where water and grass are scarce.
animals	Man domesticates animals.	Life, movement, and feeling.	Sheep eat grass.	Sheep may die of hunger.	Sheep's wool protects from weather.	Navaho melt snow for sheep to drink in winter.	There is not much game to hunt in Navaho land.
plants	Man cultivates plants.	Animals depend on plants.	Life, not movement or feeling.	Plants living on Navaho land, are very different from those in Massachusettes.	Corn needs at least a 90-day growing season.	Absence of leaves on cactus slows loss of water.	Grass, cactus, etc. are thinner ground cover in Navaho land than in Massachusettes.
life	Man's life may be very hard or easy.	The life of animals is in continual danger.	Plants live by adjustment to environment.	Birth, growth, and death	The Navaho and the sheep have some needs in common.	In Navaho land there is little water life, few streams, etc.	Navaho regulate the use of scarce resources like grass and wood.

need	Man needs food, water, and shelter.	Animals need protection from weather extremes.	Some plants need a long growing season.	All living things function to fulfill basic needs.	For wellbeing, survival, and functioning.	Water is needed in making some wool products.	Navaho need fewer furnishings, etc. for their way of life.
water	Man needs water and conserves it.	Animals need water to drink.	Plants conserve water.	Much life occurs in bodies of water.	Water is needed in many simple and complex industries.	Snow, rain, ponds, river, etc.	There is only a little more rainfall on Navaho land than in the desert.
scarcity	Fewer men live where basic resources are scarce.	Where water and plant life are scarce, there are relatively few wild animals	There are fewer plants where water is scarce.	Man can increase the amount of life where resources are scarce.	Man acquires fewer needs where resources are scarce.	Water is scarce in some regions.	Not many, not plentiful.

MANKIND'S DEVELOPMENT: A FOCUS FOR STUDY An interesting social science curriculum plan for the grades has been prepared by Educational Services, Inc.,[18] under the guidance of Jerome Bruner, entitled "Man: A Course of Study."[19] The underlying thematic questions of the course are: What is human about human beings? How did they get that way? How can they be made more so?

The concept themes for the study are instinctual and social learning in animals and the five great humanizing forces: toolmaking, language, social organization, the management of man's prolonged childhood, and man's urge to explain his world.[20] These are studied in the contexts of salmon–herring gull life cycles, baboon troops, the Netsitik Eskimo and his life in land, camp, and on the sea ice.

The main pedagogical strategies are the juxtaposing of contrasting contexts to encourage classifying and categorizing processes; the stimulation and use of informed guessing, hypothesis making, and conjectural procedures; and the "use of games that incorporate the formal properties of the phenomenon for which the game is an analogue."

The master units include statements of the ideas to be developed, the contextual contrasts that will provoke queries, and devices that have the quality of puzzles. Highly artistic and dramatic film loops have been prepared of the contrasting situations with the intention of "asking questions and posing riddles." One unusual feature of the plan is the supplying of documentary videotapes showing teachers with groups of children working through the educational problems of the unit.[21]

ASSESSMENT Unique among many published curricula (both in text and in "packaged" forms of related readings, film strips, and manipulative materials), *Man—A Course of Study* has been evaluated quite extensively. The evaluation pattern is one that can be applied to assess the impact of substantive textbooks or teacher-made curricula if their aims are similar to those of this course. The evaluation was built upon implementation of the seven instrumental or pedagogical aims of the course and five questions about the implementation.[22] The aims and questions are prototypic of modern substantive curricula and can serve as a base for evaluating curricular programs that strive for the expansion of language and thinking in school.

---

[18] Renamed Education Development Center, Newton, Mass.

[19] Jerome Bruner, *Toward a Theory of Instruction* (Cambridge, Mass.: Harvard University Press, 1965), Chap. 4.

[20] Bruner, pp. 74, 75.

[21] Bruner, pp. 92, 98, 100.

[22] Education Development Center, *Man—A Course of Study: An Evaluation and Evaluation Strategies* (Cambridge, Mass.: Education Development Center, 1970); D. Whitla, J. Hanley, E. Moo, and A. Walter, evaluators.

The pedagogical aims are actually *process goals*:

(1) To initiate and develop in youngsters a process of question posing (the inquiry method); (2) To teach a research methodology where children can look for information to answer questions they have raised and use the framework developed in the course (e.g. the concept of life cycle) and apply it to new areas; (3) To help youngsters develop the ability to use a variety of first-hand sources as evidence from which to develop hypotheses and draw conclusions; (4) To conduct classroom discussions in which youngsters learn to listen to others as well as to express their own views; (5) To legitimitize the search; that is to give sanction and support to open-ended discussions where definitive answers to many questions are not found; (6) To encourage children to reflect on their own experiences; and (7) To create a new role for the teacher in which he becomes a resource rather than an authority.[23]

The evaluation questions deal with pupil gains in accurate knowledge on the specific topics and the ability to go beyond the knowledge and apply it. They also focus on any changes the teacher may have made in his teaching style and in what ways the course has impacted on youngsters of differing backgrounds and abilities. The mechanisms for gathering assessment data include child- and teacher-interview guides, classroom environment checklists, creative writing production and content questionnaires that pose situations similar to those studied. There was a good deal of evidence that many of the aims were being met. Questions were raised about the effectiveness and impact of some of the materials and methods that suggested alterations and alternatives for further implementation of the curriculum and for any redesigning. Adding strategies for values clarification was suggested.

A SEQUEL The next cycle on a spiral of increasingly sophisticated concepts in widening panoramas of mankind's activities as a modern human being was built around People and Technology.[24] This curriculum course for the upper grades and junior high school has three large sections following an introductory phase of observing, manipulating, and building various types of tools called "Tooling Up": (1) "Using Tools" with the whaling industry as the prototype; (2) "Acquiring Energy" with the building of the Volta River Dam in Ghana and its impact on people as the context; and (3) A community study to be developed locally around the technological systems that have impact there upon the people and the environment. The pedagogical aims are the same as those of the earlier course but the conceptual schema—point-of-view, assumptions, and specific substantive instructional goals are appropriately different. Some of the assumptions for youngsters and teachers to consider are as follows:

[23] *Man—A Course of Study*, p. 5.

[24] Peter Dow and Ruth MacDonald (directors), *People and Technology: A Course for the Middle Grades* (Cambridge, Mass.: Education Development Center, 1973).

Technology comes of people; it is part of his humanity. Within limits man can control technology, for he is its creator.

. . . Social and political forces determine its use.

Different people view technologies in different ways depending on their own needs and values.

Technological systems and social systems are closely interwoven; each affects the other. In working out that adjustment between systems, we must consider and be responsive to human and environmental needs.

. . . Change can be achieved through knowledge and understanding. . . . people can come to use technology in socially positive ways.[25]

The program includes many thought-provoking materials. In the whaling unit a fine original film of one of the last old whaling expeditions has been restored and diaries of persons involved in all aspects of the industry and its influences have been collected and edited for youngsters' study. A curriculum development team visiting in Ghana brought back taped interviews with all kinds of persons involved in the construction of the great dam or with its impact upon the life of the local communities and country as a whole. A popular and economical newsprint format is used for some of the materials that explicate concepts through comic strip and informational column devices.[26] One such piece is called, "What is Technology?" It is the kind of material that any teacher could devise and reproduce for explaining a key concept. Through straight-forward text with accompanying cartoons the curriculum designers explain the expanding concepts of tool, machine, tool systems and technologies, using simple examples such as knives, egg beaters, automobiles and the postal system. The local community phase is a new venture for national curriculum projects in that the units will be designed and used by local teachers with assistance and guidance of the national group of consultants.

The Future: A Focus for Study

Since the appearance of Alvin Toffler's provocative book *Future Shock*, many educators have stressed the need to prepare curricula with a *futuristic* orientation.[27] The argument for such programs emphasizes the need for education to keep pace with the tumultuous social, political and economic changes of the era of the technology revolution, not to mention the need for education to absorb the knowledge explosion by some means. Even edu-

---

[25] Dow and MacDonald, p. 7.

[26] "What is Technology," *Social Studies Program* (Cambridge, Mass.: Education Development Center, 1972).

[27] Alvin Toffler, *Future Shock* (New York: Random House, 1970). Also see Toffler (ed.), *Learning for Tomorrow* (New York: Vintage Books, 1974). For a discussion of socioeconomic, cultural, and psychological trends with implications for curriculum planning, see Harold Shane, *The Educational Significance of the Future* (Bloomington, Ind.: Phi Delta Kappa Educational Foundation, 1973).

cated people today can merely react to events as they pass by. They are not prepared to cope with them, much less mold them. Schools have until now educated children in the experience and knowledge of the past with reference to present human situations and predicaments. Preparation for the future, even though it is unpredictable, can be accomplished by educating youngsters to look for alternatives, consider them, and practice making judgments about them; such findings must be on a humane value system and upon as sound a prognostication of the future as can be seen through present trends and historical patterns of man's reactions to events. History can become a basic study for future living if it is used as a study of both man's actions in various described situations and the alternatives that might have been taken. Crises such as those in energy, political trust, and pollution can be studied in terms of their causes, the means to meet them, and alternative actions to avoid them in the future. Value decisions can be analyzed as to rationale and effects upon all segments of society and upon the environment. The automobile may or may not be a technological system of the future but study of that system's impact on the mores, economics, and value orientations of different cultures across the world and upon various environments can be valuable; such work can prepare youngsters to meet the impact of tomorrow's technological systems and to deal with them more intelligently than does the present generation. It is also possible that wiser decisions will be made as new conditions arise in the world and that people can learn to shape the forces released by fast-changing conditions. Curricula based on such themes require a reflective mode of study and an action form of instruction, with teachers and students learning together as they prepare to take actions that will, if only in small ways, have impact upon changing events.

Relating Curricula to Stages of Educational Development

Many of the British curriculum projects developed by the Schools Council in its extensive program of teacher-oriented curriculum development have been based on the stages of child thought and language development proposed by Piaget and his colleagues. At the least they offer suggested instructional activities that suit the various conceptual and thought-process stages of youngsters. Rooted in the belief that teachers make the ultimate decisions on their classroom curriculum, regardless of established texts, materials, or packaged plans, the Schools Council teacher-dominated Governing Board has set the general format for their projects in terms of curriculum guides for teachers.

The project teams are generally composed of experts in the particular fields of study, educational psychologists and evaluators, and a majority of classroom teachers. As they propose objectives and learning processes, they also suggest many tried and tested instructional activities for use with youngsters at various stages of educational development, and provide economical materials and resources and/or recommend ways for making suitable materials. Each program is served by an evaluator who makes certain from the beginning of the project that evaluation and assessment procedures are used and then made available to teachers. The resulting programs of many interrelated instruction units are disseminated through the local education authorities and the teachers' centers. School faculties with their "head" teacher, which are quite autonomous in Britain, may choose to adapt the program to their local setting or disregard it for another or for a program of their own. Sometimes interesting local curriculum programs are considered for national development by the Schools Council.[28] For example, faculties can develop their own set of work or activity cards and accompanying packages of reading and pictured materials. Teachers become the curriculum innovators in a real sense.

For the *Science 5/13* curriculum the Schools Council Project Team has developed over twenty units for teachers for the different levels of educational development.[29] A sample of the topics gives an idea of the range and imagination incorporated into these units; Mini-beasts, Working with Wood, Children and Plastics, Coloured Things, Science from Toys, Holes, Gaps, and Cavities, and so on. Also, for the teacher there are background publications such as *With Objectives in Mind, Evaluation and Science 5/15*, and *Investigations*.

FORMING OBJECTIVES A useful chart of objectives is developed by taking each broad aim that deals with an aspect of the scientific process and subsuming the appropriate learning objectives for each stage of thought development. For example, under the broad aim of "Posing questions and devising experiments or investigations to answer them," the following sample educational objectives are subsumed: For the *intuitive stage*, "Make comparisons in terms of one property or variable"; for the *stage of concrete operations*, "Select a suitable degree of approximation and work to it"; for the *abstract thinking stage*, "Visualize a hypothetical situation. . . . construct scale models for investigation."[30]

EVALUATION With objectives like these in mind evaluation strategies were developed that not only assess learner outcomes but also look at influences on the learning environment and on ways teachers perform. Some achievement testing was done in the form of film loops of an incomplete science manipulative demonstration with follow-up questions. Instrumented Teacher Style Preference Forms and Diagnostic Record Sheets of actual learner responses to materials were developed and used. Scheduled visitor

---

[28] Schools Council Publications, London, 165 Great Portland St., 1970.
[29] Len Ennever (director), *Science 5/13* (London: Macdonald Ltd., 1971–1973).
[30] Ennever, "Objectives in Mind," p. 78.

observations and interviews with teachers and learners were devised to check written data and add information to the evaluation system. Similar evaluation systems for assessing the impact of substantive and process-oriented curricula in the sciences and social sciences and for open-inquiry teaching have been developed by the Education Development Center, Education Testing Service and others.[31]

Teachers can adapt some of this evaluation methodology to aid them in assessing the effectiveness of their studies with children in terms of concept development and use of inquiry processes. Piaget-type interviewing of individuals or small groups of learners is an effective means for sampling the concept- and generalized learning of students who are trying to meet expressive objectives in a substantive curriculum area. The interviewer-teacher sets up a manipulatory situation with pertinent objects and asks the learner to do the task and explain what he is doing and why. For example, after instruction in the attraction capabilities of magnets the teacher can present the learner with a box of materials similar but not exactly the same as those used in instruction. The child is asked to hypothesize about the attraction and give reasons for it. He is then asked how he would set up an experiment to check his hunches.

Teacher-Made Curricula

Teachers working by themselves or preferably in teams can develop their own local curricula with some assistance from appropriate consultants along the lines of these prepared programs. One of the best ways to begin is to collect a cluster of children's books at various reading levels around a topic and build a long-range plan from the ideas developed in those books. For example, there is an attractive series on careers called *You Can Work*.[32] These and other books on the same topic could become the basic materials for a local career-education curriculum in the middle grades. There are many children's books available on the theme of "building your own thing." These books include many involving activities that teachers can adapt for instruction.[33] *Certainly one of the main professional roles of a teacher is the making of the curriculum; if the teacher is to be accountable with other school personnel for the accomplishments and achievement of learners, he needs to know how to build curricula and devise the operational plans to implement them.*

There is no single cycle of generalizations and concepts, nor one set of

[31] D. Whitla, J. Hanley, E. Moo, and A. Walter, *Man—A Course of Study: An Evaluation and Evaluation Strategies* (Cambridge, Mass.: Education Development Center, 1970). Edward Chittenden and Anne Bussis, *Analysis of An Approach to Open Education* (Princeton, N.J.: Education Testing Service, 1971).

[32] Betty Warner Deitz, *The You Can Work Books* (New York: John Day, 1970).

[33] An example: Forrest Wilson, *Build Your Own Moon Settlement* (New York: Pantheon Books, 1973).

thought-process goals, nor any particular contexts that would make the ideal curriculum in any of the content areas or in a combination of them. The *spiral-curriculum* concept depends on the imagination and ingenuity of the school, university faculties, and specialists assigned to the curriculum-making task. They can select viable themes and pre-think the ideation and suggest instructional strategies with materials. However, the teacher is the actual curriculum maker in the classroom, and he needs to be involved in the process mostly by learning how to adapt the curriculum to his situation.

Models for Curriculum Resource Studies

After the broad outlines of a curriculum, with its recommended instructional processes at various levels, have been sketched, sample resource studies in depth need to be made to guide the teacher in planning his own work with a particular group of students. Resource studies should be an aid to the teacher in developing ideation in relation to particular contexts. They should also suggest strategies of instruction and processes of investigation which might illuminate the ideas, and materials to be collected for use by the teacher and the students. The teacher, then, would set up his own *expressive objectives* (cognitive, lingual, symbolic, and affective) and *action objectives* (doings, manifested behaviors) for his pupils and plan his instructional tactics from there.

The following extracts come from a sample resource study prepared by a teacher.[34]

"CONSERVATION AND BALANCED USE OF NATURAL RESOURCES": A RESOURCE STUDY FOR THE MIDDLE GRADES

I. Frame of Reference: *Educational Goals*

In general, our schools try to give the child the habits, ideas, and techniques he needs to continue to educate himself to become a good citizen. As educators, we should endeavor to strike a healthy balance among three principal educational goals: intellectual development, self-development, and social responsibility in our students. They must acquire concern for public service and the common good of man. Conservation of natural resources is the responsibility of good citizens. The one hope for the future of our world and its natural resources lies in education. Youngsters can learn to discover conservation problems in their own environment and begin to recommend solutions based on findings in their own investigation.

II. The Themes: Scope in *Terms of Instructional Objectives*
Expressive Objectives

A. Realize that nature has been generous in providing man with an abundance of natural resources through search and reporting.

B. Appreciate the long, slow process by which our natural resources were formed through fact finding and drawing conclusions.

[34] Adapted from a study done by Norine Donaldson, Wayne State University, Detroit, Michigan.

C. Observe the laws of nature and man in balance. See the beauty and design of nature. Reflect these observations in speech, writing and/or other symbolic forms.

D. Observe, record and analyze man's dependency on natural resources and the impact of over-supply and under-supply on his life ways.

Action Objective

E. Act responsibly in the conservation of our natural resources. Demonstrate a concern for the general welfare and a respect for the laws that protect his own rights and the rights of others in the sharing of resources. Show concern and responsibility by actually acting as a conservationist each day.

III. Sample Ideation: *Thematic Development from the Natural and Social Science Disciplines*
Logical Generalization Clusters

A. Nature has provided man with an abundance of natural. resources depending on his livelihood needs at a certain time in history and his particular socio-cultural, economic, and political setting.

1. The earth is made up of water, land, and air masses that include matter, living things, and energy sources. It is part of a solar system of additional matter, forces, and energies, particularly solar energy.

2. Three quarters of the earth's surface is covered with water, a resource that can be used and reused.

3. The soil is the meeting place between the atmosphere above and the mineral products of the subsoil.

4. There are many kinds of ecological areas—woods, meadows, swamps, marshes, lakes, coastlands, deserts, mountains—that suggest a variety of living resources.

5. Man is one of his own very important resources for the labor of minds and hands for processing resources into products.

6. Resources are described by natural physiological means, but their discovery and use are dependent on who wants them, at what time, and with what means for securing them.

B. The process by which our natural resources are formed is a long, slow one.

1. Under normal circumstances physical and biological forces require a long time to make good soil; for example, topsoil measures only an average six inches, taking thirty generations to form only one inch.

2. Our best soils were built on the grasslands. Once native grasses have been exterminated in a region as a result of burning, plowing, or overgrazing, it takes a long time to re-establish them.

3. An individual species of plant or animal exists because of the operation of natural forces for millions of years. Man cannot make these species. Once a species is destroyed, it is improbable that it will ever again be evolved in nature.

4. Our mineral resources were formed during our geologic past taking eons of time. The deposits of mineral and nonmineral materials are not renewable. Once they have been used they are gone, except as they can be recycled from used products.

C. There is an orderliness and design in nature that gives it beauty and wonder.
   1. The sun's energy is converted in a plant. When a plant dies, it becomes humus. Soil with humus retains water, thus permitting the emergence of new life.
   2. Forests and grasslands are reservoirs of water and guardians of the soil. Forests in a distant locality may play an important part in the life of a region that is not wooded. Animals in a region are directly or indirectly dependent upon the plants.
   3. Man lives in a web of interrelationships and interdependencies with his environment.
D. The health, welfare, and happiness of a community is dependent upon the supply and quality of its natural resources.
   1. Many of the activities of people on the earth depend on where they live, how long many people have lived there, the climate, the kind of soil there is, the number of streams, the surface of the land, and what will grow on it.
   2. People who do not understand a new environment upset the ecological balance. Man has the power to destroy. Man has the power to create. Man sometimes upsets nature's balance and he must weigh the consequences.
   3. Some practices help prevent erosion; some reclaim or make better use of the land.
   4. Air pollution and water pollution have become a serious hazard in some communities.
   5. The world's population doubles once every 40 years. We have reached the stage of a population explosion.
   6. Resources have value only as they contribute to the welfare of man at a certain stage in his evolution.
E. Each of us has a responsibility to do our utmost for the conservation of our natural resources.
   1. Man cannot control the weather, but he can do his best to prevent its destructiveness and to make it work for him and his ends.
   2. Each person who has any land should learn the best ways of caring for it. Through the science of agriculture man can do much more about improving the soil than was formerly thought possible.
   3. As we become more urban, we tend to become less concerned with conservation.
   4. There is apathy of the general public toward conservation because we still have "lots of everything."
   5. High competition of companies in our free society affects conservation practices.
   6. It is man's task to use the natural processes and resources in such a way that he secures what he needs for a very high standard of living without jeopardizing the welfare of future generations.

IV. *Sample Concept and Value Descriptions*
   A. *Natural resources* are matter and energy sources found in the earth's land, sea, or atmosphere that can be connected through the application of technology and engineering to production for man's use and consumption.
   B. *Human resources* are worker potentialities for accomplishing the needed production. Workers include professionals, technologists, paraprofessionals, and skilled and unskilled laborers.

C. *Pollution* of the environment are the results of upsetting the natural balance in a given situation to the point where the side-effects of production or the use of a product mar the environment for human life functionally or aesthetically.

D. *Depletion* of the environment is the unalterable loss of a natural resource through an uneconomical process of production or a wasteful process of consumption.

E. *Conservation* of resources and energy is a process counter to over-productivity, which saves resources for the future, slows down technological recasting of nature, and preserves natural forms for aesthetic as well as practical reasons. Its practice depends on man's critical judgment regarding the consequences for production and for depletion or aesthetics.

V. *Some Idea Sequences for Teachers to Consider in Combination for Making Day-to-Day Plans*
Sample Logical Sequences: Interrelating Disciplined Ideas

1. The earth has a geologic history that goes back through billions of years. The earth is a store house of materials important to man's welfare. He should use these materials without wasting them.

2. The knowledge and methods man is accumulating in science has much to do with the use of resources. Since prehistoric times man has been discovering new and better ways to use such resources as water, soil, and forests. These ways have their benefits and drawbacks, depending on pollution side-effects.

3. Conservation differs with each resource from place to place, region to region, state to state, country to country, depending on human needs and environmental situations.

Sample Psychological Sequences: The Student's Point of View

1. Children miss swimming in a river or pond when it becomes polluted.

2. In our country there are many wonderful things that help us to have comfortable, happy lives. We should enjoy these things, but not waste them. We should try to leave some of these so others who live here later can have comfortable, happy lives, too.

Sample Contextual Sequences

The above sequences can be developed within such contexts as

1. Local lawns, gardens, and farmlands where there are signs of erosion and poor husbandry.

2. Water and air pollution situations, local and national.

3. The science of conservation: the water cycle, chemical change, etc.

4. Laws, proposals and institutions concerned with conservation problems and questions.

VI. *Suggested Sample Teaching Strategies Using the Contents of "Forests and Grasslands, Tree Farming, and Ranching"*
Forests and grasslands are reservoirs of water and guardians of the soil. Forests in a distant locality may play an important part in the life of a region that is not wooded. (Teachers would develop their own expressive and action objectives with appropriate instructional tactics to meet them based on these suggestions and others they might devise.)

A. *Perceiving Phase:* Confronting and heightening awareness

1. Visit a pasture lot or small meadow. Look for evidence of erosion —the heavier the covering of grass, the greater the protection. Is it covered with grass or weeds? Has it been overgrazed?

2. Visit some rolling topography with fairly steep surfaces that show little or no gully action because the owner has kept a good covering of grass.

3. Find a like topography with little or no covering. Visit it during a windy day; a rainy day. Compare amount and kind of runoff to grass-covered slopes. Compare cleanliness of air in both areas on a windy day.

4. If this is not possible, run water from a hose over two sloping surfaces—one with soil exposed, the other with a thick mat of grass covering to demonstrate the value of grass in the conservation of soil.

5. Also, direct a fan toward some bare dry earth, then over sod. Compare results.

6. Visit and study the steep slopes of a road cut, map the erosion patterns, and hypothesize causes.

B. *Ideating Phase:* Problem finding, building dialogue, and problem solving

1. Let children study and report on: the various aspects of agriculture and grazing in our plains states during the 1800s; causes of dissension between sheep herders and cattlemen; effects on the ecology of an area when ranchmen and farmers declared war on such predatory animals as wolves and coyotes and what did this mean for the grass.

2. Ask a farm agent or conservationist to speak on the conservation problems they deal with.

3. Visit a woodlot on a rainy day. Notice how the rain falling on a thick carpet of leaves and needles is more likely to soak into the ground than that falling on the barren earth where there is no vegetative covering. How does a canopy of leaves protect the soil from rain, sun, wind?

4. Study the nature of the litter on the forest floor. What is underneath? Observe that the decaying vegetation forms natural pockets for the storage of water.

5. Notice water in puddles on sidewalks, the playground. What happens to it when it disappears? Compare to the forest floor.

6. Collect pictures of grasslands and forests. Contrast with pictures of denuded areas. Categorize, discuss, and generalize.

7. Study the botany of trees. Discuss and exhibit some of the many products that come from trees. Read about tree-farming and selective cutting. Plan the operations for making a forest into a tree farm.

8. Read laws and proposals from conservation agencies. Discuss rationale.

C. *Presenting Phase:* Rehearsing, applying, and summarizing

1. Plant a tree and grass on bare spots in the schoolyard, explaining in an assembly the reasons for doing so.

2. Show a film like *The River* or the TV show "Grand Canyon" by Joseph Ward Krutch. Write and illustrate persuasive stories for propagandizing conservation practices.

3. Study a collection of pictures of the results of poor conservation and have children intuit stories of the causes and make recommendations for improving the situation.

4. Study fossil-fuel energy sources and the processes of extraction and production. Apply and adapt the generalizations found in the study of "forests and grasslands."

5. Develop and play a simulation game based on the conflict between

ranchers, farmers, miners, power plant owners, and naturalists in hypothetical situations in the Sierras, the Great Lakes, the Main coast, and near home.

VII. *Sample Bibliography*
- A. *For the Teacher*

  Allen, Shirley W. *Conserving Natural Resources.* McGraw-Hill, New York, 1955.

  Carson, Rachel. *Silent Spring.* Crest Books, New York, 1964.

  Colman, E. A. *Vegetation and Watershed Management.* Ronald Press, New York, 1953.

  Dale, Tom, and Carter, Vernon Gill. *Topsoil and Civilization.* University of Oklahoma Press, Norman, Okla., 1955.

  Lyons, Barrow. *Tomorrow's Birthright.* Funk and Wagnalls, New York, 1955.

  Meyer, H. Arthur et al. *Forest Management.* Ronald Press, New York, 1952.

  Rosen, Jacob, and Eastman, Max. *The Road to Abundance.* McGraw-Hill, New York, 1953.

  Thomas, William L., Jr., et al. (eds.) *Man's Role in Changing the Face of the Earth.* University of Chicago Press, Chicago, 1956.

  Wentworth, D. F. et al. *Pollution: Examining Your Environment.* Holt, Rinehart and Winston, Toronto, 1973.

- B. *For the Students*

  Adler, Irving and Ruth. *Tree Products,* John Day, New York, 1966.

  Bronson, Wilfrid Swancourt. *Freedom and Plenty: Ours to Save.* Harcourt Brace, New York, 1953.

  Dowdell, Dorothy and Joseph. *Tree Farms: Harvest for the Future.* Bobbs Merrill. New York, 1965.

  Moore, Alma. *The Friendly Forests.* Viking Press, New York, 1955.

  Muir, John. *The Yosemite.* Anchor Books, New York, 1962 (1912).

  Murphy, Robert. *The Pond,* Avon Books, New York, 1966.

  ————. *A Certain Island,* Avon Books, New York, 1968.

  The Sierra Club Wilderness Handbook, ed. by David Brower. Ballantine Books, New York, 1968.

  Wall, Gertrude W. *Gifts from the Forest.* Charles Scribner's Sons, New York, 1952.

  Booklets and pamphlets by the Forest Service, the Soil Conservation Service of the U.S. Dept. of Agriculture, Washington, D.C., and Sierra Club and Nature Conservancy.

- C. *Films*

  Arteries of Life. Encyclopedia Britannica.

  How Trees Help Us. Coronet.

  Seeds of Destruction. Encyclopedia Britannica.

  Yours Is the Land. Encyclopedia Britannica.

- D. *Filmstrips*

  Muddy Raindrops. Society for Visual Education.

  Soil. Jam Handy.

VIII. *Sample Process Goals for Investigation*
- A. *Inductive* reasoning by looking at eroded situations and inducing what may have happened.
- B. *Deductive* reasoning by taking the concept of tree farming and applying it to cattle raising in the grasslands.

C. *Classifying* trees according to their productive uses, *reclassifying* them according to their types in the natural evolution of forests.
D. *Hypothesizing* about the effects of water on a certain plant situation and *developing* a *research design* for *testing* the *hypothesis.*
E. *Value clarifying* through open discussion of situations dealing with such questions as the admissibility of using real or plastic Christmas trees.

IX. *Sample Competency Objectives: Expressive and Action Objectives and Assessment Means*
   A. *Expressive Objectives*
   Explain through writing and diagramming the evolution of a coal field. Create pictures in words, paint, and/or film of a forest fire, showing the effects upon the environment and people.
   B. *Action Objectives*
   Keep a journal record for two weeks of each time you do an act of conservation, i.e., turning off lights or water, keeping off grass, saving paper wood pulp for recycling, etc. Also keep a record of when any of your classmates demonstrates knowledge of conservation through his actions or fails to do so. Make conservation or anti-pollution signs to be used in a nearby park area.

A LITERARY APPROACH TO PLANNING A RESOURCE STUDY

Teachers have different ways of planning, depending upon their particular interests, inclinations, and capabilities. The following extract from a resource study for an urban-metropolitan setting is by a city English teacher and is written in his mode.[35]

"RACIAL, CLASS, AND CULTURAL HATREDS— THEIR IMPACT ON US": A RESOURCE STUDY FOR LATE ADOLESCENTS OR ADULTS

I. *Frame of Reference: Educational Concerns*
   Still believing, though passioned by a deep pessimism that man is cruel and selfish, I hope that the goodness inherent in man shall be a new life-force. That warmth is true and exists in the core they call men's souls. But knife-sharp in my hope is the real, where men on padded feet rip asunder the world with hate and hurt.
   A teacher must offer to students the possibility . . . that they are biased, that their dislike for other people is returned, and that others can help it no more than the student can.
   The student must be made to see that, far from loyalty to one's own group, prejudice is the insecure need to discard another human. Its form is the same: One must out-*wop*, out-*jew*, out-*limey*, out-*nigger*, out-*greaser*, out-*spic*. Racial hatreds are not confined to interrace, but exist more often intra-race or within the same, small, ethnic group. The conflicts in Nigeria, Ireland, Haiti, and Burundi are all examples.
   This bump in the night does more than raise the hackles. It wastes the talent and time of all men. It provides the ready rationale for a class/caste system, which destroys the incentive, morals, and values of all people touched.
   Teachers must provide an alternative—the realization that to exist with

[35] Adapted from a study done by Harry Woods, Wayne State University, Detroit, Michigan.

other people is to understand and peer into their differences. That the cry in the night is torn from the threats of all men.

II. *Ideational and Value Themes*
Logical Ideation: Man's Predicament

Man is prejudiced. He rides the toboggan of his own dreams. His worth is computed, programmed, and spindled, but only within his own eyes. Crying to be heard, he is Ellison's "The Beast Who Shouted Love at the Heart of the World"; he is Pandora's Box.

His prejudice dies and is re-born by word of mouth, turn of a phrase, black hand on a white knee, daughter stolen in the dark.

He is more than prejudiced. He widens the gap of similarity by casting mockery upon another's strangeness. Middle Eastern brothers threw rocket and mortar fire across the Sinai at each other. The Orange and Green of Ireland have been involved in the greatest butchering in Europe since 1945. The city becomes a great beast whose throes tear the very fabric of our lives. Nigerian, Biafran, and Yoruba have died by the tens of thousands in the hot jungles of the old Slave Coast. The disparity prompted by male chauvinism is world-wide and within all ethnic groups.

Yet the student is all and none of the whole. He has different rules and values. Why must he be his father?

Psychological Ideation: Where the Student Is Coming from

The student lives in a world that too is macrocosmic; its limits or pe-ripheries shift and wax, become static and wane. He is a pale imitation of adults. He is both Chesterton and Ralph Ellison's *Invisible Man*. He is shadow-stuff, spending as much energy in knowing himself as he must in the awakening of sex. . . .

The student is keenly aware of how he is treated by adults. He must stop talking on command as his teacher talks inanely or chats with the instructor from across the hall. He is not expected to have opinions, which, when offered, are ridiculed or tolerated. He watches his father drunkenly tell him not to drink. . . .

The student is aware of prejudice; it is barbed and has torn his flesh. Collectively, he has thrown and spewed the vaunt of who and what he is. Nudging aside his memory of young peoplism. He indiscriminately pigs and spits, niggers and turns his face ad nauseam, honkies, whiteys, and slaps palms. But he must be made to remember. . . .

He must recall the lies told in defense of his own, both silent and vocal. Because students must cast their dies together and are our hope, he must recall. The blind eeny-meeny-minny-moe path of his father is not his path. He must be more than man; he must be human.

Contextual Ideation: Life

Normally when men have joined together to create war whether it be actual or sports, a team relationship begins to unfold that embraces others who are different. Enlarge upon it, let students who are athletes lend credence. Use resource people who are cops, servicemen, fireman, travelers, who have worked with different teams of men to influence students.

Resource studies can be composed in a variety of formats, but they will not upgrade the intellectual component of classroom studies (units of work) unless their composers tackle the development of ideation in some disciplined form. Organizing ideation for teaching is a laborious task, but the rewards for doing it are high. *When teachers involve themselves in formulating resource studies, they advance their own learning and also gain intellectual excitement about what they will teach and how they will teach it.*

section 3

Devising Pedagogical Tactics: Pretests, Objectives, Discovery Activities, Learning Centers, Work Cards, Contracts, and Rehearsal

The teacher needs to organize his ideation ahead of classroom presentation through participating in curriculum development and through his own preplanning of resource study units. He then collects or prepares the materials for instruction: books, articles, pictures, filmstrips, films, maps, diagrams, informational scripts, simple bibliographies, guides, and manuals for groups and individual study and so on. However, once he meets a particular group of students, he must devise the tactics of instruction. Examples follow.

Concept Survey Tactic

First the teacher needs to take an immediate check on the level and character of his pupils' ideation about the subject of the study he has planned. He can pretest the class for their conceptual sophistication in the subject area by making some kind of a concept survey of the class. This can be done by paper-and-pencil tests or by individual and group interviews. The following example of a group interview is from a low fourth-grade situation.[36]

> This was done in preparation for a study of prejudice against a white minority. Contemporary life in one of the European countries from which many immigrants came to the United States was to be the context of the study. This immigrant group is making its way in the American system, but they still find prejudice against them.

Question: Where did the people come from who live in this country?
Children's Answers: People came from different countries, all over the world. Some from France, Italy, Germany, and lots of other places. Some people come from uncharted islands, from Italy, and most come from the East and the Indians lived here first.
Question: Where is Italy?
Children's Answers: It's in the United States. It's not in the United States, It's

---

[36] Haig Derderian, collected as part of a master's thesis, Wayne State University, Detroit, Michigan, 1967. Adapted version.

far from here. It's in the eastern part of our country. Part in Africa, from the other side of the world.

Question: Do the people who came to this country from another country live the same way here as they did in the old country?

Children's Answers: No, in the old country they might have a well, while here we have water faucets. No, because in the other place, women wear long dresses and there is no television, no cars; they use horses. I don't think so because I don't think any other countries have to make their own stuff but when they are here they buy the stuff. They don't have stores like we do, and when they come here they go shopping and buy things instead of making them. Their food is different than ours because we have many things in cans and they make theirs a different way. They wouldn't be used to our writing because they have different writing than ours. They have different money than ours.

Question: What kind of people are the Italians?

Children's Answers: People who like spicy foods and they dress in different costumes and they are not free. They like to do things old-fashioned. They don't like to be called "dagos" and they make good bread. Italians just wouldn't understand us because we do a lot of things that they don't, such as we eat different foods, dress differently, live in different kinds of houses. Sometimes they got different names. They have an Italian look on their faces, sorta dark faces. Most of them don't have automobiles, they have donkeys and carts and things like that, and cars are different. They like to eat spaghetti and pizza.

Question: Do they speak the same way as Americans who have been here a long time?

Children's Answers: No, because they have a real accent when they talk. If they just got here they wouldn't because they have to learn English. They could learn English and sometimes they talk Italian but not all the time. If they are together in a family they talk Italian when they get together.

Question: What kinds of jobs do they look for when they get here?

Children's Answers: A bakery. Fixing cars. It depends which job they want. Work for a steel company. Work in a pizza place. They work at restaurants, but they cook and serve.

With this kind of data on the students' preconceptions, the teacher is able to build his classroom plans for developing ideation, from where the students are in concept development rather than from where he vaguely thought they might be. He knows that he must correct some misconceptions and clarify vaguenesses before he can begin building the concepts and attitudes he has in mind.

Planning Instructional Tactics

The teacher needs to take one generalization or cluster of concepts and develop an operational plan of activities that will include a focusing of the ideation, teaching–learning objectives, contexts, materials, instructional tactics, and evaluation. Such plans will vary in format, style, and content, teacher by teacher, depending upon the resources and materials in the situation, the status of the learners, and the interests and knowledge of the teacher. Two examples are presented using different approaches and formats while dealing with the same essentials.

EXAMPLE OF AN OPERATIONAL PLAN FOR THE TEACHING OF THINKING AT HIGHER LEVELS THROUGH UNDERSTANDING PRINCIPLES OF LOGISTICS

I. *Ideation: Conceptual-Valuative Scheme*
   A. *Generalization:* Basic principles of logistics for exploration travel and settlement apply across the centuries to every expedition despite differences in mode of transportation and sophistication in technology. (Interdisciplinary: history, anthropology, biology, physics)
   B. *Concepts:* "Logistics" are guidelines for planning and executing an expedition that are drawn from consideration of interrelated factors such as time, space, environment, and the basic needs of food, water, and shelter.
      "Exploration" is a scientifically planned expedition both to verify postulates about unvisited places and to gather information that might alter the postulates or cause new ones to be developed (discovery).
   C. *Values:* Respect for scientific planning and analysis of results, admiration of the scientific explorer's courage considering risks taken to test hypotheses and for those who have to migrate.
   D. *Processes:* Fact clustering, generalizing, inferring, speculating, and applying.
   E. *Relevances:* Planning camping trips, summer vacation trips, families moving from southern rural areas to northern cities.

II. *Teaching-Learning Objectives*
    A. *Expressive Objectives*
       1. Students will compare and contrast the logistical problems of Columbus's voyage and Apollo moon landings.
       2. They will draw inferences about logistical principles from their comparing and contrasting statements.
       3. Using logistical principles they will analyze why certain items must be taken on the voyages.
       4. They will speculate on what items would have to be taken on a manned spaceflight to Mars, or on Columbus's voyage had he known how far India was.
       5. They will apply logistical generalizations to other situations like a camping trip or migrations.
    B. *Action Objectives*
       1. Students will prepare a chart of necessities to take on a moon trip, on the Santa Maria, and on a canoeing trip on the Mississippi.
       2. They will make up a version of the NASA game that forces small groups of role-playing astronauts to decide which items from a soft crash on the moon they will most need to take on a trip to locate their mother-ship 200 miles away. They will play the game with another group in the class and then play the game the other group made up.
       3. *Contexts:* Columbus's first voyage as reported by his son Fernando Columbus, and documents about the Pilgrim's first settlement.

The Apollo missions as recalled from TV accounts and from written magazine accounts.

4. *Materials:* Pictures of Columbus's ships, Apollo spacecrafts, the Mayflower load diagram, Lunar Module and Lem on the Moon, Pilgrim houses, Okies on the move in the 1930s. (References: E. B. Smith and Robert Meredith, *Quest of Columbus*, Little, Brown; F. Wilson, *Build Your Own Moon Settlement*, Pantheon Books.)

III. *Sample Teaching–Learning Tactics:*

Pretest and warm-up: Discuss the problem, "Suppose you were leaving tomorrow on a motorcycle camping trip across the Mojavi Desert. What would you need to take and why?"

A. *Opening:* Show contrasting pictures of Columbus II voyage and Apollo moon trips focusing on the Nina and the LEM. "What is similar, what different?"

B. *Developing:* (a) Read excerpts from the "mutiny" passages in *Quest of Columbus*, and discuss whether the crew or Columbus was right. (b) List reasons why the astronauts could not remain on the moon any longer than scheduled. (c) Correlate these two exercises and note likenesses and differences.

C. *Concluding:* (a) Draw generalizations from comparing and contrasting logistics of Columbus voyage with that of "moon walks." (b) Create a "We Were There" mock television show (on VTR), combining the Columbus and moon voyages.

D. *Management:* In the opening use a "picture sort" with small groups of five, then total group sharing. In "developing" (a) use pairs or triads with specific passages reproduced; (b) use other pairs or triads to "brainstorm" reasons; and (c) bring everyone together for reporting and correlation. In "concluding" (a) use a "what goes together" technique with lists of similar and differences taken from the small groups for each individual to do. In (b) small interest-groups will prepare the mock TV shows for VTR around the points they choose as important.

IV. *Evaluation*

A. *Competency Indicators for the Teacher*
1. Using different levels of questioning at appropriate places.
2. Listening to learner responses and developing them into expanding ideas or questions encouraging classifying, labeling, subsuming, and generalizing.
3. Engaging more than half of the group in the discussion to keep most of the group attentive.
4. Using materials and verbal examples that solicit contrasting and comparing argumentation.
5. Shifting to different contexts after exploring one; applying and re-constructing generalizations in new context.

B. *Competency Indicators for Learners*
1. Making contrasts and comparisons.
2. Posing their own questions for furthering the cross-cultural and cross-time study.
3. Stating examples from their own experiences.
4. Drawing some kinds of inferences from slightly different contexts.
5. Suggesting other contexts in which the same generalizations might apply.

C. *Possible Assessment Procedures and Situations Using Indicators*
   1. Piaget-type interview of small groups of learners using pictures similar in concepts but different in contexts from those used in the teaching-learning situations; i.e., a Rocky Mountain pack trip.
   2. Small group interviews with pictures about the Rha expeditions and ascents of Mt. Everest.
   3. Each student makes a list of items and amounts for a three-day back-packing trip in a wooded area he knows and can describe.

EXAMPLE OF AN ACTIVITY PLAN: COMMUNITY BUILDING ACTIVITY[37]

I. *General Purpose and Ideation*
   To assess the learner's concept of a community, note elements omitted, and provide initial information for expanding and clarifying the concept of community depending on age levels and experiential backgrounds of learners.
   A. *Definition:* "Community" is a sociocultural structure of interrelationships between individuals, families, and neighborhoods in a certain geophysical setting for mutual assistance toward survival and common welfare resulting in institutional formations, patterns of building structure, transportation, communication, and governance.
   B. *Generalization:* A functioning community is dependent upon a planned interplay of social and cultural forces that can provide shelter, food, protection, employment, commerce, transportation, communication, recreation, and spiritual uplift for all.

II. *Specific Objectives*
   1. Students will construct a model of a community using geoblocks, paper, and crayons.
   2. Students will identify and label elements essential for the community's successful operation.
   3. Children will observe, compare, and note differences between their community and the other models.
   4. Based on their observation of the other models, children will include in their model any essential items they have omitted.
   5. If different types of communities (rural, suburban, urban, industrial, residential, etc.) are represented by the models, the students will differentiate and label the types of communities.

III. *Assessment Procedures to Determine Readiness*
   1. Ask children to note the different kind of buildings found in their community and state their functions.
   2. Ask children to list on paper the essential elements for a community.
   3. Have the children demonstrate an ability to work cooperatively in groups?

IV. *Description of Activity*
   A. *Materials:* For each group of six to nine children, have available one box of geo-blocks or similar wooden blocks of various sizes and shapes, one six-foot sheet of butcher paper, crayons, and a yardstick.

[37] Adapted from mimeographed materials prepared by Richard Snell, Macomb Intermediate School District, Michigan.

B. *Procedure:* Each group of children is given materials and asked to construct a community. Upon completion of initial activity, each group inspects the other group's community and takes note of missing components that make the community less than self-contained.

In large groups, the components necessary to make a self-contained community are listed on the board. With this data, the teacher may then assess the children's concept of community.

V. *Description of Alternative Activities for the NonReady*
1. If children have not demonstrated an ability to work cooperatively in groups the teacher may:
   a. Provide the block/street outline for the community and ask children to place their building models on it individually or in groups of two or three.
   b. Design an activity with the specific purpose of developing cooperation skills.
2. For children who cannot read and/or write, the teacher might ask them to bring pictures from magazines that would illustrate the essential elements of a community.
3. Organize groups on the basis of teacher awareness of individual abilities. Do a task analysis of activity and organize a group so that;
   a. The group can successfully complete the task.
   b. There is some specific contribution for each member of the group.

VI. *Initial Evaluation*
1. *Group.* The community model was recognizable and contained provisions for: shelter, obtaining food and water, employment, transportation (accessability and mobility), police–fire protection, mailing, telephoning, recreation, commerce, and religion. (*Note:* Depending on the developmental level of the children, the provisions may be expanded. If the community model does not contain provisions for the "aha" experience, it is the teacher's responsibility to make available information through which the eight criteria can be developed.)
2. *Individual*
   a. Did each child contribute to the activity?
   b. Could each child identify the essential elements of the community?
3. *Activity*
   a. Did students indicate an interest in continuing activity through related activities or elaborations?
   b. Did students suggest any related/elaborative activities?

VII. *Suggested Related Activities*
1. The teacher may wish to make available material (pictures, books, magazines) for inquiry related to necessary components or a self-contained community that were noticeably lacking.
2. Children may be alerted to look in their community and elsewhere for items missing from their models.

VIII. *Questions and Statements for Inquiry*
How many people live in this community? How might we find out? This could be accomplished by assuming four people for each single unit dwelling. The number of people for each apartment complex could be estimated by counting four people for each single unit dwelling volume equivalent within the apartment house. This could be done by manipulating

either the blocks directly or by numeral manipulation depending on the instructional level of the children.

Where does this community get its water supply? Explain. Does this require additional buildings? If so, where would they be located?

How will a lighting system for the community be provided?

What form of government does your city have? What are the possibilities? Explain (orally or in writing).

If more people move to your city, where would they live? How is this determined?

What would have to be available before more people moved to your city? Can you make those provisions in your model?

If there is a river in your city, what problems might you encounter? Can you propose solutions to the problems?

How do you suppose your community looked in 1900? 1940? 1950? On what do you base your assumptions? Can you construct models representing these times?

Where is your community? What is the weather like?

Are there rich people and poor people in your community? Where do they live? Why?

What products are produced in your community? How does the industry get the materials it needs for production? How does the industry get its products out?

Is it necessary that each of your communities be self-contained? Should your communities be combined? Should your communities share facilities and services? Which ones?

When would the community build new schools? Where would they be located?

Can you draw a picture of one of the buildings as it would look from the top? Sides? Front? Could someone else build an identical building using your drawings as a model?

The Discovery Tactic

Once the teacher has made a judgment about the level and nature of his students' thinking and made some operational plans, he will then want to use a tactic that will encourage his students to discover new concepts and generalizations or to extend those they already know.

Appropriate variations of those processes used by the scholars in the related disciplines should be considered. Taba says the act of discovery occurs

at the point in the learner's efforts at which he gets hold of the organizing principle imbedded in any concrete instance, can see the relationship of facts before him, understands the why of the phenomenon, and can relate what he sees to his previous knowledge.[38]

Children will discover the concepts and the generalizations in the instances of the context by inductively deriving them from a series of instances or by

---

[38] Hilda Taba, "Learning by Discovery," mimeographed lecture (San Francisco, Calif.: San Francisco State College, 1961).

deductively making a hypothesis and looking for working examples of it. The specific procedures of the mother discipline can be employed when they are not too complex. For example, a fourth-grade class studying the mobility of families in their community devised a sociological kind of questionnaire and interview that the children used in house-to-house canvassing. They found the rate of families moving in and out of the community, the general class of employment of the father, and the reasons for the moves. From their data they generalized that theirs was a "bedroom" community that was transient as the fathers moved upward in job placement in national businesses.[39] The class made a film that showed the typical housing in the community and the method of their interviewing. The discoveries came as they put their data together and began to reflect upon the results.

Discoveries are made as students find clues while observing and manipulating particular materials placed in the environment by the teacher. The following excerpt from an account of Karplus's work in *The New York Times* demonstrates discovery tactics and quotes the language that the children used. This example highlights the significance of language in science discoveries.

In San Francisco, under a National Science Foundation grant, Karplus trains regular public school teachers to start a typical lesson by showing the class two drawings. The first, labeled "Before," shows a beaker half-full of colorless fluid, with a small cube resting at the bottom. Bubbles are rising from the cube. The second picture, labeled "After," shows the beaker, still half-filled with fluid, but minus the cube and bubbles. Question: What has happened?

The following responses were given by different children in one class:

Pupil: It's sugar. It's a sugar cube. A sugar cube breaks up in water.
Pupil: It's ice, and the ice melts in water.
Pupil: It's not ice. Ice would float at the top.
Pupil: It looks like sugar. It's a sugar cube because it is square.
Teacher: Could ice be square?
Pupil: Yes, but not all the time, so it's probably sugar.
Teacher: Will sugar float at the top?
 (The children say not, sugar will not float at the top, but they do not seem entirely ready to accept this idea.)
Pupil: It's a dice.
Pupil: No, dice doesn't melt!
Pupil: Somebody might have taken it out of the water.
Pupil: It's soap, because of the bubbles coming off.
Pupil: It's not soap, soap takes too long a time to dissolve, and anyhow it forms lots of bubbles and lather.
Pupil: I measured, the height of water in both is the same—about 16 inches.

The teacher writes down on the board all the things the class thought might be in the jar. The next day she places three jars of water before the children and has them try out each of the possibilities. One of the children who thought

[39] Lilja School, Natick, Massachusetts, 1960.

the object in the jar was ice obtains a piece from the school cafeteria for the experiment. Others bring a cube of sugar and a piece of soap. After observing and discussing the experiments, the class decides for sugar. Apparently the telling clue is the fact that the sugar cube in their own experiment gives off bubbles like those shown in the picture the day before.

The teacher could, of course, have given the children the relevant facts at the outset. Instead, thirty third-graders spent a considerable time observing, analyzing their observations and using them to defend or modify their conclusions.[40]

The discovery tactic is actually a holding tactic on the part of the teacher. He sets the stage for the discovery but refrains from demonstrating the discovery himself.

"Lifting of Thinking" Tactics

The chief instructional tactic for developing concept formation and generalizing in the Taba program is the *lifting of thinking* by moving learners from the level of information gathering and categorizing through explaining phenomena to generalizing about it.[41] The process is started by encouraging learners to develop categories and category clusters under differing themes through a process of comparing and contrasting in at least two different socioenvironmental situations. As an *opener* the teacher presents an open-ended question that leads youngsters to list and enumerate what they have observed or previously known through a process of differentiating one event or fact from another. For example, in a study of "wood products" the teacher might display a table, a breadboard, a block of fire-starter, a newspaper, a pressedwood block, charcoal, a toothbrush, an Indian woven basket, and a nylon stocking; he would then ask youngsters to submit their hunches on a slip of paper as to which objects are wood products and which are not and place them in a slotted box. These hunches would be tallied and presented to the class, leaving the disagreements unresolved at the moment. Then the teacher would ask the group to list on the board or on big sheets of paper everything they can think of regarding "wood." All responses are accepted.

Next, in a *development* part of the teacher's plan, the question of "what belongs together" is raised as learners group the items by identifying common properties and relationships. They categorize by finding and labeling superordinates and what belongs under what. In the "wood" example many categories might emerge to be labeled, such as soft woods, hard woods,

[40] Ronald Gross, *New York Times Magazine*, September 6, 1964, pp. 10–11. © 1964 by the New York Times Company. Reprinted by permission.

[41] Hilda Taba, *Teachers' Handbook for Elementary Social Studies* (Palo Alto, Calif.: Addison-Wesley, 1967). Ideas in the next several paragraphs summarize strategies developed more fully in the handbook.

wood processing, woodworking tools, old uses of wood, new uses, and so on.

Another part of the lifting of thinking strategy is the *interpretation of data*. Again a differentiating process is employed as students identify the main points of what they observed, collected, and categorized. The *differentiating* begins when items are found in two or three categories and the question why is asked. Then students have to debate rationale and make decisions about relabeling classes and then seeing what other items would fit in the new category. Some question would certainly arise in the wood episode about why wood was used differently in olden times. Why are some items that were made of wood in olden times or in other cultures not made of wood now? The question of why did these things happen is asked to encourage the relating of one point to another and raise the issue of *cause and effect* in an *explaining* activity. The mental processes of extrapolating and making implications help teachers and students make inferences that can then be developed into hypotheses to be tested, problems to be solved by asking the question: What might happen if _____? In the wood study the following problem question might emerge: What would happen if there were a great blight and most of the world's fir trees died?

The *concluding* stage is the application of principles by finding support for predictions and hypotheses, and finding causal links through asking the question, why do you think this would happen. An example of an application question about wood: Given the facts of the reforestation cycle of soft woods and hard woods and modern needs for wood, what would you advise legislators in heavily forested states to recommend for laws governing the exploitation of forests?

Finally there is a *verification* activity that asks the question: What would it take to make this proposition probably or generally true? Sufficient conditions would need to be found. For instance, is it generally true that all wood products burn at a certain degree of heat? The lifting of thinking is advanced mainly through asking the key questions at the crucial points in the study or picking up cues from the students that will advance the thinking. In a class discussion about forests and the use modern men make of wood products, a teacher tried to deepen the reiteration of numbers of wood products by posing the following question, "If you were cavemen and you lived in forestland, what good would the trees be to you?" The responses came quickly, "wood for fires, branches for lean-tos, sticks for digging," etc. Then the teacher asked, "Does that suggest anything that we use wood for today?" The comparisons were being made when one child interrupted, "but the caveman didn't have education," and a whole new level of thinking was generated that could take the group into the effects of formalized education on tool making and shelter construction, etc. New *inferences* could be made and tested and so the thinking process is continually expanded as it is lifted.

PICTURE-CARD SEQUENCES One of the most convenient tactics for initiating the lifting of thinking is the device of picture card sequences. Although there are commercial sets prepared around various topics such as urban life and rural life, pictures can be collected, pasted on index cards or larger pieces of cardboard, and laminated so that children may handle them as frequently as they would playing cards. Large pictures in portfolios can be used as the focus for small- and large-group discussions that "take off" from the interpretations of what various members see in the pictures. The discussions can lead to values clarification and to problem finding for social science studies. They can also be used for pre-testing conceptual levels about some topic. In any event, the pictures need to be provoking in the sense that they reveal incidents that have ambiguities in them which allow for raising questions and making inferences. For example in the picture series *People in Action*[42] there is a picture that shows three children on the steps of a public library in San Francisco. One of them is holding a torn book and they all look worried as they peer through the large library window at the reflection of a busy adult. All sorts of responses emerge if the teacher is accepting of everyone's comment about what is happening. A questioning sequence is advised following the encouragement of pupils and teacher to act out the situation. What do you think will happen now? Are there other ways to solve the problem? How would you decide? or What do you think would really happen? The teacher moves from soliciting facts to having the students suggest inferences and then make value judgments as they explore the incident together through role-playing and the sharing of feelings. Through such pictured episodes youngsters are provided opportunities to talk with a sympathetic adult, to share responses with their peers to universal problems, to explore alternative solutions, and to build better self-images. Racial and cultural differences can be faced and talked out. Substantive questions may also be treated. This library picture can lead learners into questions about the need for public institutions such as libraries and citizen responsibilities toward them. The library as a service institution can make a fascinating study.

Small picture-card sequences provide another approach to the lifting of thinking. They are sequenced in broad and then narrowing categories with an ambiguous, contrasting, or wild card thrown in here and there. For example, a curriculum consultant[43] developed several sets around the themes of "artifacts," "environments," and "animals." The artifacts sequence was subcategorized into art objects and manufactured products. They were all from different historical periods although some were from the same period.

---

[42] Fannie and George Shaftel, *People in Action: Roleplaying and Discussion Photographs for Elementary School Social Studies* (New York: Holt, Rinehart and Winston, 1970), Teachers Guide, p. 2.

[43] Richard Snell, Macomb Intermediate School District, Michigan.

Some interesting and useful cards were pictures of barbed wire that looked like modern objective art, of coins dated 1971, of a Victorian wind-up grandfather clock, and of a frieze of an Egyptian pharaoh's household at work. Already it is obvious how much interplay of ideas could be generated from involving youngsters with this set of picture-cards. They can be used in several ways, depending on the teacher's objectives, by posing different task questions. For example, the teacher can ask students to sequence them according to the oldest and the newest. Questions of why they place a card here or there inevitably result in important discussions that involve evidence and good or bad hunches. Another fruitful question to ask is, "Pick out those which have similarities." In one instance students picked all the artifacts that had wheels including wheels used as gears. The resultant discussion about gearing added insights for students and teacher. The gear is a beautiful tool extension of the wheel.

Picture-card sequences can be used in the opening confrontation stage of a learning episode, but it can be used as well in developing the dialogue of ideas such as investigating the invention of barbed wire and then deciding where it fits in an historical sequence. In some instances it could be used for testing a student's understanding of concepts. Can he file the artifact pictures in a historical sequence and give a rationale for doing so? Certainly that performance objective would help reveal a student's comprehension of generalizations about the evolution of tools, machines, and technological systems in history.

The Game Tactic To Encourage Dialogues in Ideas

The teacher's classroom tactics need to be in tune with the "knowing cycle," and they must support the general strategy planned in the curriculum recommendations. For example, the teacher is responsible for making sure that the concepts are clear. The fifth-grade theme in a social studies curriculum was "Man's attempts to cope with his world led to his ventures of the spirit." One of the contexts for this study was the travels of Marco Polo. An essential concept to be developed was "trade." One of the teachers found that her group of children were very vague about this term. They certainly had heard it, but they did not seem to be sufficiently aware of its ramifications. The following account describes one teacher's tactics for building meanings of the concept "trade."[44]

I asked myself first if the children had a basic understanding of "trade" as a concept. I felt that they did not, and upon questioning in class found that I was correct in my guess. Trading was something remote from their

[44] Ann Crile, "Trading as a Concept," mimeographed material, Wayne State University, Detroit, Michigan.

lives, something people did long ago. The trading of baseball cards was discussed but I saw in the conversation that no idea of the value of differing goods, of the problems of trade had occurred to any of them.

The next day, I brought a cardboard box to school and carefully kept it high so that the children could not see what it contained. I said that we were going to play a game and that this game, like any game, had rules that had to be followed. It was a trading game, and the first rule was that EVERYONE HAD TO TRADE THE GOODS HE RECEIVED ORIGINALLY FROM THE BOX NO MATTER HOW MUCH HE WANTED TO KEEP WHAT HE GOT. The purpose of this rule was to have each child get something else for what he had and in so doing to discover by himself some of the problems involved in trading.

The second rule was that everyone had to tell me one of the problems he ran into while trading. If his problem was a thoughtful, valid one then he would earn the right to keep his goods.

The cardboard box contained candy varied purposely in size, color, and value. Everyone had eight M and M's of different colors with the hope that some might prefer ones of all the same color and trade accordingly. Some had one or two chocolate squares, two had two-inch paper-covered chocolate Easter eggs, which, I felt, would be the most desired objects and of most value to the children. A few had Life Savers of different colors and three had lollipops. Of the thirteen children in the study group, everyone had at least three types of candy, each type being hopefully of a different value to each individual according to his preference.

I split the group in half. Those on the right side were to pretend they were from the Far East, those on the left that they were from Europe. Then they all were to pretend that they had just met in Constantinople and were trading their goods. The number-one rule, that everyone had to trade, and the number-two rule, that before the candy could be eaten a problem met while trading had to be presented to me, were repeated again. Then for five minutes everyone traded seriously, naturally, and eagerly.

They took their seats after five minutes and we spent the remaining part of the period discussing the problems they had met in trading. In only two cases were the problems entirely similar ones. Otherwise, although all the problems were similar to an extent, each had some variation. Their answers in brief were as follows:

1. *People may not like the goods you are selling; therefore you have a hard time getting rid of your goods and sometimes don't get as much for them as you feel they are worth.* This led into a discussion of the fact that when there was a demand for a certain product its prices went way up. The child who ran into this problem had wanted a chocolate egg and had found that all his goods were not enough to buy it. The chocolate eggs were a perfect example to prove this fact.

2. *Dirty goods are not as desirable as clean ones.* One boy with dirty hands had been holding his candy and it had begun to melt. He had a hard time selling his goods for this reason.

3. *The seller is disagreeable and won't reach an agreement that you are willing to go along with.*

4. *No one wants to buy your goods.* In this case the boy was not able to sell any of his goods. The class suggested the reason for this was perhaps the fact that he was not a good salesman. This led into the idea that a good salesman might sell goods for more than they were worth. We touched briefly here on the difficulty a salesman might have in persuading people to buy his goods and yet still be honest about their real value.

5. *Exchange of goods of different value: One thing is worth more than another so that perhaps you have to sell eight little things to get one big thing.* In this case the boy had traded eight M and M's and two chocolate squares for one chocolate Easter egg.

6. *The seller doesn't want to sell his goods.* One of the boys with a chocolate Easter egg didn't want to sell it and in the end in order to obey the rules had simply exchanged eggs with a boy who had the other one. This led into the idea that if you were a real trader what would you have gained by such a transaction? The children commented on the fact that you trade because you need things you don't have, and if you trade what you have for that same thing then you have gained nothing and there is no point of trading.

7. *If a seller has poor quality goods then you don't want to buy.* Someone felt that because the other person's lollipop was broken it wasn't good. This brought up the idea of whether that person should have sold his lollipop for less or not. It was decided in the case of the lollipop that the value of it had not really been changed by the crack.

8. *Some people put different value than others on different goods.* This question of the problems connected with the value seemed to make the biggest impression on the group as a whole. One boy loved the cinnamon Life Savers and was willing to trade two chocolate squares for one Life Saver. He ended up with just Life Savers. Someone suggested that if certain goods are not highly valued (the M and M's because they were so common) then their price goes down, and if they are valued their price is high. The idea that value is relative to the goods and to the need for the goods was clearly established by the experience almost each one of them had had in his trading.

9. *When goods are wrapped up then you don't know what is inside.* The fact that you could cheat and put something different inside your goods than what you said was in them was raised because one boy in selling his chocolate was selling half a square as a whole square. If we had had more time this could have led to a discussion of our contents inspection laws today.

10. *How can you decide what the equal worth of different types of goods is?* After quite a lengthy discussion the children decided this was a question of judgment between seller and buyer. Most of them had trouble in pricing their goods and all gained a real appreciation of the difficulty in putting a set price to one's goods. Whether three M and M's were worth one Life Saver or two they finally discovered varied with the value the seller or buyer put on his goods.

After all the problems had been presented, and while the children were eating their candy, we transferred the problems they had met to ones that traders in Constaninople might have met, too. They all felt that the same problem of the differing values of different goods would be the main difficulty. Dirty goods, poor salesmanship, not knowing what was inside wrapped-up goods, disagreeable seller, all the categories seemed to hold.

The game tactic is only one of many that teachers can use to clarify concepts and generate reasoning. Modified forms of "twenty questions" can be used for practice in categorizing. Detective games can be arranged by placing clues in a classroom environment in such a way that a search is begun. One teacher set up a mock camping site in his classroom that included clues as to how some campers might have upset nature's cycles by leaving the site somewhat despoiled. Another teacher took his class to an old cellar hole to make some guesses about how the people had lived from assessing the artifacts they found in and near the cellar. Many imaginative simulation games have been commercially prepared. However, they are particularly effective when the teacher and groups of students develop their own games to be played by fellow students. Games that veer too far away from life situations may replace intrinsic concept reinforcement with an extrinsic goal of winning.

Independent Learning Tactics: Learning Centers, Work Cards, Job Sheets, Contracts, and Programmed Instruction

The teacher who wishes to move into open-inquiry education needs to develop over several years a system of independent study tactics for individual learners, pairs, and triads of learners. The open-inquiry programs with their self-selecting and self-directing study formats can only be held together by strands of focused and thematic learning that students can tie into at various levels and interest points; otherwise the student is left to a chaotic situation of whim only. In that case it would be best to let the youngster fend for himself outside of a school without its resources and the guidance of a knowledgeable and sympathetic teacher. Since the economy would not bear the expense of a one-to-one tutorial system in public school, a plan of instruction needs to be devised whereby students can work as independently as possible, learning from cleverly arranged materials for self-teaching, from each other through peer interaction, and from teacher guidance at the most crucial point of a learning episode.

A methodology and classroom management structure base were evolved for fostering open-inquiry education as an outgrowth of experimental teaching in several areas: the curriculum reform projects of the sixties, the team-teaching and programmed-instruction experiments, and British efforts to accomplish an "integrated day" in the primary school program.

There are two approaches based upon two different psychological motivation theories: (1) behavior modification using an immediate reward system through an *operant conditioning* process (B. F. Skinner); and (2) intrinsic motivation through self-discovery of meaning, based on an intrinsic human desire to explore and become competent in one's world. The latter approach is in tune with a psychobiological process of thought–feeling–value generation through the process of "assimilation" and "accommodation" (J. Piaget and R. White). Teachers can draw upon both of these approaches for organizing independent and self-directed study.

PROGRAMMED INSTRUCTION Much skill learning and practice can be accomplished through the programmed-instruction approach. Acquisition of the number facts, certain simple concepts and computational skills in mathematics, and the basic facts needed for conceptualizing and generalizing in the sciences or social sciences can be programmed; this permits each student to proceed through a set of exercises at his own rate while checking his own progress. The teacher may intervene at points for diagnosing when the student needs additional information or encouragement not offered by the program, and at various "terminal performance" assessment periods in the program. There are highly sophisticated programs that use the assistance of the computer to help in record keeping and pointing out where diagnosis and prescription are needed in an individual's learning profile. Teachers can develop their own local varieties of programmed instruction provided they adhere to the basic format of stating performance objectives, devising a pretest, entry activities, step-by-step exercises with immediate feedback between steps, and "terminal performance" tests.

LEARNING CENTERS Open-inquiry education is best advanced through the learning center with its packages or collections of materials and resources, and accompanying work or activity cards for short learning episodes, and job sheets for longer-ranged study. Learning centers focusing on science, social studies, language arts, literature and reading, mathematics, and the arts may be organized in corners of a classroom or located in different classrooms or in clustered areas of a building (mini-schools at the primary and middle grades levels) or in sections of a large school *resource center*. In any event they need to have the materials conveniently available that are needed for studying a focused theme and/or set of skills. They also need the related mechanisms of work cards and/or job sheets for guiding learning activities. These work cards and/or job sheets must suggest manageable tasks, be clear in direction, and foster an inquiry approach.

Work cards and *job sheet contracts* concentrate on guiding students through learning tasks that have focus and contribute to extending and enriching a learner's concept–value scheme and related skills. They need to include not only the search tasks usually posed by inquiry questions and the materials needed, but also methods for recording results and sharing them with others. A summarizing activity that can be evaluated for conceptual understanding and skill attainment needs to be included. Sometimes the cards can refer to familiar and easily accessible materials and resources such as in the commercially boxed ECO-LAB,[45] which has sets of thematically interrelated activity cards about urban and rural environments. When there are several tasks involved and the activities can extend over several days or weeks the job sheet contract is a convenient device. A study card or job sheet in a suburban school setting might read as follows:

Confronting and Gathering Data: (1) Accompany your parents to your neighborhood shopping center. (2) Draw a map in scale of the center, including

[45] J. L. Johnson and J. Mann (eds.), *ECO-LAB: A Study of Rural and Urban Environments* (Toronto: Learning Concepts, 1971). For further information on setting up learning centers see Thomas Davidson et al., *Learning Centers: An Integrated Approach* (Pacific Palisades, Calif.: Goodyear Publishing Co., 1975).

each store, its approximate size, the parking areas, the walking areas, and the delivery areas. (3) List for each store the categories of products it sells. (4) Look at a film-strip of a country store in a small town at the turn of the century (prepared by the teacher from photos taken at a historical reconstruction site). (5) List the products it sold and diagram their placement in the store. *Inferring and hypothesizing:* (1) Share your data with a classmate who has collected similar data. (2) Ask yourselves the questions: What are the similarities and differences between the shopping center and the country store? What are the reasons for the differences and similarities? *Problem finding:* (1) Together write down a question or two that you would like to investigate. (2) List the materials, resources, and techniques you need to get at answers. (3) Choose the question for investigation that you could accomplish in school and/or in the neighborhood in a reasonable length of time. *Problem solving:* (1) Write down an hour-by-hour and day-by-day plan and schedule of work; discuss this with the teacher and get approval to go ahead. (2) Do your investigation and gather new data. *Summarizing and Reporting:* (1) Put your findings together into charts, graphs, pictures, and story form. (2) Prepare a presentation to other members of the class. *Evaluating:* Write in your own study record book a summary of what you learned and what questions you did not answer and would like to investigate later on. (The teacher uses the report and the account in the study record book as bases for assessing the learning gains from the accomplishment of the activity card. The materials prepared by the students and the study record book are available for parents to see on visiting day.)

Briefer work cards can be devised for less elaborate activities for shorter time blocks and for younger children. For example the teacher can prepare a packet in a see-through bag or container so that youngsters can locate easily materials, which will include a metric ruler, simple fulcrum made of a small triangular block of wood, and three pennies. The work card would include the following: (1) Find as many ways as you can for balancing the ruler on the triangular block with the pennies on top of it. (2) Draw little pictures of the ways you tried. (3) Explain to a classmate in talk or in writing why you think it balanced each time when it did. Another independent work aid for student and teacher is the *retrieval chart*, in which together they list the references in texts, trade books, filmstrips, and so on, for discussions of certain key concepts.

The structure that holds together an open-inquiry classroom is composed of such pedagogical mechanisms, which allow students to accomplish their learning goals somewhat independently of each other. These devices absorb the attention of the youngsters and set the pattern for their concentrated learning activity. This approach is not "free school" but an orderly educational program that involves students in more self-selected and directed learning activity than is possible in conventionally organized classrooms. Success in these endeavors depends largely on the ingenuity, imagination, and thoroughness of the teacher's preplanned independent instruction devices and routines. When this system works, the teacher is freed to become an adult learner along with his students as well as a true guide for helping them advance their learning.

The Rehearsing Tactic: A Means
for Summarizing and Assessing Ideational Gains

Child conceptions that are confused, too narrow, or disparate can become better delineated and then reinforced through the classroom procedure of *rehearsal*.[46] This is a means for presenting to children the opportunity to use and redefine a concept in a context that is different from the one in which the concept was initially developed but that is similar enough to reveal pertinence.

Both Taba and Grannis recommend strategies very like "rehearsal" in their experimental programs for developing concepts in the social sciences. Taba suggests that after "confronting" children with a social situation that causes "bafflement" and that in turn encourages "discovery" of the underlying concept, the teacher can "rotate" from this inductive process to a deductive procedure. In the deductive phase the child is "confronted" with a comparable situation in which he is expected to apply the concept previously discovered.[47] Concepts are rehearsed as different settings are introduced. Grannis, in his curriculum planning, built a cyclical series of social contexts in which an expanding cluster of interrelated concepts and generalizations are developed in complexity over time as children study in each new context. Previously learned concepts are rehearsed while extensions and modifications of them are developed.[48]

Frank suggests that more use should be made in the classroom of miniature toys such as plastic models of farms or frontier towns to give the children the opportunity to rehearse or play out the concepts they have been gaining about farming or life on the frontier. He refers to this learning activity as analogical operations.[49] The toys in combination become analogues of life-situations. This type of learning is in contrast with digital operations, which deal with discrete logical steps as seen in arithmetical computation. The analogue is something felt, seen, or heard in its whole and is applicable at all age-levels of learning. It is a model toy, a picture, a film, a sculpture, a play, or it can be a model of atomic structure or a diagram of mathematical combinations. The learner can manipulate it, or see it over and over again, or dramatize with it.

The analogical operation is a means for rehearsing concepts. Language is integral to the manipulation rehearsal. The learner talks about it while

---

[46] Lawrence K. Frank, *The School As Agent for Cultural Renewal* (Cambridge, Mass.: Harvard University Press, 1960). The concept of "rehearsal" is an essential part of the argument of this lecture.

[47] Hilda Taba, mimeographed lectures, San Francisco State College, San Francisco, Calif., 1962.

[48] Joseph Grannis, "The Framework of the Social Studies Curriculum," *The National Elementary Principal* (Washington, D.C.: Department of Elementary School Principals, National Education Association, April 1963), pp. 20–26.

[49] Frank, pp. 31–37.

he is doing it. The conceptions are repeated, re-formed, and encoded in language during a rehearsal operation. Communication is set up between classmates as they play out their conceptions with toys or other analogues. The language is repeated and restated as the teacher plans for a "calculated redundancy"[50] that will insure that various pupils with differing views and abilities will build the conception as different approaches develop through the natural expansiveness of children's play.

Since Froebel discovered the learning potential in children's play, educators have known that the chief mode of children's learning is play. Yet how rarely is this essential instrument for children's cognitive development used beyond the kindergarten program? Older boys to the age of at least 12 continue to play with miniature toys of all kinds, from toy spacemen to electric trains, while girls continue to furnish their dollhouses into pre-adolescence. The play world is the real world of childhood, and it should be tapped for educational purposes in the school setting without robbing children of the spontaneity of out-of-school play that is so essential to their psychic and cognitive development. Modern plastic manufacturing could make cheaply any kind of miniature toy that the teacher could use.

Play episodes can be the contexts for concept rehearsal when the teacher accepts play as a learning situation. Sand table models, miniature diaramas of historical or social events, or small-scale constructions of buildings can serve as the instruments of rehearsal if the children are allowed to talk as they play. Puppet plays, creative dramatics, and role playing can also serve the purpose of concept rehearsal when the teacher sets the stage and the limits but leaves the children to play out the substance of the event.

At upper school-levels *simulation games* serve as an excellent means for rehearsal. A commonly used one is a mock international situation involving several small countries that have special environmental and socio-economic problems creating shortages and/or over-production of certain materials and goods. The game is played by setting up delegations from each country who must work out the conflicts caused by the disparities. The delegations receive message cards from time to time about changing political situations, and, while trying to keep peace, they must decide what their spokesmen will say at the international confrontation meetings. Other kinds of simulation games, about response to polluting factors in a community or to changing real-estate patterns, can be patterned after the commercial game *Monopoly*. However, in any educational game the enlightening discussion while playing is more important than the winning.

Rehearsing can serve as a clarifying process because concepts of one child are tested against those of other children and against knowledge from the disciplines as presented by the teacher. The process of trying out the idea by writing it down is another form of rehearsing concepts that aids

---

[50] Frank, p. 25.

clarification. To think out loud on paper or on a typewriter is a playful act, especially when the author–pupil starts developing a story that becomes a variation on the original context. New life is fused into conceptions as they are put to work by being rehearsed in changing contexts and situations.

Matching educative strategies and teaching tactics to the children's "knowing cycle" and their individual patterns of coming to know is the greatest challenge to the educator who makes curricula and to the teacher who devises instructional plans. Thus can education become knowing.

section 4

Utilizing Language Strategies: Soliciting and Structuring, Managing and Evaluating, Questioning and Explaining

Bellack, in his investigations of classroom teaching, found it convenient to view teaching and learning as episodes of "language games" between the teacher and his pupils.

In his [Wittgenstein's] view, "The speaking of language is part of an activity, or of a form of life. . . ." Wittgenstein referred to these activities as "language games," a metaphor used to point up the fact that linguistic activities assume different forms and structures according to the functions they come to serve in different contexts . . . learning the language rules that govern the use of words in these activities [is necessary for] successful communication.

Language of Soliciting and Structuring

The teacher's questions and comments about events presented to students tend to *solicit* from the children certain kinds of responses or replies, and particular language forms are expected and used.[51] If the teacher is searching for propositions, he will formulate his comments in such a way as to *solicit* a hypothetical statement from the students. The teacher will ask, "What do you think is happening here and how could we be sure?" And the students will make reasonable guesses in the form of conditional statements.

The *structuring* strategy is used when the teacher is organizing his pupils' work for a period of time in relation to accomplishing tasks. The teacher might say, "This morning we are going to take out our arithmetic books and do the review examples of subtracting numbers having zeros in them." The students would react dutifully by opening to the page, but one might ask, "Do we have to do all of them?" Instead, the teacher might place the burden of *structuring* on the students by saying, "Some of you

[51] Arno Bellack and J. Davitz, *The Language of the Classroom,* U.S. Office of Education Cooperative Research Project No. 1497, Washington, D.C., 1963, pp. 4–9.

had trouble with the handling of zero in subtraction yesterday. What might be our plan for today in attacking this problem?" Such various language games invoke different cognitive patterns. The quality of the classroom discourse is lifted when the teacher's soliciting and structuring abilities are such that they provoke independent thinking and study planning on the part of children.

The following example is taken from a discussion in a first-grade class that was studying animal fur as insulation. It shows the teacher soliciting responses and structuring the situation with the intent of having the children plan their own structure of investigation.

> A caged hamster had been brought into the room. It was being handed around as the teacher asked for observations. The children noted that he was furry and when asked if he felt warm, they all agreed.

> **Teacher** (*Soliciting*): I'll ask you another question. How many think that hamsters would feel warm in winter when it is cold?
> **Pupil** (*Responding*): Just like a cat doesn't [feel cold]. Some things are furry so that when they go out in the cold they don't feel cold.
> **Teacher** (*Structuring*): I am going to get you something. (*She brings over a picnic cooler with ice cubes in it. The children show excitement.*)
> **Pupils** (*Reacting*): An animal in there! On ice? Must be.
> **Teacher** (*Soliciting and Structuring*): One thing is whether a hamster would be warm or cold when outside in the winter. In the box we have something to help us find out.
> **Pupils** (*Reacting*): I didn't see. Ice. Ice cold. Ice cubes. I knew it was ice.
> **Teacher** (*Structuring*): The hamster, when not in a room, lives where it is cold. When he goes outside, what does he do, how does he feel? How can we find out?
> **Pupil** (*Structuring*): We could put him in the box of ice.[52]

Imaginative soliciting and clever structuring of the situation that foster causal, relational, and hypothetical thinking from students are the teaching strategies that Taba calls "lifting" the level of cognitive activity among the pupils.[53]

Language of Managing and Evaluating Pupil Performance

Marie Hughes's[54] studies have highlighted the importance of language in all aspects of teaching. Even giving directions and admonishing children in management of the classroom can be either destructive or constructive,

---

[52] From protocols gathered at the Summer School Elementary Science Study, Summer 1963.

[53] Hilda Taba, *Thinking in Elementary School Children,* U.S. Office of Education Cooperative Research Project No. 1574, 1964.

[54] Marie Hughes, "What Teachers Do and the Way They Do It," *NEA Journal* (September 1964), pp. 11–13. Her studies of teaching reported in various journals are revealing as to the kinds of language used in classrooms.

depending on the language used. Children were found to respond negatively to the little language subterfuges the teachers often use to keep children in line. Typical are "Look how nicely Johnny is working this morning" or "Let's remember that we are all going to behave like the grown-up second-graders that we are when we go to assembly." These directional admonishments either set one child against others or suggest that children are not going to meet the standard. The language of directions should be direct; that of admonishments should be straightforward.

The language a teacher uses to evaluate children's work has an effect upon their attitude toward study. The offhand statement of mild praise does not have the educational effect of a thoughtful comment about a child's work that includes an assessment of strengths and weaknesses to be improved in terms of a problem to be faced. Instead of "That's nice, Jimmy," the teacher should say, "I like your ideas here but they seem a little repetitious. Can you think of some way of saying them so that all your sentences don't start in the same way?" Admonitions that make a student look foolish and deter him from exploring alternatives should be avoided.[55]

The crowning result of invoking artful language strategy in the classroom is the releasing of students to become their own problem solvers, "self-sufficient learners." The goal is to have students "participate in the process that makes possible the establishment of knowledge. Knowing is a process not a product."[56]

Questioning in Teaching[57]

The most common language strategy used by teachers in the classroom is questioning. Unfortunately, the type of question most frequently used is one that simply requires either a "yes" or "no" answer or the response of one word or a single fact. Teachers need to consider a wider range of interrogation strategies.

Questioning has been considered a method of teaching since Socrates asked, "What is good?" The recitation format with a question followed by a memorized response is as old as ritualistic teachings like the catechism. The two main conventions of instructional interrogation are based on the logic-

---

[55] Jerome Bruner, "Needed: A Theory of Instruction," *Educational Leadership* (May 1963), p. 526.

[56] Jerome Bruner, "Some Theories on Instruction Illustrated with Reference to Mathematics," *Theories of Learning and Instruction,* NSSE Yearbook 63 (Chicago: University of Chicago Press, 1964), pp. 319, 335.

[57] This section was written in collaboration with Lawrence Gagnon. Reference: A. Lawrence Gagnon, "An Analysis of an Experimental Methodology in Teaching Thinking and Clarifying Values," unpublished doctoral dissertation, Wayne State University, Detroit, Michigan, 1965.

probing strategy of the Socratic dialogue and on the fact-questing format of the recitation. To these two ancient customs of instruction, a third has been added in modern times—the nondirective question developed in psychotherapy for encouraging free-associative thinking. From these older interlocutory conventions, the modern educator has devised three kinds of strategies for instructional questioning, which, when placed in artful interplay, will foster divergent or open-ended thinking when appropriate and will encourage convergent or step-by-step thinking when that is advantageous. In these ways the teacher can stimulate and direct the "mental play" of the classroom.

to call up the correct response to the previous question and to extend it one
    PROGRAMMED QUESTIONING When the recitation format is scientifically organized by experts using the best knowledge of psychological operant conditioning, programmed instruction is the result. By adapting the basic tenets for "programming" to the particular classroom setting, teachers can devise written programs or oral-questioning strategies to accomplish the logical development of interrelated factual material into generalizations. Published programs can be used judiciously in developing a particular sequence of ideas. In each step, the questions are framed in such a way as step further. Reinforcement is gained when the student uses the previously learned response to answer the question. Typically, programmed questions are of the variety that state a "given" or a condition and that then request response by filling in a missing key word or by answering with "yes" or "no." The questions are phrased for "eliciting desirable responses"[58] and in turn "reinforcing" the desired response by giving the student a sense of having successfully learned an item that will assist him in learning the next one.
    The questioner must select only the items that are most pertinent and that are necessary for understanding what is to follow. "Programmed" questioning should be efficient, because the instances raised in questions are carefully selected for their pertinence to a developing concept or generalization. The program of questions will be in small sequential steps, each carrying a cue that will suggest the correct answer.[59] Programmed questioning is most suited to structured presentations such as in demonstration teaching when one element of a science phenomenon is shown at a time, and questions are asked following the addition of each new element. A good workbook or laboratory manual could use this kind of questioning.

> Fill a beaker with water, and place an elastic band around the side at the top of the water. Drop a large cork into the water. Does the water rise or stay at the same level?

[58] Lauren Resnick, "Programmed Instruction and the Teaching of Complex Intellectual Skills," *Harvard Educational Review, 33*, No. 4 (Fall 1963), pp. 441–442.
    [59] J. W. Brown, R. Lewis, and F. Harcleroad, "Programmed Instruction," *A. V. Instruction: Materials and Methods*, 2d ed., (New York: McGraw-Hill, 1965), Chap. 11, p. 251.

"It rises a little."

Take the cork out and drop in a piece of plasticine of the same shape and size. How high does the water rise now?

"It rises a lot further than with the cork, and the plasticine sinks to the bottom."

Why does the cork float and the plasticine sink?

This questioning strategy is generally one of narrowing the field, limiting the factors, and moving in on one aspect of a phenomenon at a time: If we stop thinking about that but look just at this, what do we see, what can we find? What happened just at that point? How would you describe only the one event? Now given this event and that event, what do they mean exactly when put together?

Step-by-step questioning is useful only so long as there is no room for speculation and when informational data have to be organized into workable clusters. For example, a student cannot speculate about the causes of the Revolutionary War until he has some grasp of the continuity of events leading to it and of how one developed from the other. Programmed questioning can assist him in organizing his data, but for the tasks of conceptualizing, generalizing, and intuiting from these data, the teacher will need to use another strategy of questioning called inquiry. *This is not to say that programmed questioning, which assists convergent thinking, is any less important than questions of inquiry, which foster the divergent aspects of thinking. In teaching, both strategies need to be used to provide the interplay of investigation and data processing.*

INQUISITIVE QUESTIONING As described by the philosopher James Jordon, the Socratic dialogue is not a method of teaching but is one of inquiry. Students and teachers become involved in a search for truth. The teacher is a co-inquirer with the student.[60] Jordon points out that the Socratic method is used only with adults who can draw upon substantial experience for deliberation, and, therefore, concludes that it is not a method appropriate for teaching children. Even though a pure form of Socratic method cannot be used with children, the spirit of inquiry in search of truth need not await fostering until adulthood. Children can inquire at their own level and can find reason and purpose within the limits of their capabilities. The teacher's questions should serve as a catalyst for the inquiring process among the students. He should also contribute his experience to the discussion when that seems appropriate.

[Socratic method] is a method of inquiry in which one seeks to determine what the true nature of things is. The object of the inquiry is a definition that captures the very essence of a thing. Definitions are tested by seeking

[60] James Jordon, Jr., "Socratic Teaching," *Harvard Educational Review, 33,* No. 1 (Winter 1953), pp. 97–98. See also Harry S. Broudy, "Two Exemplars of Teaching Method," *Theories of Instruction* (Washington, D.C.: Association for Supervision and Curriculum Development, 1965), pp. 8–17.

their consequences for different cases. . . . It is not an inquiry into things that have not been experienced but an inquiry into the meanings of experience as it is presently held. . . . The first principle of the method is to begin with a trial definition and to test the definition against the combined wits of those engaged in the discussion. The procedure is necessarily unstructured because the direction of the inquiry depends on the trial definition.

If one learns anything from the Socratic method, he probably learns to bring forth counter-instances. He learns that what one does with a definition is test it by examples from his experience and imagination.[61]

Inquisitive questioning in the spirit of the Socratic method can be used when common experiences have been gained and their meaning in life is to be considered. After an eighth-grade class has visited a juvenile court with their teacher, made observations of the neighborhood where the court sits, and read something of judicial procedures, they cannot turn from the questions: What is delinquency? What is lawful? and What is just? This is the time when the teacher helps students propose trial definitions and asks the kinds of questions that encourage checking instance against instance from their observations and from their own experience with limits and approbations imposed by society.[62]

SCIENTIFIC INQUIRY There is another kind of inquiry that probes toward discovery of unknown and possible new combinations. This type of inquiry is exemplified by the part of the scientific method in which the scientist plays with possibilities suggested by given data. He follows hunches and lets his mind wander over the probabilities of finding a clue if he turns his attention this way or that. Like the Socratic method, the inquiry in scientific method is an occupation of sophisticated adults. Even granting their limitations in experience and thinking, however, the spirit of open-ended, intuitive inquiry can be encouraged in children. They will inquire in their own manner and in their own world.

The climate for discussion must be permissive and accepting, allowing for both the wild guess and the critical challenge. The questions asked by the teacher need to be of the open-ended variety: What do you think about that event? Where will that idea take us? What would happen if we tried it this way? Can you think of any other ways we could do it? Inquisitive questioning suits both an open and exploring activity in the mode of scientific discovery and a closing-in activity in the mode of scientific validation.

EXAMPLES OF SPECIAL QUESTIONING STRATEGIES THAT ENCOURAGE DIALOGUE Language strategies in teaching can contribute as much to the process of knowing as does the strategic manipulation of

[61] James Jordon, pp. 102–103.
[62] Suggested by an actual eighth-grade study developed by William Steel at the North School Country Day School, Winnetka, Ill.

materials for discovery. For example, J. Richard Suchman's special science-teaching strategies for "learning through inquiry" create a language game of dialogue. He requires the child to talk as he explores a scientific phenomenon, so that the teacher gets a picture of his thinking.[63] By setting up the classroom dialogue in such a way that the child is always asking questions about an observed film clip of a physical phenomenon, Suchman emphasizes "that the direction and control of the data flow are mostly in the hands of the child. Students are in this way helped to develop a set of skills and a broad scheme for the investigation of causal relationships."

Suchman divides an inquiry episode into three stages through which the teacher guides the questioning after the children have witnessed a filmed episode of natural phenomena (for example, the bending of two thin metal strips under heat and in cold water).

> *Stage I.* A verification of facts as the child identifies the objects and the conditions under which they have been placed.
> *Stage II.* A determination of relevance as the child manipulates one variable at a time while the others are controlled, and an identification of conditions that produce the outcome.
> *Stage III.* A discovery of physical principles and relationships that govern change.

The children are restricted to asking questions of the teacher that have a "yes" or "no" answer, very much like the game "Twenty Questions." This forces the child to talk out his thinking about the general question, "Why?" Suchman found in his experimentation with this particular language strategy that it "had a marked effect on the motivation, autonomy and question-asking fluency of children." "They clearly enjoyed, he said, having the freedom and power to gather their own data in their quest for assimilation."[64]

In another of the experimental science programs (the Elementary Science Study), an open-ended approach was used. Instead of building question sequences around a structured episode, the children were confronted with materials strategically chosen for the conceptualizing potential in the relationships that can be made among them. Then the students were permitted to manipulate the materials freely, to talk among themselves and with the teacher about the relationships, and to hypothesize possible explanations and ways of finding causes. "Enlightened opportunism" described this methodology, which allows the child to meet an event in his own way, assuring that he builds a preconceptual background of identification with the feel, the look, and the smell of objects as they appear in space and time before he conceptualizes the relationships that begin to have meaning

[63] J. Richard Suchman, "Learning through Inquiry," *NEA Journal* (March 1963).
[64] J. Richard Suchman, *The Elementary School Training Program in Scientific Inquiry* (Urbana, Ill.: College of Education, University of Illinois, 1962), p. 81.

for him. The teacher, after having set the stage for this kind of exploration, responds to the manipulation he observes and the talk he hears by summing up the children's findings and by reviewing the situation at which they have arrived. He uses a questioning voice as if to say "What does that mean?" and "How could we find out if that would happen again?" The ideation and the process for investigation are "discovered" by the children as they work and talk together.

At the fifth-grade level, previous experience and concepts gained from it emerge as the children are presented with an experimental situation and as they talk about it:

Temperature regulation in animals is the frame of reference when a hamster and a dipsosaurus lizard are brought into the classroom, each caged in an ice chest. The children pick up the animals and respond:

Pupil: Why is the cage so cold?

Teacher: Interesting [*question*]. Does the cold do anything to them?

Pupil: Dipsosaurus was colder, more like the air as cold as in the chest.

Pupil: Hamster was hotter. Dipsosaurus is a reptile; hamster is a mammal.

Teacher: Learned that somewhere else? What caused this?

Pupil: Because one is cold-blooded and the other is warm-blooded.

Teacher: Here are some more words. My goodness, how many have heard them before? Which is cold-blooded and warm-blooded?

Pupil: Cold-blooded is the dipsosaurus; the hamster is warm.

Teacher: Do these mean something?

Pupil: Cold-blooded—it means that body temperature will be the same as air around us.

Teacher: So dipsosaurus will be the same?

Pupil: One [is] not as cold as in one of those boxes. How if it got warmer?

Teacher: [It would be] interesting next time if we let him get warm. Would it change with temperature?

Pupil: We could put it [the hamster] in a hot place and then take him to a cold place and it would still be warm.

Pupil: It [the hamster] would be cold but warmer than the dipsosaurus.

Teacher: We'll put them in a warmer place.

Pupil: Feel warmer.

Teacher: How does he do that? If you were in these [ice chests] would you stay warm?

Pupil: I guess I'd feel sort of cold. If I went out on a winter's day with a summer dress, I'd feel cold. I would think it was cold. My body temperature would be the same inside but outside would be cold and I would get goose pimples.

Pupil: Anything you did you would stay warm.

Teacher: Next time you can tell me whether they stay warm in the room. See what observations you can make. How can that hamster stay warm in here [ice chest]?

Pupil: Maybe it is the same with the hamster as it is with us, warm on a summer day. His blood is the same but his outer covering would be cold [on a winter's day].

Teacher: How many agree? We don't seem to be sure. Douglas says we can experiment.

Pupil: If you had a drop of blood, see if it freezes up?

Teacher: We could test their temperatures.
Pupil: We stay the same temperature.
Pupil: I don't know about cold outside; have to work harder.

Teacher and children devised an experiment to check out hunches.[65]

Sometimes a concept, which has already been discovered in the classroom, can be extended to a generalization by proposing a novel occurrence and by inviting talk about other possible novel situations.

> In a seventh grade which was studying light and shadow, the teacher said, "Last night I had dinner at an outdoor restaurant. It was raining, but I ate under a rain shadow."
> The students were pleased with the new situation and recalled sun shadows under beach umbrellas. They were then divided into teams and asked to write down as many other kinds of shadows as they could construe. Some of the responses were as follows:
>
> A space ship makes a radiation shadow.
> The nose cone of a space capsule makes a heat shadow.
> A diving bell makes a water shadow.
> A bullet-proof vest makes an energy shadow.
>
> The teacher asked, "What is a shadow then?"
>
> **Pupil:** Blocking out something.
> **Pupil:** A shadow is the absence of something, a light shadow is the absence of light.[66]

The artfulness of the teacher who uses "enlightened opportunism" is found both in the proper timing of his questions or reflections on the student's comment, and in his phrasing so that the children carry on the dialogue and make the discoveries theirs.

The skillful teacher uses open-ended questions or nondirective comments that reflect the pupil's statement, to encourage divergent thinking in combination with closure questions, which bring about convergent thinking. *A rhythm of expansive exploration and narrowing specificity promotes a progressive flow of constructive thinking as the discipline of education takes place.*

THE CLARIFYING QUESTION There is an objectivity about inquiry that does not always touch personal conceptualizing and commitment. A third type of questioning is needed to strike at personal involvement—the clarifying question. The neo-Freudians were concerned with helping psychologically disoriented individuals to clarify their value orientation to life; from this approach a format of questioning has been developed that permits free association of ideas and feelings. Psychologists have proposed that the

---

[65] Record of a fifth-grade science class discussion, Elementary Science Study.

[66] Record of a seventh–eighth grade science class discussion, Elementary Science Study.

individual can incorporate only the ideas, feelings, and concepts into his personality that can be brought to personal awareness and can be freely accepted by him. A nondirective approach is the only way to place the burden of acceptance upon him.

These are your feelings?

Carl Rogers,[67] one of America's most outstanding clinical psychologists, emphasized the need for client-centered therapy. In his clinical process, the therapist mirrors the client's reactions with such questions as:

You feel that [*he repeats the client's statement*]?
What are your reactions?
You would feel thus and so [*he summarizes the client's reactions*]?

This strategy of nondirective questioning in a permissive interview situation, when no judgments of actions or feelings were made by the therapist, served well the purpose of forcing clients to work out their own value judgments in emotionally charged situations. Later, Rogers and others suggested that the therapist might participate more in the interview beyond reflective questioning by sharing with the client similar experiences he had had or had heard about. The decisions made by others could be mentioned, but the therapist was always careful not to tell the client what to do or to challenge him with direct questions that required direct conventional answers.

Rogers extended his theory and procedures to the teaching situation, noting that the teacher is not concerned with intricacies of personality adjustments in psychotherapeutic situations but, rather, is concerned with normal personality development in which personal valuing decisions are involved. The nondirective approach and the open-ended nonevaluative question become a strategy of the classroom teacher to encourage independence in decision making. This technique places upon the student the burden of thinking about value judgments and about the significance of what he is learning. If, as stated earlier in the chapter on coming to know, the acquisition of knowledge is a personal process of conceptualizing, then a nondirective approach in teaching would seem to be most appropriate at certain crucial stages in the teaching–learning process.

Louis Raths and his followers have taken this approach in attempting to develop a teaching strategy of questioning that will encourage pupils to examine and clarify their values as they deal with subjects that have personal and social implications.[68]

---

[67] Carl Rogers, *Client Centered Therapy* (Boston: Houghton Mifflin, 1951). The theory and practice of client-centered therapy are expounded, including implications for the teaching situation.

[68] Louis E. Raths, "Clarifying Values," in Robert S. Fleming (ed.), *Curriculum for Today's Boys and Girls* (Columbus, Ohio: Merrill, 1963). See also Louis Raths, Merrill Harmin, and Sidney Simon, *Values and Teaching* (Columbus, Ohio: Merrill, 1966); Sidney Simon et al., *Values Clarification: A Handbook of Practical Strategies for Teachers and Students* (New York: Hart Publishing, 1972).

Some activities helpful in value clarification are (1) question-and-answer discussion periods involving moot questions[69] for the class to consider, (2) role-playing situations where questions of value are raised and then played, and (3) discussion of a classroom social incident. The teacher needs to inject the clarifying question into these situations. Most teachers tend to ask questions only when they possess the answers.[70] The key criterion for selecting clarifying questions is that they must be questions for which *only the student knows the answer*.[71] Educators who have worked with this level of questioning suggest that the questions are more effective when asked in a nonjudgmental manner. The following types of clarifying questions have been used in the classroom:

> Reflect back what the student has said and add, "Is that what you mean?"
> Reflect back what the student has said with distortion and add, "Is that what you mean?"
> "How long have you felt (acted) that way?"
> "Are you glad you think (act) that way?"
> "In what way is that a good idea?"
> "What is the source of your idea?"
> "Should everyone believe that?"
> "Have you thought of some alternatives?"
> "What are some things you have done that reflect this idea of yours?"
> "Why do you think so?"
> "Is this what you really think?"
> "Did you do this on purpose?"
> Ask for definitions of key words.
> Ask for examples.
> Ask if this position is consistent with a previous one he has taken.[72]

A questioning attitude among students needs to be implemented within the classroom environment. *The dignity and acceptance of any question asked by a student as one that is worthy of an answer is an idea that needs to be encouraged by teachers.* If teachers brush aside questions, they can deter the questioning process of students. The teacher should ask some clarifying questions of students that show him in agreement with them as well as some that show him not in agreement. The development of skill in questioning techniques by both students and teachers will depend, to a degree, on the ability of individuals to maintain open minds during classroom interaction.

Another one of the techniques for encouraging the clarifying process is the coding of written work. Coding can be used to clarify values and to sharpen the student's insights into his own thinking. A $V+$, for a positive

---

[69] A moot question: Are athletes better than scholars?

[70] Raths, p. 513.

[71] Raths, p. 513.

[72] Raths, p. 513.

value, and a $V-$, for a negative value, are symbols that can be marked in the margin of a student's paper whenever the teacher sees an indication of attitudes, feelings, beliefs, aspirations, and the like. The student learns to identify these symbols as representing two questions the teacher is asking. They are "Do you believe this?" and "Do you want to change it?" As the student reflects and responds to the questions, he is thinking and valuing. The clarifying question can serve to raise the level of the "mental play" in the classroom, insuring to some degree the personalization of concepts and the commitment of students to a value orientation. In the social studies and science areas, questions about "segregation," "peace and war," or the "uses of atomic power" need to be explored in this manner by interweaving clarifying questions with inquiry and fact finding. Thought-provoking pictures showing racial, ethnic, or socioeconomic conflicts can set the stage for a values clarification discussion.

QUESTIONING LEVELS Sanders in *Classroom Questions*[73] presents a hierarchy of types of questions based on classifications of educational objectives related to the advancing levels of the higher thinking process. He encourages teachers to frame questions at the appropriate moment of thought development in a teaching episode that will lift the level of the students' thinking.

Hunkins in a useful book on the techniques of questioning focuses his attention particularly on their use in inquiry-oriented curricula.[74] He sets some criteria for the framing of questions such as: Is it clear on what is expected both cognitively and affectively of the student? Does the wording allow the student to respond with optional productivity? Does it give him adequate direction and permit him freedom to interrelate ideas? Hunkins recommends a simple Teacher–Pupil Question Inventory Form that teachers can use with student-teachers or among themselves for looking at the levels of questioning they use and the levels of response they get from pupils. The observer can simply indicate the level of each question and response by teacher and pupils as a learning activity proceeds. The code is based on the cognitive levels from Bloom taxonomy: (1) memory, (2) comprehension, (3) application, (4) analysis, (5) synthesis, and (6) evaluation. A matrix can be formed of the pattern, and this becomes a basis for discussion of questioning strategies. An audio- or videotape recording taken at the same time would be useful for an analysis of the different types of questions and the responses from the youngsters.

---

[73] Norris Sanders, *Classroom Questions: What Kinds* (New York: Harper & Row, 1966).

[74] Francis Hunkins, *Questioning Strategies and Techniques* (Boston: Allyn and Bacon, 1972).

Expert searching with questions by the teacher-scholar can imbue students with a love of investigation. Inquiry and clarification can electrify learning and make moments of teaching exciting.

Exposition in Teaching

The art of questioning is crucial in the teaching act, but the communicative arts of presenting and explaining information and ideas are equally pivotal. Not much work has been done on this latter aspect of teaching at any school level because most theoretical positions about school teaching have been stated in every possible way to avoid the impression that teachers might lecture to their pupils. In teacher education great care is usually taken to break the neophyte of the habit of talking to youngsters in a lecture style learned from hours of listening in college halls. As a result, many new teachers leave the teacher-education institution with the impression that they should never talk to the students but that they should always be soliciting talk from them. They are drilled on the adage, "When tempted to tell, think of a question instead." This is good advice for checking teacher talk and forcing a focus on the child's language and thought. However, when the importance of language interchange and the dialogue between the child conception and the adult scientific and public concepts are stressed, then teachers' language presentations to children become crucial.

Teachers need to consider ways to present information and ideas both effectively and artfully. The presentations of the teacher must be prepared in such a way as to follow the psycho-logic of the content from the point of view of the child as well as the natural logic of the subject matter. The child's experience of seeing puddles evaporate fast on a sunny, windy day (psycho-logic) must be woven into the logical, scientific explanation of evaporation. Means for involving the child directly in participation, and indirectly in silent parallel thinking activity, are a problem of teaching tactics. When no further questions can be raised or considered until the pupils have more information, or when added information is needed to provoke further questions or to challenge premature judgments, the teacher must plan his own presentation.

The temptation to translate the material to be presented into "baby terms" or childish language should be avoided. As in the making of good informational books for children, simplification is not the main task, but, rather, the presentation of the material in a mode that children will comprehend. Operational descriptions and imagery-evoking presentations are preferable to logical argumentation for explaining events to most elementary school children. Building sequences of concrete examples that lead to an inductively derived generalization for the pupils to locate and express are effective in science or social science presentations by the teacher. The opposite, deductive structure, beginning with a restated generalization just learned, could be used as a challenge for the pupils to locate examples in other settings. The teacher might in another instance present an overview of a subject to be studied to give a total frame of reference in which learners would investigate the specifics that would lead them to some principles. Geographical studies, for example, can be approached in this way, with the teacher using pictures, films, and recordings as well as exposition in his initial presentation. Such introductions to a study should not present the generalizations or the conclusions, for then there would be no reason to study. Instead, they should present impressions, descriptive statements, and feelings about the subject from which learners can draw their own generalizations through questioning.

After learners have investigated, made some propositions, and raised some questions, there will be need for more information and explanation. Teachers need to be wary of giving out too much unstructured, diffuse, and unrelated information unless the strategy calls for the pupils to assemble and structure the facts on their own in a kind of mental game. Usually, the teacher needs to think of himself as programming the information for presentation. With some kinds of content, such as the explanation of a computational process in mathematics, a step-by-step logical structure would be effective. With other sorts of content (for example, an exploration of a scientific concept) the teacher might isolate variables and not introduce more than one or two at the same time out of consideration of children's limited ability to hold different factors in mind while they consider others.

Repetition, a studied redundancy, may be necessary, and points should be summarized at regular intervals. The technique of class response can be useful as explanations proceed. The teacher should call for restatement and for questions that will focus on elements that still need explanation. Whatever the teacher's presentation is, it should provoke pupil questions and statements for further investigation. In this way the dialogue of the classroom occurs.

ment. At other times, the teacher's compositions are improvised on the occa-
simplicity of a Francis Bacon. The whole rich fabric of the English language
flexibly planned for the turn of events that will come from pupil involve-
Sometimes his compositions are prepared ahead of time, but they are always
As a composer in the literary arts, he may use the poignant story to good
effect as did the teachers of biblical times. He may use the extended meta-
sion. He is a composer in all the arts of presentation and communication.

As Huebner suggests, the teacher can be conceived of as a composer.[75]
phor or the rhetorical question to the advancement of learning as did
Socrates. Or he may use exposition and argument with the directness and

[75] Dwayne Huebner, "The Art of Teaching," mimeograph. Teachers College, Columbia University, 1962.

can be at his command. In the visual arts he can compose imaginative collages and scenarios of pictures for bulletin boards or classroom presentations. With miming and gesturing, the teacher can dramatize a point or create impressions of attitude. *There are worlds of language, of illustration, and of imitation at the teacher's beck and call. From these treasure troves of human ingenuity he can compose "letters to the world" that speak to the generations of students and lead them in their knowing.*

20

Analyzing the Language of Teaching

This book has attempted to present some of the knowledge about language that is useful to teachers. Study of language and literature should be a required ingredient in the education of teachers. An equally important educational experience should be the analysis of teaching itself, so that the neophyte has an opportunity to see the effects of certain kinds of language behavior by the teacher upon the classroom situation. Only then can he discover cause–result relationships in teaching and experiment with alternate language–behavior tactics.

section 1

Systematic Views of Teaching

For the purpose of analysis, teaching can be viewed as being composed of a series of interrelated language–behavior "action systems" that are intended to induce learning by the pupils.[1] Various investigators of the teaching act have focused their study on certain action elements, all of which involve language. Teaching in reality is a *gestalt* of all these elements, but it can be conceived for purposes of analysis as (1) interaction systems, (2) com-

[1] B. Othanel Smith and Robert Ennis, *Language and Concepts in Education* (Chicago: Rand McNally, 1961), p. 91.

munication systems, (3) decision-making systems, and (4) language–thinking systems. Each view of teaching helps illuminate the whole process of teaching. As a whole teaching, like language, of which it is mainly made, has a surface structure and a deep structure that are intertwined. The surface structure is manifested in the skills of management and organization of learning resources, while the deep structure is reflected in the higher processes of teaching that engender thinking and valuing in the classroom.

Teaching As Interaction Systems

Marie Hughes looks at the acts of teaching as *functions*: "The teacher cannot speak or act in the teacher–learner situation without performing a function for someone in the situation."[2] This view is derived from the fact that the teacher is an authority figure in the classroom who wields power and responds with power to the pupils' reactions to that power. The teacher may respond by controlling and limiting or by accepting, clarifying, and exploring.[3] In the following three short sentences, the teacher has performed four such functions:

VERBAL DATA	*FUNCTIONS*
I enjoyed listening to the stories the boys told this morning.	(Support-specific)
They told them very well.	(Evaluate-positive)
I wonder though, John, what kind of sharing ought to take class time.	(Standard set-recall) (Regulate-closed)[4]

The advantage of viewing teaching as a series of functions is that each function can be isolated and analyzed for the reaction it receives, and the alternative ways of functioning can then be considered in the light of the possible reaction they may receive. The concept of *power wielding* as one type of function is useful because teachers often tend to hide this reality rather than learn to face up to it. If they accept their power-wielding function and then consider the best ways to use this power for setting the atmosphere and the stage for learning, they can open up the situation for learning rather than close it down to mere answer-calling.

The concept of *responsiveness* is even more significant, for it is the teacher's mode of responding to students that really opens the way to in-

[2] Through every verbal and physical act of the teacher he performs a function for someone in the class.

[3] Marie Hughes and associates, *Development of the Means for the Assessment of the Quality of Teaching in Elementary Schools* (Salt Lake City, Utah: University of Utah, 1959), pp. 41–46, 215–219. Marie Hughes, "Utah Study of the Assessment of Teaching," in Arno Bellack (ed.), *Theory and Research in Teaching* (New York: Bureau of Publications, Teachers College, Columbia University, 1963), pp. 25–36. Ideas on these two pages are summarized from the above references.

[4] Marie Hughes and associates, p. 43.

vestigative learning. He can respond in an accepting, open-minded fashion that will encourage exploration, elaboration, and clarification of ideas, or he can curtail dialogue with the powerful phrases: "Not now," "You are interrupting," or "No, that's not what I had in mind." He can also cut a dialogue off by making no response at all, leaving the child dangling and feeling that perhaps his remark was worthless.

Flanders and Amidon stress the *influencing behavior* of teacher talk.[5] This *talk* may have a *direct influence* on the pupils or may have an *indirect influence*. *Direct influencing* occurs through giving directions, ordering, criticizing, justifying, lecturing, or expressing one's own ideas or through asking rhetorical questions. *Indirect influencing* develops from accepting and clarifying pupil questions, praising and encouraging students, or using ideas of students to elaborate on an idea or from asking questions in such a way that the pupils initiate ideas. The indirect mode of influencing seems to have more promise in it for expanding the possibilities of pupil learning than does the direct approach. Probably, the teacher can directly feed in information and ideas when *indirection* has created a situation in which the pupils are soliciting guidance from the teacher. Broad or narrow questions can either encourage student's thinking or restrict it.[6] The broad question opens up possibilities and challenges one to start probing, whereas the narrow question, although useful to pin down a point after exploration has started, can inhibit thinking and may even stop it entirely. It is the difference between "What do you think about _____?" *or* "What is your reaction to _____?" *as against* "What is the date of that happening?" *or* "Who did that?"

Pupils interact with the environmental setting established by the teacher and with the language actions of the teacher. When this interaction is open and expansive, when the teacher responds to his students and employs *indirect influence* to a large degree and in appropriate relation to judicious use of *direct* modes, the induced-learning action of the pupils can increase and improve in quality. These interactions can be categorized in an efficient manner for observation of a teaching episode, and then the teaching actions can be analyzed for their effect.[7]

---

[5] Ned Flanders, "Teacher Influence in the Classroom," in Arno Bellack (ed.), *Theory and Research in Teaching* (New York: Bureau of Publications, Teachers College, Columbia University, 1963), pp. 37–52. Flanders, Address, Association for Student Teaching, Chicago, February 1964. Edmund Amidon, *Using Interaction Analysis at Temple University*, a working paper presented to a conference on interaction analysis, University of Rochester, Rochester, New York, January 1966.

[6] Ned Flanders, "Intent, Action, Feedback: A Preparation for Teaching," *Journal of Teacher Education, 14*, No. 3 (September 1963), 259.

[7] See the specific interaction analysis techniques of Hughes and Flanders in the above references and in Edmund Amidon and Elizabeth Hunter, *Improving Teaching: The Analysis of Classroom Verbal Interactions* (New York: Holt, Rinehart and Winston, 1966).

Teaching As Communication Systems

If teaching is viewed as a message-making and receiving system for the *transmission of information*, in which the teacher is both an encoder of messages to learners and a decoder of their messages to him, then the teacher must be alert to the subtleties of classroom communication systems that may facilitate or restrain such a process. He should recognize that in addition to the basic communication systems components of sender–message–receiver, his functioning in the learning situation involves concern for the three *message elements*:—sender–receiver cognizance of message elements, congruence of message elements, and feedback.[8] Communication is a condition that may be *approached* or *avoided,* depending upon the ability of teacher and student to facilitate effectively the solving of the problems caused by the three variables. An understanding must be achieved by the teacher that the communication condition which exists in the learning environment will be influenced by his perceptions of self, his personal and cultural biases, his awareness of the situation in which he is functioning, his feelings toward the information to be transmitted, and his perceptions of those who will receive and decode his messages. He must also be aware that these same influences are at work within the learners and that he, in turn, as a decoder of messages from learners, is influenced by these same elements. The events to be perceived in a learning situation must be made available to the learner, and they must be selected from the buzzing confusion of all possible events, with consideration given to all possible influences, in order for the learner to attend. Consideration of the context within which an event is placed by the teacher, of the conditions for communication in the environment, and of the frame of reference within which the event is interpreted is crucial to good communication. The way a teacher focuses on an event, from which direction, and with what highlights may cause distortion (*restraint*) or clarity (*facilitation*) in messages in much the same way that a photographer, by the way he directs lights on a face and uses camera angle, may create a portrait that conveys the character of the person or distorts the message from the face. To become a facilitator of communication the teacher must become both a scientist and an artist. As a scientist, he must be one who "assesses the truth qualities of information and the validity of assumptions, contexts and points of view implicit in statement." As an artist, he must be sure that he uses his skills and materials to express true and valid beliefs in clear and convincing focus.[9]

---

[8] For a full account see Anita Simon and Yvonne Agazarian, *Sequential Analysis of Verbal Interaction* (Philadelphia, Pa.: Research for Better Schools, 1967).

[9] George Gerbner, "A Theory on Communication and Its Implications for Teaching," in Louise Berman (ed.), *The Nature of Teaching* (Milwaukee, Wisc.: University of Wisconsin–Milwaukee, 1963), p. 44. His view, summarized here, is treated extensively in this lecture and in his other writings.

The teacher, in this view, needs to be an artistic and effective encoder of messages that blend picture, language, diagram, and demonstration in such a way that learners perceive what is meant and attach value to its meaning. In receiving the messages from learners, the teacher must be aware of the assumptions on which they have based their messages in order to grasp their meaning and to value the learners' intent. He must also be sensitive to the varied channels they use to communicate their messages. Classroom communication systems can be analyzed by plotting the encoding and decoding process in a teaching–learning event, by examining the assumptions behind each message, by determining the encoder–decoder of message content, and by judging the *congruence* within and between teacher messages and pupil messages. An example of lack of message cognizance and incongruence would be a middle-class–oriented teacher who presented concepts from his cultural point of view; they are misunderstood by a group of children from the slums who, in turn, send back messages that either shock the teacher or whose referents are unknown to him. The city-park–oriented teacher mentioned earlier who did not think that her children from Appalachia would know about squirrels is a case in point. She did not expect to receive the message back that squirrels are to be shot and eaten.

ANALYZING TEACHER–PUPIL COMMUNICATION If the teacher can become sensitive to the communication between himself and learners, the result will be an improvement in the process. And, if he can acquire data as it occurs, he can take steps to improve the process. Knowledge of a theory of communication, such as that outlined by Yvonne Agazarian[10] and expanded by Agazarian and Simon,[11] and training in the skills of communication facilitation according to the theory can be a start. The teacher can, through simulation and role playing with peers, begin to recognize the subtlety of the transfer of topic (what one is speaking about) and personal information (what one is saying about oneself within a single message. Through one-to-one peer activities, the teacher can begin to recognize how messages can be *congruent* (topic and personal information in agreement) or *ambiguous* (the two elements dissonant).

In group simulated problem-solving situations, the teacher can be helped to see the roles of different types of information (topic–task or, personal–interpersonal) and the influences they have on group behavior. Informal analysis of scripts of group interactions can be used to assist the teacher in conceptualizing the problem-solving nature of communicative behavior. Further, this type of activity can be used with the teacher to examine the emotional climate within groups and to determine both the goal priorities that exist during group operations and the effects of these elements

[10] Yvonne Agazarian, "A Theory of Verbal Behavior and Information Transfer," *Classroom Interaction Newsletter, 4* (1969), pp. 22–33.

[11] Simon and Agazarian.

on the communication. He may collect data by himself, after training in an interaction analysis with an appropriate system,[12] and from audio-tapes plotted on a matrix and analyzed for build-ups in specific cells of the matrix. He may wish to alter his behavior or the behavior of members of the classroom group in light of the analysis. Through this type of activity, the teacher becomes more than a transmitter of knowledge—he becomes a facilitator of the transmission of information about *what* the human beings in his classroom are talking about, *who* the human beings are, and how they *feel*.

Ryans in his investigations takes the view that teaching is an *information-processing* system. Ryans's formulations for research are complex because of all the variables in the teaching–learning situation, but he suggests a basic pattern of communication. He pictures the teacher as first sensing, then filtering, clarifying, and analyzing input from the children and the situation in which he and they are. Then the teacher begins to process that information into decisions about what to put out and how to channel the reorganized information for pupil input. The teacher arranges for further "feedbacks," and the process continues.[13]

It might be possible for a teacher-in-training to view the "feedback" that he or an observed intern teacher was getting from a class and then to look at the subsequent actions of the teacher to see whether the information had been received and processed with some effectiveness as output. The teacher who received the shocking information about squirrels and then halted any further discussion of the subject was not processing information as an educational expert.

Teaching As Decision-Making Systems

Close to the view of teaching as information processing is the one that emphasizes the teacher as an on-the-spot maker of curricular and instructional decisions. After careful preplanning by organizing ideas for presentation around *centers of educational objectives*[14] or around conceptual

---

[12] For an explication of training systems see Simon and Agazarian. Also see Thomas Davidson, doctoral dissertation on "The Effects of Training in the Concepts of the Sequential Analysis of Verbal Interaction Communication Theory on the Teaching Behaviors of Prospective Elementary School Teachers," Wayne State University, 1971 (a basis for this part).

[13] David Ryans, "Teacher Behavior Theory and Research: Implications for Teacher Education," *Journal of Teacher Education, 14*, No. 3 (September 1963), 274–293. David Ryans, "A Model of Instruction Based on Information System Concepts," *Theories of Instruction* (Washington, D.C.: Association for Supervision and Curriculum Development, 1965), pp. 36–61. Information coming in to the nervous system not only has to be separated from noise and compressed, it also has to be scanned for relevance to on-going activity.

[14] Virgil Herrick, "Teaching as Curriculum Decision Making," *The Nature of Teaching* (Milwaukee, Wisc.: University of Wisconsin–Milwaukee, 1963), pp. 66–80.

themes,[15] the teacher is faced, then, with a specific classroom situation and has to make tactical instructional decisions. This view takes into account the background of the teacher's preparation and of his expected posture to behave partly in terms of a curricular framework known by the teacher well ahead of the teaching act. All moves in the classroom are made in terms of this prior curricular agreement among a teacher's colleagues or with his administrator. When a pupil raises a question or expresses a concern in class, the teacher immediately decides whether the student's point can be used to move the class toward predetermined educational goals. If the teacher is working toward "process goals" (that is, the development of certain inquiry procedures or methods for attacking a problem), he then decides to direct the classroom activities toward the use of the process he is cultivating. An example of this activity of the teacher would be an instance in an arithmetic class when a pupil asks the question, "How do you get the answer?" and the teacher replies, "Let's stop a minute and see how many ways we can figure out to attack the problem." Many of these decisions directly affect classroom management and control. A decision to involve students in structuring their own learning tasks will tend to effect orderly management.[16]

It is possible to review the transcript from a classroom observation and locate the points where the teacher has made a decision, and it is possible from his statements and actions to describe the decision that he made. The students of teaching can, then, discuss alternate decisions that might have been made at that point, provided they are in tune with the goals for the lesson decided upon in curriculum preplanning. This is one kind of professional decision teachers have to make. There are others dealing with diagnosis of educational problems and prescription for their solution. "A teacher is professional because he can solve problems concerned with instruction better than someone without special preparation."[17]

Teaching As Language and Thinking Systems

Teaching can be conceived as verbal transactions prompted by the teacher, who is responsible for them. He expects his verbal actions to induce verbal responses from his pupils. The teacher is an agent taking action with language that may be spoken, written, or gestured.

[The teacher] acts with language, using it in the performance of almost all those actions describable as teaching. . . . [He] studies and interprets verbal

[15] Joseph Grannis, "Team Teaching and the Curriculum," in Henry Olds and Judson Shaplin (eds.), *Team Teaching* (New York: Harper & Row, 1964), pp. 124–138.

[16] Jacob Kounin, lecture, Wayne State University, Detroit, April 1965.

[17] Nicholas Fattu, "Explorations of Interactions among Instruction, Content and Aptitude Variables," *Journal of Teacher Education, 14,* No. 3 (1963), 244.

action. . . . The teacher's control over his dealings with language thus determines in large measure his success (or failure) to induce the educational results. . . .[18]

The teacher's language thus functions as verbal operants. He intends to have it *operate* in the classroom to produce responding actions. These are symbolic *transactions* that are mainly in verbal form. They are tactically planned by the teacher to promote intellectual activities (namely, thinking and valuing).

In effective teaching, the teacher *structures* his verbal actions in such a way as to confront his pupils with a need for them to do their own structuring for their own studying. He *solicits* responses from them in a way that will encourage them to search, to elaborate, and to clarify. Through language he brings their personal knowing into dialogue with established knowledge and thereby lifts their thinking.

Two possible ways to open a classroom study of the colonizing period in American history follow. In this case the teacher should begin ·

Not by saying: "Today we start reading about the colonies, first Jamestown, then Plymouth, and so on. You will want to get the dates fixed first and then find out about which people colonized which section and why."

But by saying: "Let's go back about three hundred years and think about who was around here and what the countryside must have looked like. Were your ancestors here then or did they come later? What brought them here? If we could talk about these questions for a while maybe we could get some ideas about what a colony was."

By keeping a log of verbal transactions in a classroom teaching episode and by analyzing the teacher presentations in light of the pupils' responses, teachers-in-training can see the effects of their verbal moves in the language game of teaching.

section 2

Assessment of Teaching Performance: Competency Indication of the Higher Processes of Teaching Transactions[19]

Performance in teaching may indicate competence, or it may not indicate anything more than habit—unexamined techniques that the teacher has always used or seen other teachers use. A "performance only" view of

---

[18] Mary Jane Aschner, "The Language of Teaching," in B. O. Smith and R. Ennis (eds.), *Language and Concepts in Education* (Chicago: Rand McNally, 1961), pp. 124–125.

[19] This section was written with the assistance of Gary Kilarr. Gary Kilarr, "A Process Model for Teaching and Learning," a doctoral dissertation, Wayne State University, Detroit, Michigan.

teaching may be adequate for "assessing" some straightforward teaching behavior that researchers now believe will improve teaching effectiveness, such as "eye-to-eye" contact, moving around the classroom instead of standing up front, asking an indirect question instead of always telling, and so forth; but performance alone cannot reveal the intelligence or the value or attitude in the teaching–learning transaction. A performance of discrete acts of teaching cannot account for the total act that involves an integrated series of thought–value judgments brought to insightful application in style and content. The competent teacher formulates and applies *conceptual–valuative schemes* (ideational structures) derived from both professional and academic knowledge at the same time. A teacher may perform a described task involving language, thinking, and valuing but not indicate whether he is basing his behavior on knowledge (a supporting conceptual–valuative schema). If he is not, he may perform the same teaching act in a different situation where the act is inappropriate and even detrimental to the new learning situation. The *quality of his ideation* in using "content" for teaching could be inadequate. Professional and academic thought, value, and attitude cannot be separated in the reality of teaching.

For example, a teacher from a white, middle-class speech community would automatically use his speech pattern in a phonics activity with second graders who speak the same dialect. Because pupils and teacher are in speech "accord," there is no confusion about the sounds of the "endings" being studied. Does his use of the same dialect, however, indicate any knowledge of different speech patterns or of the application of this knowledge to language teaching in the schools? He might very well be placed in a black, inner-city class setting and confuse his pupils by responding negatively and with faulty technique to the alien dialect. He would be performing on the basis of habit, not knowledge.

Other examples could be given where the teaching performance might be based on teacher folklore or on misconceptions such as, "Poor black kids are low in intelligence and cannot learn except by repetitive drill." Sometimes teachers do the right thing for the wrong reason, but such inconsistencies and ignorance do not denote professionalism in their performances. There is no assurance that the wrong reason might not lead the next time to the wrong act. A social studies teacher who has an inadequate and distorted view of Negro slavery in America and is not aware of present-day racism-free scholarship about the topic could use all the best pedagogical methods and perform at a high technical level while teaching misinformation and prejudiced viewpoints. Much that passes for science teaching in the schools is at best pseudoscience. Because of inadequate conceptualizing by the teacher, misconceptions or oversimplification (such as the infallibility of technical progress without consideration for environmental effects) can be taught.

Instead of relying only on overt performances as a basis for assessing teaching, the evaluator must try to get *behind* performance and attempt to find out what knowledge and values are being applied. He can do this by systematically searching for indications of the application of thought and values to teaching in situations that present the teacher candidate with opportunities to express and apply his professional and academic knowledge. Because a teaching performance is of little value unless it exhibits many competencies, known and applied at particular times, there is no way to describe one "end" performance or "exit" performance that designates accomplished teaching. Only the tasks of teaching can be described. The *competency* or *quality indicators* in such tasks can be based on professional knowledge and value schemes and can be named. Possible preinstructional planning, instructional or postinstructional feedback situations can be anticipated in which competencies might be indicated. Reliable observational schedules can be devised for noting competency indications, and consistent reportorial means can be used for describing the indications of competency at a certain time in the professional growth of a teacher and in certain kinds of instructional situations. These objective descriptions, combined with professional judgments of those who assess the descriptions for "competency indication," can serve as an assessment of a person's teaching along a continuum of professional-life development. Continuous guided self-evaluation of one's teaching is the goal.

A conceptual–valuative scheme of academic and professional knowledge of the teaching of language and thinking can be developed from the ideas generated in this book and others like it. An example of aspects of a language scheme follows.

Language is never an end in itself but always a means to an end. Language learning must always be related to meaningful and relevant experiences for the learner.

All children develop language.

A. Children are competent language users by the time they are 5 to 7 years old.
1. They control the phonemes and rules for generating the language.
2. Their vocabulary will be relative to their cultural experiences and interests.
B. The language the child learns is the language of the home and is the one best-suited for survival, communication, and obtaining knowledge in his culture.
C. Receptive control precedes productive control.

Language constantly changes. At any one point in time there will be multiple and systematic varient forms of a language.

There are social attitudes toward language variation that reflect the varying social status of the language users. People tend to view variations of their own language ethnocentrically.

The receptive and productive processes are not mirror images of each other.

All language has structure. The structure of language is grammar.

Linguistic performance is an end-product of the language process. Control over that process is linguistic competence.

Reading is meaning, reading is thinking. Listening is thinking, speaking is thinking.

Thought and language develop through stages. There are levels of higher thinking processes.

Language, art, music, dance, and mathematics are all symbol systems for thinking, creating, and communicating.

Teachers may apply this knowledge and value orientation in their teaching, and these applications can be observed whenever they plan, instruct, and assess their instruction. A teaching plan can be evaluated for competency indication of knowledge of youngsters' thinking levels and processes. The instructional act can be recorded and later assessed for indications of an understanding of the different levels of thinking and the questioning language used to gain those levels. After a teaching episode is over, the record of that episode can be analyzed, and comments by the teacher about rationale and alternative approaches can either indicate or not indicate competent understanding of the professional and academic knowledge needed.

SOME COMPETENCY INDICATORS FOR THE APPLICATION OF LINGUISTIC AND THINKING KNOWLEDGE TO TEACHING

1. Recognizing language community differences in speech, and showing sensitivity toward the speaker in terms of analysis of his speech pattern
2. Demonstrating an understanding of what learners from an unfamiliar speech community are saying
3. Accepting and encouraging learners to make use of their own speech pattern while expanding it at will
4. Building pride in the learners' speech community by respecting consistent features of learner speech
5. Extending language patterns of learners by expanding learners' experiences and talking about them, and by introducing them to other speech patterns—especially those most generally used in business, literature, and other "formal" exchanges
6. Encouraging every possible use of language interchange, for example, by stopping a formal lesson to share language and thinking about a subject or object
7. Using other than language symbol media for creating and communicating thought and feeling
8. Lifting questioning levels to foster higher levels of thinking
9. Planning units of study that show accurate and current ideational structures drawn from the several disciplines
10. Setting up situations for values clarification.

Observational schedules need to be devised to provide opportunity to evaluate systematically the various competency indicators through speech, demeanor, acting, writing, gesturing, and logical argument. Instructional teams of observers-analyzers drawn from colleagues and supervisory staff can carefully note the indicators in the instructional situations as performed and thereby encourage a systematic yet self-evaluating process.

section 3

Supervision of Teaching by Analysis
in Cooperative Teaching Centers

The core of any teacher-education program, preservice or in-service, is the competency gains made through the practice and study of teaching. On a minimal level, supervision gives a practicing teacher some outside evaluation of his performance. The supervisor gives him support if he tells the teacher that he is doing well, and undercuts his confidence if he says he needs to improve. Evaluation of teaching should not be the first and only purpose of supervision. Before evaluation is even suggested, supervisory visits and follow-up conferences should focus on an analysis of both the teaching observed and the interaction data gathered.[20] After an analysis of what happened and a consideration of teaching alternatives have been discussed, then some long-range evaluation in terms of where the teacher started and where he is heading can be introduced. The practicing teacher's actions need to be analyzed, not criticized, if an understanding of teaching is to result and if he is to gain the skills for self-evaluation.

Observations and analyses need to be structured so that some consistency and objectivity can be achieved. Some of the patterns for researching teacher activities have been adapted by researchers and their followers for supervisory use. The categories in Ned Flanders's "Interaction Analysis" and his system for tabulating them into a matrix have been extensively used with effect.[21] In like manner, Donald Medley and Harold Mitzel have listed three categories of teacher behavior: emotional climate, verbal emphasis, and social organization. Their structure for recording data by a technique of time-sampling observations is nicknamed OSCAR (observation schedule and record). This procedure permits an observer to capture the behavioral trends of the teacher in teaching–learning situations.[22] Morton Waimon has developed a simpler schedule of larger categories of teaching behavior to be used by students in analyzing videotaped accounts of teaching episodes.[23] He divides teaching behavior into two major functions: (1) initiatory

[20] Virginia Morrison and W. Robert Dixon, "New Techniques of Observation and Assessment of Student Teachers," *The College Supervisor*, Association for Student Teaching Yearbook 43 (1964), Chap. 9, pp. 91–106.

[21] Ned Flanders, "Intent, Action, Feedback: A Preparation for Teaching," *Journal of Teacher Education, 14*, No. 3 (September 1963), 254–257.

[22] Donald Medley, "Experiences with the OSCAR Technique," *Journal of Teacher Education, 14*, No. 3, 267–273.

[23] Morton Waimon, "The Study of Teaching Behavior by Prospective Teachers," address, University of Rochester Conference on Teacher Education, Rochester, New York, January 1966.

behavior, determined by the teacher's goals, and (2) reflexive behavior, determined largely by the pupil's responses. These two functions appear in three types of teacher statements: (1) procedural, (2) substantive, and (3) rating (mostly reflexive). By labeling and then categorizing these teacher statements, the student can begin to see the intricacies of the teacher's instructional role.

A Composite Schedule of Teaching Actions for Use in the Assessment of Teaching

Each of the methods for observing and analyzing teaching has certain advantages because of its particular focus. Depending on situational, temporal, and training factors, these various techniques can be made operational. However, for practical use, an informal combination of some of their categories may be sufficient. The following pattern is suggested for observing and analyzing teaching episodes. For the purpose of teacher education an episode can be defined as a planned and continuous teaching–learning situation that inscribes the systematic development of preselected ideas, concepts, or skills. Generally, an episode will have three interlocking sections:

1. An *opener* in which the leader confronts the pupils with the question, problem, or skill to be considered, and pretests for prior knowledge and experience;
2. A *development* section in which the teacher presents information and ideas, solicits response, and engages in a dialogue of clarification and elaboration with the pupils;
3. A *recapitulation* in which ideas or skills are repeated, reinforced, summarized, and extended for later consideration.

The matter of a teaching episode can be categorized in three dimensions or a mixture of these three: (1) *cognitive* (facts, concepts, ideas, generalizations); (2) *affective* (feelings, attitudes); and (3) *sensorimotor* (actions, doings). The recognizable media by which the behaviors of teachers and pupils are expressed are (1) *language* (grammar of meaning, vocabulary, and intonation), (2) *gesture* (facial or body), and (3) *action* (doing, moving, acting out).

Seven basic *activity systems of teaching* can be isolated for observation, even though they often occur simultaneously as well as in the order designated; the abbreviations may be used for "quick hand" recording in the margins of classroom data protocols.

1. *Managing* (Mng.): wielding power by setting the stage for learning (climate, tone, environment, and grouping);
2. *Confronting* (Cnfr.): inciting curiosity, upsetting equilibrium, posing a problem, tapping a concern or interest;

3. *Structuring* (Str.): organizing for work and study, suggesting approaches and methods;
4. *Soliciting* (Solct.): questioning, pleading, opening up possibilities;
5. *Presenting* (Prsn.): stating, defining, opining, relating to previous experience and learning;
6. *Responding* (Rsp.): clarifying, elaborating, classifying, opening new avenues;
7. *Summarizing* (Sum.): pulling ideas together, tying new ideas to old ones, looking ahead to new problems, questions, and concerns.

The observers and analyzers will need to distinguish the three modes in which the teacher performs these various activities and the reflexive effects they have upon the pupils. The three modes consist of:

1. A *direct* mode (D): telling, proclaiming, manipulating, ordering, demanding; also explaining, narrowing the focus, coming to the point;
2. An *indirect* mode (I): getting the pupils to think and do, postulating, posing, hypothesizing, accepting, encouraging, guiding, leaving things open-ended;
3. A judicious mixture (M) of these two modes.

Pupils' reactions (activity systems) in response to the teacher's activities can be coded in the same categories as those used for teaching. Modes of performance by pupils can be distinguished as:

1. *Convergent* (Cn.): copying, repeating, quoting, reciting, closing in on an idea, conforming;
2. *Divergent* (Dv.): imagining, raising questions, hypothesizing, exploring;
3. *Placid* (Pl.): sitting, doodling, gazing, daydreaming, clamming up, ignoring;
4. *Distractive* (Dt.): talking off the point, interrupting with extraneous remarks, acting out aggressions, fooling around, disrupting other's work.

There are two kinds of data to be analyzed: (1) that which the teacher intended to do (his plans), and (2) the data from the classroom dialogue and activities. For written recording, children's responses can be placed in quotation marks, classroom actions can be placed within parentheses, and then all other data will be what the teacher said. In the margins can be placed the abbreviations for activity systems as judged at the time of observing. They will be cues for the analytical discussion of the teaching episode to follow. Matrices of activities can be devised for showing teaching tendancies.

Analytical Conferencing for Professional Development

Work with simulated analyses from videotapes prior to on-the-job observations directed by a trained supervisor will alert both beginning and experienced teachers about descriptions of teaching systems, the appropriate observational data-collecting instruments, and their use in analysis. Planned team supervision that uses verbal and action classroom data as bases for critique conferences can be an effective way to instruct in teaching.[24] A team of supervisors composed of a clinical professor, a supervisory clinical teacher or school supervisor, a representative from the appropriate subject area, a colleague, and educational psychologist can observe and collect data from an episode of teaching. The teacher presents the team first with his objectives and general plan of action. Following the recorded episode of teaching, a conference is arranged; the one who taught opens the analysis session by presenting his perception of what happened. The observer-supervisors, referring to the data they collected, focus attention on tactics used by the teacher and on the responses made by the pupils in light of the teacher's objectives. Content analyses of the logical flow of thinking in the teacher–pupil interactions can be made. Then the observer-supervisors can discuss the effects and possible alternative tactics that might have been used. The teacher's regular supervisor or chosen colleague guides the discussion and interjects evaluative comments in support of the observed teacher's general progress. Once trained, groups of teachers may pursue self-supervision by using a colleague team approach.

When applied to preservice teacher education, the orientation differs— the role of the clinical professor in the team supervision of teacher candidates within a group of clinical supervising teachers and their students changes to the role of educational coordinator for the clinical observation and analysis of practices in teaching. While being responsible for a group of teacher candidates, the clinical professor directs the planning and execution of a program of teacher education for the teacher interns with the help of a selected corps of sponsoring clinical teachers and with the occasional help of a small team of specialists in curriculum areas and educational psychology.[25] He becomes both a "clinical professor" of teaching and a coordinator of a teaching clinic. The team may be just a group of colleagues who tackle agreed-upon teaching problems in an analytical way, using observation and pupil feedback schedules and VTR to gather data for a *clinical conference.*

These kinds of cooperative supervisory practices, which are carefully planned and scheduled in a true classroom laboratory situation, can only be accomplished when public schools and universities join in a partnership for teacher education. These cooperative ventures are built on mutual respect between the school (bound to the practical) and the university (devoted to the theoretical). Both the practical and the theoretical are needed in teacher preparation and in the examination of the work of experienced teachers. To the round table of clinical discussion of teaching, the school worker can bring wisdom from enlightened daily practice, while the college professor of edu-

[24] Morris Cogan, "Clinical Supervision by Groups," *The College Supervisor,* Association for Student Teaching Yearbook, *43,* (1964), 114–131.

[25] E. Brooks Smith, "The Case for the College Supervisor," *The College Supervisor,* Association for Student Teaching Yearbook, *43* (1964), pp. 166–173.

cation can bring the objectivity and collected knowledge from foundational disciplines. The curious schoolteacher studies teaching in the everyday world of school, while the professor of education studies theories of teaching from the vantage point of the academic world of the disciplines. Both schoolteacher and professor need to meet frequently to share ideas and experiment in the crucible of the classroom as they focus together on teaching teachers and on improving the education of children in a great cooperative and professional venture.[26]

Teachers Centers

Obviously some interinstitutional mechanism is needed for accomplishing cooperative and analytical studies of teaching. Although the analysis of teaching can be used to upgrade present instruction it is a limited exercise unless it can be tied to comparative endeavors in the development and redevelopment of curricula. Instructional improvement in a vacuous curriculum of isolated skills or in a routine, misconceived, or irrelevant curriculum is of little value. The teacher is the curriculum maker no matter what is handed to him at the door of his classroom in the way of text series or flashy packages of teacher-proof materials. Ultimately he uses, abuses, ignores, or adapts what is offered on the curriculum platter. The teacher and his professional organization need to become more deeply involved in curriculum development with school administration, university consultants in content and pedagogy, and with community and students if the educational program is to be improved, especially in the language and thinking areas where many misconceptions persist. Thinking cannot be lifted unless there is something significant in the curriculum to think and talk about.

The emergence of the Teachers' Center in Great Britain suggests a model that can be adapted to involve teachers in their own professional development through cooperative work and study for curricular and instructional improvement. In reporting about the history of a British Teacher Center's involvement in a regional curriculum development program, Bill Greenwood expands the idea of curriculum development being a necessary feature of the teacher's life, both in and out of school time. In drawing a

[26] E. Brooks Smith, H. Olsen, and C. Barbour (eds.), *Partnership in Teacher Education* (Washington, D.C.: American Association for Colleges of Teacher Education and Association for Student Teaching, 1967); H. Olsen, C. Barbour, and D. Michalak, *The Teaching Clinic: A Team Approach to the Improvement of Teaching* (Washington, D.C.: Association of Teacher Educators, 1971); also see *A Guide to Professional Excellence in Clinical Experiences in Teacher Education* (Washington, D.C.: A.T.E., 1973); also, E. Brooks Smith, "A Collaborative Effort," in R. Edelfelt and M. Johnson (eds.), *Rethinking Inservice Education of Teachers* (Washington, D.C.: National Education Association, 1975).

distinction between the passive in-putting of inservice education and the dynamic activity of teacher curriculum development, he says:

> It is the curriculum development element, with its creative involvement of individuals, with which centres should primarily be concerned; it is the involvement in creating which will give the teachers the new horizons and strengths necessary if the teacher's centre movement is to be concerned with *innovating for change rather than innovating for continuity*.[27]

Through such procedures as team supervision and such organizations as cooperative centers for the study of curriculum and teaching—and there can be many variations of them—the beginning teacher, the experienced teacher, and the professional educator can become students of teaching and scholars of the language processes in education.

Language can be a masterwork of men when teachers understand the nature of its potential and imagine the many ways it can foster individual and societal fulfilment as they and their students come to know their world. Teaching and learning are mainly language games in which the stakes are high—a true education.

Testing Ideas against Reality

Curriculum and teaching have been explicated along with methodology, but some further practical suggestions are presented.[28]

PUPIL FEEDBACK QUESTIONNAIRES and INTERVIEW GUIDES can be devised for direct or indirect response from learners and for use in the lower grades as well as with high school students. For the younger children happy- and sad-face drawings can be used in place of written responses. Teachers can make up their own questionnaires, depending on the situation and what they want to find out. They may present the questions themselves if they tell the youngsters the need for having the information and ask them to print and not sign their names. A colleague can be asked to present the questionnaire and do sample follow-up

[27] Bill Greenwood, "Regional Curriculum Development through Local Teachers' Centres: Some Reflections," in Geoffrey Mathews (ed.), *Teachers' Centres* (London: Darton, Longman & Todd, 1973), pp. 96–110. Also see A. J. Light, *Curriculum Development with Teachers: The British Experience*, published lecture, Wayne State University, 1975.

[28] Prepared wtih the assistance of Greg Davenport, Wayne State University, Detroit, Michigan. Two useful books are: *Diagnosing Classroom Learning* by Robert Fox, Margaret Barron Luszki, and Richard Schmuck (Chicago: SRA, 1966). *Looking in Classrooms* by Thomas L. Good and Jere E. Brophy (New York: Harper & Row, 1973).

interviews while the teacher works with the other class. Sample direct questions follow:

1. When talking and helping students my teacher usually:
   ____favors girls, ____favors some girls, ____favors some boys, ____favors boys.
2. My teacher shows he likes me:
   ____always, ____a lot, ____a little, ____sometimes, ____never.
3. My school work in (SUBJECT) is:
   ____very interesting, ____interesting sometimes, ____sometimes dull, ____very boring.
4. When disciplining, my teacher is:
   ____too easy, ____just right, ____too hard.
5. When giving an assignment, my teacher's directions are:
   ____very clear, ____fairly clear, ____not so clear, ____confusing.
6. In discussions, my teacher allows me to talk:
   ____not at all, ____very little, ____just the right amount, ____too much;
   (NAMES) ____ and ____ are allowed to talk too much;
   (NAMES) ____ and ____ do not talk at all.
7. My teacher wants me to learn new ideas:
   ____yes, ____no.

INDIRECT QUESTIONING can help teachers find out about their pupils' feelings toward them. One way to do this is to ask each student first to think of himself as the teacher and, second, to think how he would feel as that teacher. Sample indirect questions follow:

For the following statements, indicate your teacher's agreement as either strong or weak.

1. Pupils should help other pupils do their work except for tests.
2. Students usually want to learn and can be trusted to do their work.
3. Students should speak out and tell other students off.
4. Teaching is a drag.
5. Repetition is the best form of practice.
6. Youngsters of this age are fun to work with.
7. To learn is exciting.

OBSERVATION-OF-TEACHING FORMS can be used by a colleague-teacher-consultant observing in a classroom or by a teacher observing a videotape of his classroom teaching. Checklists can be devised for the observer to use when rating the teacher on such teaching actions as:

Calls on the same pupil or pupils.
Praises student or students.
Rephrases questions.
Allows for student options.
Modulates voice.
Prepares pupils for transitions.
Interrupts students.
Tells the answer.
Probes for deeper thinking.
Keeps eyes on all parts of the room.
Is courteous yet firm.
Is ambiguous in direction or responses.
Moves about the room.
Names student before asking question.
Uses incorrect language or uses improper spelling.
Overuses a phrase like, "you see."
Talks down to students or over their heads.

Simple OBSERVATION SCHEDULES can be devised for focusing on one or two aspects of teaching. For recording questioning and responding in group discussion, several levels of questions and answers can be described; factual questions with memory responses, compare-and-contrast questions with categorizing responses, probing questions with the making of inferences, and preference questions with the making of value judgments.

A schedule can be arranged for the observer to check the occurrence of each type of question and each type of response along a time continuum. This will give a picture of the variety or lack of it in both the teacher's questioning style and the students' responses.

Turning Ideas into Practice

TEAM INTERNSHIP Set up a preservice clinical teaching laboratory by forming a team internship situation in place of conventional student teaching. Two back-to-back classrooms can be combined under the coordination of one experienced clinical teacher. In place of the other teacher four intern teachers can be assigned each semester to the coordinating teacher with stipends equal to one-fourth of a beginning teacher's salary. The difference between an initial salary and an average one can be set aside for special materials and resources such as renting portable video-taping equipment and/or extra services of the coordinating teacher. A college clinical professor working with three or four such modules in different but nearby schools can spend sufficient time in load to develop with the coordinating teacher and interns an experimental teaching, analysis, and evaluation program trying out new curricular modules and instructional strategies. Therefore, six professional personnel at different levels of experience are working regularly with the double classrooms. Opportunities are thus multiplied over conventional situations not only for various instructional team combinations, but also for thorough planning, for teaching analysis and evaluation, and for advancement of pupil learning.[29]

COMBINED INSERVICE-PRESERVICE MODEL Invite teachers of a school faculty to volunteer for working on some aspect of their instruction that they want to improve. Ask them to do a needs assessment and then work with them on setting objectives for themselves and their pupils that are attainable within a semester's time. Team each teacher on a volunteer basis with an advanced student or intern teacher to serve as a team associate to that teacher during the term and to be available as a relief teacher in that classroom under the supervision of a college clinical professor assigned to that project school. The interning teacher when ready would work with the class independently one morning per week, while the inservice teacher works in a seminar and/or workshop updating and reorganizing his conceptual schemes, teaching plans, resources, and materials to meet his objectives. The School district consultant and the clinical professor would work with the teachers in the morning seminar, with the interning teachers in a parallel after-school seminar, and with teachers, interns, and pupils in a clinical setting during the afternoon school session. The seminars can deal with innovative teaching ideas and their theoretical base, with planning classroom activities to implement the ideas and with evaluation strategies for assessing impact on pupil accomplishment and teacher effectiveness.[30]

[29] See reports of the Wayne State University–Detroit Public Schools, *Team Internship* program by Robert Olberg, Thomas Davidson, David Wallace, and Jean Fuqua.

[30] See reports by Pierce McLeod and Richard Snell, Macomb Intermediate School District, Michigan; and E. B. Smith and David Wallace, Wayne State University, Detroit, Michigan.

Afterword

Sense of Wonder

A child's world is fresh and new and beautiful, full of wonder and excitement. It is our misfortune that for most of us that clear-eyed vision, that true instinct for what is beautiful and awe-inspiring, is dimmed and even lost before we reach adulthood. If I had influence with the good fairy who is supposed to preside over the christening of all children, I should ask that her gift to each child in the world be a sense of wonder so indestructible that it would last throughout life, or an unfailing antidote against the boredom and disenchantments of later years, the sterile preoccupation with things that are artificial, the alienation from the sources of our strengths.

If a child is to keep alive his inborn sense of wonder . . . he needs the companionship of at least one adult who can share it, rediscovering with him the joy, excitement and mystery of the world we live in. . . .

Those who contemplate the beauty of the earth find reserves of strength that will endure as long as life lasts.[1]

The child is surely at the center of the learning process, for he will only learn what he can incorporate into his knowing. The teacher is certainly at the center of what will be taught, for he alone can prepare the environment and set the stage for instruction. *But language is central to the interaction of teaching and learning that produces knowing.* This book has attempted

[1] Rachel Carson, *The Sense of Wonder* (New York: Harper & Row, 1965), pp. 42–44, 88.

428

to remind teachers of the centrality of language in the teaching–learning process and, in the light of modern language scholarship, to suggest ways for improving the instructional program so that children may go forth from school "cautiously peering, absorbing, translating," still with the sense of wonder they brought to school.

Index